*Chronicles of a Vicar*

Fred Secombe was born in Swansea in 1918 and ordained in 1942. The vicar of various parishes in Wales, and a Prebendary of St Paul's Cathedral, he was also a founder of three Gilbert and Sullivan societies and won the Waterford International Festival of Light Opera Award for *Utopia Ltd* in 1968. The elder brother of Sir Harry Secombe, he now lives in Cardiff.

Also by Fred Secombe:

*Chronicles of a Curate*
*The Changing Scenes of Life*
*Mister Rural Dean*

# CHRONICLES OF A VICAR

## Hello, Vicar!

## A Comedy of Clerical Errors

## The Crowning Glory

### FRED SECOMBE

Illustrated by Maxine Rogers

**Fount**

*An Imprint of* HarperCollins*Publishers*

Fount is an Imprint of
HarperCollins*Religious*
Part of HarperCollins*Publishers*
77–85 Fulham Palace Road, London W6 8JB

*Hello, Vicar!* first published in Great Britain in 1993 by Michael Joseph Ltd,
and in 1994 by Fount Paperbacks. Copyright © 1992 Fred Secombe.

*A Comedy of Clerical Errors* first published in Great Britain in 1994 by
Michael Joseph Ltd, and in 1995 by Fount Paperbacks.
Copyright © 1994 Fred Secombe.

*The Crowning Glory* first published in Great Britain in 1995 by
Michael Joseph Ltd, and in 1996 by Fount Paperbacks.
Copyright © 1995 Fred Secombe.

This edition 1999

3  5  7  9  10  8  6  4  2

Fred Secombe asserts the moral right to be
identified as the author of this work

A catalogue record for this book
is available from the British Library

ISBN 000 628135 4

Printed and bound in Great Britain by
Caledonian International Book Manufacturing Ltd, Glasgow

# CONTENTS

# Hello, Vicar!

To all those curates who
suffered at my hands

# 1

'Who'd be a vicar's wife?' sighed Eleanor after closing the door on a Liverpudlian tramp who had been supplied with a cup of tea and some spam sandwiches. He was reeking of meths to such an extent that to strike a match in his vicinity would have produced a fireball on the vicarage doorstep. Unshaven, with watery blue eyes set in a florid punchbag of a face, and clad in clothes which appeared to have been stolen from a scarecrow, he was not the most prepossessing of characters.

He had rung the doorbell halfway through *In Town Tonight*, one of our favourite wireless programmes. 'Good evening, Father,' he slurred, as his opening gambit. 'I wonder if you could give an old sailor who has been through the war the price of a cup of tea and a night's lodging.' I was about to put my hand in my pocket when my wife arrived at my side.

'You can have a cup of tea and some sandwiches,' she had said firmly, 'but you will not have any money from this house and you can pass that message to all your friends. Pontywen vicarage is not the place for a soft touch.'

'God bless you, madam,' he replied, through gritted teeth.

As my wife returned to her armchair, I said, 'You have been a vicar's wife for just three weeks; and who'd be a doctor's husband for that matter? I've answered so many phone calls for you that I might as well be your receptionist. If you had let me give him a bob you wouldn't have had to go to the trouble of making tea and sandwiches.'

'Fred, you will thank me for tonight in the years that lie

ahead. I know you. You are definitely a soft touch. Once that got around, this vicarage would have become a Mecca for all the hobo fraternity in South Wales. It's a good thing I happened to be in when he called, otherwise there would have been a queue of applicants in a few weeks' time. As for being a doctor's husband, I would have thought that taking calls for errands of mercy would have been most appropriate for a servant of the Lord, especially since he did not have to respond to the call for help himself.'

Not for the first time in my short married life, I found myself unable to deny the truth behind my wife's arguments. For someone who had been convinced that his way of thinking was always in line with God's purpose this was a bitter pill to swallow, even if it was administered by a doctor.

It seemed only yesterday that I had been inducted into the living of Pontywen with Llanhyfryd, in the presence of a crowded congregation and a plethora of parsons – the youngest incumbent in its hundred-year-old history. Furthermore it was the first time since the diocese was established in the nineteen twenties that an assistant curate had been elevated to the status of vicar in the same parish, after the appointment of the previous incumbent to another benefice. This made headlines in the local press.

My euphoria at the induction service had vanished by the next morning when I was faced with the necessity of drawing up a rota of services for the three churches in my charge. Pontywen, population six thousand, was a typically drab valleys town, with a colliery and a steelworks on its outskirts. It was served by two churches, St Mary's and St Padarn's, five chapels and a gospel hall. Llanhyfryd was a rural community, population two hundred and fifty-three, some four miles distant from Pontywen, with an ancient parish church, St Illtyd's. Until three years ago, it had enjoyed the luxury of having its own vicar. Admittedly he had been there for thirty-nine years and was suffering from senile decay. However, he was their vicar, living next door to the church. Now they were shepherded by a parson who lived four miles away, and who might as well have been four hundred miles away as far as they were concerned.

To minister to three diverse congregations would tax the

patience of any saint, let alone a parish priest. When the only assistance available to him was provided by a young clerical misfit and an elderly lay reader whose lengthy sermons were a cure for insomnia, to compile a rota of services presented a puzzling exercise in damage containment. After three weeks the natives were already restless.

Disquiet was most evident in St Padarn's, the daughter church where I had been in charge as a curate. They expected me to give them priority over the parish church. The most vociferous objector was Bertie Owen, their church-warden, who was equally voluble at the Pontywen steel-works where he was a shop steward. When I was a curate he had been my staunchest supporter; now that I was the boss I was somebody to confront. It was impossible to reason with Bertie. As Idris the Milk said of him, 'Everytime he starts shouting about something you can hear the echo in his head.'

'I tell you what, Mr Secombe – I mean, Vicar . . .' It was the morning after the tramp episode and Bertie had button-holed me in St Padarn's vestry after the Family Communion Service. 'If you are going to spend nearly all your time up in St Mary's, you are going to have a strike on your hands here. We've had Mr Wentworth-Baxter for three Sundays running. On the first Sunday he found he had left his sermon in his digs and he tried to make one up as he was speaking in the pulpit. He spoke for about two minutes and repeated himself about a dozen times. The next Sunday he got here ten minutes late, announced the wrong hymns and passed by Mrs Collier at the altar rail. Last Sunday –'

'All right, Bertie,' I replied, 'you need not say any more. I shall have a word with him tomorrow morning. Just remember I am no longer attached solely to St Padarn's. I have three churches to look after. If I could cut myself in three my life would be much easier. Since that is impossible I am afraid you will have to put up with Mr Wentworth-Baxter for most of your Sunday services. There's one thing. Life will never be dull as long as he is taking the service. It will be full of the unexpected.'

'Well, I tell you what you can expect and that is an empty church if this goes on.' With these words Bertie stalked out of the vestry, slamming the door behind him to give dramatic effect. Charlie Hughes, his elderly fellow churchwarden, who was counting the collection shot up from his seat and adjusted his hearing aid.

'What's the matter with that dull bugger now?' inquired the old man.

'He's annoyed that you have to put up with Mr Wentworth-Baxter but I am afraid there is not much I can do about it for the time being,' I replied.

'Don't worry, Vicar. Of course you've got to be up at the parish church more than here. He ought to know that but there you are, there's none so deaf as him who won't listen. That's him all over. The trouble is that he's stirring up the others. Still, it will sort itself out in time.' Charlie patted me on the shoulder and went back to his counting.

I decided to read the riot act to Charles Wentworth-Baxter at our Monday-morning meeting in the vicarage. This was not an unusual occurrence for him. I was the fourth successive vicar to apply such treatment to my hapless assistant. The son of a parson, he had been dragooned into holy orders. While intellectually capable of getting a second-class degree in English at Oxford, he suffered from a stunted growth in common sense and a permanent adolescence in affairs of the heart. On two occasions I had had to rescue him from calf love obsessions with local schoolgirls. It was small wonder that my wife had christened him Peter Pan.

We were seated in my study after nine o'clock matins. It was not so long ago that I had been ushered into that room as the apprehensive young curate. Then the many book-shelves had been packed with volumes, most of them with leather-bound backs, early twentieth-century specimens, un-opened for many years. Now most of the shelves were bare, revealing the new decorated wallpaper. The rest were occupied mainly by the colourful paperbacks I had accumulated over the years, Penguins and Pelicans stacked in neat rows.

There was one resemblance to the late Canon Llewellyn's study and that was the big mahogany leather-topped desk which I had bought at an auction. Behind it was a wooden armchair with a leather-topped seat surrounded by brass studs. This had come from Pontywen Lodge, formerly the workhouse and now transformed into Pontywen Hospital, by courtesy of the Welfare State. The chair had accommodated a generation of geriatrics awaiting their final call as they sat each day staring into space. After an application of varnish it looked worthy of its promotion to a vicarage.

An imposing desk nurtures a power complex in the man behind it. At the age of twenty-eight, given the responsibility of a town parish, my ego burgeoned behind this piece of wood as I surveyed the sloppily dressed individual slumped in the leather armchair opposite me.

'Look at you, Charles. If ever there was a pathetic spectacle, you're it,' I pontificated. 'A priest has an obligation to be presentable in his appearance. You could not care less. In the same way that you could not care less about your administration of the sacraments or your preaching. You come late to service and afterwards escape from the vestry like a bat out of hell. It is no wonder that Bertie Owen is yelling for your blood.'

I felt a warm glow of self satisfaction at my tirade. It vanished in a flash as the worm turned. Raising his head he looked me in the eyes.

'Don't try to be a Canon Llewellyn, Fred,' he said quietly. 'You're only the same age as I am. I could take it from him and Father Whittaker. They were men with a lot more experience than you. Up until your – er – elevation, I was your friend. Now I am your doormat. I'm sorry but I can't take it. I shall have to resign my orders and try school teaching instead.'

The very thought of Charles in front of a class of schoolboys would have induced peals of laughter from me under normal circumstances, but not now. It appeared that I had overplayed my hand and hurt him deeply. There was a long silence as I struggled for a reply. I stood up and came around the desk. I sat on its edge, still silent. His head was bowed.

'I'm sorry,' I murmured, 'I should not have been so insulting. It's amazing how a little power can turn one's head. There is no need to resign your orders or to leave this parish. All I ask is that you make an effort to support me. Now that I am the vicar I get all the flak when things go wrong and that is difficult to take at my tender age. Shall we shake hands and forget the incident?'

I held out my hand. He raised his head, with a broad smile on his face, and shook the proffered token of reconciliation energetically.

'Thanks, Fred,' he said. 'I knew that was not the real you a minute ago.'

It was then that I realized I had been trapped by the soft-touch syndrome once again. Charles, like Eliza, had come to stay. If there had ever been any deep hurt, the wound had been healed miraculously in a matter of seconds. I decided that I would say nothing to Eleanor about the episode. She regarded Charles as a walking disaster area, whose removal from Pontywen should be an occasion for the Te Deum not the Miserere.

Only minutes after my colleague's departure I watched an ancient Austin Seven pull up outside the vicarage door. A tall grey-haired, bespectacled man in his fifties, dressed in tweeds, alighted from the machine. He carried a briefcase and looked like a representative for sheep dips or cattle cakes, the type I had encountered at farms in Llanhyfryd.

'Good morning, reverend sir, may I see the vicar, please?' He spoke with a West Country accent which had been softened by a good education.

'You are looking at him,' I replied.

His face reddened. 'My apologies, Canon Llewellyn. I must admit I did not expect to see so youthful a canon of the diocese.'

'I am afraid Canon Llewellyn departed this life some two years ago. Since then there have been two incumbents. I am the second and my name is Secombe.'

'This is what comes from using a dated clerical directory,' my visitor went on. 'My further apologies, Vicar. May I introduce myself? I am Walter Polkinghorne and I am compiling a monograph on the church bells of this diocese. From my records it would appear that you have two medieval bells and one seventeenth-century bell in the tower of St Illtyd's Church.'

'Would you care to come in, Mr Polkinghorne?' I said.

As we sat drinking coffee, I confessed my ignorance of

the treasures in the belfry at Llanhyfryd. 'To me, the bells have sounded somewhat tuneless. Perhaps it is the way that Tom Cadwallader, the sexton, rings them. He pulls one with either hand and has the bell rope of the third tied around his foot. It is something of a circus act to see this big oaf of a man engaged in ringing three bells at the same time. Apart from that there is very little pleasure in the sound that emanates from them.'

'The medieval bells probably came from a primitive foundry. The mixture of tin and copper to make the bronze cast may not have been of the right proportions. The late-seventeenth-century bell comes from a well-known founder in Gloucester, according to my notes, and should have a much better tone. Anyway, I should like to have your permission to visit the tower to examine them and to make drawings of them. Perhaps you might like to come with me?'

'Well, I was due to do some visiting this afternoon but I can postpone that until tomorrow. In the meanwhile I am afraid I cannot offer you lunch. My wife is a doctor. So we have an evening meal. You are welcome to a tuna sandwich and a cup of tea.'

'That is very kind of you. How unusual for a parson to have a wife who is a doctor. I suppose you have to get domestic help of some kind.'

'Not as yet, but we have a lady coming for an interview this evening.'

'Will she do the cooking for you? Or is your wife fond of cooking?'

By the time we had finished our sandwiches Mr Polkinghorne had delved into my background to such an extent that he could have written a monograph on the life of Frederick Thomas Secombe.

'I hope you don't mind me asking all these questions. I am as much interested in people as I am in bells. I suppose it comes from living in a small community. I live in a village outside Taunton. There everybody knows everybody else. They even know when you've changed your socks.'

He said this as he was driving me to Llanhyfryd, looking at me more than at the road, in a most unnerving fashion.

'How claustrophobic,' I replied. 'I should hate to live in a place like that.'

'I don't find it a bit claustrophobic. In any case it keeps everybody in line, if you know what I mean. You wouldn't dare to stray from the straight and narrow in our village and that's a good thing, surely.'

As we went up the church path he took a small hammer from the pocket of his coat. 'One of the tools of the trade,' he said. 'And here's another.' This time a torch was brandished. 'Belfries are dark places; a torch is essential.'

I led the way up some steps to what was the ringing chamber many years ago. Nowadays the bell ropes continued down through holes made in the floor to enable the verger to ring the bells at ground level. A ladder leaned against the wall near a trap door in the ceiling.

'Here we go then,' said Mr Polkinghorne. 'Would you mind holding my briefcase while I open this trap door?' To open the door was no easy task; after several attempts to push it open, the bell expert was sweating profusely at the top of the ladder, despite the late January cold.

'Evidently this has not been opened for some time,' he gasped.

'Shall I go and get the sexton?' I asked.

'Let's have one more shot at it,' he said. He took a deep breath and gave the recalcitrant piece of wood a mighty blow with the flat of his hand. It flew open and almost threw him off balance on the ladder.

'Right. Stage two coming up,' he announced. He hauled himself up into the top of the belfry, grunting and puffing as he did so.

'Phew!! What a mess,' he exclaimed. 'It looks as if the birds of Llanhyfryd have been using this as a hotel for several generations. Would you give me my briefcase, please?'

Gingerly I climbed the ladder. I never did like heights, even small heights. I handed him his briefcase.

'Thank you, Vicar,' he said. 'Now then, let's get you up here. Put your bottom on the floor and swing your legs around.'

I was beginning to regret my acceptance of his offer to accompany him. After two abortive attempts to follow his instructions I managed to get aloft. The floor was littered with twigs, some parts to a depth of several inches. There were enough bird droppings to manure all the gardens in the village.

'We had better replace the trap door for the time being, in case we forget there is a hole in the floor. There is a good iron ring on it to pull it back up when the need arrives.'

He closed the door with a bang and turned his attention to the bells. The faint winter sunshine filtered through the louvres.

'There you are, Vicar. See the inscription on this bell. "Laus Deo, Abraham Rudhall, Gloucester 1699." You see it's a somewhat different shape from the other two and so will its quality of tone differ. Listen.' He gave the bell a sharp knock on its side with the hammer. The sound penetrated my ear drums. 'Isn't that lovely?' he asked, as if it were a snatch of Beethoven or Mozart.

'Beautiful,' I said.

'Now these other two bells are much more ancient but comparatively tuneless.' He struck them with the hammer and assaulted my ear drums once again. The belfry was becoming as claustrophobic as his village.

'If you don't mind, I shall make some sketches of the bells and note the markings on them. It will take about half an hour at most.'

The minutes dragged by as he examined the markings on the bells by the light of his torch and then proceeded to make sketches of them. I occupied my time by peering through the louvres at the countryside and by watching the sun begin to dip behind the hills.

'That's it,' he said and closed his sketch pad with a flourish. 'Thank you very much; most interesting. Time to go home.'

He knelt down by the trap door and tugged at the iron ring. He was unable to raise the door, which remained as firmly shut as if it were cemented into the floor. The more he tugged, the less inclined the wretched bolt-hole was to respond. Mr Polkinghorne began to panic.

'Does anybody know we are here?' he asked anxiously.

'Of course not,' I replied curtly. 'As you know we came here directly from the vicarage. I suppose the only thing we can do is try to attract attention. I'll keep an eye open from here if you will keep trying to raise the confounded contraption.'

He took the hammer from his pocket and put the shaft through the ring, pulling desperately. It was to no avail.

Suddenly in the gathering dusk I saw through the louvres an old lady walking in the church yard. I thrust out my hand and shouted 'Help!' She stopped in her tracks, looked up, let out a scream and hurried off through the lych gate.

'A fat lot of good that has done,' I said. 'She thinks she has seen and heard a ghost. Why not use that hammer to bang on the bells? At least it will attract attention.'

In an instant he was transformed into a Quasimodo. He began to play tunes on the bells which Llanhyfryd had never heard before.

'If you give me your torch I will keep flashing it on and

off,' I suggested. He paused in his labours, handed me the tool of his trade and went back to a frenzied attack on the ancient bronze with the other tool.

By now dusk had given way to darkness. I put my hand out through the louvres and kept switching the torch on and off. To my intense relief I saw another torch advancing up the path to the church. I realized how they must have felt in Mafeking.

A few minutes later there was a heavy tread in the ringing chamber beneath us.

'Anyone up there?' inquired Tom Cadwallader, the sexton. A senseless question since the demon bell banger had only just ceased his frenetic activity.

I shouted, 'Tom. It's me, the vicar. This trap door is jammed and we can't get out.'

'What are you doing up there, Vicar?'

'Never mind what I'm doing up here. You push that door open, please.'

There was a silence in the course of which the sexton's brain was coming to terms with the predicament. Then he shouted, 'Hold on, I'm coming.' Up the ladder he came and smote the trap door with a furious blow. It burst open immediately. Tom's hand was more potent than a sledge hammer. His full-moon of a face with a few straggly hairs over his bald head appeared at the top of the ladder. He stared in wonderment at the bell expert, clad in his white coat.

'What's the vet doing up here?' he inquired.

'This gentleman is not a vet. He is an expert on bells and he is writing a book about all the bells in the diocese.'

'Old Rhiannon Morris went into the post office and said there were ghosts in the church. Then the bells started playing and frightened everybody. So they came and asked me to see what was happening.'

'Well, Tom, you can tell the village that the church is not haunted and that you rescued the vicar and a campanologist from a fate worse than death. In the meanwhile if you will come down from the ladder, we should like to return to civilization.'

As the Morris Minor pulled up outside the door of the vicarage, my wife appeared on the doorstep.

'Where on earth have you been?' she asked as I emerged from the car. 'I finished my surgery half an hour ago and found the place in darkness . . .'

'My apologies, Mrs Secombe,' said Mr Polkinghorne through the opened window of the Morris Minor. 'I'm afraid it was my fault. I invited your husband to join me in an inspection of the bells in St Illtyd's Church where an unfortunate happening trapped us in the bell tower.'

'Mr Polkinghorne is a campanologist and is doing a monograph on the bells of the diocese,' I explained. 'The trap door in the bell tower refused to budge, and Tom Cadwallader had to rescue us eventually.'

'A likely story,' she replied, 'if it were not corroborated by your campanologist companion. Would you care to come in, Mr Polkinghorne, and join us for our evening meal?'

'I should love to,' he said, 'but I am afraid I am due in Abergavenny where I have booked a hotel room and dinner for this evening. Thanks all the same.'

Once the car disappeared down the drive, Eleanor turned to me. 'I wish you would leave a note when you disappear unexpectedly. As far as I knew you could have been trapped in some designing female's boudoir, not St Illtyd's bell tower.'

'No such good luck,' I replied.

She caught hold of my jacket by its lapels. 'Good luck doesn't enter into it when you have so charming a spouse. That would be bad luck, believe me.'

'I believe you,' I said, 'and to prove it, take this.' It was such a long lingering embrace that she had to break off with a cry that she could hear the potatoes boiling over on the gas stove.

'As you said this morning, who'd be a vicar's wife,' I shouted after her as she ran into the kitchen.

Promptly at eight o'clock that evening, the doorbell rang to announce the arrival of the applicant for the post of a daily help at the vicarage. Since I had come into the category of an incumbent with a stipend which was more than double that of a curate, and my wife's income was considerably more than mine, we decided that we could afford domestic assistance, perhaps even to the extent of a housekeeper. For the time being we deemed it advisable to be content with someone who would clean the house and would do the laundry. To that end we had advertised in the local newspaper. We received one reply. It was from a widow who claimed that she had 'done cleening for a bank manidger and his wife'.

'I don't like the sound of that letter,' I said to Eleanor.

'Because she can't spell,' she replied, 'it does not mean that she can't clean or wash. Let's wait and see.'

On the doorstep was a little middle-aged lady with horn-rimmed spectacles. She was bare-headed and carried a man's umbrella to protect her from the snow which had begun to fall. Her grey hair, which sported several clips, had been cut à la pudding basin mode.

'I'm Mrs Watkins,' she announced. 'I've come about the advert in the paper.'

'Come on in Mrs Watkins,' I said. 'Leave your umbrella in the porch. It will be quite safe here.'

'I 'ope, so,' she replied. 'It's my late 'usband's and I wouldn't want to lose it.'

She followed me into the sitting room where Eleanor was pouring out a cup of tea for the interviewee.

'Hello, Mrs Watkins,' said my wife and shook her hand. 'Take off your coat and come and sit by the fire. You must be frozen on a night like this. A cup of tea will warm you up.'

I took her coat which was liberally covered with snow-flakes despite the umbrella.

'It's going to snow a lot, I think,' forecast our visitor. 'I do always get shivers running down my back if it's going to snow heavy and I can tell you, I've 'ad them all day today, I 'ave.'

'Well, I hope not,' replied Eleanor. 'It's difficult enough to fit in all the visits to patients, without being hindered by snow as well.'

Mrs WAtkins proved to be a non-stop talker, despite the handicap of an ill-fitting upper set of false teeth which kept slipping in a disconcerting fashion in the middle of a sentence. By the time she left she had given us a vivid description of her late husband's last hours and of his life since early childhood. As she went out into the driving snow, we retired to the peace of the sitting room.

'Quiet after the storm,' I remarked. 'I don't know whether I can cope with a never-ending stream of conversation.'

'The point is, dear Frederick,' said my wife, 'that you will not be here to listen to it and neither shall I. By the time we come back to the house at lunchtime she will be just about ready to leave. Anyway, we'll try her and see how it goes. I tell you one thing, she has a very reliable forecast in her shivers. It looks as if we are going to have an extremely heavy snowfall.'

We awoke next morning to discover that Pontywen had much in common with the North Pole. The vicarage drive had disappeared and so had the stone wall which bordered the garden. That was the view from the bedroom window. When I came downstairs, I found that I could not open the back door because the snow had piled up against it to form an impenetrable barrier. Fortunately the porch had protected the front door but even there the snow was a few inches deep. There was no electricity in the house and the telephone was dead. According to the battery wireless set I owned, most of South Wales had more or less come to a standstill, ravaged by blizzards.

'It's a good thing, Mr Polkinghorne did not accept your invitation to dinner last night. Otherwise we might have had a semi-permanent non-paying guest, by the look of things,' I said.

'What is more to the point, if we did not have an Aga cooker, we should have been living in a refrigerator instead of a kitchen and there would be no boiled eggs for breakfast,' said my wife. 'In any case, blow Mr Polkinghorne! How on earth am I going to get my car out of the garage and what is more, if I get out, how am I going to drive it through that wall of snow?'

'I'm afraid, my love, it will have to be shanks's pony for

both of us and even that pony will have great difficulty going any distance.'

We were now a two-car family. Eleanor had given me her old Morris Minor and had purchased a brand-new Ford 8, which was kept in the garage. The Morris had disappeared under the snow at the front of the vicarage.

'I don't care whose pony it is, but before we get cracking we shall have to remove some snow from the drive. How do we manage that?'

'With a shovel, dear Liza, with a shovel.'

'Then how do we get it, dear Frederick, dear Frederick? It's inside the garage.'

'Well, that means I shall have to use the brute strength of my bare hands to carve a way.'

'Two things, love. You will not use your bare hands. You will wear gloves and forget the "brute strength" bit. It is going to be a combined operation, once we have got our wellingtons and macs on.'

It took us half an hour to move round from the front of the house to the back, where snow drifts several feet high had piled up, and to open the door of the garage sufficiently wide to get the garden spade.

'Now then, Hercules,' ordered Eleanor, 'let's see what you can do with the shovel for Liza.'

After an hour, between us we had managed to dig a single-file trench halfway up the drive.

'Isn't it deathly quiet?' said my wife, as we stood exhausted and breathing clouds of vapour into the air.

'"And all the world a solemn stillness holds",' I quoted.

'I tell you one thing;' she replied, 'it's too cold for the beetle to wheel its droning flight. Its wings would drop off. Let's go in and warm up with a cuppa. Then I'll see if I can make my way down to the surgery. Perhaps the phone is working down there.'

'Don't expect to find any patients. If they are well enough to struggle to the surgery, they can't be invalids, that's for sure.'

'Believe me, we have some very tough invalids who would trek to the North Pole for their free bottle of medicine. It's not the regulars who are worrying me but people like Mrs

Ellis in Sebastopol Street. She is forty years old, with a family of eight children, and she is expecting her ninth any time now. The poor woman is not very strong and should go to a maternity hospital but she insists on having the baby at home.'

As we sat drinking our tea by the warmth of the stove, I said to Eleanor, 'There's one person who will be glad to see the snow bringing the town to a standstill – the perfect excuse for staying in and doing nothing.'

'You are not alluding to Charles, by any chance,' she replied.

I was about to assure her that she was on target when the front doorbell rang. Startled, we looked at each other.

'It's never Charles,' I said. 'It can't be.'

The bell rang again and yet again.

I hurried to the front door to be confronted by a cap-and-mufflered man wearing a mac speckled with snow who was in a highly agitated state.

'Is the doctor in?' he gasped.

Eleanor appeared alongside me. 'Mr Ellis!' she said. 'Your wife has started labour?'

'Sorry to trouble you 'ere. I went to the surgery and it was all shut up. She've 'ad the pains some time but you know what she's like, Doctor. She wouldn't let me come until now. She's worried about you coming through the snow.'

'If you can get through the snow, Mr Ellis, so can I. Hold on. I'll get my bags, and I'll be with you in two ticks.'

A few minutes later she was ploughing through the snow, following in the footsteps of our visitor. I went back to my excavating work and managed to reach the gates of the drive, where I stood exhausted. As I surveyed the fruit of my labours, my ears were assailed by a shout from behind me. To my amazement there was Charles almost knee-deep in snow and grinning from ear to ear.

'Isn't it great?' he enthused and attempted to sing 'Walking in a Winter Wonderland'.

I had forgotten that he was Peter Pan and that to him the deep snow had turned Pontywen into a playground.

'Moelwyn says that he has a sledge in the outhouse and

that I can borrow it for tobogganing with some of the young people from St Padarn's, when I can get it organized.'

'In that case, Charles, it will be the first organizing you will have done since you have been in Pontywen; a momentous landmark in your career. More to the point at the moment is the need to clear a way up the church path.'

The smile disappeared from his face.

'Couldn't Full Back Jones do that? It's more like his job than mine – digging, I mean.'

'With snow like this, it is everybody's job to help clear it. So, shall we make a start?'

Suddenly the winter wonderland had turned into a chore for Charles. The one thing which he detested above all else was a chore, especially one which involved manual labour. After ten minutes' half-hearted use of the spade, he was seized by a pain in his back. Then he informed me that he was beginning to shiver and that the cold was getting into his bones.

'I think I had better get back to my digs. There won't be any visiting today, will there? So perhaps I can spend the afternoon preparing my sermon for next Sunday.'

'Don't be so facetious. When did you ever begin writing a sermon in the first part of the week? You had better come into the vicarage and have a cup of tea in the warmth of the kitchen. We can discuss what we are going to do if this snow continues.'

He followed me down the vicarage drive, like Shake-speare's schoolboy creeping like snail unwillingly. As the kettle sang on the stove, I went to the larder to discover that there was only enough milk for two cups of tea and that we were down to the last crust of bread.

'A sign of the times,' I said as I came back into the kitchen. 'The milk has almost disappeared. Just one crust of bread left. There are only two candles. There will be no supplies coming from Newport or Cardiff today. The town is cut off. I expect Jones the Dairy is being besieged, not to mention Phillips the Bakery. Once we have had our cup of tea I shall have to do some shopping; that's if there is any left. What with no electricity and our phone out of order, we are back to primitive times.'

22

'The only thing to do if it keeps on like this,' suggested my colleague hopefully, 'is to cancel service on Sunday.'

'No such luck for you, Charles. What ever happens we shall have to keep the services going. We shall have to switch Evensong from six thirty p.m. to the afternoon, if there is still no electricity.'

'That means there will be no Sunday School,' interjected Charles eagerly. He was even less enthusiastic about Sunday School than he was about the Sunday services.

'For someone who wants to go tobogganing with the young people from St Padarn's, you sound quite glad there is to be no Sunday School.'

'By young people, I mean the girls from the Gilbert and Sullivan and some of the young men who have joined this year – not the kids from the Sunday School.' His lip curled at the very idea of a romp with the eleven and twelve-year-old boys who plagued his life every Sunday afternoon.

I had formed a Gilbert and Sullivan Society some eighteen months previously which had staged a successful production of *The Pirates of Penzance* and, after a hiatus caused by my elevation to the status of vicar, had begun rehearsals of *The Gondoliers*. The Society was based upon a benevolent despotism. I chose the cast, directed the opera and played the tenor lead opposite Eleanor, who was an accomplished soprano lead. We had debated whether we could afford the time because of our respective careers, but our love for the Savoy operas won the day. Charles had already had an adolescent passion for one of the more nubile schoolgirls in the first production, which had almost ended in disaster for him. Later he had embarked upon an association with another schoolgirl who was a Sunday School teacher in St Padarn's. That ended abruptly when her father committed suicide. It was small wonder that Eleanor had christened him Peter Pan.

'What I thought to do,' he went on, 'was to ask how many would be willing to make up a toboggan party when we meet tomorrow evening.'

'Charles, why did you mention the girls first and the young men second? For heaven's sake, grow up, man. You have had enough experience with schoolgirls to last you a lifetime – I am quite prepared for you to organize something for the young people but get your priorities right, first of all. It is not in order for you to play the field but rather to create a fellowship to grow into the worshipping community at St Padarn's and the parish church. Anyway, if this snow continues, how many will turn up at St Padarn's tomorrow evening and how many candles will be needed to provide illumination for the rehearsal? I think we had better finish our conversation and get down to the shop before everything is snapped up.'

'If you don't mind, perhaps I had better get back to my digs. My trousers are very damp around my legs and, in any case, it's nearly quarter past twelve. Myfanwy always has dinner ready at one o'clock prompt.' It was a sullen curate who made his way through the trench in the snow of the vicarage drive and into the chaos of the Pontywen streets.

Chaos indeed reigned supreme in the little valley town – drifts six or seven feet high dominated the sky line at the end of some streets where the funnelled wind had driven the snow into grotesque statues. Shoppers queued outside the dairy and the bakery in the town square where the towered clock looked down on a scene which resembled a Brueghel painting. Roberts the ironmonger was besieged by customers in search of candles. 'Now then, ladies,' the old man was shouting over the clamour in his shop, 'only six each. That's your ration. I've got to be fair to everybody.'

By the time I had finished my shopping I had arrived home with a carrier containing, one loaf of bread, one bottle of milk, six candles, a pound of potatoes and a tin of tuna. It had taken me an hour and a half to collect such meagre provisions.

Eleanor had not returned. I made myself a cup of tea and spread some fish paste on the crust of bread left over from the day before. She did not arrive until half past three, announcing her arrival by banging her wellingtons against the step outside the back door.

'I'm back,' she shouted as she came through the door.

'So I heard before you came in,' I said, as I came to greet her. 'Is all well?'

'I'm afraid not, love. It's a breech birth and the poor woman is having a terrible time. She should be in hospital but how can we get there? The roads are blocked so no ambulances are available. I've come back for a cup of tea and a sandwich. It is worth braving the snow for that. The little house is full of kids and is far from clean. I've left Nurse Foley there in charge for the time being. She brought me into the world quite successfully. If she could do that, I'm sure she can cope with anything.'

'Is Mrs Ellis in any kind of danger?' I asked.

'No, she's not but the baby is. Because the head of the child is the last to come out of the mother sometimes the umbilical cord gets caught around the neck of the baby and causes asphyxiation. It's a very tricky operation, I can assure you. When you're trying to cope under difficult circumstances, it is even trickier.'

'Go into the sitting room, my love, and put your feet up for five minutes. Frederick will make you a cup of tea and supply you with tuna sandwiches, made from fresh bread collected this morning.'

When I arrived with the tea and sandwiches sometime later she was stretched out on the settee, fast asleep. I tapped her gently on her cheek. She opened her eyes.

'Wake up, Sleeping Beauty, Prince Charming here,' I announced.

'Some Prince Charming you are,' she murmured. 'You are supposed to kiss Sleeping Beauty not slap her face.'

'Correction,' I replied and kissed her firmly. 'You needed that. Your lips are quite cold.'

'But not my heart. Come here and give me a cuddle as an aperitif to the tuna sandwiches.'

As we sprawled on the settee with our arms around each other, I said to her, 'There's one thing. If the baby does die, there are plenty of other children in the family to make up for the loss of that one.'

'If you were a doctor, my dear, you would never say that. It means that you have lost a life when your job was to save it. Not only that, Mrs Ellis is such a good mother that even if she had twenty children, she would still grieve over that loss, as if the child were her only one.'

'Never a day goes by without another display of my ignorance of medicine and the medical profession.'

'Why not put it another way, Frederick? Each day you learn more and more. Be positive, Vicar.'

An hour later she went out into the darkness, guided by the torch I had kept since my air raid warden days in Swansea.

The six o'clock news on the wireless was full of doom and gloom. It appeared that the electricity would be cut for up to twelve hours a day, caused by the strain on the power houses. We had no electricity at all in Pontywen, since the power lines had been brought down by snow, so it mattered not.

I sat in darkness savouring the warmth of the kitchen, and waiting for the sitting-room fire to light up. There was no central heating in the vicarage. The Church expected its clergy to be Spartans as well as Christians. The darkness and the warmth combined to send me to sleep on the kitchen chair, with my head on the table. My siesta was interrupted by the continuous ringing of the door bell. Only half awake, I stumbled my way through the darkness to open the front door. Standing on the doorstep, looming above me was PC Will Davies the local policeman, known to everybody as Will Book and Pencil, his torch directed down at his large feet.

'PC Davies here, Vicar,' he said. 'You are wanted urgently. Mr Collier, your organist at St Padarn's has been found dead in the snow. His widow is asking for you.'

Five minutes later he led me by the light of his torch, down to the Collier residence in Taliesin Road. Apparently the organist had collapsed and died on his way from work as a clerk in the Pontywen Colliery.

Agnes Collier was a thin little lady, with sparse grey hair surmounting a sallow bespectacled face. She was the leading soprano in the church choir, jealous of anyone who might dare to usurp her position as soloist or as organizer of church decoration. Now this formidable figure in St Padarn's was slumped in her chintz-covered armchair, apparently a broken reed.

I was shown into her presence by Mrs Annie Jones, her soprano rival, who had the unusual habit of taking out her dentures before singing the hymns. Despite the rivalry, Annie professed to being Agnes's best friend.

'Here's the Vicar, Ag,' whispered Annie, in deference to the sad occasion. Normally she had a bell on every tooth.

Agnes continued to stare at the floor.

Annie decided to use her bel canto to repeat the introduction.

The widow's head jerked up.

'There's no need to shout, Annie. I heard you the first time.'

Annie gazed up to heaven and shrugged her shoulders.

'Sit down, by here, Vicar.' Agnes indicated a vacant dining-room chair by her side.

I obeyed and sat down beside her. I would have taken her hands but they were firmly clasped in her lap.

'I'm so sorry about the news, Mrs Collier,' I said. 'It must have been a great shock for you. Mr Collier always appeared to be in good health.'

'Ah!' she replied. 'That's where you're wrong. He used to get terrible indigestion but he'd never go to the doctor. I've told him time and time again to go but he was so stubborn. Just like this morning, I told him not to go to work with all that snow about but off he went. They sent him home early because so few of the miners had turned up. He used to take a short cut round the back of Sebastopol Street. Some children playing snowballs found him dead in the lane. We got Dr Hughes but he said he had been dead for some time. Why do men have to be so stubborn?'

There was not a tear in her eyes, only anger against the mulishness of men.

'And look what happens,' she went on. 'I'm left on my own. No children. My parents are dead. So are his. I've got a sister in Liverpool but I never see her. His brother went out to Canada before the War. I don't even know where he lives. All I've got is the church and now you've become Vicar, we are left with that Mr Wentworth-Baxter for all that he's worth.'

It was evident that any further attempt at sympathy would elicit another catalogue of reasons for self pity. An uneasy silence followed; Annie Jones came to my rescue.

'Would you like a cup of tea, Vicar?'

'Yes, please, Mrs Jones.'

'What about you, Ag?'

'Not for me, Annie. I don't feel like eating or drinking anything at the moment. There's some biscuits in the biscuit barrel. It's on the top shelf in the cupboard by the sink. Mr Matthews the undertaker has been round. They've laid him out. He says that because of the snow, it may take some time to have the funeral.'

She spoke in the same tone about her late husband as she did about the biscuits.

'If we have a change in the weather, then the snow will soon thaw,' I said, stating the obvious to cover my mounting embarrassment.

'I can't see that happening what with the weather forecasts and that. Anyway I want him buried in the parish churchyard. We've got a grave there. Our little girl was buried in it thirty years ago. We had a full-depth grave so that we could be buried there as well. Beryl was only four and she could be alive today if it wasn't for old Doctor Phillips who was here then. She had terrible stomach ache. Give her opening medicine, he said. We did. What the old fool didn't realize was that she had appendicitis. The appendix burst and she was dead two days later with peritonitis – that's men for you.'

By now I was wondering why she wanted to see me urgently. I was a man and apparently she despised men. Perhaps because I was a parson, I did not come into the category of men. I was some neutral being to whom she could pour forth all her bitterness, as if she were talking to herself.

Annie Jones came in with a tray on which were the cup of tea and a few ginger biscuits on a plate.

'You could have used the best china, Annie. That cup's got a chip off it,' chided the widow.

Annie's face reddened as she fought a battle for self control.

'I did look for your tea service, Ag, but I couldn't find it.'

'It's in the china cabinet in the middle room.'

'Well, that's why I couldn't find it in the kitchen. Sorry, Mr Secombe. Shall I take it back and give you a fresh cup?'

'Not to worry, Mrs Jones,' I replied. 'I'm sure the tea will taste just as good in this cup.'

'Go on, Annie. Take the cup and saucer back and give him a fresh cup in the best china.'

Annie took the offending china from me without a word but with a look which spelt volumes.

'As I was saying, Vicar,' continued the very recently bereaved, 'life has dealt me some hard knocks. It's a good thing I've got the strength to fight on. I'll need that more and more now. Why don't you have a biscuit while you wait for your cup of tea.'

I was glad of the biscuit. It gave me something to do while I listened to the monologue.

'Yes, my husband would never go to the doctor, especially after our little girl died. Perhaps if he had gone he would be alive today. Still, you never know, do you, what's round the next corner.'

Mercifully, at this stage Annie arrived with the best piece of china.

'Here you are, Vicar,' she said. 'It's milk and two sugars, isn't it?'

'It is indeed and very welcome it is, before I go back out into the cold.'

'You're not going just yet.' The widow put her hand on my forearm with the intention of pinning me to my seat for the rest of the evening.

'I'm afraid I have to get back, Mrs Collier. My wife is out on call and neither of us has had a meal. I shall have to prepare something for us both.' I spoke so firmly that she had to accept the fact of my leaving.

When I had drunk my tea, I said, 'I'll come and see you later in the week about the funeral arrangements. I expect the undertaker will be in touch with me tomorrow in any case. Is there anybody staying with you tonight?'

'I'm staying with her,' interjected Annie, 'My husband's on nights and I've left him his supper.'

'I told you, Annie, I can manage on my own.' The widow's tone of voice was sharp.

'Nothing of the sort, Ag. I've brought my nightie and things and I'm staying here. So that's that.'

Before any further argument could develop I rose from the chair and made a beeline for the door. I paused there and said, 'Goodnight, Mrs Collier. We shall remember you and Mr Collier in our prayers at church tomorrow morning.'

'Prayers won't bring him back,' was the reply.

Annie Jones saw me to the front door.

'I'm afraid the shock has left her at odds with you and me and the world in general,' I whispered.

'When wasn't she like that?' said Annie and closed the door.

Once outside I realized I had no torch. The easterly wind was beginning to rise and there were snowflakes in the air. Under no circumstances was I going to return to that house to see if I could borrow a flashlight of some description.

I blundered my way through the snow, sometimes knee-deep. It was at least half an hour before I found myself by the vicarage gates. The trench I had dug down the drive was as welcome to me as the path through the Red Sea to the Children of Israel. That razor-sharp easterly had begun to bite into my innermost being. Outside the back door I took off one wellington and began to knock the snow off against the step. As I did so, the door opened.

'Well, explain yourself,' demanded my wife mockingly.

'That's a perky tone of voice,' I said.

'Don't stand there like a stork on one leg,' she ordered. 'Come on in, sit down on the floor and take your other boot off. Otherwise you'll have two wet socks instead of one.'

'You sound as if all has gone OK with you. Mother and baby both well, I take it.' I gave a long sigh of relief as I tugged off the wellington.

'You sound as if you're exhausted. Yes, mother and seven-pound baby boy more or less exhausted like you, but safe and sound, thank God. Now tell me your story.'

'In a nutshell, you have coped with an incoming into the world and I have had to cope with the consequences of a departure.'

'Come and tell Eleanor all about it while I prepare some chips to go with our tin of corned beef.'

'Every vicar should have a wife,' I said.

# 3

It was a fortnight since the arctic weather had inflicted itself upon the Valleys and the country in general. There was still a blanket of snow everywhere and the roads were treacherous skating rinks. However, life was slowly returning to normal. The telephone lines had been restored, as had the electricity supply, except that it was subject to the twelve-hour cuts that the government deemed necessary to prevent the collapse of the system. Shops were receiving their supplies and the evening newspapers were on sale once again.

I was reading the newspaper in my study while Eleanor was preparing our evening meal in the kitchen. One of the paper's less interesting features was the Post Box, the readers' letters column, with its quota of pompous comments on world or national affairs from regular correspondents, mixed with local trivia from one-off letter writers. My eye was drawn to it by the heading 'Housing Scandal' and underneath was the following letter.

Monmouthshire Post
Tuesday 17 March

Dear Sir,

Like many of my fellow soldiers who have returned to civilian life after fighting for King and Country, I have come home to a land where there is no accommodation for me and my family. We have two children, a six-year-old boy and a five-year-old girl and have to live with my in-laws. The children sleep with us in the one bedroom and my wife has to share the kitchen with her mother who has to cook for the four of her family living at home.

In the meanwhile there are empty houses in Pontywen which have not been occupied for some time. Take for example number 13, Mount Pleasant View which has been vacant for three months and belongs to someone who has no need of it. This is a scandal. Is it any wonder that there are squatters? Is this the land fit for heroes to live in?

Yours faithfully,
A Desert Rat.

Number 13, Mount Pleasant View was the house which had been left to me by my former landlady, who had died some months previously. Shortly after I had received the unexpected legacy I was appointed Vicar of Pontywen. Events had happened so quickly that I had little time to spare on thoughts of what to do with the house.

Brandishing the newspaper, I dashed into the kitchen shouting 'Look at this!'

Eleanor turned round from the sink with a Dover Sole in her hand, half of a Friday-evening treat by courtesy of Richards the Fish whose wife was one of her patients.

'What on earth is the matter? Is the world coming to an end or what?' she looked at me, wide-eyed with astonishment.

I thrust the paper under her nose, pointing to the cause of the panic. 'Read that,' I said.

'Calm down, Frederick, and let me put this fish on a plate before I read it. Give your blood pressure a chance to subside.' She deposited the Dover Sole on a plate, washed her hands under the tap and then dried them, taking her time over her ablutions.

I gave her the paper, stabbing at the letter with my finger. She read it slowly.

'I don't think it warrants such a reaction on your part, Fred. The man does not mention your name, in all fairness, and if you were in his position, you would feel the same. This simply means you must make up your mind very quickly whether you want to sell it or let it. Now, if you don't mind, I have to get on with my culinary exercise, stage one. Pop off back to the study, love, and relax.'

She kissed me on the cheek, turned me round gently and steered me towards the door.

I slumped into the wooden armchair behind my desk and contemplated the ceiling, which proved to be devoid of inspiration. My predecessor had suggested that I might sell the house to the Church. I could not see the Parochial Church Council agreeing to that when Pontywen had no married curate. With the newspaper spread out on the desk, I turned my attention from the ceiling to the other pages. On page 5 a headline proclaimed 'OLDER MEN FOR THE CHURCH'. The article beneath referred to the influx of 'mature' men who were being given a short intensive course of training, in an effort to fill the depleted ranks of the clergy. The war years had caused a hiatus in the supply of ordinands. Married men who had spent their formative years in secular professions were being encouraged to consider whether they had a call to serve in holy orders.

'That's it,' I said to myself. In 1947 very few parishes had houses available for married curates – there were three churches to serve in Pontywen. The bishop knew what an incompetent person I had as my assistant. Perhaps he would be willing to let me have an older married man in addition to Charles.

Eleanor was most enthusiastic.

'I don't see how the bishop can refuse. You seem to be a blue-eyed boy as far as he is concerned. So go for it, Secombe.'

'There are a number of snags, love. First of all, I don't know whether he has anybody available at the moment. Secondly he might think that I would not be the right kind of vicar to employ a man much older than myself. Thirdly there is the question of grants towards the stipend of a second curate. Money from the central funds is in short supply.'

'Nothing venture, nothing win. You have nothing to lose by trying, anyway. Give his Lordship a ring tomorrow morning.'

'I thought I would write to him tonight. I can put everything down on paper, make out a good case, as it were.'

'Don't be so timid, Fred. Beard the lion in his lair.'

'That's no way to speak of the bishop. In any case, he's more like a lamb than a lion.'

'All the more reason then to speak to him rather than write to him.'

'You win, as usual. I'll phone him tomorrow morning.'

The next morning was the Saturday which Charles had chosen to be the occasion for his Winter Sports party. He had taken so long to arrange it that, had the weather not been abnormally severe, the snow would have melted long ago. The younger members of the Gilbert and Sullivan Society had shown great enthusiasm for the event which was to be rounded off with sandwiches and home-made cakes in St Padarn's. Inevitably Bertie Owen had indicated that he would be taking part, despite taking umbrage that he had not been asked to organize the jamboree. Idris the Milk and a few of the older men were also involved and had asked their wives to superintend the refreshments.

'What time is the kick-off this afternoon?' asked Eleanor as she was about to leave for her morning surgery.

'Two o'clock prompt, according to Charles, but since he is never prompt for anything, I should imagine half past two would be the more likely time.'

'That's all to the good. I don't expect I shall finish until about one o'clock, and since Mrs Watkins will not be coming this morning, I want to do some tidying up before we go. Don't forget to ring the bishop. I'll get fish and chips on my way back.'

As I waited for Charles to arrive for nine o'clock Matins, I rehearsed in my mind what I intended to say to the bishop later that morning. By the time my colleague arrived at ten past nine, I had concocted what I thought to be a reasonable case.

'Have you seen last night's *Post*?' he inquired eagerly.

'Never mind about last night's *Post*. What about this morning's service which is supposed to begin at nine o'clock *prompt*, like your big event this afternoon?'

'Sorry for the lapse, Fred.'

'Charles, you should be more accurate. You omitted "daily" from your "lapse". As far as last night's paper is concerned, I shall be doing something about it shortly. Now shall we get on with the service?'

The disgruntled curate began to mumble his way through Matins, annoyed at being devoid of a gossip about the letter. By the time the service was over, his excitement about the afternoon's proceedings had removed the scowl from his face.

'We've got thirty-five coming. I've arranged a programme of races and things. I've asked Gwen Shoemaker to be in charge of the refreshments afterwards.'

Gwen was the wife of Idris the Milk. Diplomatic and energetic, she was an ideal person to supervise the rest of the wives in the kitchen at St Padarn's.

'Good choice, Charles,' I said.

He blushed at the rare compliment.

'See you at the Tump at two o'clock prompt – I can't stop to gossip, I have an important phone call to make.'

I sat down at my desk when I returned and composed myself before making the important phone call. Then I took a deep breath and dialled the bishop's number. To my dismay the housekeeper answered. 'I am afraid the bishop is away for the day. You had better ring him on Monday morning. If it is urgent, I can take a message.'

'No, Miss Wilkinson, it is not urgent but perhaps you would leave a note that the Vicar of Pontywen will be ringing him on Monday morning.'

How I enjoyed announcing myself as the Vicar of Pontywen. The self importance vanished when she replied, 'There's no need for that, Mr Secombe. A number of clergy have rung up already. The bishop will be available for calls from half past ten until half past twelve on Monday. So just take pot luck.'

When Eleanor arrived with the fish and chips at one fifteen p.m. her first words were 'Well, what did he say?'

'He said nothing, I'm afraid; for the simple reason that he was not there. He's away for the day. I am ringing him on Monday morning, apparently as one of a queue of clergy waiting to pester the poor old boy, according to his housekeeper.

'You had better get in first before he gets exhausted, love. Give him a ring about nine o'clock.'

'Impossible, my sweet. I was told that he was available for calls from half past ten until half past twelve.'

'In that case phone him about twenty past ten. I'm sure he won't mind you being ten minutes early, especially since you are a blue-eyed boy.'

'Look, love. I don't tell you what to do about patients, so please allow me to decide when I ring him.'

She stood and stared at me, her expressive dark-brown eyes opened wide in astonishment, and then suddenly she burst into peals of laughter.

'Frederick, I never realized you could be so masterful. Let me put the fish and chips in the oven before I swoon in your arms.'

I followed her into the kitchen. As soon as she had put our lunch in the oven, I pulled her to me. She looked up at me from her five foot two inches.

'I'm sorry, love. Before we were married, I told you to check me when I get too bossy. I thought you were most impressive.'

It was half an hour before we turned our attention to the fish and chips. It was another hour before we joined the St Moritz set on the Tump. The Tump was a barren, steep slope which was topped by a small plateau running parallel with Penygraig Road and dropping down to the Recreation Ground at its foot. At one time it must have been some kind of a tip. During the summer it was a playground for little boys who wished to wear a hole in their trousers as they slid to the bottom. Now, covered in snow, it could have been taken for a Swiss ski run. As Eleanor and I neared the venue for the Charles Wentworth-Baxter frolics, we could hear shouts of encouragement mingled with shrieks of laughter. Evidently my curate's enterprise was proving to be a hit with the Gilbert and Sullivan crowd, a veritable milestone in what had been a most ineffectual ministry until then.

'I wonder what's causing the excitement,' I said. 'Is it the races or the things?'

'What on earth do you mean, you abstruse vicar?'

'According to Charles, the afternoon was to consist of races and things.'

'By the sound of the laughter, I should think it's the things, and Peter Pan might be in the thick of things.'

Suddenly there was a deathly silence as we turned the corner into Penygraig Road. 'I shouldn't have said that,' commented Eleanor, as we saw a knot of people approaching an inert figure at the bottom of the slope, watched by a small crowd of spectators at the top of the Tump. 'Poor Peter Pan,' she murmured.

We made our way as quickly as possible to the Recreation

Ground and reached the foot of the slope where the accident victim lay alongside an overturned sledge. Inevitably it was my curate there, lying in a heap. Bertie Owen was about to examine the body when Eleanor shouted 'Don't touch him!'

'Doctor, it's you,' he said. 'There's glad I am to see you – and you, of course, Vicar. The curate's had an accident.'

My wife knelt by Charles who was prostrate, face down on the hard-packed snow. Gently she turned him over. He was unconscious. She examined his shoulders and his legs. 'Bertie,' she ordered, 'go and phone for an ambulance at once. Tell them that a doctor has examined the patient and that he needs hospital treatment urgently.'

Bertie Owen skidded his way to the telephone kiosk at the corner of the Recreation Ground, falling on his posterior twice in the process.

'I think he has a broken collar bone and a broken leg,' Eleanor whispered to me.

'What about his head?' I asked.

'It looks like a slight concussion. He will probably be conscious well before the ambulance arrives.'

The words were scarcely out of her mouth when Charles blinked his eyes and returned to his winter wonderland, body all racked and aching with pain.

'Oooh!' he exclaimed as he tried to sit up.

'Lie still!' commanded Eleanor. 'We'll have the ambulance here in a minute. Till then you are not to move.'

'I won't, don't worry. The pain is too bad for that. I was trying to get the fastest time; if I hadn't fallen off, I think I would have done it, Oh!'

As we found out later, each contestant was being timed by Idris the Milk who had borrowed a stopwatch for the occasion. When Charles took his turn, Bertie Owen gave the sledge an almighty push and, according to the onlookers, Charles parted company with his vehicle when it was only halfway down the slope. It then became a toss up, which would arrive at the bottom first, the curate or the sledge, since both were descending at an alarming pace. Apparently it was a dead heat.

Eleanor and I went with the victim to the hospital while the others decided to abandon play for the day and to make their way to St Padarn's for the refreshments.

'I'm sorry about this, Fred,' said Charles in the ambulance. 'It was going so well up until then. What are you going to do about the services?'

'Never mind about that. You concentrate on getting better as soon as you can.'

'As soon as you can will be at least two months, I should think,' interjected Eleanor. 'It looks as if you have a nasty break in your left leg. Your collar bone should not be too bad. I'm afraid you will have to keep the nurses company for quite a few weeks.'

A dreamy smile spread across his countenance, despite his pain. He looked as if he would have given Bertie Owen a vote of thanks for his push on the sledge.

The X-rays bore out Eleanor's diagnosis. There was a bad break in the left leg but the collarbone fracture was mild in comparison.

We walked down from Pontywen Hospital, leaving Charles Wentworth-Baxter drooling over the nurses and evidently looking forward to his stay.

'By the time he leaves hospital he will have fallen in love once again,' I said to Eleanor.

'Not once but half a dozen times, I should think, knowing him,' she replied. 'More important than Charles's love life is the headache you are going to have over the services tomorrow and the Sunday after. What on earth are you going to do?'

'I should phone the rural dean but that would be a waste of a call. The bishop is away for two days. So that leaves the archdeacon. Perhaps he knows of a retired clergyman who might help out or perhaps a parish with a spare curate. Speaking of which, this accident will strengthen my case when I ring his Lordship on Monday morning.'

The rural dean, the Reverend Daniel Thomas, was an elderly gentleman who was rarely seen outside his parish and presided over a deanery with more than its fair share of geriatric clergy. He might be able to supply me with a stick of rhubarb from his well-stocked garden but certainly he would be unable to produce a clergyman for an emergency.

On the other hand, the archdeacon, the Venerable Griffith Williams, was an ambitious priest in his early fifties who had the affairs of his archdeaconry at his fingertips. 'You go on to the vicarage,' said my wife. 'I'll join the party at St Padarn's. I expect they will be wanting news about the demon sledger. You can come and join us with your news after your phone call.'

To my great relief the archdeacon assured me that he would see that someone would turn up at St Padarn's for the nine-thirty a.m. service and for evensong at the Parish Church at six-thirty p.m.

Armed with this information, I made my way to St Padarn's where Aneurin Williams, the musical director for the Gilbert and Sullivan Society, was conducting some impromptu singing of choruses from the *Pirates of Penzance*. Evidently a good time was being had by all, despite the curate's mishap. The MD called a halt to the music.

'We've saved you some sandwiches and cakes, Vicar,' said Gwen Shoemaker.

'What about the services at St Padarn's tomorrow?' inquired Bertie Owen.

'You're a fine one to be asking that. If you hadn't pushed

the curate so hard, he would have been taking the services.' Idris the Milk's remonstration was greeted with a number of 'Hear! Hear!'s from members of the Society.

'Those of you who worship at St Padarn's will be pleased to know that there will be a priest to celebrate the Eucharist at nine-thirty p.m. and I shall be taking Evensong. So all is well for tomorrow at least.'

As far as rehearsals are concerned,' said Aneurin, 'until I can find a pianist, I shall play the piano and conduct from the stool.'

When I went to St Padarn's to take evensong next day I had a glowing account of the morning's service from various members of the choir and the churchwardens. Even Mrs Collier, in her widow's weeds, was moved to commend the celebrant, as a postscript to some disparaging words about Miss Usher, the deputy organist, who had taken over from her late husband.

It appeared that the locum was the Reverend Dewi Jones, a retired missionary who had spent most of his ministry in China. He had regaled the congregation with traveller's tales which had held them spellbound.

'What do you think?' said Mrs Collier. 'He even brought a prayer wheel with him to show how the Chinese made their prayers to God.'

Considering what she had said to me about prayers for her late husband, when I visited her on the day of his death, I would not have thought she would have been interested.

Eleanor had decided to worship at the parish church exclusively once I had been inducted as vicar. It meant that she had only to walk a few steps from the vicarage and it also gave her an opportunity to get to know the people there, her previous acquaintance with a congregation in Pontywen having been confined to a few visits to St Padarn's.

When I returned to the vicarage, my wife was as fulsome in her praise of the preacher as they were in St Padarn's.

'He is a dear old man,' she said, 'and he had them eating out of his hand. He brought a prayer wheel with him – and had some wonderful stories to tell about life in China in the twenties and thirties. I asked him back to the vicarage for coffee but he had to get back. His wife is very frail, he said, and he doesn't like leaving her on her own too long. I have invited them both here for dinner one night this week. He said he would let us know sometime tomorrow if they are coming.'

'Charles Wentworth-Baxter is going to be something of an anticlimax when he returns if we have a succession of such star preachers at St Padarn's.'

'Let's face it, Fred, poor Charles is a permanent anticlimax. Let's hope that the bishop will turn up trumps with another curate who will at least be average in the pulpit and in the parish at large. There can't possibly be another one like Charles.'

The next morning at ten twenty-five a.m. precisely, in accordance with my wife's instruction, I made my vital telephone call to the bishop. There was no engaged tone but it was a few minutes before the receiver was picked up.

'Bishop speaking,' announced a somewhat irate voice.

My heart sank to my boots. Why hadn't I waited until ten thirty, I said to myself; this is more like a lion than a lamb.

'This is Fred Secombe, my Lord. I hope I have not rung at an inconvenient time.'

'That's quite all right, Vicar.' There was a slight moderation of the irritation in his tone. 'I am afraid I have a rather busy morning ahead of me; so if you could be as brief as possible, I should be much obliged.'

'To put things in a nutshell, my Lord, I have an empty three-bedroomed house belonging to me in the parish which could accommodate a curate and his wife. Charles Wentworth-Baxter has just broken his leg and his collar bone in an accident. A letter appeared in Friday night's *Post* from an ex-soldier complaining that Number 13, Mount Pleasant View was owned by someone who had no need of it, while he and several like him had no house in which to rear his family. Is it possible that my house could be a haven for a married man in holy orders who is desperate for accommodation?'

There was a long silence at the other end. I did not possess a prayer wheel. If I had, it would have been spinning at breakneck speed.

'You have certainly crammed much into that nutshell, Vicar. As it happens, I have a married man due to be priested at Trinity who is very unhappy about living in a rented flat, with no hope of a house in the parish; I am sure his vicar will let him go under the circumstances. There is one snag: he is considerably older than you. He is a fifty-year-old entrant into holy orders who has done a shortened course at a theological college. If you are prepared to accept him, and of course if he wishes to come to you, then he can be licensed to Pontywen. His name is Barnabas Adrian Webster and his address is 15, Merthyr Street, Cwmfelin. If you write to him, making an appointment, I shall also write to him and to the Vicar of Cwmfelin. By the way, I hope Mr Wentworth-Baxter is not too badly injured.'

'No, my Lord, he should be out of hospital in the next month or so but it will be quite a while before he will be able to resume his duties. Thank you very much for your help. I think I shall be able to work with Mr Webster despite the age difference. Anyway, we shall see once we have met and discussed things.'

'Remember, Vicar, you are under no obligation to take this man. Let me know what you have decided once you have had the interview. Now if you will excuse me I must get on with all the other calls lined up for me.'

I put the phone down and then rang Eleanor at the surgery.

'You sound excited,' she said; 'so what's the news?'

'I can have a married curate and presumably he can come as soon as possible. There are two snags. One, he will not be priested for another three months. However, I am sure we shall be able to manage until then with people like the Reverend Dewi Jones. Second, he is fifty years old and has only done a sandwich course at a theological college.'

'My dear love, I am working with someone who is nearly seventy years old. That's no great snag. In any case, he is bound to be better than Charles. Splendid news. We shall celebrate tonight and dine out. By the way what is his name?'

'Barnabas Adrian Webster.'

She giggled. 'What a pair – Charles Wentworth-Baxter and Barnabas Adrian Webster. Alike in name. I hope they are not alike in nature.'

'We'll see,' I said.

# 4

They stood on the vicarage doorstep, an incongruous couple. The Reverend Barnabas Webster was tall, well-built, fresh-complexioned and grey-haired. His wife was diminutive, thin, sallow-faced, with dark beady eyes. They both smiled nervously when I opened the door.

'Good morning, Vicar, I hope we are not too early. It took far less time to come than I thought it would.' There was a burr in his voice similar to that of Mr Polkinghorne. His whole appearance suggested a rural background, from his grey tweeds to his big black boots. A gold watch chain adorned his waistcoat.

'Yes, I was expecting we might even be a little bit late, wasn't I, dear?' Mrs Webster's high-pitched tones had a metallic edge to them. Evidently she was not the mouse she seemed to be, in her somewhat dowdy clothes.

'You were indeed. That's because you forget we've got a new car now, that doesn't loiter like our last one. It's a Riley, Vicar.' He pointed with pride at the gleaming expensive car. 'My last extravagance before entering the ministry.'

'Well, don't let's stand out here. Come on into the drawing room.' I had intended to say 'lounge' but changed the word at the sight of the Riley. If he was out to impress, then so was I.

'Please make yourselves comfortable. I'll arrange for some tea for us.' I went into the kitchen where Mrs Watkins was at the sink in her green overalls. 'When you're ready, Mrs Watkins, may we have three cups of tea, a bowl of sugar and a jug of milk; all in the best china, and some of those mixed biscuits.'

43

'What about plates an' that?' she inquired. 'An' that' featured in most of her sentences.

'Of course. That's fine, thank you. We're in the lounge.'

When I returned the pair were looking out of the big bay window at the still snow-covered lawn and flower beds.

'The garden must be very pretty in the summer,' said Mrs Webster.

'It is indeed but I am afraid it will take up a lot of time to keep it in good order,' I replied.

'I know all about that, Vicar. We had a large garden behind the village stores we used to own in Shropshire. What with looking after the shop and coupons and things it used to be quite a headache until I got a man to mow the lawn and see to the flower beds. That's what you ought to do, Vicar.'

If Barnabas is going to be generous in his advice after only a few minutes' acquaintance, what will he be like in a few months' time, I said to myself.

'Please take a seat, both.' I indicated the leather settee in front of the window, ignoring his gratuitous suggestion.

'Once we have had some tea and a chat, I shall take you to see the parish church and St Padarn's, and after that the house in Mount Pleasant View. I am afraid there is no garden at the back but there is a greenhouse of sorts.'

'That will be nice, won't it, Barney?' piped up his wife.

I was not quite sure whether she was referring to the greenhouse or to the itinerary.

Barney smiled in reply. It was more a quick flash of his false teeth than a smile.

'So you were a shopkeeper before you entered the ministry. What made you give up your village stores at your time of life to take holy orders?'

He stared at me as if it were the first time he had been asked that question.

'My uncle is a parson in Radnorshire – near retirement now but I've stayed with him many a time. I liked what I saw. He had time for people as well as lots of time for himself. I left school when I was fourteen to help in my father's shop, but when I was in my twenties my vicar asked me if I would like to be a lay reader. He helped me to study to pass the lay reader's exam and I got through. So I became the vicar's right-hand-man for twenty years. Then about three years or so ago, he asked me if I had thought about being ordained. He had a word with the bishop and the next thing I was in a theological college doing a shortened course. Now here I am. I may not have been to university but I have had better training than that, in the university of life, in the outside world.'

It was the first time I had ever heard a life spent in a village grocery store described as one lived in the outside world, the university of life. Furthermore it was apparent that he thought his 'training' was superior to mine, at university and theological college.

Before I could think of a suitable reply Mrs Watkins knocked on the door and brought in the tray with the tea and biscuits.

'This is the lady who helps in the house during the week. Mrs Watkins, this is the Reverend and Mrs Webster. They may be coming to Pontywen in the near future to work in the parish.'

Mrs Watkins wiped her right hand in her overalls and offered it to the couple.

'Pleased to meet you. Well, you couldn't come to a better place or a better vicar. What he do do for people in the parish is nobody's business, and Dr Secombe, if it comes to that – both of them always 'elping everybody an' that.'

As our daily poured out the tea, Mrs Webster embarked upon another topic of conversation,

'Of course, Vicar, your wife is a lady doctor, isn't she? It must be quite exciting to be married to somebody like that.'

'Hardly exciting. I don't think she would put her job in that category. Demanding, yes. Exciting, no. It means she has less time to help in the parish than other clergy wives.'

'In that case I would be only too ready to help in that direction if we come here.'

Mrs Barney was indeed only too ready to take charge. I began to consider the disadvantages of having a second curate, remembering a saying of the rural dean's, 'There's only one thing worse than not having a curate, and that is having a curate.' I had one prime example of that already in Charles Wentworth-Baxter.

By the time we had done the tour of the churches and an inspection of 13, Mount Pleasant View where they thought they could 'do something with it', I decided to stall for time saying that I had to talk things over with the Parochial Church Council. Then I would let them know next week whether I could offer Barnabas the curacy.

When Eleanor came back from her visits in the early afternoon she was all agog to hear what had transpired. After she had heard my account of the proceedings, she said, 'There is just one thing to remember. If you don't take the Reverend Barnabas I doubt whether the bishop will offer you anybody else. Put up with him and his pushy wife for the time being. Then perhaps you may get someone much better next time. On the other hand, they may turn out to be more of an asset than you think.'

The monthly meeting of the Parochial Church Council was due to be held the next evening. I had discussed the probability of a second curate with the two wardens already. Both Harold Jones, the vicar's warden, and David Vaughan-Jenkins, the people's warden, were enthusiastic about it and considered that the Church would be able to finance the purchase of the house, as well as a contribution to the new curate's stipend. Mr Vaughan-Jenkins was a local bank manager and therefore was respected by the members of the Church Council as the financial expert par excellence.

So it was the people's warden who swayed the meeting with his assurance that the parish could afford to buy the house and help maintain the new curate. 'The vicar is prepared to sell the house at a figure much less than he would get on the open market. I shall be able to negotiate a loan on reasonable terms and I heartily recommend the proposition to this Council.'

Inevitably it was Bertie Owen who was the only dissentient when I asked for a discussion of the proposition. 'As people's warden of the daughter church, I hope that the new man will be given the responsibility of looking after our congregation. We have never had a married curate before, except for a few weeks when our vicar was curate, that is. He'll have a wife who isn't working, not like Dr Secombe, and she will be able to take charge of the ladies.'

'Mr Owen, the purpose of this meeting is not to discuss where the new curate will be placed in the parish. That is my responsibility; you have been asked to decide whether Ponty-wen can afford a second curate and the purchase of the house.'

'Look, Vicar, I tell you this now straight from the shoulder,' Bertie pointed his finger at me, 'if you think we are going to put up with Mr Wentworth-Baxter, when we've got somebody else with a wife, who could be doing the job, then you'll find there won't be much money coming from St Padarn's towards the cost of a second curate. There won't be enough people in the congregation to help pay for one curate let alone two.'

If Bertie expected support from the other Council members from St Padarn's, he was disappointed.

'I move that we buy the house and pay for the new curate,' proposed Ivor the Milk.

'I second that,' Charlie Hughes, the vicar's warden at St Padarn's, announced.

With that the motion was passed, with only Bertie's vote against.

Next morning I wrote to the Reverend Barnabas Webster, offering him the curacy at two hundred and fifty pounds per annum with house, rent and rates free. Then I went to the hospital to see Charles and to pass on the news that he had a fellow curate. He was lying flat on his back with his leg in traction and was engaged in conversation with a pretty little nurse.

'Fred, meet Nurse Williams, my favourite nurse, the Florence Nightingale of Pontywen.'

'Don't you listen to him, Vicar! I expect he says that about all the other nurses,' she blushed.

'Knowing Charles, Nurse Williams, I am sure he does.'

She moved further down the ward.

'First of all, how are you feeling?'

'Fine. The food is good and the nurses are tremendous.'

'So I see. I have come to bring you some news. You are going to have a fellow curate very shortly.'

The effect on the invalid was startling. He attempted to sit up, causing interference with the leg contraption and a certain amount of pain for himself.

'Lie back, Charles. I didn't think that information would

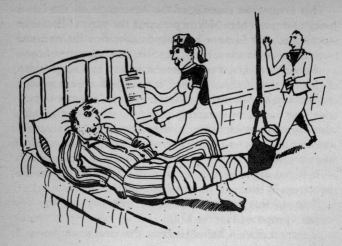

have such an effect on you, otherwise I would have broken it more gently.'

'What does that mean, Fred? Is it the thin end of the wedge for me?'

'Don't be so silly. There's no wedge involved. If you remember, there were two curates in this parish for quite a while until I was made vicar. It is just that I have sold my house to the Church, which enables Pontywen to have a married curate. Fortunately the bishop has been able to supply me with one. He won't be priested until next June but he will be moving in shortly – which is just as well with you in your present state of health.'

'Who is he? He must be an older man if he's married.'

'Got it in one, Charles – his name is Barnabas Adrian Webster, aged about fifty, a former shopkeeper who has now fulfilled his ambition, with a wife who has now fulfilled her ambition even more so – anyway, we shall see how we get on together.'

'You don't seem to be too thrilled.'

'Maybe second impressions will be better than first ones.'

'I see.' Charles sounded gratified that his future colleague was none too good a catch.

48

That evening we entertained the Reverend and Mrs Dewi Jones to dinner. Mrs Morris prepared the vegetables in the morning so that Eleanor had less to do when she returned from the five o'clock surgery. My wife had thought to cook a meal which involved rice since the Jones's had spent much of their lives in China. When I suggested that perhaps one of their happiest thoughts on leaving China was the knowledge that they were escaping from an endless diet of rice, she decided that a leg of black-market pork from the church-warden at Llanhyfryd, garnished with roast potatoes, cauliflower, tinned peas and carrots, would provide a much more acceptable main course. Our daily help had also made the dessert – jelly and blancmange, neatly formed by their moulds. She was now indispensable at the vicarage.

Our visitors arrived at seven o'clock prompt. The old missionary, tall, thin, bald-headed and bespectacled, escorted his little wife who was crippled by rheumatoid arthritis, with the loving care of a doting husband. Slowly they made their way from their car to the doorstep where I was waiting to greet them.

'Good evening, Vicar,' said my locum. 'How good to meet you in person.' He shook my hand warmly and introduced his wife who held out a hand which was half closed by the cruel malady.

'Excuse my fist, Mr Secombe. I am afraid it is more suited to a boxing ring than a dinner party.' She spoke without a trace of bitterness. It was obvious that she was fighting her handicap with a sense of humour and with a courage which transcended anything in a boxing ring.

'It's a great pleasure to have you with us. Please come in out of the cold.' I ushered them into the lounge.

'I hate the cold. It is my greatest enemy,' she said. 'On days like these I long to be back in China.'

Throughout the meal the couple fascinated Eleanor and myself with tales about their experiences in that vast country. We were surprised to know that, prior to the coming of the Communists and the Civil War then raging with the Nationalists, Christianity had played a big part in public life out of all proportion to the small number of Christians in China.

Then, after dinner, when we were enjoying a cup of coffee and some biscuits in the lounge, I mentioned that the following week the parish was about to have a married curate added to its clergy.

'In that case,' said the Reverend Dewi Jones, 'my services will be required no longer.'

'Not at all, Mr Jones,' I replied. 'The new man is not due to be priested until Trinity in ten weeks' time. Until then I shall be most pleased if you will help us with our Communion services.'

The old man seemed delighted that he would be needed in Pontywen for some time yet.

'By the way,' he asked, 'who is this new curate?'

'He rejoices in the names of Barnabas Adrian Webster and is at Cwmfelin at the moment.'

His face dropped. 'That is John Webster's nephew. John used to be in college with me and we have kept in touch ever since. I have heard all about Barney from him. From what I can gather he seems to be more in love with the status of a parson than with his duties. Apparently his wife has been the driving power behind him, longing to be Mrs Vicar one day. I tell you this in the strictest confidence so that you are fully prepared for his coming. It may be that you can make something of him by leading him in the right direction. I hope so for your sake, as well as his.

'Now then,' he went on, 'here is a little present for you and Mrs Secombe.' He put his hand into his inside pocket and produced two pairs of chopsticks. 'Would you care for a demonstration?' He broke a cream biscuit in half and then deftly used the chopsticks to pick it up. 'I shan't soil the chopsticks by putting it in my mouth – but you get the general idea.'

Eleanor picked up the method in no time. I convulsed the three onlookers by failing at every attempt to use the eating tools. It was fortunate, I thought to myself, that we had not cooked rice. Otherwise I should have been expected to use the things. If I failed with half a biscuit, rice would have been a disaster.

By the time our guests departed we were on Christian-name terms. Dewi and Rachel were destined to become firm friends of ours despite the difference in our ages. Eleanor had been able to give some helpful medical information about new tablets on the market to ease the pain for the old lady.

'There is no cure for that,' my wife told me after they had left. 'It will get progressively crippling.'

'You needn't tell me that,' I replied. 'My grandmother ended up bent in half in bed with her knees almost touching her chin and with her hands virtually closed up. My mother nursed her for some years in our council house. It is a terrible affliction.'

'I remember your mother telling me all about that. It must have been a trying time for her because shortly after that she had to go into hospital to have her kidney removed. I think Rachel and your mother have more courage than most ordinary mortals.'

'To return to ordinary mortals, what about Barney and his wife? It seems that I have bought a pig in a poke, if you know what I mean.'

'I do know what you mean, although Barney would hardly appreciate that. Well, Secombe, it is a chance for you to prove yourself. So, go to it, man.'

On the following Monday the Websters moved into 13, Mount Pleasant View. There was still snow on the ground and the roads around Pontywen were as treacherous as they had been for the past three weeks. The steep hills and icy surfaces formed a lethal combination as several drivers had found to their cost. To their number was added the Reverend Barnabas in his new Riley. His new motor car and a lamppost in Lady Smith Terrace had met each other unexpectedly. Fortunately it was more of a gentle embrace than a violent confrontation. The curate was no Jehu. However, his beloved acquisition was suffering from a damaged headlamp and a dented wing. The driver was suffering more than the car. He seemed to be on the verge of tears when he arrived at his new home, where I was waiting to greet the couple.

'I told you to take that other road, Barney,' said his wife, evidently intent on adding to his misery.

'Whatever road he took, Mrs Webster, he would have to contend with the ice. Anyway, it could have been worse.

We have a good garage here in Pontywen and I'm sure they will be able to put the damage right. Come on in and have a cup of tea before the removers get here.' My bonhomie failed to pacify the curate.

'Thank you, Vicar. The van won't be here just yet. They've stopped for something to eat at one of those road-side cafés.' He intoned the words in a manner more appropriate to a funeral service. 'I'm afraid the garage in Pontywen will not be able to see to this car properly. It will have to go back to the Riley dealers in Cardiff. What a way to begin my time here in Pontywen.'

'I hope it is not an omen. Those men have already broken some of my best china. Everything seems to be going wrong,' wailed Ethel.

'I'm afraid I don't believe in omens, Mrs Webster, especially ill omens. "Sufficient unto the day is the evil thereof." That is one of my favourite verses in the whole of the New Testament.'

She manufactured a simper.

'Quite right, Vicar. I suppose Christians shouldn't believe in omens. It has just been one of those days, but there, we have arrived safe and sound. That's all that matters, isn't it, Barney?'

'Yes,' said Barney without an ounce of conviction.

Eleanor and I had moved almost all of the furniture from my late landlady's house to help fill up some of the many rooms in the vicarage. There was still the gas stove, a few cups and saucers in a cupboard, plus kitchen table and a few chairs. I had brought a tea pot with some tea, sugar and milk from the vicarage.

'Sit down and relax,' I said to the Websters. They sat down on the kitchen chairs while I used the late Mrs Richards' kettle to boil the water for a cup of tea.

'They should have been here by now. I feel sure something has happened.' Mrs Webster was sitting on the edge of her seat, expecting the worst, obviously still affected by the omens. We had been sitting in the kitchen for an hour engaged in small talk which none of us enjoyed, while we waited for their belongings to arrive.

'I think I'll have another look at the Riley.' Throughout

our trivial conversation Barney insisted on referring to the machine as 'the Riley'. It was too upmarket to be called 'the car'.

'In that case I'll come with you, if it's only to stretch my legs.' I had no desire to be closeted with his wife who had begun to bite her nails in agonized suspense. 'Perhaps you would like to have a look around the house once again, while you wait,' I suggested to her.

'If you don't mind, Vicar, I think I'll stay where I am. All I want is for the van to arrive. You go with Barney.' She continued to chew her nails.

When I went out, I found Barney seated on the pavement, with a look of surprise on his face, his legs spreadeagled.

I had visions of another hospital case. It was enough to have one curate in traction but two would be too much.

'Let me help you up, Barney. You don't mind me calling you Barney, do you?'

'No, Vicar, everybody calls me that. I don't think I've done much harm to myself. I didn't realize the steps were so slippery.'

I put my arms around him and heaved. To my great relief, he stood on his two legs without any sign of great pain.

'Thank you, Vicar. That certainly shook me up. I think I must have bruised my posterior but that's about all. Now then, let's have another look at this damage.'

As he moved towards his prize possession, I sent up a silent prayer of gratitude. We were taught to call such a communication with the Almighty an arrow prayer. This one went with the speed of light.

We were surveying the impression the lamppost had made on the Riley when to my surprise Eleanor's new Ford drove up behind.

She was out of the car in a flash.

'This is my wife,' I said. 'Eleanor, this is Barney Webster.'

They shook hands.

'Well, Mr Webster,' she said, 'I am afraid I have to bring you some none too good news. The police phoned me a few minutes ago to say that the furniture van bringing your possessions to Pontywen has overturned on the main road a few miles away. It seems that the driver and his mate are OK and that they hope to have the van righted with a crane before long. They should be here in another hour or so, if all goes well.'

Barney's cup of misery overflowed into his face, with an expression which would not have been out of place in a condemned cell.

'I hate to think what Ethel is going to say about all this,' he moaned.

I looked at my wife. She raised her eyes to heaven.

We moved into the house, with Barney bringing up the rear at a discreet distance.

As soon as Ethel saw my wife, she stood up quickly, knocking over the kitchen chair in the process.

'Don't tell me,' she breathed, 'this is Mrs Secombe. Doctor, how nice to meet you, I've heard so much about you.'

Eleanor took the proffered hand and held on to it.

'Mrs Webster, it's a pleasure to meet you but no pleasure to have to bring you unwelcome news. There has been an accident to your removal van, it skidded on the ice on the main road and overturned. The good news is that the police say that they hope to have it upright shortly and that the driver and his mate are only a few miles away.'

Ethel was transmogrified and pulled away from my wife.

'Barney, I told you we should have had Pickford's. I didn't trust those men as soon as I saw them. I expect they were in a pub not a café. All my lovely china, let alone the furniture.' She turned to me. 'So it was an omen after all. I knew it, New Testament or not, Vicar.'

I decided that silence was the best policy this time.

# 5

'You are suffering from constipation of the intellect and diarrhoea of the vocabulary.' This pithy comment from the professor of English on the back of a fellow student's essay in my first year at college provides an apt diagnosis of the Reverend Barnabas Webster's mental condition in his first sermon in the parish church.

He took as his text the fourteenth verse of the twenty-seventh chapter of the Acts of the Apostles. 'And when the ship was caught and could not bear up into the wind we let her drive.'

'Now, my dear friends, let me explain,' he began. 'That word "drive" is a nautical expression and it means "drift". We let her drift. Drift. What one of you here this evening can lay his hand or her hand on his or her heart and swear that he or she has never drifted? Never? Drift.

'Can you say that you have never been carried along on the tide of life, not caring where you have come from or where you are going or how you got there in the first place? Drift.

'Have you never stopped to think what life is all about or are you content to carry on doing your work wherever it may be, in the mines perhaps, or the steelworks, or the office or in the home without ever saying to yourself, "What am I doing here or why am I doing it?" Drift.'

There followed a further series of pointless questions addressed to his listeners, each with the word 'Drift' as its sequence. Everytime the word 'Drift' was used, Barney would pause for several seconds. After the first ten 'Drifts' the choirboys began a guessing competition about the final total. Barry Harrington, a mischievous thirteen-year-old back in the choir stalls after recovering from a serious road accident, caused widespread amusement in the chancel by announcing in something more than a stage whisper 'This sermon comes to you by courtesy of Drift, the new washing powder.'

Eventually the sermon drifted to its conclusion which, of course, was the word 'Drift'. A silence of a minute or so ensued while the Reverend Barnabas Webster surveyed the glazed expressions of his congregation before ascribing his sermon to the glory of God the Father, the Son and the Holy Spirit. Meanwhile the occupants of the choir stalls, both young and old, indulged in unseemly mirth despite several stares from a vicar who strove to contain his own desire to giggle. I was informed by Barry after the service that 'Drift' had notched up a total of fifty-two. It was a pulpit performance which even Ezekiel Evans, the parish lay reader, could not equal for inanity. Charles Wentworth-Baxter was a model preacher by comparison.

'Secombe,' said my beloved as we relaxed before a blazing fire in the sitting room. 'You have definitely, indeed very definitely, bought a pig in a poke, as you suggested a few weeks ago. I have never heard such a comic turn on any stage as Barney's effort this evening.'

'What on earth am I to do, love? He thinks he knows it all.'

'Might I suggest for a start that you do to him what your old vicar did to you when you came here first?'

'And that is?'

'Insist that he writes out his sermon and brings it to you before he preaches it. After all, you had been ordained a priest and had served a couple of years when you arrived in Pontywen. He has only been ten months in orders. You have every right to vet whatever rubbish he intends to preach. At least that way you will know what he is planning to perpetrate on the St Padarn's congregation, or wherever, while you are in St Mary's. Not only that, but it will stick a pin in his inflated ego. He needs it.'

'It's not going to be easy. He is so much older than I, and what is more, is convinced he is so much wiser as well.'

'Age and wisdom are not the same thing, Frederick. Some people have still learned nothing even when they have reached their three score and ten. Perhaps you will be the means of injecting a modicum of sense into his thick skull. You have nothing to lose but the chains of a second impediment in the parish.'

Next morning at five to nine, Barney swished his way into church in his cassock with a cape over his shoulders. He gave the impression that he was more in love with his cassock then he was with his calling. He read the lessons as if he was intoning them. By the time the service was over his whole attitude riled me to such an extent that I was determined to act on Eleanor's advice to deflate him.

As we waited in the vicarage study for Mrs Watkins to bring us tea and biscuits, I decided to delay my offensive until I had lulled him into a false sense of self importance.

'Have you settled in now, Barney?' I asked.

'Yes, very well indeed. As you know, the furniture arrived more or less intact and almost all the china was unbroken. By the end of the week we shall be all ship shape and Bristol fashion. Ethel is working like a beaver. Once she has got the house to her liking then she will be able to help in the parish.'

The thought of Ethel let loose in the parish was sufficient to make me suddenly determined that she and her husband should be exiled to Llanhyfryd.

'I have been thinking about where you and Ethel can be of most use and I am convinced that Llanhyfryd is the ideal place. You know the country life so well. Once you have been priested you shall have charge of St Illtyd's. Until then you can help in the parish in general.'

At the thought of being given charge of a church, Barney's bosom was filled with pride.

'Thank you very much, Vicar. I'm sure I shall be able to do a fine job in Llanhyfryd.'

The moment had come to put down the mighty from his seat.

'By the way,' I said, 'I think that for the next few months I had better see your sermons before you preach them. I am afraid your contribution from the pulpit last night was rather a poor effort. I shall do all I can to help you improve.'

His face went purple and his eyes opened wide.

'What do you mean, Vicar?'

'Well, for a start, you don't gain anything by repeating a word several times. Someone counted the number of "Drifts" in your sermon. Apparently there was a total of fifty-two. Five or six times perhaps is the limit for repetition but fifty-two must be a record of word wastage.

'Then again there was no point in challenging your congregation with a series of questions which led nowhere but probably left them bewildered and, worse still, bored.'

It was at this stage of the conversation that Mrs Watkins came into the study with the refreshments.

My new curate stared glumly at the carpet as our daily help poured out the tea. 'Milk and sugar, Mr Webster?' she inquired.

'Just milk, thank you,' he grunted.

'They do say the weather's going to get warmer and put an end to the ice an' that,' said Mrs Watkins.

'Then all the trouble will begin when the thaw sets in. You're lucky that the lavatory is working and the pipes aren't frozen in our house, Vicar.'

'That's not luck, Barney. We had a primus stove going in the lavatory for weeks and the water tank in the loft was thoroughly lagged. My old landlady, Mrs Richards, saw to that.'

He sounded disappointed that the freeze had not affected Number 13, Mount Pleasant View.

After Mrs Watkins left, he launched into a counter attack.

'I must say, no one has complained about my sermons before, not my last vicar nor my vicar when I was a lay reader all those years before.'

'Hold on, Barney. I am not your last vicar nor the vicar before that, but I am in charge of you now. I am responsible for your training.'

He bridled at the last sentence.

'Whether you like it or not being a lay reader is a totally different position from that of a priest. After the bishop and the priests have laid hands upon you at your ordination the bishop will give you a Bible and say "Take thou authority to preach the Word of God." If you are going to preach the Word of God with authority, it had better be something different from the farrago of nonsense you dished up last night. So, I would like you to write out your sermon for next Sunday which you will preach at St Padarn's in the morning when I shall be present and in Llanhyfryd in the evening. I shall expect it here by Friday morning after Matins and we shall go through it together.'

Barney's visage reflected a conflict of emotions: outrage that his preaching ability had been so devastatingly criticized by someone so much younger than himself and the realization that the someone held the whiphand.

There was a silence in which his head was bowed. He looked at me and murmured, 'Well, you are the Vicar and if that is what you want, you shall have it. My sermon will be ready by next Friday.'

His capitulation was so complete that I was tempted to unbend and say that the discipline would be only for a few weeks. Then I remembered what had happened when I relented after my tirade against Charles not so long ago.

'Thank you,' I said. 'Perhaps you would like to come hospital visiting with me this afternoon. You can meet your colleague and some parishioners who are there. During the rest of the week you can do some pastoral visiting. I shall give you the names and addresses tomorrow. By the way, what day of the week do you want as your day off?'

'I think I had better have a word with Ethel about that, Vicar, as it affects her as much as me.'

When Eleanor came home for lunch I was able to announce my successful attempt at deflation.

'Well done, that man,' she said and kissed me. 'Let's hope that the process will continue. I am afraid that Barney will not be put down after only one attempt. After he has gone home to his spouse, she will see to it that his ego will be reinflated, if only to satisfy her own ego. The Websters will need watching, as long as they are in Pontywen.'

'They will not be in Pontywen, my sweet,' I replied. 'I have told him that he and Ethel are to be let loose in

Llanhyfryd once he is priested. The farmers out there will soon cut him down to size and the farmers' wives will do the same to Ethel, even more so.'

'I know one gentleman who will not be very happy about your decision. Bertie Owen will be up in arms and organizing a petition. I can see him carrying a placard outside the vicarage and chanting "Give us Webster."'

'My dear love, a couple of "Drift" sermons in St Padarn's and they would be clamouring for Charles to come back. In any case the word will get round after last night's fiasco. I don't think Bertie will have much support.'

It was obvious as soon as the Reverend Charles Wentworth-Baxter and the Reverend Barnabas Webster met that they disliked each other immediately. Charles was out of traction and was seated in a chair by his bedside with his arm in a sling and his plastered leg thrust out in front of him. He was in earnest conversation with Nurse Williams whom he had described as Florence Nightingale on my previous visit.

'Hello, Fred. How about this? I am out of bed for the first time. It won't be long before I'll be out through the door.'

The familiar greeting shocked his fellow curate. I made a mental note that Charles would have to address me as Vicar on all occasions when we were in company.

'Charles, this is Barney Webster, your new colleague.'

They eyed each other and shook hands with as much warmth as two boxers touching gloves before a bout. Charles asked Barney if he was settling in and Barney asked Charles how long he expected to be in hospital. After that they exchanged no more words for the short time we were together.

As we moved on towards the Princess Royal ward for the next stage of our visiting, a staff nurse coming in the opposite direction stopped and stared at Barney.

'Mr Webster,' she exclaimed, 'fancy meeting you. I didn't know you had become a parson. The last time I saw you was when you served me with half a pound of bacon just before I left home to do my training. Then, of course, my parents moved to Abergavenny and I've lost touch with the village. Where are you now then?'

'I'm here in Pontywen,' stammered an embarrassed Mr Webster, 'and this is my vicar, the Reverend Fred Secombe.'

'Oh! I know Mr Secombe by sight. He's often in here. How is Mrs Webster? I expect she finds it strange having nothing to do after helping you in the shop all day.'

'She's very well, thank you. If you will excuse us, we have to go on our rounds now,' replied my red-faced curate.

'Goodbye for the time being. Perhaps we can have a longer chat when I see you up here next.'

So saying she strode down the corridor, leaving behind the victim of a second deflation in the space of a few hours.

'One of your ex-customers, Barney?' I asked, rubbing salt into the wound.

He glared at me. 'Beryl is a real chatterbox. They will all know in the hospital that I was her grocer in next to no time.'

'There's no harm in that. As you told me at our first meeting, your background of customer relations is an excellent one for someone coming into the ministry. At least the staff in the hospital will know that in you they have a man of the people who should feel at home talking to the patients.'

By the time we had finished our visiting, Barney had recovered both his composure and his parsonical tones in addressing the five bed-bound parishioners on our list. The village shop was forgotten as he enjoyed the kudos of his dog collar, smiling benignly at each bedside and uttering wise platitudes.

'Would you care to come back for a cup of tea, Vicar,' he asked as we walked down the hill from the hospital.

'As long as it is just a brief stay. I have lots to do at the Vicarage.' I had no wish to be discourteous. I felt I owed him a modicum of goodwill after the morning episode.

'We shan't keep you long. It will give you a chance to see what we have done in the short time we have been in the house and Ethel will be glad to see you.'

Ethel looked far from glad on seeing me. She had to be called down from the loft where she had been depositing some suitcases. Her face was grimy as was the overall she was wearing, evidently a relic of her time in the shop.

'I wish you had told me you were bringing the vicar back with you, Barney. At least I would have been presentable.' She disappeared quickly upstairs.

Somewhat abashed, my curate led me to my old bedroom which was now converted into his study with bookshelves lining the wall, filled with dated theological works and numerous collections of sermons by preachers who had long since died. By the window was a desk and an armchair.

'This is my den,' he said proudly.

'It has certainly changed since I last slept here the night before my wedding. I have a great affection for this room, Barney. So look after it.'

'Indeed I shall. This will be my workshop where I hammer out all my sermons and do all my thinking; the most important room in the house, the dynamo of my ministry, as it were.'

'Well, let's see what this dynamo can produce in the way of a sermon by next Friday. Where did you get all these books, by the way?'

'My uncle gave me a lot from his study and I've got the rest from second-hand bookshops. I'm a great one for second-hand bookshops.'

'Some of the new paperback books would be a welcome addition, Barney. They don't cost a great deal and, best of all, they are up to date.'

'Ethel and I are going into Cardiff next week and I shall go to the church bookshop to have a look around. About that, Vicar; we have had a talk and we have decided that we'd like to have Tuesday as a day off.'

'That's fine, Charles had Thursday as his day off.'

We went downstairs to the front room which was as much transformed as my old bedroom. An expensive carpet covered the floor, with a moquette three-piece suite to match in green. In one corner was an antique grandfather clock and in the bay window was a mahogany occasional table. Two Buck prints of ruined castles adorned the walls.

A little later, Mrs Webster made a grand entrance carrying a tea tray laden with the best Royal Doulton china. She had changed into a twin set with a string of artificial pearls around her scrawny neck.

'Sorry about the delay, Vicar. If I had known you were coming I would have had everything ready. Still, there we are.'

We drank the best China tea from the best china cups and ate petits fours from the best china plates. There was no doubt that the Websters were well blessed with this world's goods, and were determined to advertise it. St Padarn's and its council estate was not an appropriate corner of the Lord's vineyard for them to cultivate, I said to myself. Llanhyfryd and its affluent farmers would be more in their league.

As if she were reading my mind, Ethel swallowed half a piece of one of her dainty biscuits and said 'I hear that you want Barney to take charge of Llanhyfryd once he has been made a priest. If there is anything I can do to help him there, I'll be more than happy to do it. How about the Mother's Union? Is there a branch there?'

'No, I am afraid there is not. Perhaps you can try to form one later this year, if you would like to do so. There hasn't been a parson's wife there for many years.'

'Oh, I should love to start one there. I used to run the branch in our church at home because the vicar was a bachelor. So I know all about what is involved.'

Evidently any pique there may have been in the Webster household over my criticism of the 'Drift' sermon had disappeared in the euphoria about Barney's future elevation as curate in charge of Llanhyfryd.

The late afternoon sun was shining brilliantly as I walked back to the vicarage. At last the arctic conditions were disappearing and the snow was turning to a grey slush on the pavements. When I came down the drive, it was a joy to see little patches of green appearing in the white blanket which seemed to have covered the lawn for ever. Spring had decided to make its appearance. With Easter just a week or so away it was time that the season asserted itself.

Eleanor's car was outside the front of the house, ready for her evening surgery. As I opened the door, I could hear her in conversation with someone in the sitting room.

'Here he is now,' she said as I walked down the hall. 'Fred,' she called, 'Mr Evans has come to see you. Excuse me, I have to rush off to surgery.'

The thought of a conversation with Ezekiel Evans was enough to dissipate any joy at the coming of Spring. 'He is yours now,' whispered my wife as she made her escape. 'Best of luck.'

'Mr Evans, what can I do for you?' I inquired.

He was sitting in the armchair by the window, apparently intent on staying there for a while.

''Ave you 'eard, Vicar, about what is h'intended for Good Friday by the Pontywen Rugby Club?'

'I am afraid I haven't. Don't tell me they are all coming to the Three Hour Service.'

'It's not funny, Vicar. They 'ave h'arranged to play their postponed fixture with Penisacoed on Good Friday morning at 'alf past eleven. H'at the most solemn time of the year they will be h'indulging in a football match. H'I think something should be done to stop it. When we're in church quietly thinking about h'our Lord's last hours on the Cross, we will be 'earing the shouts coming from the Welfare Ground. H'I think it's disgusting that we should be h'insulted in this way.'

'I quite agree, Mr Evans, that it is not funny but it is a sign of the times. There is nothing that can be done to stop it. We live in a free country and we have just fought a war to protect that freedom. I could write to the secretary of the club and point out that Good Friday is a sacred day for churchgoers. However, as far as I know none of the rugby team make a habit of coming to church. On the contrary, while we are in church on Sunday mornings most of them will be getting ready to drink in the club from twelve o'clock on. As far as Good Friday is concerned when I was a lad in Swansea, one of the trade unions used to run a "Go as you please" variety concert in the Empire Theatre on that day. Perhaps it would be a better idea to organize a Sportsmen's Service one Sunday in the summer and invite all the sporting clubs in Pontywen to attend. I don't think that banging a drum and trying to stop the match is a good idea at all.'

Ezekiel was not impressed and spent half an hour or so propounding his views. Eventually he left in high dudgeon at not receiving any support from me and hinting that he might look elsewhere for help in his campaign.

On Friday morning the Reverend Barnabas Webster produced his sermon for Sunday. It was obvious that he had copied it from one of the many paperbacks he told me that he had bought in Cardiff the day previously. A quotation from Aldous Huxley was ascribed to Adolphus Huxley. The literary style was something my curate could never achieve.

'This is word for word from a book, Barney. You could at least try to put it in your own words.'

'When I did that last Sunday, Vicar, you took it apart. You can't criticize this sermon from a preacher who is often on the wireless.'

'The point is this. It is somebody else's work. I think what you had better do on Sunday is to announce to the congregation that you are going to read this man's address. That is the only honest way you can preach it. Next week, if you don't mind, let us have something which you have written, whatever its merits or demerits.'

Like Ezekiel earlier in the week, he left in high dudgeon. With a disaffected lay reader and a disgruntled curate, life was becoming fraught.

Worse was to come. On Friday evening I received a call from the Reverend Dewi Jones asking if he might see me the following morning with some information he thought I should be given. It sounded ominous.

'This has been some week,' I said to Eleanor later that night. 'I would never have thought that I would miss Charles's presence in the parish but I can't wait to get him back. The other two members of my staff are a positive pain in the neck.'

'Cheer up, Frederick,' she replied. 'At least you are showing that you are in command in the parish. I must say I admire your courage in putting an older man than you in his place – two older men, counting Ezekiel. You will be a much better priest for all this experience.'

She gave me a hug and kissed me.

'I wonder what our friend Dewi has to tell me tomorrow. More bad news, I expect.'

'As you are fond of preaching, my love, sufficient unto the day is the evil thereof. Let's get to bed and leave that until tomorrow.'

Next morning the old ex-missionary arrived, sober-faced.

'Nice to see your lawn cleared of snow and looking so green. It won't be long before you have to have your lawn-mower at work, Fred. Happy thought.'

'Not so happy for me, Dewi. I can't say I shall enjoy pushing that machine around. We are thinking of getting someone to help in the garden.'

'I expect there are plenty of retired men who would be glad of the job, if you feel you would rather be doing something else.'

'With the kind of assistants I have, there will not be much time to spend on horticulture. Come on in, Dewi and let's hear what you have to say.'

As we sat drinking coffee in my study he launched into the reason for his visit.

'If you remember, I warned you about Barnabas Webster before he arrived here – that he would be more concerned with the trappings than the essence of priesthood. He has an exaggerated sense of his own importance.'

'I am fully aware of that, and I am doing my best to curb that sense.'

'Well, Fred, I am afraid that there is some more work for you in that direction. I don't know whether you have heard, but there is to be a rugby match on the Welfare Ground on Good Friday morning.'

'I have heard and I have been pressurized by Ezekiel Evans to try to stop it. I told him that they are entirely free to do such a thing, if they so desire.'

'In that case you will not be pleased to hear that your curate is attempting to stop it by organizing a campaign. He has written to all the ministers of the chapels, inviting them to a meeting in his house next Monday evening. I found out by chance when I met Rhodri Bevan the Welsh Baptist Minister in the paper shop yesterday afternoon. He asked me if you knew anything about it.'

As soon as Dewi Jones left me, I drove to 13, Mount Pleasant View at high speed and pulled up outside with a screech of brakes behind Barney's precious Riley. I leapt up the steps and banged imperiously on the knocker.

Ethel opened the door. Barney's voice called from his study upstairs. 'Who is that, dear?'

I did not give her a chance to reply.

'It's the Vicar,' I shouted, 'and I am on my way up to see you.'

I rushed past the open-mouthed Mrs Webster and reached my curate in a trice. He retreated into his den, I followed him and closed the door.

'Sit down,' I ordered, pointing at his armchair. He sat.

'Now then, Mr Webster. I want to know about this pro-test meeting you have arranged for next Monday.'

Wide-eyed, he stared at me; his mouth opened but no words came forth.

'Come on, please. Explain yourself.' I stood over him.

'It-it was Ezekiel Evans,' he stammered. 'He came here earlier this week and-er-asked me to get the ministers together to-er-try to stop this Good Friday football match.'

'And you thought you had the authority to do this?' I demanded. 'Did you know that I had refused to do any such thing?'

'Mr Evans more or less gave the impression that-er-, how shall I put it, you couldn't be bothered to organize anything and that you wouldn't-er-mind if somebody else did.'

'I shall deal with Mr Evans later,' I said. 'As far as you are concerned, you should have raised the matter with me first before doing anything. If this happens again, I shall have no hesitation in giving you notice. What you have to do now is to write to all the ministers concerned cancelling the meeting and take those letters around to all concerned by this evening.'

As I left the room, I collided with Ethel who was listening outside.

'Don't worry, Mrs Webster,' I said, 'I shall see myself out.'

# 6

It was my first Easter Vestry meeting as Vicar of Pontywen.
The church hall was crowded for the occasion, with a strong
contingent from St Padarn's in addition to an above-average
attendance from the parish church congregation. Charles
was absent, away in Yorkshire with relatives and convalesc-
ing after his accident. Barney, temporarily chastened after
the Good Friday protest incident, had recovered his pomposity and was enjoying his privileged position at the table
alongside the wardens and the secretary.

After the opening prayers and the reading of the minutes
I launched into my inaugural Vestry address. 'This year is
an important landmark in the history of the parish. One
hundred years ago next October 17th St Mary's Church was
consecrated. Accordingly we shall celebrate the occasion
with a series of events. Later this evening we shall elect a
committee whose task it will be to arrange a programme.

'The number of Easter Communicants was higher than it
has been for several years, both in the parish church and St
Padarn's. In a few weeks' time we shall begin confirmation
classes, as a result of which I hope that next Easter we shall
see an even bigger number at the altar rails than this year.

'As you all know, we now have an addition to our staff
in the person of the Reverend Barnabas Webster. We are
pleased to welcome him and Mrs Webster into our midst.
Before very long he will be priested and I have decided to
give him the charge of the parish of Llanhyfryd. I shall let
them know at their Easter Vestry tomorrow evening.'

Bertie Owen was on his feet instantly.

'Shame!' he shouted. 'St Padarn's needs a married man,

not a bachelor like Mr Wentworth-Baxter.' He turned round to the part of the hall where the bulk of the daughter church congregation were seated. 'Are you going to put up with this?' he demanded with a theatrical gesture. His appeal was met with a complete silence.

'When you go out from here tonight you will all be opening your mouths about the vicar's decision. Why don't you stand up now and say what you think?'

Not a voice was raised in support. Bertie slumped into his seat. 'I don't believe it. I just don't believe it,' he mumbled as he shook his head.

'It seems, Mr Owen, that you are the voice of just one crying in the wilderness,' I said. Evidently news about the 'Drift' sermon had become widespread.

'Speaking of Mr Wentworth-Baxter,' I went on, 'you will be glad to know that he is progressing very well after his accident and should be back on duty in a few weeks' time. In the meanwhile I am most grateful to the Reverend Dewi Jones for his assistance over the past month or so.'

'Hear! Hear!' came from all quarters. Dewi, who was sitting in the front row, murmured his thanks.

'Now then, we come to the election of churchwardens. I have pleasure in asking Mr Harold Jones to be my warden for the coming year.'

'Thank you, Vicar, for asking me and I shall do all I can to help you in this important year for the Church of St Mary,' he replied.

'Nominations for the post of people's warden.'

'I propose Mr Vaughan-Jenkins,' said Harold Jones.

'I second that,' said Sam Thomas, the secretary of the Parochial Church Council.

'I propose nominations closed.' This contribution came from Jim Evans, past churchwarden.

There were several people who wished to second the proposal.

Mr Vaughan-Jenkins thanked everybody for their confidence in him and pledged his wholehearted support for the vicar in the year ahead.

Next came the appointment of churchwardens for St Padarn's.

'There is only one person who can be my warden in St Padarn's and this is Mr Charlie Hughes who has been so faithful in his duties over the past years.'

Charlie adjusted his deaf-aid and stood up.

'Thank you, Vicar. You know me. Anything I can do to help, I'll do it. Thank you.'

'Now we come to nominations for people's warden,' I announced.

Once again there was a silence from the St Padarn's contingent. A red-faced Bertie craned his neck, looking for support. None was forthcoming.

Mrs Collier, widow of the former organist at St Padarn's, stood up. 'I propose Mr Idris Shoemaker.'

'I second that,' said Charlie Hughes.

'Any other nomination?' I asked.

Bertie was looking desperate.

'I propose nominations closed,' shouted Harry Williams, a member of the Gilbert and Sullivan Society who had no love for Bertie.

Once again there were several seconders and so Idris the Milk became the new people's warden for St Padarn's.

The ousted churchwarden looked a picture of misery. Good-hearted Idris administered balm to his injured pride by proposing him for the Parochial Church Council and for the Centenary Committee. By the time the meeting was over Bertie had recovered much of his composure, no doubt savouring the prospect of using both those committees as a soap box for his opinions. The thorn in my flesh had not been removed.

This became evident at the first Centenary Committee meeting. I prefaced the proceedings with 'The vicar's few words'.

'To mark this milestone in Pontywen history, we shall have a series of special services to which we shall invite former clergy of the parish as guest preachers and, of course, our bishop. I shall write a booklet recalling various events and personalities over the past hundred years. I shall be glad of the loan of old photographs to illustrate the text.

'Before I ask you for suggestions to make our celebrations worthy of the occasion, it seems to me that one suitable way to do this would be the complete redecoration of St Mary's. It is many years since the church has seen the application of a paintbrush. As you are well aware, there are patches of wall where the paint has been peeling and the pews are obviously in need of varnish. I think this is something we can do ourselves, without any great cost to the church.'

Bertie was on his feet immediately.

'What about the same treatment for St Padarn's? After all, our building is as much a part of the parish as St Mary's. I am quite prepared to make up a team of men to do this.'

'There is no reason why St Padarn's should not be decorated, Mr Owen; I am sure that a team of men could be formed to do this, but I think you had better consult the wardens before anything is done. It is their responsibility to care for the church.'

'That's all right,' he continued, quite unabashed, 'I'll have a word with Idris and Charlie after this meeting. I know where I can get paint at cost price.'

A long list of suggestions was formulated including a grand dance, a parish social, a variety concert and, as the *pièce de résistance*, a pageant which would involve adults and the Sunday School children. This last idea emanated from Mrs Powell, an elderly widow and a formidable figure, who used to produce children's operettas before the War. For this and for every other proposed event Bertie offered his services. As Idris the Milk remarked afterwards, he should have been christened Jack, after Jack-in-the-Box. He must have sprung to his feet at least a dozen times.

Bertie apart, it was a most successful meeting. There was the same enthusiasm which had prevailed at the Easter Vestry meeting. As Canon Llewellyn, my former employer, would have said, the parish was 'in good heart'. Not having the Reverend Barnabas Webster present was an advantage; much to his chagrin, I had told him that as he was to have charge of Llanhyfryd he would not be involved in preparations for the centenary in Pontywen. A further advantage was the non-participation of Mrs Webster, whose finger would have been in many pies had she been given the opportunity.

On the other hand my wife had been nominated as chair-lady for the Social sub-committee. When I returned to the vicarage with the news of her proposed appointment her reaction was not over-enthusiastic. 'Well, my love,' she said, 'it will only be possible if we are not to do *The Gondoliers* until after these celebrations are over. What with my work in the surgery, and the vicarage, there will be precious little time to do much for the centenary, if we are doing *The Gondoliers* in the previous month. This applies to you as well, don't forget.'

So it was that the Gilbert and Sullivan society went into abeyance until November when the celebrations would be over. However, a number of the soloists indicated that they would contribute items for the Variety Concert in October, and Bertie offered to 'do a monologue'.

When Charles Wentworth-Baxter returned to Pontywen after his convalescence he was highly delighted to find that the parish was busy preparing to celebrate the centenary of St Mary's. Services and pastoral visiting bored him but celebrations spelt excitement.

'Have you settled on a programme yet, Fred?' he asked when he reported to the vicarage for duty.

'More or less, Charles. Why, have you any ideas?'

'How about getting the two church choirs together to do a performance of the *Messiah*?'

'That is rather ambitious with half-a-dozen third-rate tenors and basses, four contraltos and a preponderance of screechy sopranos. We can combine the choirs to sing some anthems for the special services and that's about it. Perhaps we could invite the Pontywen Choral Society to do the oratorio.'

'If they would come, that would be great. Then we could do something dramatic like a pageant of the history of St Mary's over the past hundred years. I wouldn't mind writing that.'

'I am afraid Mrs Powell has offered to do a pageant but what kind I do not know. She says she will bring me a script in the next few days.'

Charles exploded. The lady had been his landlady for a few weeks when he first came to the parish. His incarceration had ended when she locked him out because he was not in by ten o'clock.

'That old battle axe! Whatever she concocts will be suitable only for the junior classes of the Sunday school.'

'We'll see, Charles. If it is at that level, I shan't hesitate to scrap it and you can have your chance to write something worthwhile.'

A few days later I found a bulky envelope posted through my letter box. It contained the script and an accompanying note. 'Wrote this in 1940 and was unable to do it because of the War. Have tried to bring it more up to date.'

Charles's prediction proved to be true. The 'pageant' was Mrs Powell's version of *The Pilgrim's Progress*. Its one great merit was its laughter-provoking propensity. Eleanor and I spent the evening in such hilarity that we ached by the time we had read through to the epilogue.

The author had sought to update the dialogue with such sentences as 'What sayest thou, buddy?' or 'Is it OK with thee?' There were several verses of doggerel which were to be sung to the same tunes as 'Home Sweet Home' and 'What shall we do with the drunken sailor?' Evidently she envisaged a massive stage because one scene had the stage direction 'the crowd is seen coming down the hill from the castle singing this poem set to "Men of Harlech".'

When we had finished laughing my wife brought me back to earth. 'Now you have to call on the playwright with the news that her epic is unsuitable and that her services are no longer required.'

'I think I had better do that at once. Tomorrow morning, after service. I am afraid that will certainly be no laughing matter.'

'You can say that again,' replied my wife encouragingly.

The next day the staff gathered together for Matins. Although I had said that there was no need to turn up for daily service in a cassock, Barney persisted in dressing up in his regalia, still savouring the swish it made as he walked down the aisle, to the disgust of Charles who appeared in his crumpled lounge suit. It was the end of his first week back in the parish, and already there was a large degree of antipathy between them. I was discovering the cost entailed when a curate becomes a vicar. The buck stops here, in the words of President Truman's desk motto.

As we drank Mrs Morris's coffee in my study, I told Charles that he could go ahead with a script of the history of Pontywen.

'Great!' he enthused. 'I shall go through the church records and go to the library to find out all I can about the history of Pontywen itself.'

'I am doing that already, Charles, for the publication of a booklet. You can borrow the notes I have made so far. I shall want them back as soon as you have finished with them.'

'Of course, Vicar.' He had learned to drop the 'Fred' when his colleague was present.

'By the way, Vicar,' said Barney, 'they are getting a bit jealous in Llanhyfryd about all the fuss over the centenary of St Mary's. They say that Llanhyfryd is hundreds of years older than Pontywen and that it is time that something was done to celebrate their long history.'

'Who are *they*, Barney?' I asked.

'Well, there's Mr Jones, Blaenycwm Farm for one.'

'Yes. Anybody else apart from him? He was bound to make comments.'

Barney fished in his mind for further malcontents but to no avail. He had not been expecting to give details.

'I can't think of anybody else off hand.'

'If I were you, I should ignore Jones, Blaenycwm. In a few weeks' time you will be in charge of the parish. You will have to learn who are the troublemakers if you want to be an effective parish priest and not pay too much attention to what they say. It will be your job to keep them in control, not encourage them, as you did with Ezekiel Evans.'

A few minutes later I was on my way to Melbourne Terrace with Mrs Powell's script in my hand. A tall, thin elderly lady whom I had christened Betsy Trotwood, she was a formidable figure who must have put the fear of God into all the children in her care in the Sunday School operettas. I climbed the steep steps of Number 8 and announced my presence with the aid of the gleaming brass knocker on the drab door.

I could hear her firm footsteps on the polished oilcloth and braced myself for the ordeal to follow. The door was unlocked and then opened a few inches.

'Who is that?' a high-pitched voice demanded.

'It's the vicar, Mrs Powell.'

She opened wide the portal and looked down on my five foot seven inches from her vantage point.

'Come on in,' she ordered.

I was led into the front room and waited while she raised the Venetian blinds with three quick tugs. For an elderly woman she was very agile and her physical presence was intimidating.

'Sit down, Vicar.' It was a command not an invitation. I sat on the edge of an uncomfortable leather-covered dining chair beside a china cabinet, clutching her magnum opus and wishing that the earth would swallow me.

She was still standing like a headmistress about to discipline a pupil. 'Well, when do you want me to start?'

I took a deep breath.

'To tell the truth, Mrs Powell, I am afraid it is not suitable.'

Before I could say any more she launched into an attack.

'Truth! What kind of truth is that? What is more suitable than *The Pilgrim's Progress*?'

'This pageant is supposed to celebrate the centenary of St Mary's Church. It has to be concerned with its history over the past hundred years.'

'If you expect me to waste my time on piffling material like that, young man, you can forget it. It's either *The Pilgrim's Progress* or nothing.'

'I'm afraid it isn't. Mr Wentworth-Baxter is going to write a script using the notes I have made on the history of the church.'

Her reaction was swift and awesome. With her eyes blazing and her finger pointing towards the door she spoke in a voice trembling with passion.

'You had better go, Vicar. To think that you could give the responsibility for a pageant to a young layabout like Charles Wentworth-Baxter is unbelievable. What does he know about stage work? I tell you this: I shall not set foot inside St Mary's ever again. Good morning.'

Deciding that discretion was the better part of valour, I did not stay to argue but made my exit as dignified as I could, until I tripped over the doorstep. I managed to stay upright as the door was banged behind me. It was another of those moments when I wished I was a curate again.

When I recounted the experience to Eleanor at lunchtime she was most unsympathetic. She laughed almost as much as when we had read the script on the previous evening.

'I warned you it would be no laughing matter but I was wrong. It sounds hilarious. I wish I could have been a fly on the wall. Don't worry, love. If she goes, she goes. I don't know why you agreed to her doing the thing in the first place.'

'My dear Eleanor, she is always talking about the wonderful productions she organized before the War. I had no idea how dreadful they must have been.'

'If you don't mind me saying so, Frederick, you are taking a big risk by allowing Charles to take over. He is hardly the person to inspire confidence.'

'Don't forget, love, he had a Second in English at Oxford and he's very widely read. In any case I can always vet the script and keep an eye on the production. I could never have done that with Mrs Powell.'

After lunch, we drove off in Eleanor's new car to visit her parents, our weekly obligatory visit. Dr and Mrs Davies lived some ten miles away in a mock-Tudor residence in the heart of the countryside. At one time Dr Davies had shared a practice in Pontywen, where Eleanor was born. Now his surgery was in Llangwyn, a little market town; a much more lucrative field for his medical abilities. The son of a miner, David Davies had married the daughter of a Cardiff barrister. Mrs Daphne Davies, educated in private schools, had detested life in Pontywen and was in the process of converting her husband into a pseudo squire. It was a process which he resisted gently. So far, his concessions amounted to wearing tweeds plus deerstalker hat and taking part in shooting parties. Hunting and fishing were activities beyond his ken and on no account was he going to be drawn into them.

Mrs Davies had not yet recovered from the shock of her

daughter's marriage to a curate with a working-class background. Over the past months the trauma had been relieved by the good fortune with which her son-in-law had been blessed, both by his landlady's will and his elevation to the status of vicar. Now on these monthly meetings I was privileged to receive a peck on my cheek, instead of the perfunctory handshake.

'Eleanor, darling, how lovely to see you and looking so well.' She gave her a half-hearted embrace and turned to me. 'And if it comes to that, so are you.' She obliged with a butterfly kiss. My Christian name never crossed her lips — 'Fred' was too mundane and 'Frederick' impossible, even for her, though not for her daughter in playful mood. Mrs Davies could never be playful.

'Before I forget, your father has two rabbits for your dinner tomorrow. He has skinned and cleaned them. He went out last night with his gun and brought back four of them. By the way, he has an emergency call but he will be back soon, so he said!'

'I hope I shan't have one of those. I have left your number at the surgery just in case anything happens. Fingers crossed.'

'Hands together is a better insurance,' I interjected.

'Don't be so pious, Frederick,' replied my wife. 'A little superstition never did anybody any harm. Don't tell me that you have never touched wood.'

'Touché.'

'For that, Secombe, you should have suffered the fate of my father's rabbits.'

'Eleanor,' exclaimed my mother-in-law, 'Don't say such things.'

'Only playing, mother dear. I don't wish to become a widow just yet.'

Mrs Davies shook her head in disbelief at her daughter's remarks and went into the kitchen.

'You have shocked your mother,' I said.

'It takes very little to shock my mother. She had such a sheltered genteel background. The best thing she ever did was to marry my father.'

Right on cue the front door opened and a baritone voice proclaimed, 'The wanderer has returned.'

Eleanor rushed into the hall to greet her father.

'Your ears must be burning, Dad. I was just talking about you.'

'That explains it then. I thought it was inflammation. Come here and give your father a kiss.' He caught hold of her and gave her a bear-like hug.

'And how are you, Fred? How is the parish? In good heart?'

'Both in good condition, I am pleased to say.' He shook my hand warmly.

'Let's get in the front room and have a snifter. I'll be glad of one after that call. A chap in his forties with a heart attack; he was dead by the time I got there. Three kids including a baby and a wife much younger than himself. The poor woman is beside herself. I've given her a sedative but she'll need a lot more than that in the months ahead. That's where you blokes have a big part to play, Fred.'

'I'm afraid that is the time when I feel like you, unable to offer anything more than a spiritual bromide. Nothing will bring her husband back and to tell someone in her twenties with a long life in front of her that one day she and her husband will be reunited is small comfort. All you can do is to keep an eye on her, lend a sympathetic ear and try to see that members of the congregation give her some interests outside the home.'

'My dear Fred, that is a lot more than I can do, believe me. Enough of that; a dry sherry for you both?'

We nodded.

'I expect your mother has told you there are two rabbits for you. Plenty of protein. You ought to do a spot of rabbit shooting, Fred. It will supplement your meat ration, provide you with plenty of fresh air and give you a new pastime.'

'My father used to go rabbit shooting when we were on holiday at my cousin's place in Cardiganshire. He was quite a good shot. On his last outing there he was chased by a bull and gashed his cheek on a branch of a tree. He never went out with the gun again.'

'There aren't any bulls where I go, if you want to come up here. Perhaps you would prefer to go to one of the farms in Llanhyfryd since you must know most of the farmers down there. You can borrow my single-barrel gun.'

78

Eleanor began to laugh. 'I can't see you Fred, tracking round the fields with a gun, killing innocent little creatures.'

'Not so innocent,' said her father. 'The farmers are only too pleased when you keep the rabbit population down. Anyway, think about it.'

At that moment the telephone rang. Dr Davies answered and called my wife. 'It's for you from the surgery.'

'Just my luck,' she said. She picked up the phone and as she listened her face changed colour. 'When did this happen,' and 'where is she now?' she added. Then followed 'Right, I shall be there straight away.' She put the receiver down and turned to me.

'You're not going to like this, love. It's Mrs Powell; she has collapsed with what seems to be a heart attack on her way to get her pension. She's in a neighbour's house. I think you had better stay here and I'll come back to pick you up.'

'No way, I'm coming with you. I feel responsible for this.'

'You are not responsible, Fred. It is her heart condition. If you want to come with me, do so by all means but please don't start blaming yourself for what has happened. Anyway we can't stay arguing here. Let's get cracking. Tell mother I'm sorry we have had to go, Dad. Be in touch.'

We were in Pontywen in no time. 'She's in Number 12, Melbourne Terrace,' said Eleanor. She was up the steps in a flash. The neighbour who had been standing in the bay window, waiting, opened the door before my wife could knock. 'Come in, Doctor, and you, Vicar.' We were ushered into the front room where the invalid was stretched out on the settee, her eyes closed, her face a ghostly white against the black of her clothing.

'I think she's gone, Doctor,' whispered the large lady who had taken charge of the stricken Mrs Powell.

Eleanor examined her. 'Yes, I am afraid she is dead. She seems to have been dead for a while.'

Despite my wife's protestations as I looked at the corpse, I felt like a murderer. If I had not come to her house that morning she would still be alive. It was indeed no laughing matter.

79

# 7

'For heaven's sake, love, snap out of it,' pleaded Eleanor. We were sitting on a bench looking out over the Bristol Channel at Penarth. It was a lovely summer afternoon and yachts were decorating the blue expanse beneath the cliffs of this exclusive little resort on the outskirts of Cardiff. A fortnight had elapsed since the death of Mrs Powell and I was still in the chains of a guilt complex. If it had been the Bay of Naples spread out before us, its beauty would have been no solace to my soul.

In the space of less than twelve months I had been involved in two sudden deaths which could have been attributed directly to me. The first was the suicide of a sidesman at St Padarn's whom I had caught stealing money from the collection plate. He left behind him a widow and two daughters who were unaware of his misdemeanour and of the lecture I had given him. This second death, like the first, was the result of what I had said to the victim. What rubbed salt into my wounds was the legacy that she had left to the parish church in her will. The fact that the post mortem revealed that her heart was in such a poor condition that she could have died at any time, meant nothing to me. Unknowingly I had decided the time of her death.

'I wish I had never taken holy orders. Perhaps I should resign and take up teaching instead,' I moaned.

It was the signal for my wife to launch an all-out attack on my self pity.

'What kind of a man are you, Fred Secombe? You have a lifetime of valuable service to give to your church and the people of your parish, not to mention the God who has first claim on you. You have only been ordained a few years and you are prepared to pack it in already. That is not the man I married and admired. You can't run away from the realities of life. There are times in my profession when I may make a wrong judgement, and someone may die as a result. On the other hand there are hundreds of people who will benefit from my doctoring, just as there are those who will need your ministrations. Come on, let's go home. I don't want this lovely day spoilt by your moping.'

She stood up; I caught hold of her arm.

'Sit down, please,' I said.

She looked at me for a moment and then sat down.

'As usual, you are quite right, my love; I'm sorry. That was a very good sermon; I needed it. If they were ordaining women, you would have made an excellent priest. I promise, in the sight of God, the Bristol Channel and yourself, that I shall no longer dwell on what is past and that I shall devote my life to what is present, including this.' I put my arms round her and kissed her passionately, dog collar notwithstanding. Two elderly ladies stopped and stared, at a discreet distance. I looked up and smiled at them; they turned away and walked on with as much dignity as they could muster.

'You naughty vicar!' exclaimed Eleanor; 'but carry on, if you don't mind.'

'I don't mind one bit, *cherie*,' I replied and carried on.

The Reverend Barnabas Adrian Webster was in retreat at the bishop's palace ready for his ordination as priest the following day. So when we arrived at the vicarage we were surprised to see Mrs Webster on the doorstep, looking somewhat flustered.

She came up to me as I was getting out of the car.

'What's the matter, Ethel?' I inquired.

'There are three too many for the bus from Llanhyfryd for Barney's ordination tomorrow. Mr Jones the churchwarden forgot to put their names on the list but he says they never gave their names when they went to pay him for their fares, and they've come to me to see if anything can be done about it.'

'Don't worry; they can come with me. My wife has to be on duty so my car will be able to take three. Tell them I'll pick them up outside the post office at nine o'clock.'

'Thank you so much, Vicar; that's very kind,' she gushed. 'I'll go straight away and tell them. They are waiting at our house to find out if anything can be done. Bye bye, Doctor Secombe; sorry you won't be there for Barney's big day. Still, I suppose that's one of the drawbacks of being a doctor.'

'One of the advantages, rather,' said Eleanor as the curate's wife scurried up the drive. 'I don't fancy being closeted in the cathedral for two to three hours, not even to see Barney "done".'

At nine o'clock prompt the next morning I pulled up outside Llanhyfryd post office to find the Misses Chatworthy, two elderly sisters who shared a large house on the edge of the village, and Mrs Cadwallader, the sexton's wife, waiting 'like patience on the monument'. They might as well have been monuments because they spoke no words throughout the journey. The only indication of their presence was the strong smell of mothballs from their Sunday best.

'I'll pick you up at half past two outside the Crown Hotel in the market square,' I told them as I waited for them to emerge from the back seat of the Morris Minor. They had squashed themselves together to avoid the possibility that one of them might have to sit by the driver. Suddenly one of them spoke. 'The others aren't starting back until five o'clock,' complained Mrs Cadwallader, who was all set for a day's outing, it would appear. The two old ladies nodded their agreement.

'I'm afraid I can't spare the time to stay here until then. Perhaps there will be someone else who will give you a lift; there are bound to be a few with cars coming from Llanhyfryd. Have a look around after the service. As far as I am concerned, I must leave by half past two. If you are not outside the Crown, I'll know you are coming back with somebody else.'

Already there was a small crowd of excited relatives and parishioners outside the cathedral gates. I joined the Vicar of Cwmtydfil, a big bluff North Walian who was stranded in South Wales. Ifor Morgan had a broken nose, a pot belly and a reputation for breaking-in recalcitrant curates. One of his unfortunates was being ordained priest together with Barney. There were only two to be priested while six ordinands were to be made deacons.

'Well, young Secombe, I see you have someone being priested like me. Now all your troubles will begin. Let me give you a word of advice after twenty years of hard labour coping with curates. Let them know at the outset that you are the boss, whether they are priests or not. They are the assistant priests and their job is to assist you. Put your foot down and keep it down.'

'I am trying to do that, Ifor. My trouble is the difference in age. He is twenty years older than I am.'

'In that case, my boy, put both feet down.'

At this point in the conversation there was a tap on my shoulder. I turned round to see Bertie Owen.

'Excuse me, Vicar, I've brought Miss Wilkins in the car and I wonder if she could have a seat up near the front. You know what her sight is like, let alone her legs if she wants to go up for Communion.'

Miss Wilkins was an elderly lady with jam-jar-bottom spectacles, a pudding-basin haircut and clothes that were in vogue in the Edwardian era. She was a regular communicant at St Padarn's where Bertie always made a great show of escorting her to the altar rails.

'I am sure the verger will find somewhere suitable if you ask him.'

'Righto, Vicar, I'll go and get her now; she'll be thrilled, thank you.'

'She does know the service is going to last more than two hours, does she?'

'Oh, yes, I've told her that but she was determined to be here. So what can you do?'

'Say no,' said Ifor Morgan to me as Bertie went away. 'We had better get in the vestry and start robing before there are any more interruptions.'

The vestry was full of young hopefuls among whom Barney stood out as a father figure. Vicars and rectors stood in their own groups while the ordinands were silent and apprehensive. In the inner vestry, the bishop, the dean and the archdeacon were in conversation with the bewigged chancellor who would administer the oaths of Canonical Obedience later in the service. Soon the choir entered and we all lined up for the grand entrance initiated by a prayer from the dean through his musical nose.

As we made our way into the imposing chancel of the ancient building, I could see Bertie and Miss Wilkins in a row of chairs immediately behind the reserved places for relatives of those being ordained. When the opening hymn ended, the long service began with the singing of the Litany, followed by the opening part of the Communion service. Then the six deacons were examined separately by the bishop who then laid his hands 'severally upon the head of every one of them'. After this it was the turn of the two deacons to be made priests. I moved out into the chancel with Ifor Morgan ready to join in the laying of hands upon them. As the bishop began to 'examine' Barney, who knelt in front of him, I could see a commotion in the row behind the relatives.

Bertie was assisting Miss Wilkins to her feet and attempting to shepherd her down the row of worshippers into the side aisle instead of taking her up the centre aisle on the edge of which they had their seats. No one had their eyes on the Reverend Barnabas Webster. They were watching the spectacle provided by Mr Bertram Owen and friend. By the time the couple had disappeared into the vestry, Barney's great moment had passed, unobserved by most of the congregation.

They returned in the middle of the archdeacon's sermon, to the delight of the cathedral choirboys and to the evident annoyance of the preacher whose patience was exhausted by the time they were halfway down the row. He paused and waited while Bertie apologized loudly to each worshipper they passed. As they resumed their seats the recently deposed churchwarden of St Padarn's waved his hand regally at the archdeacon as a signal that he could carry on with his peroration. The Owen show had ended, or so I thought. It was not to be. As each row of worshippers was summoned by the cathedral churchwardens to come forward to take their Communion, Bertie's row was obstructed by Miss Wilkins, who seemed to be unable to move forward once

84

she was in the centre aisle. From my vantage point in the chancel I could see Bertie at her feet, lifting first one foot and then the other, and removing an impediment: it was her bloomers, which her companion stuffed inside his waistcoat. After doing this, he escorted her up the chancel to the altar rails, smiling benignly on anyone in his view.

'I thought I had seen everything until now,' whispered Ifor.

'That is the vintage Bertie; he has always been a show stealer,' I replied sotto voce. 'His best effort was the destruction of the vicarage garage and the car inside it by lighting a garden bonfire inches away from its wooden walls. We can only hope that he will not attempt to replace the garment when they go back.'

As he came down the chancel after his communion with a protective arm round the old lady, he managed to collide with a number of waiting communicants. He must have said 'Sorry' at least half a dozen times before he reached his seat. Once there he thrust his hand inside his waistcoat and produced Miss Wilkins' item of underclothing.

'He wouldn't dare,' I said to Ifor.

He did not. Instead he handed the article to Miss Wilkins who held it while he went down on his hands and knees to recover her handbag which had been put beneath her chair. In the meanwhile a queue of returning worshippers formed outside the row causing chaos in the centre aisle. Eventually, as they passed the duo on their way back to their places, they were given a ringside view of Bertie's attempt to stuff the voluminous unmentionable into the handbag. Some were amused, but the majority were disgusted.

Among that majority after the service was Mrs Webster who was highly indignant that the limelight had been switched from her husband at the moment of his ordination.

'Why that man had to come to the service dragging that old woman with him, I don't know. It isn't as if they go to Llanhyfryd Church. All the bus load are very annoyed at what happened.'

'I shouldn't say too much about Bertie, Ethel. He is a fan of you and your husband's.'

'Oh! In that case I mustn't speak too badly of him, I suppose. After all it isn't easy to look after a handicapped old lady like that. I expect we shall be seeing him at Llanhyfryd one of these days.'

'Speaking of Llanhyfryd, do you know if the Misses Chatworthy and Mrs Cadwallader have found someone else to give them a lift. I have to go at half past two at the latest.'

'It's all arranged, Vicar. I've just had a word with Barney and he says they can come back in our car. We are all going to celebrate his ordination in the Ashgrove Café with tea at four o'clock. It would have been a pity if they had to miss it because of the churchwarden's silly mistake. Sorry you won't be there, Vicar.'

'Well, Ethel, if I had known about the party, I would have made arrangements to stay here. Next time there is any function like this, I should like to be told about it. Then I can be present.'

'Everything was done in such a hurry, Vicar. That was the reason, you see.'

The real reason was the desire of the Websters to act as the Vicar and Vicaress of Llanhyfryd. Whilst it was an advantage to have them out of the way in the country, I had no intention of giving them *carte blanche*. That could lead to parochial rivalries and unpleasantness between the two parishes that had been joined together. It was one thing for Llanhyfryd to feel that they had a married couple in semi-charge but quite another that there was now a declaration of independence.

I had a further opportunity to drive this home at our Monday-morning staff meeting. As we left the church after Matins to proceed to the vicarage, workmen were arriving with the scaffolding to be erected inside the church ready for the redecoration by voluntary effort.

'It is very important that we join the band of workers to show interest. The churchwardens have made a rota for the week. As a first stage we are going to sandpaper the pews, prior to revarnishing them. So I should like the three of us to be there tonight in old clothes ready to do our bit. After that, we shall have to see that one of us at least is there every night they are working.'

My words were not received with enthusiasm by either of my two curates.

Charles spoke first. 'As you know, Vicar, St Padarn's are also going to redecorate, since they are part of the parish. I think they are going to start next week. Apparently Bertie Owen has managed to get a blow lamp for the paint stripping; so that will be much quicker than using sandpaper.'

'For heaven's sake, Charles, don't let Bertie Owen loose with a blow lamp. It won't be a new vicarage garage this time; it will mean a new church.'

'Don't worry, Vicar. Ivor the Milk is taking charge and he has managed to find a retired painter to use the flame thrower. What I meant to say was this: I can't be in two places at the same time. So, while I can come to the parish church this week, from then on perhaps I ought to be at St Padarn's.'

'Fair enough, Charles. As long as you will be there.'

At this juncture in the conversation Barney intervened.

'We have decided at Llanhyfryd that, as the church has not been redecorated since the nineteen twenties, it is time that something was done, so we are having a meeting to decide on colour schemes and that kind of thing.'

My blood pressure rocketed to a dangerously high level.

'Have we?' I shouted. 'Now look here, Barney, I am still the Vicar of Llanhyfryd. You are just the curate in charge – curate, got that? The only body with powers of decision is the Parochial Church Council at which I must be present. Your job is to be responsible for taking the services and visiting the sick and the whole. If you wish to do anything else you must have my permission. You had better cancel the meeting as you did with the one to organize the Good Friday protest. Instead you can turn up tonight in Pontywen and help redecorate.'

Charles indulged in an ill-concealed smirk, while Barney looked at me with enough daggers to make a pin cushion out of me.

'I warned you,' said Eleanor as we ate our lunch. 'Sending Barney and Ethel into exile in the country will not remove your headache any more than a large bottle of aspirins. As long as he is your curate he will spell trouble. The only cure for the pain will come when he moves elsewhere. Perhaps because of his age the bishop will offer him a living in the very near future. In the meanwhile, as Ifor Morgan told you, all you can do is put both feet down firmly, and you seem to be doing that very well indeed. I am proud of you, Secombe.'

A motley band of workers turned up at seven o'clock for the inaugural session of the centennial clean-up of the parish church. Mr Vaughan-Jenkins, churchwarden and bank manager, appeared in spotless overalls and wearing industrial gloves. Mr Harold Jones, fellow churchwarden, local builder, volunteer clerk of the works and foreman, was clad in filthy overalls which had adorned many a building site. The only other person wearing overalls was Barney, who had brought his village-store uniform, more suitable for cutting a pound of bacon than removing a decade of dusty varnish from the pews. The rest of us wore pullovers and trousers which any self-respecting tramp would have refused to accept, while Charles turned up in clothes which even a non-self-respecting tramp would have rejected.

'Will you all come up here in the chancel!' requested Harold Jones. 'There are twenty of us here tonight and I want to form five teams of four each. Four teams to work on the ground stripping down the pews and one team to get up on the scaffolding and start cleaning the ceiling, ready for distempering later on.'

We all shambled up the aisle into the chancel where Harold had set up a trestle table laden with small blocks of wood and sheets of sandpaper.

'It's quite simple for those doing the pews. All you have to do is put a piece of sandpaper round one of those blocks like this and then rub hard until you get down to the bare wood. Plenty of elbow grease, gentlemen, and patience. This kind of job is going to take time. Rome wasn't built in a day, so they say. You are not going to finish the work in less than four or five weeks, believe me; maybe a lot more. Then I want four of you with a head for heights to come up with me on the scaffold to clean up all that muck on the ceiling and, later on, the walls. I have taken some brushes up there already.'

In no time at all the teams had sorted themselves out. I

noticed that Barney had joined up with Ezekiel Evans, no doubt informing him of how dictatorial the vicar was. Charles was working with Moelwyn Howells, his landlord, and was due very shortly to suffer from a strained wrist or perhaps blistered fingers or any excuse to opt out.

I was about to start work with my three team members when Harold approached me.

'Vicar, I think you had better come up and have a look at the ceiling and especially the east wall. I think I can see signs of some serious subsidence. If that's the case, we'll have to get the diocesan architect to have a look at it as soon as possible.'

My heart was in my mouth. To say that I was afraid of heights was a gross understatement. Yet I had no desire to appear weak-kneed. In any case it was my duty to see for myself what damage had been done to the church. I should have ignored these promptings and asked to be excused the inspection.

Very gingerly, I followed Harold up the ladder holding on to the sides like grim death and not daring to look down. As I approached the platform, I was faced with the terrifying prospect of letting go of the ladder and hauling myself on to the planks. I stood on the rung of the ladder, petrified, with my eyes closed, unable to move.

'Stay there, Vicar,' instructed Harold.

'I think I shall be staying here for the rest of the night. I can't move up and I certainly can't move down.'

'Open your eyes. Now then, give me your right hand. Come on, you won't fall. Hang on to the ladder with your left hand. Give me your hand, Vicar. Jim, you come round behind me. That's fine. Now then, Vicar, give me your right hand, please. Once you have done that you can give Jim your left hand and we'll pull you up.'

'I'm afraid I'll pull you both down on top of me.'

Jim Evans, an ox of a man, laughed loudly.

'What's your weight, Vicar?'

'Ten stone.'

'I'm fifteen stone, so don't flatter yourself. Come on, do what Harold has told you.'

I held out my right hand, which was held firmly by

Harold. Then I took a deep breath and held out my left hand, which was gripped in a vice.

'Together,' ordered Harold. And in a trice I was on the platform.

'Why didn't you tell me you are afraid of heights? I wouldn't have asked you to come up here, if I had known.'

'To be honest, I was afraid you might think me a bit of a cissy if I told you. Anyway, now I'm up here, you had better show me these alarm signals which could blight our centenary celebrations.'

With Jim and Harold on either side of me, I was guided towards the end of the platform for a view of the east wall and of the ceiling above it.

'There are the cracks, Vicar. They are not very big ones, I know, but they may be just the beginning of a lot worse. In that case the sooner it is attended to the better.'

'I take your word for it, Harold. I'll phone the architect in the morning. Let's hope it is not serious.'

I was guided back to the ladder. So far my sight had been directed upwards or at eye level. As we reached the ladder, I glanced down at the hive of industry below. My head swam. My body froze.

'I'm never going to get down from here. Never.'

'Come on, Vicar. What's that in the New Testament about "Oh ye of little faith"? Jim, you get on the ladder first, then he will know there's someone beneath him for company.'

Big Jim grinned.

'It's all right, Vicar. I'll hold you up, if you fall. Not that Vicars are supposed to fall.'

He went down a couple of rungs.

'Now then,' instructed Harold, 'turn round to me. Right. Catch hold of the ladder, hold tight and feel for the rung with your left foot. Go on, it's quite safe. Jim is there beneath you. Don't look down. Look straight in front of you. Fine. Now start going down very slowly.'

An eternity later I reached terra firma to applause from the ground-floor workers. It was then that I realized I had provided circus entertainment for them. A cold perspiration besprinkled my brow. I excused myself while I left my three team partners to escape to the vicarage for suitable refreshment.

Eleanor was mowing the lawn in the evening sunshine.

'That was a quick stint of labour. I would expect it from Charles but not from you,' she chided.

'I'm going back. I need a short break while I visit the medicine cupboard for a reviver. I have just had a nasty experience.'

'Don't tell me you have found dry rot in the pulpit or that the death-watch beetle has been confirmed in the church.'

'No, but I have had a serious attack of vertigo through examining some cracks in the east wall.'

'Secombe, you have been climbing ladders, trying to show off; It doesn't become you. I thought you looked a pale shade of green. The doctor prescribes a small tot of whisky with a couple of peppermints to follow before you rejoin your companions. It is a good thing it was you doing the climbing and not Charles, otherwise there would have been another hospital case.'

As I returned, I met Charles leaving the scene of action and looking sheepish when he saw me.

'Sorry, Fred, I'm afraid I have done something to my wrist. I think I must have sprained it. Apart from that, my fingers are beginning to blister after using that sandpaper. So perhaps I had better lay off doing any more here and wait until we start at St Padarn's next week. I thought you had packed it in. You looked terrible when you came down from that scaffolding.'

'Our late employer, Canon Llewellyn, used to say, "Carry on. Never give up." The only carrying on you know about, Charles, is concerned with young ladies. It is about time you realized that there is another meaning to the phrase and the sooner the better; you can start now. Perhaps you would like to come back into the church with me and stay until everybody else has finished. I know you don't like Barney but I am positive he will stay to the end.'

There were no protestations. The very thought that Barney had a virtue which he did not possess was sufficient to make him one of the last 'volunteers' to leave the church.

'What on earth has happened to Charles, hanging on to the last like this?' asked his landlord.

'I think it is a slight touch of Barneyitis,' I told him.

# 8

'We must get a full-time gardener,' said Eleanor when I returned from the opening night of Operation Centenary in the parish church. 'Pushing that lawn mower is excellent exercise I can do without. Now that we have decided that we do not want Mrs Watkins as a live-in housekeeper, we can afford to splash out on the garden. There is that expanse of wilderness at the back of the vicarage which can be turned into a kitchen garden. Fresh vegetables on our doorstep would be a welcome addition to our ration-book fare.'

A few days previously we had discussed the idea of having our daily help installed in the house, with her own sitting room as well as bedroom. The thought of her incessant chatter was one disincentive. Another was the impression given to the parish by such an appointment that the vicar was getting aspirations above his station because he was married to a lady doctor. In any case Mrs Watkins might not have wanted to give up her council house, despite her frequent complaints about its dilapidated condition. So we came to the conclusion that the status quo would have to suffice for our domestic arrangement.

'Old Arthur Williamson is retiring from his bread round with the Co-op at the end of the month. He is always talking about his allotment. I am sure that all his fellow choristers could give an update on the progress of his kidney beans or the size of his cauliflowers. Full-time gardening at the vicarage would be a job he would enjoy.'

'An inspired suggestion, Frederick. For his age he is remarkably fit. It is the outdoor life, I suppose. Lucky for him that he has earned his living above ground. When I see some of the poor wretches who come to the surgery, a lot younger than Arthur, with their lungs loaded with coal dust, my blood boils.'

'There's one thing, love. When the pits are nationalized there will no longer be colliery owners whose pockets are loaded with gold dust, including Sir David Jones-Williams, whom God preserve.'

Sir David was the local squire whose wealth and baronetcy were derived from the exploitation of three generations of miners and the despoliation of the lovely valley from which the coal was torn. He and Lady Jones-Williams were regular worshippers at the parish church, which was built by his forebears to the glory of God and as a sop to their conscience.

Next morning, to my surprise I had a telephone call from that very gentleman, the first I had received from him since I had become Vicar of Pontywen.

'Is that the vicar? Good. I'll come straight to the point. David Jones-Williams here; I gather that you are writing a centenary booklet about the history of St Mary's. As you are aware, it was built by my family. You will be interested in some old newspaper cuttings about the laying of the foundation stone and the consecration of the church and some of the memorabilia I have here. Perhaps you would like to come to tea tomorrow. Would four o'clock suit you? Right. See you then.'

Down went the phone at the other end. The call must have lasted little more than a minute. The Squire was a man of few words. Stockily built with a florid countenance and a bristling moustache, he was a formidable figure, feared by most of the inhabitants of Pontywen and loved by none. My first encounter with him was a collision when the vicar's car which I was driving met his Bentley round a corner. It was not the best kind of introduction to Sir David. Since then circumstances had changed to such an extent that he was not ill disposed towards me. He could never be amicable to anybody.

Later that day I went to see Arthur Williamson in his terraced house in Balaclava Street. He had just come in after stabling his horse. His bread van and his horse, Rosie, were a familiar sight in the town. A widower whose wife had died some years ago, he led a full life. Apart from working on his allotment, he was a member of the Pontywen choral society and an enthusiastic member of St Mary's church choir.

'Sit down, Vicar. Would you like a glass of beer? I always have a drop when I come in from work. Then I get my dinner ready.'

A thin little man, with a few wisps of hair straggling across his bald head, he was the reverse of Sir David, with a ready smile and a fund of conversation.

As we sat imbibing, he said, 'I'm going to miss old Rosie. She's fourteen now. I had her when she was a young mare. They're going to have a motor van for deliveries after I've gone. So she'll be put out to grass. If I had the money, I'd like to keep her. It would give me something to do during the day.'

'Well, Arthur, I have come to see you about that. How would you like to take on the job as full-time gardener at the vicarage? We need to develop a kitchen garden on all that land at the back of the house. Then there are the two lawns and the flower beds at the front. So it would be quite a task.'

His face split from ear to ear.

'Vicar, there's nothing I'd like better. I've been wondering what to do with my time. If the wife were still alive it would be different but being on my own it would be miserable if all I had to do was sit in the allotment all day. Wonderful. I can start the week after next, if you want me to.'

'Fine. Perhaps you would like to come up later this week. I can show you what is involved and we could talk about wages and so on.'

'I'm not worried about the wages, Vicar. Of course it will be great to have extra money in my pocket apart from the pension – but to have a job to do in the open air. My father and his father before him spent all their working lives down the mine. All they had to show for it when they died was the dust they had collected – not the money. My mother told my father when I was getting ready to leave school that

94

on no account was I going to go underground. What's the result? At sixty-five I'm healthier than most men of my age and some of the young ones as well. Mind, if I had nothing to do when I retired, I might have developed a beer belly.'

'With your physique, Arthur, you couldn't even develop a beer pimple. How about coming up to the vicarage next Friday evening about half past seven.'

'Righto, Vicar! I'll look forward to that. I'll bring a pencil and paper with me and we can work out what to do with this kitchen garden that you want. Best to be organized from the start.'

Our daily was leaving the vicarage as I came down the drive.

'Tell Dr Secombe I've done all the vegetables an' that; they're all ready in the saucepans.'

'You'll be pleased to know, Mrs Watkins, that next year we shall have fresh vegetables from our own garden. Arthur Williamson is coming to make a kitchen garden at the back of the house, now that he is retiring from his bread round.'

'Well, there's nice. Everybody do know Arthur the Co-op. 'E's a lovely man. Fancy 'im coming 'ere to work an' that. 'E'll 'ave that garden in shape in no time. They do say 'is allotment is a picture.'

'So I am told. He is going to start the week after next. That will be another cuppa for you to make as well as for the curates.'

'It won't be no trouble for me; I'll be only too pleased. 'E must be very lonely, looking after 'imself, love 'im. I remember when 'is wife died; very suddenly it was. Not long after my 'usband died. Mind, I was ready when 'e went, because 'e 'ad been bad with 'is chest 'an that for years.'

'I am afraid I have one or two telephone calls to make, Mrs Watkins.' I had no desire to spend precious time listening to her description of the death-bed scene which I had heard several times before.

'I'll pass on your message to my wife. See you tomorrow.'

Eleanor was delighted to have the news about Arthur and was highly amused at Mrs Watkins' reaction to it. 'And I met her in the garden where the praties grow,' she sang. 'I smell the beginnings of a romance, Fred my dear. Two lonely people in a potato patch and brought together by the vicar.'

'I don't think Arthur would appreciate your reading of the situation. He would prefer a pint of beer to Mrs Watkins anytime, believe me. If she begins to indulge in one of her monologues he will banish her to the kitchen in a trice. He will be in love with the good earth of the vicarage, not its daily help.'

'You have no soul, Secombe. If she starts plying him with her Welsh cakes he could soon be under her spell. The way to a man's heart is through his stomach, even if in your case, it was through your bottom.'

'Kindly leave the stage, madam. You are disgusting; there is no other word for it.'

She raised the glass of sherry I had poured for her.

'Here's to Arthur and-er – Mrs Watkins. We don't know her Christian name, do we? Perhaps one day we'll find out or perhaps she will for ever be Mrs Watkins. If they get married, we'll know as soon as they put their banns in.'

'This is where we came in. If you don't mind, I have to phone the diocesan architect about the inspection of the east wall and the roof. I've tried three times to get him at his office. So now I'll try his home number.'

'His wife will not be pleased; neither will he. Can't you wait until tomorrow morning?'

'Listen, Doctor Secombe. I do not tell you what to do as far as your work is concerned. I would not dare, in any case. So will you please allow me to do what I think fit, as far as my work is concerned?'

'I like you when you are masterful, Frederick.'

She kissed me. 'Go and phone him, love. I'll get the dinner ready.'

The architect's wife answered tetchily. 'He has only just come in. Would you hold on, please?' When he came to the phone he sounded hungry – impatient.

'Hello, who's that?' he snapped.

'This is the Vicar of Pontywen. We are redecorating the church and have scaffolding up in the nave. Last night when we began our work we discovered some cracks at the top of the east wall and in the roof above. I'd be grateful if you would come and inspect what we have found. I know that some of the churches in the area have suffered from subsidence and I am wondering if we have been afflicted with the same thing.'

'It sounds bad to me. I haven't my diary with me. Ring me tomorrow at the office at nine thirty and I can give you a day and time. Goodbye for now.'

He was as economical with his words as Sir David Jones-Williams and sounded as jovial.

'Well?' inquired my wife when I came into the kitchen.

'You are the most infuriating young lady I have ever known. Why must you be right every time? You are more infallible than the Pope. At least he has to sit on his throne, surrounded by his council to achieve that perfection. You can do it standing up, sitting down or in any other position.'

'In other words, you had a dusty answer to your call.'

'I have to ring him tomorrow morning at his office.'

'Since you have exalted me above the Pope, I shall refrain from saying I told you so. Your dinner is ready, Vicar, but I can assure you I have not achieved perfection in that sphere. I have overdone both the meat and the veg.'

The following afternoon I drove out to Garth Hall, the mountain fortress of Sir David Jones-Williams. It was a lovely sunny day. The hedgerows were clothed with wild flowers and the fields were a patchwork of green and yellow. One of the glories of Pontywen was its nearness to the countryside. To be able to breathe fresh air instead of the industrial effusions which afflicted the inhabitants of the little town was only a matter of minutes in a car or a couple of hours by shanks's pony.

As I turned off the country road into the squire's drive, I was aware of a young lady sunbathing on the lawn in front of the Victorian Gothic façade of the mansion. Wearing dark sunglasses, her only other covering was a skimpy bathing suit. Lying on her back with her arms outstretched in an attitude of careless abandon her appearance was greatly at odds with her prim and proper surroundings. Croquet hoops and long skirts were meant for that expanse of matured grass.

Who could she be? I asked myself, as I pulled up at the side of the house. As far as I knew Sir David and Lady Edwina were childless. She could not be a trespasser. Sir David would have sent one of his minions to remove her from the scene in quick time if that were the case. The tea party was going to be very interesting.

When I rang the doorbell the sound echoed through the building. Footsteps pattered across the hall inside and the door was opened by a maid in black-and-white livery; she was little more than sixteen and very nervous.

'Sir David is waiting for you in the library, Vicar.' She spoke her words at great speed, glad to get them over.

She led me across the spacious hall with its big open fireplace and its imposing staircase to a room whose door was surmounted with the head of a stag complete with impressive antlers. She tapped on the door and waited until she heard the bark of command from within.

'It's the Vicar, Sir,' she announced and fled as soon as I entered.

The study was several times larger than mine with an impressive array of leather-bound books, a number of oil paintings, all of them portraits, an enormous desk and six leather armchairs. Sir David stood behind the desk on which was a leather-bound scrapbook opened for inspection and what appeared to be a silver trowel alongside the book.

'Well, here it is, Vicar. A full account of the foundation-stone-laying ceremony and another of the consecration by the Bishop of Llandaff.' He picked up the silver trowel. 'This was used by my grandmother to lay the foundation stone of St Mary's Church. Would you care for a sherry before you inspect this historical record?'

'Yes, please, Sir David. Dry, if possible.'

'I don't have anything sweet,' he said curtly.

As we sat in the comfort of the large armchairs, the squire began an investigation of my future plans for the parish church.

'I hope you are not contemplating any changes to the services, dressing up or doing away with Matins and that sort of thing.'

'Certainly not, Sir David. I enjoy singing the psalms and the responses. Sunday would not be Sunday without them.'

'Glad to hear it, Vicar.' He stroked his white military moustache. 'In any case, if anybody wanted the communion service sung to that medieval dirge, they could always go to St Padarn's, couldn't they? I suppose you will not be messing about with the time of the service either. From the time that I was a child, I have always been used to arriving at St Mary's just before eleven. That becomes a part of one's life, eh?'

At that stage in the conversation there was a tap on the door.

'May I come in, Uncle David?' The female voice was seductively low and husky.

'Only if you are decently clad,' demanded the old man.

'Have no fear. I have slipped on a summer dress over my bathing costume.'

With that the door opened to reveal the sun worshipper. She was in her early twenties, it would appear; raven haired, brown skinned, slim and graceful, she floated into the room.

'This is my niece, Fiona Forbes-Hamilton. Down here for a few days. Fiona, this is the Vicar of Pontywen, the Reverend Frederick Secombe.'

She moved across to me as I stood up and held my hand, her sloe-black eyes lingering over me in an unnerving but approving inspection.

'Secombe,' she murmured. 'That's not a Welsh name, surely.'

'West Country,' I replied. 'My forebears came from Cornwall. One of them was a sailor who married a Swansea girl and settled down there.'

'How romantic,' she breathed. She was still holding my hand and I was beginning to feel like a fly trapped in a spider's web.

'We have business to do, Fiona. So I should be grateful if you would tell me yours.' His tone was acid.

'I have rung the garage and my car will be ready at half past five. I was wondering whether you might like to give me a lift to Pontywen to pick it up.' She smiled sweetly at him.

Her sweetness was wasted on the desert air. Sir David granted very few favours.

'Afraid not,' he grunted. 'Perhaps the Vicar can oblige after tea.'

Miss Forbes-Hamilton switched her gaze to me. I could feel the web tightening around me.

'Vicar, will you be a darling and oblige after tea?' Her husky tones made it sound more of an invitation than a request.

I swallowed hard. 'By all means, if you don't mind riding in a decrepit Morris Minor.'

'Not at all. I shall look forward to the pleasure of your company.' With a flutter of her eyelashes and a flash of brown legs, she twirled around and made an exit worthy of a Hollywood glamour girl.

'Back to business,' snorted the squire. 'I do not wish these newspaper cuttings to be taken from here. So I suggest that you copy them while I go and see to arrangements about tea. My wife is indisposed, I am afraid. There are some sheets of paper here and pen and ink.'

It was rumoured that Lady Edwina's indispositions, which were frequent, were due to a weakness for gin and it – more for the gin than the it. There was considerable sympathy for her in her addiction. As Idris the Milk said on one occasion, 'Anybody who has to live with Sir David deserves a medal as well as a bottle of gin.'

Once I was alone, I sat down behind the desk and read through the two news reports from the *Monmouthshire Messenger*. They encapsulated the social climate of 1846 and 1847. The first cutting referred to the foundation-stone-laying on 18 June 1846.

The weather was invitingly fine when a large concourse assembled for the ceremony. As the Vicar of Abergelly remarked in his address, he was 'fully aware of the rapid increase in the population in this part of his parish.' There are now 1,514 souls in Pontywen and soon it must have an incumbent of its own.

The Vicar had engaged one of Mr Huxtable's omnibuses to bring a goodly party of ladies and gentlemen from Newport. This left at 9.30 a.m. and arrived in good time for the service which was due to commence at 1 p.m.

Two spacious tents were erected on the grounds, above which floated the national flags. The Pontywen band was in attendance and the National schoolchildren were drawn up in order near the platform, one of the pupils bearing a banner 'Church and Queen'. The spot presented with its numerous array of carriages and fashionable visitors an exceedingly interesting spectacle.

Shortly after 1 p.m. a procession formed from the chief tent to where the foundation stone was suspended from a decorated triangle. It was headed by Lady Honoria Jones-Williams and Sir Robert Jones-Williams who had contributed £1,000 to the subscription list for the building of the church, the Reverend Septimus Jones, Vicar of Abergelly and a large body of the clergy of the diocese, several magistrates, coal and iron and other masters and gentry with several ladies, with the architect and builder. Mr Gibbs, the architect's representative, carried a richly chased silver trowel, appropriately inscribed, on a velvet cushion. Buried beneath the stone laid by Lady Honoria was a bottle containing current coins of the realm and two poems, one in Welsh and one in English. The one in Welsh was composed by Mr William Williams, churchwarden, the other was composed anonymously.

In his address the Vicar mentioned the beneficence of Sir Robert Jones-Williams, 'Be not ungrateful I beseech you for this liberality (but I would now address myself more particularly to his workmen) but by your energy, industry, regularity of conduct and obedience to his rules, enacted solely for your safety and welfare, enable him to raise a due reward for the large capital he has already expended.'

He continued his peroration with a plea for loyalty to the Queen. The whole company joined in an outgoing of fervent loyalty in singing the National Anthem and giving three times three cheers for the Queen.

The ceremony over, the crowds went into two tents. In the one tent, the gentry and their ladies were treated to an excellent cold lunch, a feature of which was the wine and also a large supply of the finest strawberries placed on the tables by Mr Ernest Jenkins, Sir Robert's head gardener. In the other tent with a commendable consideration for the working classes who were permitted by their employers to enjoy the day as a holiday, Sir Robert and other masters of the neighbourhood provided a substantial treat of roast beef, cheese, bread and beer which was partaken of with right good appetite by the workers of the wealth of the district who gave hearty cheers for the 'founders of the feast'.

It is estimated that the cost of building the new edifice will be £1,650. With donations from the gentry and the coal and iron masters, the subscription list has already reached £1,589. This bodes well for the established Church in Pontywen.

The account in the same paper of the consecration of the church on 17 October 1947, again referred to 'the fashionable concourse of ladies and gentlemen'. However, on this occasion there was but one tent 'where the party sat down to a sumptuous cold repast with choice wines and fruits and an excellent dessert; the prize grapes from Sir Robert Jones-Williams' garden, so highly commended at the Newport Flower Show, forming a rich and refreshing delicacy'. The only representatives of the working classes to be regaled were the schoolchildren of Pontywen, 'carrying gay banners with mottoes', who were given tea and cakes in the Infants' schoolroom.

It was tea and cakes, too, in the dining room of Garth Hall after I had finished my labours in the study. Sir David sat at one end of the long refectory table while Fiona chose to seat herself next to me at the other end, to the obvious displeasure of her uncle. Considering the acres of space available she placed her chair so close that her feet came into contact with mine, by deliberate intent, I was sure. I became hot under my clerical collar. The bulk of the conversation came from the young lady who evidently regarded me as a life line to rescue her from the boredom of her surroundings. Cakes and tea were ferried back and forth nervously by Rhiannon, the petrified waif in livery, adding to the tension I felt.

In a desperate attempt to shrug off the attentions of the female fatale, I spoke of my wife and how happy we were. To no avail. That revelation seemed to spur her to greater efforts to allure me, with more foot contacts and eyelash flutterings, apparently on the basis that anything my wife could do, she could do better. If she had been ugly and unattractive I would have been impervious to the blandishments. On the contrary, she was pretty and decidedly attractive – I was flattered. She knew that. The fact that I was married added spice to her amorous adventuring.

As the grandfather clock in the hall chimed five o'clock, it sounded to me like the bell in a boxing ring, saving an unfortunate from a knockout. I stood up and announced that I must be on my way back to Pontywen.

'Hold on, Vicar,' breathed Fiona, 'don't forget you promised me a lift. I'll just go and put some war paint on and I'll be with you in two ticks.'

'That child!' exploded Sir David when she had left the room. 'I must apologize, Vicar. She treats every man she sees as legitimate prey, whether married or not. She will be back in London next week, thank God. I hope you have got what you want, by the way.'

'I have indeed, Sir David. It has been a great help. Do you think we might borrow the silver trowel to put on display during the week of the centenary celebrations?'

'You must let me think about that. Apart from its worth as a piece of silver, it has tremendous sentimental value to our family.'

'Many thanks and I hope Lady Edwina will soon recover from her indisposition.'

'I'm sure she will,' he said and led me out of the dining room.

The journey back to Pontywen was a hazardous one. Everytime I wanted to change gear, it seemed that Fiona's leg was in the way. By the time I dropped her at the garage I was in a state of nervous exhaustion.

'Thank you, Vicar, very much. You have been an absolute sweetie. Do you play tennis?' she asked.

'I am afraid not,' I lied.

'What a pity! We could have had a game at Garth Hall tomorrow.'

When I arrived at the vicarage, Eleanor was in the kitchen. 'You look as if the heat has been getting at you,' she said.

'It's not the heat,' I replied, 'it's Fiona.'

I recounted the afternoon's events.

'Is she pretty?' inquired my wife.

'Very,' I said.

'And what's more she uses potent perfume. You reek of it.'

Next morning the telephone rang just before Eleanor was about to leave for work. She answered it.

'Who was that?' I asked.

'Your girl-friend. I told her you had gone away on retreat in a monastery for a few days. She sounded quite disappointed.'

# 9

'We shall go in convoy, like our ships during the war.' With those words the Reverend Daniel Thomas, the rural dean, launched the first summer outing for the clergy of the deanery since the outbreak of hostilities in 1939. This momentous occasion took place on the Monday after the commencement of the centenary redecoration work in Pontywen. What with the pulsating Miss Forbes-Hamilton episode, these were eight days full of incidents. None more so than the deanery outing.

At the last chapter meeting it was decided that we should have an outing to Hereford where we would have a sit-down meal at The Cathedral Restaurant. After that we would look around the cathedral and then join the congregation for Evensong. It was to be a clerical stag party. 'Our wives have got the Mothers' Union and that sort of thing,' said the rural dean, 'so we chaps will come in our own cars and meet outside The Bull Inn, and start off at eleven o'clock prompt.'

Lined up outside The Bull Inn, Tremadoc ready for the safari to Hereford were five cars worthy of any vintage rally. In prime place was the Reverend Arthur Powell's Sunbeam open tourer, with its spare wheel attached on the running board. Smoking a cigarette in a long holder, with his grey hair parted in the middle and plastered to his head with brilliantine, he looked like another edition of Edgar Wallace the crime writer. Arthur Powell, in his sixties, had come to Tremadoc from a town parish and had big ideas for building a church hall and renovating his church, but with no money to carry them out. Apart from Charles and myself, he was the only one to be wearing his college blazer which was now in a state of terminal decay.

Alongside him in the front seat, sitting bolt upright and looking terrified, was the Reverend Williams-Evans, a whippet of a man in his seventies. All his travelling was done by bus, including his yearly visit to Cardiff to bring back books from which the clergy would choose one to study. The thought of travelling in such a monster of a car, driven by his extrovert companion, was apparently causing him to look death in the face. It was not so much an outing as an ordeal.

Behind the Sunbeam was an ancient Ford Eight, with the spare tyre on the back. At the wheel was the Reverend Isaiah Jenkins, a tiny garden gnome in his late eighties, with a tendency to drive on the wrong side of the road. Sleeping in the front passenger seat was the Reverend Evan Hughes, a nonagenarian, the Rip Van Winkle of the deanery. The old man was never awake for more than five minutes at a time whenever the chapter met. It was said that he would fall asleep during a hymn and would have to be roused to carry on with the service.

Next in line was a venerable Singer with an engine taken from a sewing machine by the noise that it made. This belonged to the Reverend Amos Morris, chapter clerk, a beanpole of a man whose thin face was dominated by a long red nose, unkindly christened Rudolph by Charles. He had collected his neighbour, the Reverend Elias Jones who supplemented his income by keeping a few sheep and cattle on land rented from a parishioner. In his tweed suit and his Sherlock Holmes hat, he was enveloping Amos in clouds of tobacco smoke from his Sherlock Holmes pipe.

Then came my 1931 Morris Minor, a gift from my wife who had bought herself a brand new Ford 8. My passenger had been press-ganged into joining the party. Not only was Charles bored to tears at every chapter meeting, but of late he had developed a romantic relationship with Bronwen Williams, who had nursed him during his spell in Pontywen Hospital. This new episode in his love life was more promising than his two previous love affairs with schoolgirls. At least Bronwen was much nearer his own age and was already beginning to smarten him up. He had been hoping to be given the Monday-afternoon visiting at the hospital. Instead I had given that duty to Barney Webster. It was enough for me to have to bear with my fellow incumbents without having to put up with Barney's presence as well. So it was a very morose Charles at my side.

The last car in the convoy was the bull-nosed Morris belonging to the rural dean. It was his pride and joy. If there was the slightest shower when the car was on the road he would return home as soon as possible to dry and polish its exterior, in case of rust. Fortunately for him the day of the outing was dry and sunny. 'I am coming last so that I can keep an eye on you chaps, like a shepherd to the convoy,' he said, mixing his metaphors and driving solo.

At eleven o'clock precisely the 'convoy' moved off, after a signal from the rural dean's horn to Arthur Powell who roared away as if he were in a road race. In no time at all there was a large gap between his Sunbeam and the Ford Eight which was meandering over the road like a drunken tortoise. A cattle lorry coming in the opposite direction found great difficulty in taking avoiding action. As it passed us I could see the driver's face was ashen as a result of sparring with the Reverend Isaiah Jenkins.

Half an hour later four cars were still in convoy with a considerable tailback behind us and with the leading car much nearer to Hereford than the rest of us. The hedgerows were a riot of colour and through the open car window came the scent of wild flowers mingled with the effusions of the exhausts ahead. It was a lovely hazy day of sunshine, unappreciated by Charles who sat in sullen silence, bereft of contact with his beloved Bronwen. Suddenly the Ford Eight stopped, fortunately on the left-hand side of the road. The other three cars pulled in behind, allowing a stream of frustrated drivers behind us to overtake, shaking their fists as they passed.

'Now what?' said my curate.

Ahead of us, the Reverend Isaiah Jenkins and the Reverend Evan Hughes disembarked and made their way through a farm gate into a hay field. The rural dean appeared at the window. 'Bladder bother, I expect. I think I'll join them.

You two are all right, I expect. It looks as if the Vicar of Tremadoc has disappeared. I only hope he knows the name of the café in Hereford where we are to go.' He stopped at Amos Morris's Singer and was joined by its two occupants in a visit to the field.

Five minutes later we resumed our journey. 'I don't think we shall ever reach Hereford,' prophesied Charles. It was at twelve twenty that we came to a halt again. This time the reason for our stop was immediately apparent. Clouds of steam were billowing from the Ford Eight. 'Radiator trouble,' I said to my passenger knowingly.

'I know a good way to stop that,' said Charles. 'Chewing-gum.'

'That is ingenious,' I replied. 'And which one of our convoy use chewing gum?'

Once again the rural dean appeared at our window.

'I don't suppose you have any water on board.'

He was still persisting with his naval terminology.

'I am afraid not. I expect we shall have to find a house somewhere but more important something to plug the leak.'

'They do say that chewing-gum is good for that but I suspect none of the chaps has any.'

After a minute he was back.

'I wonder if your curate would try to find somewhere where he can get water. Abergavenny is only about five miles away but Isaiah will never make it.'

'Charles will be pleased to help, I am sure,' I said. He glared at me and then glared at the rural dean. Slowly he arose from his seat and made his way out into the rural wilderness. There was not a house in sight.

As he disappeared into the distant landscape, a car pulled up beside me.

'Trouble, Vicar?' inquired the driver.

'Yes, I am afraid. We are on our way to Hereford and one of our cars has a radiator leak.'

'Not to worry. Glad to help on the road to Damascus-cum-Hereford. I always carry a can of water with me in case of accidents or leaks. What is more I have the remains of a tin of Radweld with me which should do the trick.'

He drove his old Wolseley in front of the Ford Eight and

pulled up the bonnet. By now the two old men were surrounded by the remainder of the convoy. Evan Hughes was still asleep, blissfully unaware of the hiatus in our journey.

'We had better let it cool down before doing anything,' suggested the rescuer. He waited for a while before removing the cap of the radiator and inserted what was left of the tin of Radweld. Next he poured in a canful of water and waited to see if it came out through the hole which had caused the trouble. To everybody's great relief the radiator remained intact.

'You can get on your way, reverend gentlemen, and may God be with you.' There was a faint hint of mockery in his tone of voice. As he moved away I recognized him as the Marxist lecturer who had been invited to debate the existence of God in my third year at college and had almost succeeded in making as many converts to atheism as the organizers of the debate had hoped would move in the opposite direction.

'That's someone I would call a good Christian,' said the rural dean. 'Let's move on or we are going to be late.'

'Hold on, Mr Rural Dean. Don't forget you asked my curate to go and fetch some water. If you want to go ahead do so by all means, but it will be minus the Pontywen contingent.'

'Oh! I had forgotten Mr Wentwood-Baxter.' He could never remember names. 'Of course, we'll wait for him. After all he is on an errand of mercy, isn't he? Hold on, Isaiah, we had better not dash off without him.'

Before Isaiah could make a dash in his Ford Eight, Charles appeared on the horizon accompanied by someone who was carrying a can in each hand. Slowly the pair made their way towards us.

'This is Mr Richards, Grove Farm,' said my curate. 'He has brought plenty of water.'

'Thank you all the same, Mr Bentworth-Waxford, but some good Christian soul has come to our rescue. I am very sorry, Mr Grove. It is very kind of you to help like this – but there you are.'

It is a pity that I had no camera available to capture the looks on the faces of Charles and his farmer friend. I have never seen looks speak so many volumes – enough to stock a library.

As we set off towards Abergavenny I felt as if I had an unexploded bomb beside me. Not a word escaped his pursed lips. In any case I made no attempt at conversation. I had no desire to detonate the device.

Led by the zigzagging Isaiah Jenkins at a speed which merited a man with a flag in front, the convoy crawled into the narrow streets of the little market town. The few shoppers stopped and stared at the sight of the clerical collars in the four cars, especially since the leading car appeared to have an aversion to pedestrians.

Charles spoke for the first time since his unnecessary errand of mercy. 'Look!' he said as we were moving towards the Hereford road. He pointed to a somewhat dishevelled Arthur Powell, who was waving frantically as Isaiah Jenkins and Amos Morris totally ignored him, grimly intent on their journey.

I waved down the rural dean behind and pressed hard on the horn button to warn the front two cars. Apparently they were deaf because they still made their way down the road towards the beckoning countryside.

'Don't worry,' said Charles, 'we'll soon catch them up. It will take them half an hour to go a couple of miles.'

'I've blown a gasket,' explained the demon driver when we joined him. 'My car is round the corner in a garage. Williams-Evans and myself had to push it about half a mile through the streets.'

The reason for the stares from the shoppers became obvious. Evidently it was not long since they had seen two clerical collars pushing a big Sunbeam tourer. The sight of seven more parsons in an erratic procession was a cause for wonderment and speculation.

'Blown a gasket!' exclaimed the rural dean. 'Well! Well! Is that bad? Can it be cured.' He spoke as if the Vicar of Tremadoc were suffering from a serious illness.

'Oh, yes! But at a cost to my pocket. They say it will be ready by five o'clock. So if you don't mind, Mr Rural Dean, we shall have to travel with you to Hereford and pick up the car on the way back.'

'Where is your passenger, then, so that we can start off again? We are going to be very late getting there at this rate.'

'He has gone to the public lavatory. I think the worry has upset his stomach.'

'Fright, more like; plus Powell's tobacco,' commented Charles quietly.

Arthur Powell had discarded his cigarette holder and was chewing a cigarette rather than smoking it.

'I hope he will not be long, that is all I can say. By the way, Vicar, if you are going to come with me – no smoking, please. My wife can't stand the smell of tobacco in the car. She has got a nose like a hawk; she would know straight away if you had been smoking.'

The stranded motorist puffed furiously at his cigarette, determined to reduce it to a butt before discarding it. This was just as well because the thin form of the Reverend Williams-Evans appeared from around the corner, with his arm across his stomach and the look of a martyr on his countenance.

'Here he is,' said the rural dean. 'Now we can set off again on our joy ride. Get in, Rector. I hope you are feeling better. It's a good thing there was a lavatory handy. Once we get moving, you will be all right. Think of that nice meal waiting for us in Hereford.'

The Reverend Williams-Evans turned green and tottered back to the refuge he had left a minute ago.

'Would you never!' the dignitary exclaimed. 'Where has he gone now?'

'To that handy lavatory,' I said.

'We can't wait here much more. Go and see how long he is going to take, Vicar.'

Arthur Powell seized the opportunity to take out another cigarette before checking on his passenger. Ten minutes later he was back, supporting the broken reed with one hand and using the other to finish off the remains of his stub.

This time the human wreck had a face no longer green but ashen instead. He was deposited on the back seat of the car while his erstwhile driver sat in front with the impatient rural dean who had instructed me to 'step on it'.

My old car could manage fifty miles an hour at most, and involving such rattling that it was in danger of shaking to pieces. In any case, as my curate had said, it would not take us long to catch up with the other two members of our party. So once I had reached forty miles an hour I made no attempt to increase my speed. In the meanwhile the bull-nose Morris was so close behind me that, if I had stopped suddenly, its nose would have been buried in my back seat.

It was then that I caught up with a funeral procession headed by a hearse proceeding at a pace which would have been approved by the Reverend Isaiah Jenkins. There seemed to be about a dozen cars in the cortège. In my rear-view mirror I could see the tortured expression on the face of the Reverend Daniel Thomas BA, RD.

'How far is it from Abergavenny to Hereford?' inquired Charles.

'Twenty-three miles, and if we are to stay behind this lot all the way it will seem more like a hundred and twenty-three miles,' I replied. 'I don't think they will even catch up with Isaiah. There are far too many cars to overtake. Anyway this old crate is incapable of passing more than one at a time.'

Suddenly there was a blast on the horn behind me and the Morris pulled out. It managed to pass three cars before pushing into the cortège as oncoming traffic forced it to take cover.

To my great relief, about a mile further on I could see the hearse turning right from the main road.

A minute or so later, the ruridecanal road hog put his foot on the accelerator. To my great surprise he was followed by the three cars he had overtaken, with me bringing up the rear. It must have been five or six miles further on that we met up with the other cars of the 'convoy', which had pulled in to the side of the road. The bull-nose drew in behind them. To my even greater surprise, the three cars pulled in also. As I left my car to find out what was happening, I overheard the black-suited driver of the car immediately behind the rural dean saying to him, 'It looks as if we are going to be late for the funeral.'

'I don't know what funeral you are talking about. All

I know is that we are going to be late for our outing to Hereford.'

'You are not going to Grosmont churchyard then? You are all parsons. The late Mr Philpott was highly respected and I thought you must have been late catching up with the procession.'

'Excuse me,' I said. 'The rest of your cortège turned right off the road some six miles back.'

By now we were joined by the mourners from the other two cars.

'They are not going to the funeral; they're off to an outing in Hereford. We've got to go back down the road six miles and turn off there,' said the driver of the first car. He turned to the rural dean. 'You should have known better, a man of the cloth like you, butting in among the mourners. If it hadn't been for you, we would have been at the church-yard by now.'

'Not at the speed the hearse was going,' I ventured to say. 'If you drive at a reasonable rate I am sure you will be there in time.'

'Perhaps you are right, Reverend,' he replied. 'Come on, let's see if we can beat them to it.'

They were gone in a flash.

'I have never heard anyone talk about getting to a funeral in those terms,' commented Charles.

'More to the point for us,' I said, 'what has happened to the Ford Eight this time?'

As we went towards it, the reason was obvious. The spare tyre had been taken off the back of the car. The Reverend Elias Jones, with his pipe in his mouth and his hat on the back of his head, was endeavouring to use a foot-pump to inflate the ancient rubber relic.

'Good heavens, Isaiah, when did you last put some air into this tyre?'

'It's like this, Elias: I never use it anyway, so I don't bother.'

'Don't tell me you have never had a flat tyre before today.'

'Yes, of course, but somebody always comes to help. People are very kind like that. The last time was just after war broke out.'

'Nineteen fourteen or nineteen thirty-nine?' inquired Elias.

Eventually the tyre was inflated and put on in place of the punctured tyre, which was attached to the back of the old car after much manipulation of rusty nuts.

The rural dean extracted his gold hunter watch.

'A gift from grateful parishioners when I left my last parish.'

This ambiguous announcement was made to an audience who had heard it many times before.

'Good gracious me!' he exclaimed, 'It is gone two o'clock. What time did you tell the café we would be there, Mr Chapter Clerk?'

Amos Morris spoke as slowly as Isaiah Jenkins drove his car. He paused as if he had been asked a thought-provoking question.

'Round about one o'clock, Mr Rural Dean,' he drawled.

'They will think we are not coming. We had better stop at one of those telephone kiosks when we see one. In that case you had better lead off so that you can communicate as quickly as possible.'

Amos was incapable of doing anything as quickly as possible but undertook to lead the way, followed by Isaiah who had a front-seat passenger blissfully unaware of the day's exciting incidents. As far as I could see, the Reverend Evan Hughes was still in a deep sleep.

The convoy crept along the road to Hereford causing traffic chaos for miles until it ground to a halt by a cross roads which boasted a telephone box. It was now twenty past two and our destination was still seven miles away.

There was a long hiatus while the chapter clerk searched in his pocket for the letter from the Cathedral Restaurant and for change to make the telephone call. Eventually he emerged from his car and ambled to the means of communication. Once inside we could see him fumbling for his money and dropping the letter in the process. Eventually he began to dial and we waited to see his response to the call. As Charles said afterwards, Amos Morris would show as much reaction to the news that the world was going to end as he would if he was informed by his wife that he needed a haircut.

The rural dean had his nose pressed against the window of the box like a schoolboy eyeing a display of sweets in a shop. A conversation ensued for minutes before Amos put down the receiver and made his exit.

'Well?' demanded his superior of the chapter clerk.

'I am afraid, Mr Rural Dean, that they close at half past two and that they will not open again until six o'clock. The lady suggested that our best policy would be to try one of the transport cafés on the way into Hereford.'

The effort entailed in speaking the two sentences seemed to have exhausted his strength and he leaned against the door of the telephone box.

'Transport café!' bellowed the rural dean. 'I had just got my mouth in shape for the rainbow trout; perhaps we can try somewhere else in Hereford.'

'She said that no restaurant will be open when we get there. Our only hope would be to wait until six o'clock.'

'I have to be back in Abergavenny by five o'clock to pick up my car,' said Arthur Powell. 'Blow the rainbow trout; I'll settle for sausage, bacon and egg. My stomach is beginning to feel my throat is cut.'

'And what about our visit to the cathedral for evensong at three thirty p.m.?'

'At the rate we are going, we wouldn't be there in time anyway.'

Arthur's patience was at an end, and he was not the only one.

The Officer Commanding could see that a mutiny was impending in the ranks of the convoy.

'Very well,' he breathed. 'Perhaps we had better call it a day and look for one of those cafés. You never know, we might have a good meal.'

Half an hour later we arrived at the Roadside Café, among a conglomeration of pantechnicons and lorries. As we entered the low-roofed building redolent with the smell of fried food, a score of eyebrows were raised at the sight of nine clergymen walking up to the counter to place their orders. It was not long before the place was empty as the drivers shovelled down their food in order to make a quick escape from such an intrusion of holiness upon their privacy.

I have never known bacon, sausage, egg and chips to be so tasty.

'Was it Socrates who said that hunger was the best sauce for the appetite?' said Charles in an effort to be erudite.

'By the look of the plates left on the tables, I would have thought it was tomato ketchup,' I replied.

'You have no soul, Fred.'

'Don't speak like that to your vicar or I'll stop your hospital visiting permanently.'

It was a threat which silenced him for the rest of the meal.

An hour later the convoy made its way back to Abergavenny, with Rip Van Winkle resuming his siesta as soon as he got in the seat of the Ford Eight. Arthur Powell collected his Sunbeam and roared off with his captive while the rest of us dawdled our way back to the Bull Inn.

'I am very sorry that we didn't get to Hereford,' said the rural dean before we went our different ways. 'We must start earlier next year.'

'Wouldn't it be wiser to hire a small bus and perhaps take our wives with us?' I suggested.

'Maybe we could get a little bus but I don't fancy bringing

our wives with us. You know what women are like; it would stop us having a good time.'

Charles and I were in danger of exploding from suppressed laughter, which manifested itself in a fit of coughing.

'Don't forget to get that tyre repaired and that radiator seen to, Isaiah,' said Elias Jones.

'One of these days, if I can remember. That's the trouble.'

'If you don't remember, you'll have plenty of trouble.'

Isaiah never had any more trouble. He died a week later.

# 10

'We must ask Charles and his young lady to dinner one of these days,' said Eleanor. We were driving back from her parents' home after our weekly obligatory visit. 'He is such a different person since he has taken up with her, apart from the improvement in his appearance; we must do all we can to encourage the relationship.'

'Amen to that,' I replied. 'Nowadays he is even on time for our daily service. Before very long he might develop into an asset instead of a liability. I never thought that would happen. What a difference the right woman can make.'

'You should know that, Frederick.' She put her foot down on the accelerator as we swung from the side road into the main road to Pontywen.

'And you should know that self praise is no recommendation, even if it happens to be true. More to the point, what about inviting them to come one day next week.'

'It had better be the Saturday evening to give us time to give them a reasonable meal. Now that my father has lent you his precious shotgun you might bring back a pheasant or two; you never know.'

On the back seat of the car reposed my father-in-law's single-barrelled shotgun. It was the first one he had ever purchased and it had a great sentimental value for him. At shooting parties he used his double-barrelled firing piece, keeping his first love for the occasional foray of rabbit shooting. A box of Eley cartridges was given to me as a present to commemorate my baptism of fire. He had instructed me on how to load the gun, how to hold it and how to aim at the target. All I had to do now was to obtain permission from one of the farmers in Llanhyfryd to shoot on his territory.

I was beginning to feel the complete parson: vicar at a tender age, happily married, with a parish totally under control. Over the past few weeks life had been very satisfactory. The cracks in the roof and the wall of the parish church were dismissed as insignificant by the diocesan architect; preparations for the centenary were going apace; I had finished writing the booklet containing the history of the parish; and Charles had produced a promising script for the pageant. Now I was about to add another string to my bow by becoming a clerical marksman.

Next morning I telephoned Evan Jones, Blaenycwm Farm, churchwarden of Llanhyfryd, to obtain his permission to shoot on his land. Evan had been a troublemaker until Eleanor had restored his sick wife to full health by the application of the latest available drugs on the market. Since then I had no more aggravation from him. Another reason for this was the removal of Charles from the scene at Llanhyfryd and the arrival of their own curate-in-charge.

'G-good morning, Vicar. T-to what do I o-owe the p-pleasure of this c-call?' he stammered.

'I was wondering whether you would give me permission to shoot some of the rabbits on your land. My father-in-law has lent me his gun and given me some cartridges.'

'B-by all means. I n-never knew you were a sh-shooting man.'

'To be honest, I have never handled a gun before. I thought I might like to have a go.'

'W-why not. You had b-best come up about eight o' c-clock tonight and I'll sh-show you where to go.'

Charles was delighted to have the invitation to dinner at the vicarage. 'Bronwen will be thrilled,' he said. 'She has met Eleanor a few times at the hospital and thinks she is an excellent doctor, apart from being a nice person. There's only one snag, though. I haven't told you this before, she is a Welsh Baptist, a practising one too and very strict about drink and so on. So, if you were thinking about having wine with the dinner, perhaps it would be better if you didn't, if you know what I mean. It's up to you, of course.'

When I told Eleanor, she was highly amused.

'I think we shall fill our glasses with white wine before-hand and pour lemonade into their glasses. That should do the trick. With a bit of luck there will be little difference in colour.'

'You are a very devious lady but I love you,' I replied.

At half past seven that evening I set out for Blaenycwm Farm, fully equipped for my first shooting expedition. It was a lovely late summer evening with barred clouds blooming the soft dying day. Eleanor had kissed me goodbye and wished me good luck. The world was my oyster. I drove up the farm track from the main road and pulled up outside the farm house trying to suppress my excitement which was mingled with a certain amount of apprehension. As I left the car, Dell, the black and white farm dog who had once bitten me, came towards me menacingly. Deciding that discretion was the better part of valour I dashed back to the safety of the Morris Minor.

At that moment the farmer emerged from his front door.

'I hope you are going to shut him up while I am out in the fields,' I said. 'Otherwise I don't know who would be the more scared, the rabbits or me.'

'D-don't worry, Vicar. I'll tie him up now and then c-come and show you where to g-go.'

A minute later he was back.

As he led me into the fields, he said, 'I hope you d-don't m-mind me mentioning this, Vicar, but a lot of p-people in the church are g-getting f-fed up with being b-bossed about by Mr W-Webster and his w-wife. She is even w-worse than him; the w-women can't stand her.'

'I am surprised to hear you say that. I thought you were only too glad to have your own man and not to be tied to the coat tails of the vicar in Pontywen. Charles Wentworth-Baxter was not a bossy type by any means but you couldn't wait to get rid of him. So what do you want?'

'P-perhaps you don't know w-what has been g-going on. He has s-sacked Miss Owen from the organ and p-put Mrs W-Webster in her place. She is a m-much worse organist than Miss Owen; c-can't even p-play the psalms. W-we-'ve got to s-say them now, and she has t-taken charge of the flower rota and altered everything. N-now he has started d-dressing up.'

'What do you mean, dressing up?'

'You know – p-putting on that old n-nightgown with that p-pinafore thing over it. Ianto Lewis and his w-wife have stopped c-coming and s-some of the others say they are not g-going to come anym-more while he's here.'

'This is all news to me, Mr Jones, and you can tell everybody else that I shall be looking into the matter.'

'Thank you, Vicar. W-well this is the p-place to be. G-get behind this hedge and l-lie low. You'll see the r-rabbits come out in n-no time.'

So saying, he left me to the beginning of my new career in field sports. First of all I took out the cartridge with its pink cardboard holder tipped with its shining brass base. Nervously I broke open the gun and inserted the missile into the breech, snapping back the weapon into its loaded position. I began to breathe deeply, acutely aware that I had a means of destruction in my own hand. While I was doing this, my blood began to boil at the treachery of Barney who had betrayed the trust I had put in him.

Then I crouched down and began to patrol behind the hedge, occasionally peeping over the top to see if there was any prey in sight. The first few peeps produced no sight of a rabbit. In a way I was relieved. I could go back and say that they had all stayed in for that night. My next sniping manoeuvre over the green parapet made my heart stand still. There appeared to be a family outing from one of the warrens. There were five rabbits – two large and three small ones.

I remembered what I had said to my father when I was a three-year-old in Cardiganshire as he was about to go rabbit shooting. 'Don't shoot the little ones, Daddy.' I pulled back the trigger and aimed at one of the big ones. For what seemed an eternity I tried to position the little raised piece of metal at the end of the barrel between the two sighting pieces at my end. I closed my eyes and squeezed the trigger. The impact of the firing was so unexpected that it almost knocked me over.

When I opened my eyes, to my horror I could see one of

the little ones on its back with its legs kicking, in an empty field. I scrambled over the hedge and stood over the dying creature. My immediate thought was to put it out of its misery. Wildly I began to strike the poor animal with the barrel of the gun instead of the butt. It refused to die until I had hit it several times. Eventually it lay completely still. Exhausted by my murderous exertions I was unable to bring myself to look at the corpse. Instead I looked at the gun. My father-in-law's precious possession had suffered as well as the rabbit. The barrel had been bent to such an extent that any cartridge I would have put in it would have been fired into the field to my side instead of the one in front of me.

It was quite a while before I could bring myself to pick up the mangled remains of what had been a young frisky member of a family, innocently enjoying itself. I shuddered at the contact with the warm corpse. Hurriedly I made my way to the gate, determined to get away from the scene of the crime as quickly as possible. I put down the misshapen gun and the even more misshapen rabbit. Frantically I tried to open the heavy iron gate which was chained to the gate-post. Suddenly it swung back knocking me over and landing me face down into the mutilated animal. My stomach heaved.

I stood up and braced myself to handle the thing once again. I removed it into the lane, together with my father-in-law's precious possession. After several attempts I managed to close the gate. Now I was faced with the problem of what to do with my prey.

Under no circumstances could I return to the vicarage with the 'hunter home from the hill' attitude, providing the dinner for tomorrow. Was I to leave it in the lane or perhaps take it back with me and give it a decent burial? Should I slink off from the farmyard without saying goodnight to Evan Jones or should I tell him what had happened?

First I decided I would go to Evan Jones and confess that I was not 'a shooting man' as he would put it. Secondly I would take the body back with me and give it a decent burial in the kitchen garden. Thirdly I would tell Eleanor that it was the last time I would fire a gun. Fourthly, and this in some ways was the most painful of all my decisions, I would have to go to my father-in-law with the battered shotgun and confess my complete inadequacy.

The farmer emerged from his house when the dog's bark announced my return.

'I s-see you've g-got a r-rabbit. N-not very b-big is it?' He grinned.

'I'm afraid, Mr Jones, this is my one-and-only attempt with a gun. I had to kill the poor thing by beating it to death. That is something I never want to do again. Now I have to go back to my father-in-law with a badly damaged shotgun.'

He looked at it and whistled his amazement at the extent of its malformation.

'Th-there is one thing, he'll n-never be able to use th-that again. I d-didn't think you were the k-kind to g-go about with a g-gun, that's for sure.'

'It is a bit late to find that out now. Anyway, thank you for letting me have the use of your field. I think I had better be off back to the vicarage and face the music.'

'I b-bet it w-won't be "Home s-sweet Home", Vicar.'

With those words ringing in my ears I drove down the farm lane and out on the road to Pontywen. By now it was dark. It is just as well, I told myself. With a bit of luck, Eleanor will not hear me arrive. I shall creep round the back to the garden shed, pick up the spade and bury the remains in the bottom of the garden. That way I shall not be obliged to see the full horror of my victim's wounds in broad day-light, and my wife would be unaware of my mindless excess of cruelty. It would be bad enough to have to tell her about the mess I had made of her father's favourite gun.

'The best laid schemes o' mice an' men gang aft a-gley.' Since my scheme was not best laid, I suppose it was inevitable that it would gang greatly a-gley. I managed to park the car by coasting down the vicarage drive with the engine shut off; and taking with me the dead rabbit, I went around the garden shed and quietly opened the door. Fumbling around in the dark, and moving further into the outbuilding to feel for the spade, I kicked over an empty bucket. There was a loud clatter. The next instant the kitchen light was switched on. The back door opened. I was trapped in the act, illuminated as I stood in the entrance to the shed, with the wretched thing dangling from my left hand.

'What on earth are you doing?' demanded my wife.

'I am-er about to bury this animal,' I stammered.

'You are supposed to eat it, not bury it. Have you been drinking some more of Evan Jones's scrumpy?'

'No, love, honestly. Let me bury it and I'll explain when I come in.'

'Can't you explain now? It can't be all that complicated a story.'

'That's what you think,' I said. 'So, if you don't mind, I'll get the spade and bury it.'

I turned back into the shed, whose contents were now discernible in the light from the kitchen. Grabbing the spade I made off down the garden path, while Eleanor stood bewildered, wondering if I was suffering from a brain storm.

It did not take me long to dig a small hole of sufficient size to contain the rabbit. I threw a few clods of earth over it and made my way back to the shed. By now my wife had gone back into the house. I decided to leave the gun in the car until the morning. It would be sufficient for me to explain the burial first.

'Well?' said Eleanor as I came into the kitchen.

'Let's go into the sitting room and I'll tell you all about it,' I replied.

We sat side by side on the sofa and I held her hand.

'It's like this: I am afraid I am not cut out to be a sporting parson. I shall never again fire a gun. My one-and-only shot was aimed at a large rabbit, probably father. Instead it struck junior but failed to kill it outright. I had to jump over the hedge and attempt to put it out of its misery as it lay on its back, kicking its legs in the air. I went berserk in my anxiety to end its suffering. All I managed to do was to inflict an excess of injury on the poor thing before it finally breathed its last. The reason I wanted to bury it was in atonement for my mindless beating. I was grubbing around in the dark to avoid you seeing what I had perpetrated on the victim. I am afraid that is not the end of the story.'

'What do you mean love? You are in a state, aren't you? Let me pour you a medicinal whisky before you tell me any more.' She kissed me on the forehead.

'While you are doing that, I'll get the gun from the car,' I said.

I came back into the room with the gun behind my back. Eleanor came towards me with a tumbler of whisky in her hand.

'I was not going to show you this until the morning but now that you have heard chapter one you might as well see the embodiment of chapter two.'

When I produced the twisted wreck of a gun, her eyes opened wide.

'Frederick, what have you been doing? My father will not be able to use that piece of scrap iron anymore; and to think it was his pride and joy.'

'Can you imagine how I feel about it? I used the barrel of the gun in my panic instead of the butt.'

'Here, sit down and drink this.' She put her arm round me and led me to the sofa. 'I am glad you didn't let me see the full extent of your attack on the creature.'

'Your father will never forgive me for this.' I gulped down a mouthful of whisky.

'Of course he will, once he knows the circumstances. To be truthful, I'm glad that you have found out that you are not the kind to indulge in bloodsports; I was surprised that you thought you might be.'

'Do you know what? I feel much better already, thanks to you.' I kissed her.

'I expect the whisky has helped, too. Did Evan Jones see the result of your night's work?'

'He did indeed; he said he didn't think I was a shooting man. Speaking of Evan Jones, he gave me some very disturbing news about our friends the Websters.'

'You amaze me,' said my wife. 'Come on, tell me more. You have had a rotten evening by the sound of everything.'

'He says that Barney has started wearing vestments, or "putting on that old nightgown with that pinafore", as Evan put it. He has sacked Miss Owen from the organist's job and our friend Ethel has taken over. Apparently she has also taken over the flower rota and altered everything. In other words, he is causing chaos.'

'I think, my dear, you had better have a word with the bishop.'

'I'll have a word with both. First of all with Barney after Matins tomorrow and with the bishop later on. Where on earth did he get the vestments?'

'Perhaps Ethel made them for him. She is very handy with the sewing machine.'

'In that case, it's small wonder that Evan Jones talked about the nightgown and a pinafore.'

'Finish up that whisky, love, and let's go to bed. Little man, you've had a busy day.'

Next morning I was up early, fired with indignation at Barney's duplicity and ready to administer a drastic dressing-down coupled with a threat of dismissal.

'You're hardly in the right frame of mind to approach the throne of the Almighty, my love,' said Eleanor. 'Don't you think you had better have a quiet quarter of an hour or so in church to calm down before the two curates arrive for Matins? You will need a cool head when you put Barney in his place, otherwise you might say something you will regret afterwards.'

I took her advice and spent half an hour on my knees in my stall. The stillness of the chancel was a balm to my injured feelings. By the time I began the service I was in full control of myself. At least, I thought so. When Matins was over, I told Barney that I wanted a word with him in the vicarage.

'Can't it wait?' he replied; 'I promised Ethel I would take her to Cardiff as soon as I came back from service.'

'No! It can't wait!' I exploded. 'I want you in the vicarage now. Ethel can wait.'

His ruddy complexion turned a deep purple and his mouth resembled that of a fish out of water.

'If you say so, Vicar,' he stammered.

I marched out of the church and into the vicarage, followed by an apprehensive curate who was beginning to suspect that I had found out what had been happening in Llanhyfryd.

Once in the study I took my seat of authority behind my desk and motioned him into the armchair in front of me. Not a word had been spoken since we left the vestry.

'What in heaven's name have you been doing in Llanhyfryd?' I demanded.

'What do you mean, Vicar?' His face was at odds with his verbal attempt at innocence.

'You know perfectly well what I mean, Barney. Since when did I give you permission to wear vestments in St Illtyd's? Why did you sack Miss Owen from her job as organist when she had been doing it quite satisfactorily for the past thirty years? Since when has Ethel had the authority to commandeer the flower rota and make changes where the women have had their own Sundays down through the years? You are acting like a bull in a china shop.'

'Hold on, Vicar,' he blustered. 'You told me I was in charge of Llanhyfryd.'

'When I said that you were in charge that did not mean you could act like a tinpot dictator without telling me what big changes you were making. I am still the incumbent at Llanhyfryd – not you. Any authority you have is only delegated by me and nothing on the scale of your actions over the past weeks should have been done without reference to me. Where did you get the vestments, anyway? I hope you did not buy them with the St Illtyd funds?'

'Certainly not, Vicar. Ethel made them from designs she had made after seeing them in church catalogues. We have paid for them ourselves. They are a present to the church.'

'Well, Barney, you can keep the present at home. You will not wear them in St Illtyd's. As for Miss Owen's dismissal, I shall call and see her. If she is prepared to come back as organist, I shall reinstate her. As far as the flower rota is concerned, I shall call a meeting of all those who place flowers on the altar and sort that matter out.'

His risen hackles were painful to behold.

'In other words, Vicar, you are going to make me look a fool, not to mention Ethel.'

'Barney, you have made a fool of yourself.'

'Under the circumstances, I think I had better resign from my curacy. There's no point in staying where I am not wanted.'

'Before you do that, I think you should know that I am going to phone the bishop later today and inform him of all the happenings in Llanhyfryd. If you resign formally, that will place you in a very awkward position. On the other hand, if I suggest to the bishop that, because of our age difference, it might be better for you to be with an older man, or possibly even to be given complete charge of a small parish somewhere, you will be in the clear.'

There was a long silence as he struggled with his emotions. It was not the first time that I had punctured his ego. This treatment from someone who was more than twenty years his junior he found difficult to bear. On the other hand, the possibility of complete charge of a parish was something he could not afford to dismiss out of hand.

'Very well, Vicar; I'll wait to see the outcome of your conversation with the bishop. I shall want to speak to him as well, to put my side of things.'

'Do that by all means but wait to see what happens after I speak to him this morning. I shall let you know immediately I have phoned him.'

An hour later, after I had made up my mind what I would say to his lordship, I rang him.

'I don't know whether I should come to see you, my Lord, or whether I can discuss this on the phone.'

'If you can possibly give me an idea of what is involved, Vicar, I shall judge for myself. I have some time to spare at the moment.'

'It is about Barnabas Webster. I am afraid I have given him far too much rope at St Illtyd's. As a result he is in the process of hanging himself and most of his congregation with it.'

'Could you be more precise?'

'In the space of a few weeks he has imposed vestments on his bewildered flock, sacked the organist, and installed his wife in that position. She has taken charge of the flower rota and alienated all the ladies.'

'And you knew nothing about this?'

'Nothing, my Lord. He resents being told what to do by someone so much younger than himself. Quite honestly I think it would be better for him that he was elsewhere.'

'Dear me! He has only been with you five minutes, as it were.'

'I realize that, my Lord, but I can assure you that it would be better for St Illtyd's and for himself that he and I part company as soon as possible.'

For the second time that morning I was met with a long silence.

'Right, Vicar, leave the matter with me. Will you please tell him that I wish to see him at eleven a.m. next Wednesday? How is Wentworth-Baxter behaving himself?'

'He is much improved in his ministry, my Lord, I am glad to say. He is a different man since he has taken up with a nurse at the hospital. She has done wonders for him.'

'It is just as well. With the old Wentworth-Baxter plus Barnabas Webster you would have been in great difficulty. Don't worry, I shall see what I can do to ease matters for you.'

The bishop was true to his word. When Barney returned from his episcopal interview, like Charles he was a different man. He drove his precious Riley down the vicarage drive at a rate of knots, pulling up with a screech of brakes. I saw this performance from the study window and hurried to the door to find out what had caused such untypical behaviour.

He advanced towards me, with a wide grin on his countenance. 'I have been offered the living of Llangelli,' he announced. Llangelli had a population of three hundred and was hidden away in an outback of the diocese. To an aspiring curate it would have meant exile; to Barnabas Webster it meant he was lord and master of his own parish; to the bishop it meant that the Websters were out of harm's way; to me it meant the removal of a headache far worse than Charles had ever given me.

# 11

As soon as Charles appeared in the vestry on Saturday morning it was obvious that a very large cloud had obscured the sunshine that had brightened his life in recent months. His gloomy face was in direct contrast to the beaming visage of Barney, whose not inconsiderable ego had been boosted by his elevation to the rank of incumbent elect.

When the service was over Charles asked if he might have a word with me in the vicarage. As soon as Barney had left, he launched into his tale of woe while we walked down the drive. 'I don't know how to tell you this, Fred, but Bronwen and I will not be coming to dinner with you tonight?'

'What on earth has happened? Have you quarrelled over something?'

'Worse than that. We have parted for good.'

I felt that any minute he would burst into tears.

'Go into the study and sit down while I make a cup of coffee. Eleanor has gone to the surgery. I shan't be a minute.'

When I came back with the two cups of coffee, he was sitting in the armchair with his face buried in his hands. I handed him his cup. His hand was shaking as he took it and it was plain that he had been weeping. I brought the other armchair alongside him.

'Come on then, Charles; out with it. Tell Uncle Fred.'

'I think I told you that she was a very strict Welsh Baptist, regular at worship, dead against drink and that sort of thing. Well, she has suddenly decided that she has a call to join a medical mission in Central Africa. She is going for an interview next week. Last night she told me it is better we part now because there is no future for us together, especially since I am an Anglican priest. All this has come out of the blue and I'm devastated. I love her so much and I thought that she loved me.'

'More than likely she does but being a high-principled girl she feels that her love of God takes precedence over her love for you. She is prepared to sacrifice her personal feelings to respond to the call of the missionary field. There's only one hope for you.'

He looked up at me as if I had found a way out from yet another impasse for him.

'What's that, Fred?'

'Perhaps the Mission Board will turn her down for one reason or another. It may be that she is not fully qualified or maybe she is not physically fit to endure the rigours of life in Central Africa. In that case she stays in Pontywen Hospital and you can take up where you left off.'

His face embodied the emotions of a drowning man, clutching at a straw which he had magnified into a lifeboat.

'I had never thought of that possibility. She is not sitting her SRN until next March. Perhaps they will tell her to wait until then and, as you know, she is only a little slip of a girl who may well not pass the compulsory medical.'

'So, there is a little light at the end of the tunnel, Charles. Do you feel like coming on your own this evening for a meal?'

'No, thanks. If you don't mind, I'll wait until we can come together.'

He left the vicarage in a much happier frame of mind, apparently convinced that the interview would turn out to be the answer to his prayers rather than those of Bronwen.

I rang Eleanor at the surgery to tell her that the dinner with the two was off.

When she had heard this further instalment of the Wentworth-Baxter love story, she said, 'What on earth are we going to do with the food I have got in?'

'Why not ask your parents to come, if they are free. It will be an opportunity for me to make peace with your father, since they had to cancel our visit to them this week.'

'Secombe, I have always said you are devious; this proves

it. Right! I shall ring them up immediately. It may be that they are otherwise engaged but it's worth a shot, if you will pardon the expression.'

Ten minutes later she telephoned to say that her father had answered the phone and had persuaded her mother to join us for dinner.

As the time for Eleanor's parents to arrive drew near I began to feel more and more apprehensive about exhibiting the mangled piece of metal which had been the barrel of her father's gun. I knew how I would have felt if someone had destroyed something which had held great sentimental value for me. Her father was a person whom I admired and respected, which made matters worse.

When the front-door bell announced the arrival of my in-laws, my heart was pounding and my mouth was dry. Eleanor was in the kitchen.

'Go and let them in, love,' she shouted. 'Take them into the sitting room. I'll be with you in a minute.'

My father-in-law was his usual good-humoured self, which made the confession of my misdeed all the more painful to contemplate. Mrs Davies was her usual vinegary self, which also added to the prospect of discomfiture for me later in the evening.

As I poured them a sherry, I debated with myself whether I should produce the evidence now or later in the evening. Discretion being the better part of valour, I came down in favour of a delay until dinner was over and the wine had mellowed the occasion.

Eleanor had excelled herself with the main course of grilled pork chops and braised pineapple, by courtesy of Protheroe, the butcher (for services rendered), and Evans, the grocer (ditto). After the apple tart baked by Mrs Watkins, with apples from the vicarage garden, and coffee, supplemented with brandy (also for services rendered), I felt emboldened enough to lead my father-in-law from the dining room into my study, while Eleanor was engaged in conversation with her mother.

'A delightful meal,' commented Dr Davies. 'Evidently my daughter is an excellent cook as well as an excellent doctor.'

'I'm afraid your son-in-law will never achieve excellence with the gun,' I began nervously.

'You mean you missed your target,' he said with a smile.

'I wish it were just that,' I replied. 'I am afraid I hit something which was not intended. If you sit there, I'll bring you the result of my marksmanship with the deepest apologies on my part.'

A question mark furrowed his brow as I left the room. I went into the shed and brought the damaged weapon into the kitchen. As I looked at it yet again, my resolution began to waver. Then I realized that it was too late to draw back from the inevitable. Holding the gun in my hand as if it were some monstrous creature, I entered the study.

'Good God!' said my father-in-law. 'What have you been doing with it? Trying to turn it into a pruning hook?'

'I'm terribly sorry. Instead of hitting the rabbit I aimed at, I hit the baby of the family. It lay on its back writhing in pain and I attempted to put it out of its misery by beating it with the barrel instead of the butt. By the time I had finished it off, I realized what I had done to the gun. I'll buy you another one with pleasure, if you will accept it. I know that will never replace the first love, but it is the least I can do. All I can say is that I shall never ask you or anybody else for the loan of a gun. That was my one-and-only attempt at being a sporting parson.'

He looked at me long and hard; then he stood up and took the gun.

'I may be able to do something with this. I am sure the gunsmith in Cardiff can, if I can't. The important thing is that you have found out that you are not meant for blood-sports. You must leave that to callous idiots like myself and the rest of the shooting fraternity. Don't worry, son.'

With that he shook my hand.

'Perhaps it is better I put it in the boot of the car before my dear wife sees it. What the eye does not see, the heart does not grieve.'

There the matter rested.

On Monday morning we had our usual chapter meeting in the vicarage. Barney was like an excited child. 'The date of my induction has been fixed for two months' time. We have been up to inspect the vicarage. It is a lovely old house with big grounds. There's a paddock and a long drive. It could do with resurfacing, mind, but apart from that every-thing is most impressive. Ethel can't wait to move in.'

'I'm sure she can't,' I said.

'Oh! and by the way, Vicar, there's no need for you to come to Llanhyfryd; we have sorted things out. Miss Owen is back at the organ and Ethel has put the old flower list back up in the porch. In any case she will be far too busy now to be bothered with running things at St Illtyd's.'

'I didn't know that she was running things at St Illtyd's, Barney; I thought that was your job, not hers.'

His smile vanished and his colour deepened.

'Anyway, thank you, Barney for putting things right. In that case I shall not go to Llanhyfryd today. I'll do the hospital instead. You can do some visiting on your patch, Charles, for a change.'

He looked up at me with that wounded-spaniel expression which was his speciality. For months it had been his Monday treat to visit the hospital and Nurse Williams in particular.

He waited behind after we had finished our meeting.

'I wanted to see Bronwen especially today. It is my last chance to do that before she goes for that interview.'

'My dear Charles, I am doing this for your sake. I don't want to interfere in your affairs, if you will pardon my phraseology, but I thought it would be an opportunity for me to press your suit, as it were.'

'What do you mean?'

'I am not talking about smartening you up. Bronwen seems to have achieved that in any case. It will do no harm if you are not present this afternoon. Absence makes the heart grow fonder. On the other hand it will give me an opportunity to have a few words with her about the serious-ness of the step she intends to take and to stress the strength of your feelings about her.'

'If you put it like that, Fred, then how can I object? I'll call round later to find out what has happened. Thank you for your help.'

'Don't expect miracles, Charles.'

'No, of course not.' It was obvious by the jaunty way he went up the vicarage drive that he was not truthful in his reply.

At lunch I told Eleanor about what I had done.

'You rotten thing,' she said, 'depriving poor Charles of his last glimpse of his beloved before she has her interview. What is more, he will be expecting you to wave your magic wand once again. I'm sure you can do very little in the few minutes she will be able to spare you.'

'Nothing venture, nothing win,' I replied.

I found Bronwen in the Princess Royal ward, appearing from behind a curtain and carrying a bed pan. 'See you on your return,' I said. She seemed somewhat embarrassed, either because of what she was carrying or because she suspected I had come to see her rather than the patients; possibly for both reasons.

Whilst she was out of the ward, I did the round of the beds, exchanging pleasantries with the middle-aged and elderly ladies. I had long since ceased to inquire what illness had brought them to hospital. In this particular ward the bulk of the patients were there for what they would simply describe as 'internal' reasons. Bronwen was away for such a long time that I was running out of small talk. I began to think that her absence was not caused by duty but by a desire to avoid meeting me.

Just as I was about to give up my mission, she reappeared and drew back the curtains surrounding the bed-pan lady. I made a beeline for her before she could disappear once again.

'I know you must be busy, Bronwen, but do you mind if I have a few words with you before you move off.'

'They will have to be very few, I'm afraid, Vicar. I'm sorry about last Saturday. I expect you know why I was not there.'

'Yes, of course. Charles is very upset about your decision but he respects your dedication and your courage. I'm sure he was hoping that you could join him in serving the Lord here in Pontywen rather than going solo to Africa to do it. Still, if you do not feel strongly enough about him to do that, then it is better that you part.'

'Oh, but I do feel strongly about Charles, very strongly. It is simply that I have this overwhelming urge to give my life to God in the mission fields. Over the past weeks it has become irresistible. I can't be deaf to the call any longer. I am desperately sorry for Charles but what can I do?'

'I see your plight, Bronwen. I don't wish to pry into your

affairs but would you please answer this question? What will you do, if for one reason or another the Mission Board does not select you?'

'Well, Vicar, there is only one answer to that. I shall have to pray about it.'

'When you do pray, under those circumstances, please include Charles in the forefront of your prayers. He will be more than ready to help you serve God in a little house in Mount Pleasant View and in St Padarn's Church. I apologize for poking my nose in; I just felt I had to do so. I'll leave you to get on with your work now.'

She stared into my face. There was a hint of puzzlement in her eyes.

'Thank you, Vicar. I'll think about what you have said.'

With those words she made her way to the far end of the ward where an elderly lady had started to call for her assistance.

As I left the hospital it dawned upon me that I had offered her the tenancy of 13, Mount Pleasant View as Charles's wife when they were not even engaged or in any way attached. My ruminations were halted by a shout from across the road.

'Vicar! Hold on. Do you mind if I have a word with you?'

It was the unmistakable voice of Bertie Owen, who was getting out of his car which was parked opposite the hospital entrance. He came across the road to me.

'Mr Wentworth-Baxter told me you were in the hospital, visiting, so I've been waiting for you to come out.'

'What's the urgency, Bertie?'

'Well, it's like this, Vicar. I'm working nights this week. I hate that shift but never mind. Anyway, I looked in at St Padarn's this afternoon to do a bit of painting because I can't be there tonight with the others. I had the shock of my life. It's been broken into. I thought you ought to know at once.'

'Of course. Have you told the police?'

'I thought I'd see you first. You're the boss. Can I give you a lift, Vicar.'

There was no alternative but to accept, despite the effect the ride would have on my stomach. Bertie had a habit of driving in fits and starts. As he talked to his passenger his foot would come off the accelerator. When he realized the car was slowing down, he would press the pedal down to the floor board, jerking his victim forward and propelling him towards the windscreen.

'You had better take me to St Padarn's and from there to the police station.'

'Right, Vicar, that's what I thought; whoever it is, they've been drinking the Communion wine and they've been scribbling all over the services register. The hassocks are all over the place. I don't think anything has been stolen, though. Sorry, Vicar.'

The car jerked forward. I had my hands on the dashboard to prevent me disappearing through the windscreen. By the time we reached the church a few minutes later, my stomach was nearer my mouth than my midriff.

He took me around to the back of the church where the kitchen window had been used to gain entry. A few panes of glass had been broken to unloose the catch. Inside, hassocks had been thrown about the church as if there had been the equivalent of an ecclesiastical pillow fight. The altar and its candlesticks were untouched. An empty bottle lay on the draining board in the kitchen beside cups which had been used as receptacles for the Communion wine. In the vestry, cassocks and surplices were strewn upon the floor. The register lay open on the desk and crude drawings were scrawled over several pages. A pool of ink surrounded the pen which had been employed for the artwork.

'Children,' I said.

'I was wondering if it was a tramp,' replied Bertie.

'He would hardly use two cups to drink the Communion wine and I am positive he would not waste his time drawing stupid pictures in the register, let alone throwing hassocks all over the place.'

'Perhaps you're right,' he said.

'It's a good thing the tins of paint are put away in the cupboard, otherwise there would be paint all over the place as well. You had better ask Idris to get Roberts the Ironmonger to replace the panes of glass.'

'I'll go to Roberts's, Vicar; it won't take me two ticks.'

'Idris is the warden, Bertie, and that's his responsibility.

What you can do now is fill the gaps in the window with some cardboard for the time being. Don't bother to take me to the police station, I'll see Will Book and Pencil later.'

I could not face another stop-start journey and in any case the crime was not of such a serious nature that urgent police investigation was needed.

On my way back to the vicarage, I called at Idris's house to inform him of the break-in. The little milkman was enjoying his siesta in front of a blazing fire in the hearth and awoke with a start as his wife tapped him on the shoulder.

'Wake up, sleeping beauty; you've got a visitor.'

His glazed eyes focused on me.

'What a nice surprise,' he croaked in a voice hoarsened by his open-mouthed snoring.

'I can't stop long, Idris,' I said. 'I'm afraid there has been a break-in at St Padarn's. Nothing serious. Children, I think. They have emptied the wine bottle and drawn faces in the register. That's about all. The panes of glass need to be replaced. I've told Bertie to ask you to do that but I thought I had better let you know now. I'll see Will Book and Pencil later this evening. By the way, how did Bertie come to have a key? I hope he is not holding one he is not entitled to.'

'I know that, Vicar. No, it's all right. I lent him the key last night after church so that he could get on with a bit of painting this afternoon. I wonder who the little devils are who've done this. The Morris kids from Maes-y-Coed Avenue were playing round the back down there last Saturday when some of the men were painting the walls.'

Maes-y-Coed Avenue was part of the council estate adjoining St Padarn's. Built in the early thirties it was now a slum where the children ran riot on most evenings. Matthew and Ben Morris had come to Sunday school at one time out of curiosity, but with no encouragement at home they had lost interest. Their father had served a sentence for desertion from the army but was now back with his family, if that could be said of someone who was in the pub most of the time.

'Perhaps I should have a word with Matthew and Ben first. If I can avoid bringing the law into this, so much the better. I shouldn't like to see them brought to court.'

'If you are going to do that, you will have to be careful how you do it, Vicar. Dave Morris has a very nasty temper and wouldn't take kindly to having his boys accused of doing something criminal – not that he's got anything to be proud of, with his record.'

'With a bit of luck, Idris, I should be able to meet them as they come out of school now. I shan't accuse them of anything, believe me, but I could put the fear of God into them, in a diplomatic way of course. That is, if they show signs of a troubled conscience.'

I hurried to the Brynglas School just in time to meet the exuberant swarm of uncaged juveniles who were pouring from the entrance. One of the first out was Matthew who had pushed his way to the front.

'Matthew,' I shouted.

When he saw me, his face coloured. He turned round and began to barge a path back into the school. If ever there was an admission of guilt, I said to myself, this was it. I decided to wait; Ben, the younger brother, would be out soon, in any case. The minutes ticked by but there was no sign of Ben. Most of the teachers had emerged and there was only a trickle of pupils. Either Matthew had waylaid Ben in the corridor or perhaps Ben had made himself ill by drinking the Communion wine and was not in school. As far as I knew this entrance was the only means of exit. Sooner or later he would have to reappear.

Another quarter of an hour passed by. Joe Llewellyn, the caretaker, appeared in the doorway.

'Hello, Vicar!' he called out. 'Waiting for somebody?'

I walked up through the playground to speak to him.

'As a matter of fact I am, Joe. I want to see Matthew Morris but he doesn't seem to have come out yet.'

'Hold on, I'll have a look inside. As far as I know the school is empty. He hasn't any right to be here now anyway. Has he been up to something again?'

'Let's put it like this, Joe. I suspect he might have been. He saw me when he was coming out earlier on and then went back into the school.'

'If he's hiding, I'll flush him out. Mind, he might have got out through the boiler-room door and climbed the railings at the back. Stay here and I'll go through the classrooms and the cloakrooms.'

Some time later he came back.

'The little bugger has got out through the boiler room; the door is open. If you want to see him you'll have to go to his home.'

After what Idris said, that was a confrontation I did not want but it was something I had to face. It was obvious to me that Matthew had broken into the church. That was too serious an offence to ignore. If I went to Maes-y-Coed Avenue straight away, it was more than likely that he would not be there. On the other hand if I went later in the evening his father would be out in the pub and it would be much easier to interview the miscreant in the presence of his mother.

When I arrived at the vicarage I found Charles waiting for me, anxious for news about my meeting with Bronwen.

'For heaven's sake put him out of his misery, love,' whispered Eleanor when she met me at the door. 'I hope you've got something worthwhile to tell him – like she's thrown up the idea of going to the jungle and that she's ready to marry him tomorrow. I have got to go to surgery now. Tell me all when I return. Don't forget to lay the table. The dinner's cooking in the oven.' She kissed me and ran out to her car.

'Well?' said Charles, as soon as I entered the study. He looked like a little boy waiting to see what Father Xmas had brought.

'Well,' I replied, 'I have told the apple of your eye how much you dote upon her. In fact I went much further than that; I promised her residence in 13, Mount Pleasant View if she decides to marry you. I never thought I would play the role of a marriage broker as part of my ministry. I hope you're satisfied.'

'Fantastic, Fred! You are a brick. But how did she react to all this?'

'She said she would think over what I had said. Earlier she said that she had this irresistible urge to serve the Lord in the mission field. She also said she felt very strongly about you. That's about it.'

'I can't thank you enough. Do you think I should see her tomorrow before she goes to London for the interview on Wednesday?'

'That's up to you. As long as you do not pressurize her, it might be a good idea. Look, Charles. The time has come for you to make your own decisions. I have done all I can do. From now you must make your own judgements.'

When Eleanor returned from the surgery later, I gave her a full account of my efforts on Charles's behalf and then told her about the Matthew Morris episode.

'If I were you, I should let young Matthew stew in his own juice for tonight and call round tomorrow evening instead, when his father will be out, as you say. He will have twenty-four hours of waiting for the axe to fall. That will be punishment in itself.'

'Thank you, Vicaress,' I said and took her advice.

# 12

It was with a certain amount of apprehension that I knocked on the door of 20, Maes-y-Coed Avenue. The last time I had done that was when I had to call at the house on behalf of the Soldiers Sailors and Airmen's Families Association, the welfare body which cared for dependants of servicemen. My vicar had sent me to inquire into the financial circumstances of Mrs Morris whose husband had deserted – the house was filthy and unkempt. What made my visit uncomfortable was not only the wayward spring in the decrepit armchair which bored its way relentlessly into one of the cheeks of my posterior, but also the smoker's cough from a man behind the closed kitchen door. The wife was on tenterhooks, anxious to get me out through the front door as soon as possible. It seemed obvious to me that she was sheltering her erring husband.

That was two years ago. Now the house appeared even more unlovely. Two rusty bicycle wheels with spokes missing and a punctured football kept company with a number of squashed tin cans on top of the dried mud patch which served as a garden. The front door's green paint was peeling and its bottom edge was beginning to splinter as a result of the kicking it had received. The downstairs front window was encrusted with dirt and two ragged pieces of cloth were pathetic representations of curtains. Upstairs the bedroom windows had newspapers pasted on their bottom halves to provide covering. It was a picture of utter desolation.

As I waited for someone to answer my knock I felt that the culprit was not in that house but in a pub somewhere in Pontywen. Eventually there was the sound of an inner door opening. Mrs Morris appeared before me, her greasy hair straggling down the side of her face which showed no sign of recent contact with soap and water. Her dress, which had large apertures under both arms, seemed two or three sizes too small for her ample frame and clung to her in such a way that it indicated she had been inside it for several days. The many stains bore further witness to its long uninterrupted use. She was bare-legged and bare-footed. Her eyes were dead orbs in her pallid face and showed no surprise at seeing me.

'What can I do for you, Reverend?' she asked in a toneless voice.

'Is Matthew in? I'd like to have a word with him, if I may,' I asked.

A baby began to wail.

'I'll get him for you now.' This was said in a tone of voice which implied that there had been other requests for a word with him.

'Matthew!' she shouted with a ferocity that any sergeant-major would envy.

The miscreant emerged unwillingly and stood behind his mother for shelter.

'What's 'e been doing now?' she inquired.

'Nothing, mam. I 'aven't been doing nothing.' He was still hiding behind his mother.

I had no desire to enter the house, which reeked as soon as the door was opened, but I felt it would be impossible to carry out my mission on the doorstep.

'Do you mind if I come in and speak to Matthew on his own for a minute?'

The baby's cries were now louder than ever.

'Take the Vicar into the front room,' she ordered.

I was led into the 'parlour' whose furniture still consisted of the two rexine-covered armchairs which had been there on my last visit, now even more battered.

'I'll leave you to it,' she said and went into the kitchen to deal with the baby.

Matthew stood behind one of the armchairs.

'Why did you run away when I called to see you outside the school yesterday?'

'I 'ad to go back in for something.'

'You know that's not true because the caretaker told me you had gone out through the boiler-room door to avoid meeting me.'

There was a silence as Matthew hung his head.

'I have come to ask you if you know anything about a break-in at St Padarn's last Sunday night when somebody got in through the kitchen window, drank the Communion wine and scribbled all over the church register. There were two cups which had been used to drink the wine.'

He was still looking down at the floor.

'Somebody saw you and Ben hanging around the back of the church on Saturday night. That's why I have come to ask you if you know anything about what has happened. You see, it's a very serious thing to break into a church. If I ask the police to find out who did it they would have to put them in prison. So far I have not gone to the police station but if I can't find out who did it I shall have to call the detectives in. They will find out in no time.'

He raised his head and looked at me defiantly.

'You 'aven't got no proof. I'm not saying nothing.'

His head dropped again.

Suddenly there was the sound of a key being inserted in the lock of the front door. My heart missed a beat. Evidently the dreaded Dave Morris was returning from his drinking sooner than I had expected.

'That's my father,' said Matthew. 'I'll tell 'im what you've been saying that I've done.'

He shot through the door into the passage. I felt as if I wanted to shelter behind one of the armchairs.

'Dad, come on in 'ere. The Vicar 'ave come and said that me and Ben 'ave broke in 'is church.'

A bleary-eyed figure stood in the doorway. Dave Morris, red-faced, purple-nosed and built like a tank, presented an awesome sight to someone who was only five foot seven, ten stone and non-combatant. He advanced on me, his beery breath strong enough to knock me out.

'Are you accusing my sons of – er –' He paused to think what the accusation involved. 'Of – er – consecrating your church?'

His face was thrust so close to mine that I felt he was going to head-butt me.

I retreated a few steps.

'Hold on, Mr Morris. So far I have not accused Matthew of anything. I have simply asked him if he knew anything about the break-in.'

'Why pick on 'im?' he roared.

'Somebody saw him and Ben around the back of the church last Saturday evening. I don't want to drag the police into this.'

'I'll drag you through that door and out into the street if you say any more.' He came towards me again. I was about to take evasive action when the kitchen door opened.

'Stop it, Dave!' shouted his wife.

'You keep out of this, woman. I'll deal with this creep myself.' He pushed her out of the way.

'Dave, they did do it. Ben 'as just told me. 'E was sick all Sunday night because he drank that Communion wine.'

This revelation stopped him in his tracks. His befuddled brain wrestled with its implication. After a few seconds, as the realization began to dawn upon him that his sons were in the wrong, he made a lunge towards Matthew who side-stepped his father and ran out into the street.

'Vicar,' he said, trying to stand still and to look apologetic, 'what can I say? I try to bring them up in the – er – right way and look what they do.'

His wife raised her eyes to the heavens.

'Leave them to me. I'll deal with them, the buggers – I beg your pardon, Vicar.' He was about to put his arm around me. I emulated Matthew's side step and made for the door. 'Very well, Mr Morris. I'll leave them to you. Don't be too hard on them. They are more to be pitied than blamed.' With those words I made my escape, taking deep gulps of the polluted Pontywen air as if it were champagne.

'Don't tell me,' exclaimed Eleanor when I arrived back at the vicarage, 'you have seen a ghost. You look so pale.'

'I saw something more substantial than a ghost and a lot more frightening. It was called Dave Morris. I don't wish to repeat that experience, believe me. However, I think we can consider the break-in at St Padarn's as case closed.'

When she had heard all the details and supplied me with my second medicinal whisky in the space of a few days, she proceeded to lead me to my armchair. 'Sit down, Sherlock Holmes, and listen to some good news. Charles has been here. He and Bronwen are going out for a walk tonight to talk over their future. She is still going up to London for her interview tomorrow but she realized that it was a mistake to have broken up their relationship in such a high-handed fashion. Your curate is convinced that you are some kind of miracle worker. You are never going to get rid of him, I can assure you. Charles Wentworth-Baxter, perpetual curate of this parish.'

'Perpetual, my eye,' I replied. 'If he and Bronwen get wed, that girl has enough backbone in her to see that he stands on his own two feet and moves on!'

'Frederick, that whisky is playing havoc with your metaphors but I know what you mean. Let's hope that he does that and doesn't tread on her feet too often, which is more than likely.'

Since Wednesday was his day off, I did not see Charles until Thursday morning when he appeared in the vestry like a Cheshire Cat who had been given a saucerful of double cream.

'If you are not careful, boy,' I said, 'you will split your face. Come on, out with it. Let's have the good tidings you bring.'

'I'm engaged.'

I stared at him. 'You're what?'

'I'm engaged.'

'How on earth have you managed that?'

'Well, first I went up to London before Bronwen; I thought I would give her a surprise. I was waiting at the station when she arrived.'

'I bet she was surprised.'

'She certainly was, and pleased too. Anyway, we found the way to the Missionary Society headquarters and we arranged to meet at a café opposite at half past twelve. I went off to Foyle's bookshop and browsed through a few volumes to pass the time away. When I got back to the café at a quarter past twelve she was already standing outside, looking very down in the mouth. We went in and ordered a meal. While we were waiting for it to be served, she told me that they felt she should wait until she had her SRN before she should consider going into the mission field. I told her it sounded as if God was not calling her in that direction and that perhaps He was pointing her in my direction instead. By the time we reached Cardiff, I had proposed to her in the train corridor and she had accepted. Isn't life wonderful?'

'Not only wonderful, but breathless as well. So I suppose you will be thinking of an early marriage date and a move into 13, Mount Pleasant View. I know Barney and Ethel have been a pain in the neck, but I must admit they have transformed the place since they have been there. So you will have a freshly decorated house awaiting you.'

'We have decided to delay the wedding until she has sat her SRN and then get married at Easter. That will give us time to get some furniture. I don't care if it's only a few boxes and a mattress, as long as we are together.'

'I can't see Bronwen being content with that. She looks like the kind of girl who would have saved something towards her bottom drawer. I don't expect you have saved much, Charles.'

'Not exactly but I shall save all I can over the next months. Perhaps my father can give us some of his furniture from his vicarage. He will be retiring before long and he will not need much when he moves into a smaller house.'

'Let's hope he can give you something. You will not find any decent modern furniture. It all appears to be made of plywood with a gloss of paint to deceive the customer. Well, that is enough marriage talk. What about moving into church for Matins? You have plenty for which to thank God, so come on.'

It was a happy service which Charles took. He read the prayers with a fervour he had never shown before, especially the General Thanksgiving which he decided to include, directly after the third Collect. As we knelt in silence at the end of the prayers, the door at the West End of the church opened noisily. Startled, I looked up to see Full Back Jones standing in the aisle, clad in his filthy old mackintosh, the battered trilby on his head and his muddy wellington boots to complete the outfit.

'You had better get back to your digs, Charles,' I said. 'Evidently there is an emergency in the churchyard.'

I went down to the gravedigger, whose toothless grin was conspicuously absent. His face was contorted with a deep frown.

'Boss,' he lisped, 'sorry to trouble you but I've got to get rid of that Ernie. I'm doing that grave for the three thirty tomorrow.' He made it sound like a race at Newmarket. 'That boy is there sitting on a gravestone and watching every spadeful of earth I dig up. 'E don't say a word, just watches. I can't stand it anymore. 'E's been doing that for the last six months ever since the Griffithses 'ad 'im back from the institution. It's like 'aving blessed Dracula keeping an eye on you.'

'Blessed' was his euphemism to me for 'bloody', which would have been much more appropriate.

Ernie Griffiths was a mentally handicapped young man in his late twenties. He was the only child of his elderly parents, born when his mother was in her forties. For a while he had been in the local mental hospital but was now restored to the bosom of his family. For some strange reason he was fascinated by death and by the dying. If he heard that someone was seriously ill he would sit outside the house of the invalid on the garden wall and wait in the hope that the undertaker would arrive. Day after day he would keep watch. Relatives would move him away but he would only retreat to another vantage point where he could see what was happening. Then when the grim reaper took his toll, he would turn his attention to the digging of the grave and, of course, the filling in after the funeral.

'What do you want me to do about it?' I asked. 'Ernie will not listen to anything I say. The poor man is not a rational person. Believe me, he will come back and hide behind trees or tomb stones in the churchyard. I should hate to think that I was responsible for him going back into Cefn Bryn.' Cefn Bryn was the local mental hospital.

'Can't you 'ave a word with 'is father and mother, boss?' After all, they are supposed to be looking after 'im. 'E's really getting on my nerves.'

'OK, Full Back, I shall go and see them later today, but I can't promise anything.'

When Eleanor came home from her rounds at lunchtime I told her about the engagement.

'There's one thing to be said about Charles,' she replied, 'he never wastes time in his love affairs. It only took him six weeks to get engaged to that precocious sixteen-year-old Elspeth Evans and less than a fortnight to fall in love with that other schoolgirl. I trust this is a case of third time lucky.'

'At least Bronwen is in her twenties and is very mature in her ways. She is just what he needs to make him grow up and become a responsible person. I know you call him Peter Pan but I have a feeling that this is the end of his extended adolescence.'

'To a degree, Fred. In some ways he will never grow up but now he has found someone who will not only be wife but mother, too. As long as she is prepared to put up with that for the rest of her life, all will be well.'

'Oh, by the way,' I said, 'Full Back Jones turned up in church at the end of Matins this morning. He wants me to have a word with Ernie Griffiths's parents about his ghoulish habit of watching him at work gravedigging. It is a wonder that no one has come to see me about his hanging around houses where someone is very ill. That is much more distressing than being a spectator at a graveside. Relatives must feel that his presence is a sign that the patient will never recover.'

'I know it must be very upsetting, but apart from Mr and Mrs Griffiths locking him in his room, it seems to me that there is not much they can do about it. Perhaps a psychologist might be able to cope with the problem without putting the poor young man back in an institution. I should think that is their only hope. In any case it is more than likely he has been seeing a psychologist already.'

Later that afternoon, I climbed up the hillside to Bryn Road. As I made the steep ascent I sympathized with the elderly couple I was about to visit who had to make that journey every day whenever they went shopping. It was a row of stone-built houses, exposed to the prevailing south-west winds which brought the rain to the valley. Number 7's exterior was in excellent condition. It looked as if the woodwork had been repainted recently, a rarity in those days. The brass knocker gleamed in the afternoon sunshine, as if daring anyone to use it. I felt as if I should wipe my hands with my handkerchief before fingering it. Gingerly I raised the shining object and gave a gentle tap. It brought an immediate response.

A little white-haired lady, neatly dressed in skirt and blouse, opened the door and greeted me with a smile. 'Hello, Vicar! How nice to see you. Come on in, please. I was in the passage, just about to put on my coat to go shopping.'

'Don't let me hold you up,' I said. 'I can come back later.'

'The shopping can wait. It is not often I have the pleasure of a visit from the vicar.'

She led me into the front room, which merited the description of a parlour with its three-piece suite in green moquette, expensive rugs on the linoleum and a large aspidistra on a stand in the corner by the window.

'Would you care for a cup of tea, Vicar?' She fingered the necklace around her scrawny neck.

'Yes, please, but don't put yourself out.'

'It will be no trouble at all. I'll go and get my husband. He can talk to you while I'm making the tea. Sit yourself down.'

She disappeared into the middle room. I went over to the mantelpiece to examine the photographs which were flanked by two china dogs. One of them was of a soldier in the khaki battledress of the First World War, evidently Mr Griffiths, another of the happy couple outside the church after their wedding, and a third was of a smiling chubby baby now grown up into the scourge of Full Back Jones.

As the middle-room door opened, I subsided into one of the armchairs.

A tall, slightly bent, sallow-faced thin man in his seventies was preceded by his wife. 'This is my husband, Jim.'

I stood up and offered my hand which was met with an arthritic paw. His fingers were unable to clasp mine.

'Pleased to meet you, Vicar. Sit down, make yourself at home.' I sat back in the armchair, while he manoeuvred himself into the armchair opposite me.

'You two have a chat while I make the tea,' said Mrs Griffiths and left the room humming a little tune.

'It is not often we have visitors. The last time we had the vicar here was years ago – Canon Llewellyn. So it's good to know we have not been forgotten, even if we don't go to church. I don't think I could sit through a service now anyway with this old arthritis.'

I began to feel most uncomfortable. How on earth was I going to explain that this was not a social visit? For the time being I decided to ignore the reason for my call and indulge in pleasantries. It transpired that Jim Griffiths had been employed in the steelworks all his working life after being demobbed from the Welsh Guards in 1919.

'A fat lot of good I'd be there now. I used to work on the furnace; heavy, sweaty work. It is more than likely my arthritis was caused by that but you could never prove it.'

At this juncture in the conversation Mrs Griffiths came in with a tray loaded with her best tea service and a plate of biscuits. While we were drinking our cups of tea, I pointed at the wedding photograph.

'Is that outside St Mary's?' I asked.

'Yes, of course,' said my hostess. 'We have lived in Pontywen all our lives. That was June 1923. Canon Llewellyn married us. He was not a canon then, mind. He used to be very good looking. He didn't have that goitre at that time.'

'I was good looking then too,' interjected Jim Griffiths, 'and I didn't have arthritis. What's more I wasn't a bad back-row forward.'

'Stop bragging, Jim. The best thing about you is that you haven't been a bad husband, thank God, and you certainly haven't been a bad father with all the trouble we've had with Ernie.'

I seized the opportunity to bring up the reason for my visit.

'Oh, by the way, I hope you don't mind me mentioning this but I have had a complaint from the gravedigger that Ernie is forever hanging around when he is digging a grave. I suppose I should also tell you that he is hanging around houses where there is somebody who is very ill and expected to die. I know what a trying time you must have caring for

Ernie but the relatives of invalids resent his continual presence.'

They looked at each other. 'You explain, Dorothy,' said Jim.

'Vicar, we know what he is doing. We have tried to talk him out of it but it's just like water off a duck's back. I am sorry for those poor people who are pestered by him, very sorry, but what are we to do? I don't want him to go back to Cefn Bryn. That would break my heart.'

'Is it possible that a psychologist could do something for him?'

'My dear, he has been seen by psychologists at Cefn Bryn. That's why he went there. They thought that he was fit to come back to us six months ago. We have tried keeping him in the house, but as soon as our backs are turned he is out again. He is as slippery as an eel. Apart from this thing about death, he is easy to handle. He is never violent and he loves us deeply – as we do him. If anyone comes to you, could you explain that he means no harm? We'll do what we can. What more can I say? We waited years and years for a child. Then, when we thought we would never have one, Ernie was born. It was so wonderful, a miracle – but look what kind of a miracle it has turned out to be.'

She began to weep. Jim clambered out of his armchair to sit alongside her on the settee, his arm round her.

'Mrs Griffiths, I must apologize for bringing this up. I should have known you would be aware of the situation. I'll have a word with Full Back Jones and if anybody comes to me with a complaint that Ernie has been hanging around a house, I shall ask them to try and understand. The last thing I want is to see Ernie back in Cefn Bryn.'

I went back to the churchyard as soon as I left their house. Full Back Jones was still inside the unfinished grave, watched by Ernie who was sitting on a headstone.

'Ernie, your mother wants you at once. If I were you, I would go home as fast as you can.' He stared at me.

'Go on,' I ordered; 'off you go as quick as you can.'

He stood up and slowly made his way to the churchyard gate, looking back from time to time.

The gravedigger leaned on his shovel and grinned up at me.

'Thank you, boss. I hope that's the last I see of 'im.'

'It won't be, I am sure, but I think that from now on when he hangs around it would be a good idea to have pity on him instead of getting annoyed. He can't help being what he is but you can help getting annoyed.'

The grin vanished as he picked up his shovel and attacked the bottom of the grave.

# 13

I was sitting in the barber's chair at 'Dai Tonsorial's', suffering the discomfort caused by his bad breath, his incessant chatter and the occasional nip from his misdirected clippers. David Williams had acquired his nickname from his frequent use of the word with reference to his trade. 'We in the tonsorial profession are artists in our own right. The artist creates a portrait with his pen. We create tonsorial portraits with our scissors,' he told me once. Since everybody who entered his premises left with the same short-back-and-sides haircut, his claim to be an expert was somewhat extravagant.

'How's the parish, Mr Secombe?' He had cut my hair ever since I came to Pontywen as a curate and he could not bring himself to call me vicar. Dai spoke with the speed of a machine-gun, never waiting for an answer to his questions. 'Won't be long now, Mr Secombe, before your centenarian anniversary, will it? Had your curate in last week, Mr Secombe; got engaged, I hear. When is the other one going, Mr Secombe? Going into the country, Ezekiel Evans told me; says he will be taking his place out in Llanhyfryd, he expects.'

A month had elapsed since Charles had announced his engagement and during that time his enthusiasm for the centenary pageant had waned considerably. The coming milestone in his own life was far more important to him that the milestone in Pontywen church's life. Once again it looked as if I was going to be left holding the baby. There were only three Sundays left before Barney and Ethel Webster were due to leave for their new parish. After all the trouble they had caused, the piece of information about Ezekiel Evans' expectations was sufficiently disturbing to make me leave the barber's shop in haste to telephone the Reverend Dewi Jones. The worst possible scenario to follow the Websters' departure was one in which the lay reader was let loose in Llanhyfryd.

It was some time since I had been in touch with the retired missionary and for weeks I had been intending to ask for his assistance at St Illtyd's. 'Fredericus Cunctator' was the name Eleanor gave me at times: Frederick the De-layer. It was an unfortunate habit which had been with me since my student days. Most of my 'exam' work was of the last-minute variety, as were most of my sermons. 'One of these days,' my wife warned me, 'you will be too late.' So it was with some trepidation that I rang his number.

'How nice to hear you, Fred. What can I do for you?'

'I hope and pray that you can help me out at St Illtyd's when Barney Webster leaves in three weeks' time.'

'Your luck is in. Jim Thomas at Begelly had asked me if I could do a locum for him when his curate left, but apparently his man had second thoughts about leaving and turned down the offer of a curacy elsewhere. I had heard that Webster was leaving. Quick work that, wasn't it? Though I am not at all surprised. I bet you are glad. I haven't forgotten his attempt to stir up trouble over the Good Friday rugby match.'

'Dewi, you are a pal – you have saved Llanhyfryd from a second fate worse than death. I have just heard from the barber that Ezekiel Evans had informed him that he expected to be taking Barney's place in Llanhyfryd.'

'They are two lovely berries moulded on a single stem, as the Good Friday trouble proved. How are the preparations proceeding for the centenary celebrations?'

'The men have done a fine job in the parish church. All the scaffolding is down now and the inside has been trans-formed. It is worth putting up with the smell of fresh paint to worship in such pleasant surroundings. They have not quite finished at St Padarn's but they hope to have it com-pleted in a fortnight or so. How is Mrs Jones?'

'I am afraid the arthritis is progressively worse but she remains as bright as a button through it all. I sometimes think that women have far greater courage and ability to bear pain than men. I expect she will accompany me occasionally to St Illtyd's. By the way, how is Wentworth-Baxter these days? Still as lazy as ever?'

'Well, there has been a marked improvement. He has become engaged and will move into 13, Mountain Pleasant View after his marriage at Easter. As usual with Charles there is a snag. He is so besotted with his lady love that his preparations for the pageant are suffering from lack of interest. It looks as if I shall have to take over his script, which is quite good, and do the rehearsals myself.'

'That is probably just as well, Fred. I must ring off to get the dinner ready. Love to Eleanor, God bless.'

No sooner had I put the telephone down than there was the ring of the doorbell. Standing on the doorstep was Ezekiel Evans in his lay reader's pinstripe suit plus Anthony Eden hat, looking every inch the next spiritual overlord of Llanhyfryd. 'May h'I 'ave a word with you, Vicar?'

'By all means, Mr Evans. Come along into the study.'

When he had sat down in the armchair opposite me, cradling his trilby, he launched into the reason for his visit. 'No doubt you will be h'expecting me to 'elp you out at Llanhyfryd. H'as you know, h'I 'ave no transport but h'I 'ave been talking this h'over with the Reverend Barnabas Webster h'and 'e 'as 'ad a word with George Griffiths, Yew Tree Farm. 'E says 'e will pick me up and bring me back if the church will pay for 'is petrol.'

'That is very good of George Griffiths,' I replied, 'but it will not be necessary.'

'Why is that, Vicar? 'Ave you h'arranged for somebody else to pick me up?'

'Your kind offer of help will not be needed. The Reverend Dewi Jones is going to take charge of the services at St Illtyd's. In any case, it was not up to Barnabas Webster to make arrangements for what was to happen after he had left the parish. It would have been wiser for him to have consulted me first.'

Not only did I relish every word of my reply but also the dumbfounded look on his face.

'As you know, Mr Evans, I should have had to find a priest to take the Communion services. As it is, the Reverend Dewi Jones will take Evensong as well. Since he has his own car, the question of transport will not arise. Any way, thank you for your readiness to assist.'

'May h'I inquire what is the point of me 'aving a licence to take services h'if h'I can't use it?'

'Mr Evans, the point of you having a licence is your availability to help when needed. As things stand, you are not needed. I am only too happy to have you read the lessons here in the parish church and occasionally to read the prayers after the third Collect.'

He left in a state of high dudgeon, a chronic condition in his case. As he stalked up the vicarage drive, I uttered a short prayer of thanks for my eleventh-hour deliverance. It was a great relief to know that I could concentrate on preparations for the centenary, knowing that Llanhyfryd was in the safe hands of Dewi Jones.

Next morning I asked Charles what progress he had made with casting the participants in the pageant and whether he had made a schedule of rehearsals for the coming weeks.

'Sorry, Fred, but you know what things have been like over the past month or so. To tell the truth I haven't done anything yet.'

'Charles, we have little more than two months left. Does Bronwen know that you are supposed to be producing the pageant? I bet you have not told her. She is too conscientious a girl to keep you from your duties.'

'As a matter of fact, I haven't. There's so much to do before you get married, as you are aware.'

'I am fully aware of that but, as you are not getting married until Easter, you are hardly pressed for time. However, rather than have a dog's dinner of a pageant, I am prepared to take over the casting and the production, on condition that you provide the accompaniment for the Gilbert and Sullivan's Society Concert, both at rehearsal and for the performance. I think you owe it to me to keep your word on that.'

'Of course I will. Thanks, Fred, you are a pal.'

'What you mean is that I am an idiot, a complete and utter idiot.'

'I wouldn't say that under any circumstances.'

'You wouldn't say it but you would think it.'

My wife had no hesitation in saying it when I told her at lunch what had happened.

'Secombe, you are an idiot. That man gets away with murder. You have already written your booklet. As chairlady of the Social Committee I have booked the Pontywen Silver Band for a concert, booked the Red Coats Dance Band for the grand dance, and booked those dreadful Fol-de-Rols for a variety concert. I have formed a Catering Sub-Committee, not to mention another committee to arrange a flower festival, and what has he done?'

'Well, you must admit that he has written a good script for the pageant.'

'Entirely based on your booklet. How much research did he do himself? None. I think you should make him contact everybody in the Gilbert and Sullivan ready for the first rehearsal, as well as acting as liaison officer with Aneurin Williams.'

'OK, boss. I'll do that. I only hope that we can rely on him to do it.'

'My dear Fred, you are his boss. You have to make him do it, not just suggest it.'

I promised I would be a man of action.

Later that afternoon I went to see Idris the Milk who had awoken from his siesta and was about to visit Daisy, the mare who pulled his milk cart around the streets of Pontywen.

'Just caught me in time, Vicar. I've got to go and feed Daisy.'

'Do you mind if I come with you for a walk and I can tell you the purpose of my visit as we go?'

'By all means; it will be a pleasure. I won't be a minute. I've got to get a bucket full of leftovers from dinner together with cabbage leaves and carrot tops. She enjoys a treat like that on top of a dollop from the sackful of oats in the stable.'

As we walked up the hillside past the hospital and then on the mountain track to the allotments where Idris had his stable, I told him that he had to be responsible for Scene 3 in the pageant, the erection of St Padarn's, the corrugated-iron edifice which was to be a temporary building until a stone church would replace it. That was in 1907 and a stone church was no nearer a reality in 1947.

'If we had a stone church, St Padarn's would no longer be the homely place it is now,' said Idris.

'You are probably right,' I replied. 'In any case, what is a church? It is only a shelter for an altar and for those who worship around it.'

We looked down on Pontywen snuggled in the valley, with its rows of terraced houses flanked by the big wheel of the colliery on the one side and by the belching chimneys of the steelworks on the other.

'I don't think a brand-new stone church would fit into that picture, do you, Idris?'

'I tell you one thing, Vicar. It wouldn't look brand-new for long.'

'By the way, keep a tight rein on Bertie Owen as far as the pageant is concerned. If he were to be in charge, it would develop into a pantomime, not a pageant.'

'Don't worry, Vicar, I'll see to that. I've had to do that with the redecoration. Twice the men have had to go over some of the pews he is supposed to have painted. I've told him that from now on he can only do the painting when everybody else is there and not on his own. Anyway, I'll call a meeting of everybody interested in taking part in the pageant after church next Sunday.'

'I'll come down to St Padarn's for the meeting after I've taken Evensong at St Mary's. Another thing, I shall want the Sunday School children to join the parish church Sunday School for the opening scene of the pageant. We can arrange that next Sunday afternoon. I'll ask Charles to get the children to stay behind for a moment.'

Idris coughed.

'To tell the truth, Vicar, he has not been at Sunday School for quite a few Sundays. Bertie has been acting as supervisor. Not that he minds, he loves it.'

When Daisy had been fed and we were on our way down, I decided to call in at the hospital to see if my lovesick curate was there. The time had come for my role as a man of action.

As I entered, I almost collided with the matron. It would have been a painful encounter since Miss Eunice Bevan was built like a battleship.

'Oh, Vicar!' she said 'I'm so glad to see you. Would you

mind coming into my office? I should like to have a word with you.'

I followed her into the austere surroundings of the small room, most of which was occupied by a large desk covered with folders. She eased her ample frame into the wooden armchair behind it, and motioned me to sit on one of the chairs on the other side.

'To come straight to the point' – it was obvious that she was a woman of action – 'I am afraid that your curate is becoming something of a nuisance. He is haunting this hospital and Nurse Williams in particular. I know they are engaged but that doesn't give him *carte blanche* to be hanging around here every day. I am sure that Bronwen is not encouraging him to do this. She is a very conscientious nurse and keen to get her SRN next month. Unless he stops being so obsessive and taking up so much of her time, she will not get her certificate. Since you are his employer, perhaps you can see that he pays more attention to his job and less to Nurse Williams.'

'I shall certainly do so, Matron. As a matter of fact, I have called in to see if he's here and to have some serious words with him. His work in the parish is suffering as a result of this obsession, as you call it.'

'You will be doing us all a favour if you put an end to his behaviour. I have already had a complaint today from the sister of the Princess Royal ward. You will probably find him lurking in the corridor in its vicinity. I am sorry to trouble you like this but you can see my position.'

I assured her that I could see her position and left to look for my erring curate. The matron's pointer to his whereabouts was on target. There was Charles lolling against the wall outside the Princess Royal ward.

'It is only a few weeks ago,' I said, 'that I had to put an end to a young gentleman's haunting of graveyards and invalids' houses. I never thought I would have to come to the hospital to put an end to another young gentleman's haunting of hospital corridors. There is one big difference: Ernie Griffiths is mentally handicapped; you are a parish priest in full possession of your faculties, or so I presume. Charles, I have just had a complaint from the matron about your continual presence in this hospital. It has got to stop. I tell you one thing, if you keep on mooning around Bronwen, you will find the engagement will be off and you will be back to square one with nobody to blame but yourself. What is more, if you persist in neglecting your parochial duties you will find there is no place for you in Pontywen. I understand you have not been near the Sunday School for weeks. For heaven's sake, grow up, man, and get out into the parish to do some work.'

This had an electrifying effect on the Reverend Charles Wentworth-Baxter who made no reply. He strode off down the corridor and skidded on the polished floor into a trolley laden with cups of tea and plates of biscuits. His legs went from under him as the chinaware and its contents showered down upon him. The little auxiliary nurse behind the trolley let loose a scream which, combined with the noise of the disintegrating crockery, caused the three doors in the corridor to open simultaneously. The sister, the doctor and the nurse, wielding an empty bed pan, were confronted with the sight of my curate, drenched with hot tea, and surrounded by the debris of broken china, looking dazed as he lay on the floor.

'Not you again!' said the doctor. 'You must be accident-prone. It seems only yesterday that we mended your broken leg.'

He went to his side and knelt down.

'Feel any pain anywhere?'

Charles shook his head.

The doctor stood up. 'In that case you had better get to your feet.' Suddenly he was aware of my presence. 'Hello, Vicar; I thought for a moment you were going to lose the assistance of your curate for another few months.'

By now Charles was standing and brushing the remnants of the biscuits from his suit which bore the marks of the spilt tea.

'Sorry to cause so much trouble,' mumbled my curate. 'I didn't realize the floor was so slippery. I think I had better go and change my suit.'

The sister shook her head in disbelief and went back to her ward. The nurse returned her empty bed pan to its repository and the little auxiliary began to pick up the remains of the afternoon tea.

As Charles disappeared round the corner, the doctor turned to me. 'You have my sympathy, Vicar. So has Nurse Williams to whom he is engaged, I understand. He is what North Country folk call gormless.'

When I told Eleanor of the afternoon's accident, she was highly amused but when I told her of what had preceded it she was deeply concerned.

'That idiot could not only lose Bronwen her SRN but even her job in the hospital. Apparently you have had your say with Charles but, since you have had several 'says' with him to no avail, there is no guarantee that this one will be any different. If you don't mind, I think the time has come for me to have a say with his fiancée before it is too late. This Saturday let's have them to the dinner we should have had a month ago.'

It was not the most congenial of occasions. Charles was still smarting from the tirade I had unleashed at him in the hospital and Bronwen seemed to be a shy young lady with whom it was difficult to make conversation.

'Where is your home, Bronwen?' asked my wife at the dinner table.

'Trefelin; a little village outside St David's.'

'I know it,' I said. 'I was in the Canonry, in College in St David's. It is a lovely part of the world.'

'Yes, it is.'

'Did you go to school in St David's?'

'Yes, I went to the Grammar school there.'

'How long were you there?'

'Until I sat my Higher Certificate.'

'What do your parents do?' Eleanor inquired.

'They have a small farm.'

'I worked on a farm in St David's during vacations,' I said. 'They were Welsh Baptists like your parents. Very strict they were; I remember whistling on a Sunday and I had a row for doing it.'

'My parents would be the same.' She did not say whether she approved of this or not.

After this there was a period of what an aunt of mine would describe as 'no talking, only eating'. When the meal ended, Eleanor suggested that I might like to take Charles into the study for coffee while she and Bronwen had a women's chat in the lounge. It was a suggestion for which my curate showed little enthusiasm but one which his fiancée seemed to welcome.

'Would you like a glass of port or a whisky?' I asked Charles when we were alone.

'No thanks! Bronwen would smell it on my breath. I have told you what she is like about drink.'

'So that means you are going to be a teetotaller for the rest of your life.'

'Look, Fred. I would rather give up drink than give up Bronwen. She means much more to me than a glass of port, or whatever.'

After that remark, we lapsed into silence, a silence which was accentuated by the sound of animated conversation punctuated by laughter coming from the other room.

'They seem to be getting on together very well,' I said.

'I think I have told you before that she thinks a lot of Eleanor as a doctor and a person,' he mumbled.

'She sounds a lot happier than you look, Charles. For heaven's sake, cheer up. You are getting married soon to a girl whom you obviously adore.'

'That's the point. I can't bear to be out of her company. That is why you found me up in the hospital.'

'What you do not seem to realize is that you will kill any love she has for you if you persist in hanging around her all the time. You will give the poor girl claustrophobia. That is why I had to let rip at you in the hospital corridor. It's for your own good as well as hers.'

These words spoken in a kindly tone had much more effect on the lovesick swain than the angry lecture I had delivered earlier in the week.

'Thank you, Fred; I see what you mean. I must take a grip on myself. After all, it is not fair to you or the parish either if I carry on as I have been doing these past weeks.'

'You can say that again, boyo.'

For the next half hour or so we had a relaxed conversation about the parish and about the Websters' imminent depar-ture into the wilds of the diocese. By the time Charles and

Bronwen left, the ice had been broken completely. The apparently shy Welsh Baptist was now an animated young lady with a ready laugh. She gave the impression that she would be able to cope with her fiancé's excess of attention without any help from me or the matron.

As Eleanor and I were doing the washing up, she gave me a report on the 'women's chat' she had had with Bronwen. Apparently, after the incident in the corridor, the sister on her ward had given her a graphic account of what had happened. As a result, Bronwen had given Charles an ultimatum that either he stopped trying to see her at every possible opportunity or he stopped seeing her altogether. This was the reason for the freeze on conversation with which the evening had begun.

'From what I can gather,' said my wife, 'she has every possible chance of getting her SRN. Charles is a lucky man. He has found someone who has all the moral fibre that he lacks. What is more, she is very much in love with him. Perhaps after the promise he made to you about keeping a grip on himself and Bronwen's ultimatum, we shall see a change in Charles in the future.'

It was an immediate change. Next evening when I went down to St Padarn's for the centenary meeting after evensong at the parish church, I found my curate in an ebullient mood. He had recruited all the children in the Sunday School for stage one of the pageant and had delivered a powerful sermon at Evensong in the course of which he had made a strong appeal to the congregation to make the centenary celebrations worthy of the occasion. As a result there were fifty people who had stayed behind for the meeting. Idris the Milk told me it was the best sermon he had preached since he had been in charge of St Padarn's.

Then came the biggest surprise of all – Charles took me aside before the meeting and informed me that he was prepared to take over the production of the pageant so that I could devote more time to the other events in the celebration.

'Are you sure you are ready to do this?' I asked.

'Positive!' he replied. 'Bronwen told me I should do it, after the chat she had with Eleanor last night. I gave her my promise and I shall keep it.'

# 14

It was a very wet late afternoon. Clouds had engulfed the hilltops and, to quote the psalmist, 'the pools were filled with water'. Twenty wet passengers crowded into the little bus belonging to Pontywen Motors on their way to the induction of the Reverend Barnabas Webster to the living of Llangelli. Originally a forty-seater conveyance had been ordered but only twenty names were collected, and most of those were only given after pressure had been brought to bear upon them by Bertie Owen, who had volunteered his services as organizer. The four parishioners from Llanhyfryd were coming by car.

Eleanor and I saw the dispirited contingent off and then sped ahead of them in her car. Some of the roads were partially flooded and we made our way cautiously along these until eventually we came to the signpost directing us to Llangelli along a single track road. The luxuriant hedges seemed to have an attraction for each other on either side of the narrow way and were reaching out across our watery path.

'You had better say a prayer that nothing comes in the opposite direction,' suggested Eleanor.

'I think I had better reserve that for the bus when it arrives here,' I replied.

After three miles of a snail's-pace journey, the road opened out into a settlement of a dozen houses, a pub and a grocer's shop-cum-post office of the type which would be familiar to Barney. There was no sign of the church.

'What happens now?' I asked.

'You had better brave the elements and inquire in the shop where we can find the church,' ordered my wife.

I dashed out of the car, putting my foot in a puddle as I disembarked. When I pushed open the door, a bell with the tonal quality of a tin can announced my arrival. There was no one to be seen in this rural Aladdin's cave. Goods were suspended from the ceiling. The counter was cluttered with half-empty cartons of sweets and chocolates. In one corner behind a glass shield was the post office with official notices tacked to the wooden partition. From a back room emerged a small dumpling of a lady with rosy cheeks and horn-rimmed spectacles underneath a scarf which ill concealed a set of curlers.

'Afternoon, Reverend.' Her high-pitched voice had the burr of the countryside. 'Come for the service, have you?'

'I have indeed,' I said. 'Can you direct me to the church, please?'

'Certainly, Reverend. Where have you come from, if I might ask?'

'I have come from Pontywen. The new vicar was my curate.'

'If you don't mind me saying so, you look young for a vicar. A lot younger than the Reverend Webster.'

I was not quite sure how to answer that question. After all, I had only come in to find the way to the church.

'Well, I started earlier in my life than your new vicar. Where did you say the church is?'

'I didn't, Vicar, but it's another half mile up the road. You'll be able to see it in the field.'

'In the field?'

'Yes, you have to park at the side of the road and then go along the path to the church. You'd better mind that wet grass.'

'I shall certainly do that and thank you for your help.'

'That's all right. I'll be seeing you soon. I'm the organist.'

When I arrived back in the car, I said to my wife, 'I have just met the organist. She is still in her curlers with less than half an hour to go.'

'You know what they are like in the country, love. Llan-hyfryd should have taught you that. More to the point, did she tell you how to find the church.'

'It is half a mile further up the road and we shall be able to see it in the field.'

'The field?'

'Yes, you have to park at the side of the road and then go along the path to the church. Oh, and by the way, we had better mind the wet grass.'

'If I had known, I would have come in my wellies. I can see the steam arising from the congregation as the service gets under way. You will have half the Pontywen lot down with colds next Sunday.'

We drove the long half mile up the road and out of the mist we could see the tower of the church. When we pulled up by the gate, we could see Barney's car parked much further up the road, leaving room for the expected congregation.

'Do you think he has left enough space?' I said to Eleanor.

'Blessed is he that expecteth little,' she replied, 'because little is what he is going to get.'

'We had better move away from outside the gate to allow his lordship's car to take its proper place,' I suggested.

She drove on a few yards.

'I tell you one thing,' she said. 'His lordship is going to get his gaiters wet by the look of that grass, not to mention the dampness for the rest of us who are gaiterless.'

As we made our way along the narrow path with the rain beating down on our umbrella, the verdant pasture soaked our legs. By the time we had entered the porch our extremities were exceedingly uncomfortable. A mingled odour of paraffin, mustiness and fresh flowers greeted us at the open door.

The interior of the church would have graced the Chelsea Flower Show. There were flowers everywhere – around the font, on top of the font, on every window ledge, even at the end of every pew in the form of attached posies. Attending to the altar floral decoration was Ethel Webster, with floral costume to match, complete with some form of floral hat. It was difficult to tell which were the flowers and which was Ethel.

'If she is not careful,' whispered Eleanor, 'she is going to suffer from a nasty attack of greenfly.'

'Hello,' she called as we came down the aisle. 'How nice

to see you.' Her intonation and her appearance came into the dowager duchess category.

'My word,' I said, 'your parishioners have worked hard with the decorations.'

'The parishioners have had nothing to do with it. I have done it all myself. I have been up since six o'clock this morning. Most of the flowers are from the vicarage garden.'

'In that case, well done, Mrs Webster!'

'Barney's round the back, stoking the boiler to try and

get a bit of warmth. I am afraid it is a bit past it. One of our first jobs is to try and get a new one. That's after we have got rid of these old oil lamps and put in electricity.'

It was obvious that many other tasks lay ahead of them. Damp had made inroads into the plaster on the walls. The tower was in need of repainting. The pews had fallen prey to woodworm. Since there was every evidence that any effort would have to be that of a one-man band, or to be more exact, a one-couple band, the Websters faced a challenge of mountain-moving proportions.

By the time Barney had emerged from his exertions with the boiler, the bishop and the archdeacon had arrived. With a quarter of an hour to go before the service was due to commence, the churchwardens were still absent, together with the organist who must have been engaged in taking the rollers out of her hair.

The rain had dampened the dignitaries' spirits as well as their gaiters. Pools of water emerged from their umbrellas after they were placed in a corner of the vestry. The archdeacon, the Venerable Herbert Davies, was a burly figure with a broken nose acquired during a distinguished career as a back-row forward. Under normal conditions he had a keen sense of humour but the deluge was sufficient to quench it. As soon as the bishop had gone out into the chancel, he began to browbeat Barney.

'The service is due for seven o'clock, isn't it, Webster?' he demanded.

'Yes, Mr Archdeacon, of course,' replied Barney in deferential tones.

'Well, where is everybody? It's not the kind of night to hang around in wet clothes. The churchwardens should have been here by now. You will have to get them to pull their socks up, won't he, Vicar?'

This question addressed to me of all people was a barb into Barney's soul.

'I am sure he will be able to do that, Mr Archdeacon, once he has settled in. It looks as if he has a big job ahead of him to get this building into a fit condition for worship. So I suppose he will have to woo them rather than bully them.'

My ex-curate gave me a silent vote of thanks for the unexpected support.

'The carrot rather than the stick, eh? Well, if the carrot doesn't work, sooner or later it will have to be the stick.'

At this stage in the conversation, the bishop came back into the vestry accompanied by the rural dean, the Reverend Tobias Evans, better known in Abergavenny cattle market than he was in his deanery.

'The rural dean tells me that your warden has helped him out by towing his car out of the ditch into which he had skidded on his way here. He was due to pick up the other warden and they both should be here any time now,' said the bishop to Barney.

The archdeacon said nothing.

A loud hubbub at the back of the church announced that the Pontywen contingent had arrived. I took the opportunity to leave the vestry. Inevitably Bertie Owen had taken charge of the books at the back of the church and was ordering his bus load not to occupy the first two rows of the pews. 'They're always reserved.' Ethel and Eleanor were still engaged in earnest conversation inside the sanctuary. Suddenly there was a surge of humanity in the doorway.

'Excuse me that's my job,' said a large red-faced man elbowing Bertie out of the way. Two self-important gentlemen in their tweeds, evidently the wardens, marched up the aisle and into the vestry. The post-office lady waddled to her place at the harmonium in the chancel. The Llangelli congregation had arrived, all fifteen of them, together with two of the neighbouring clergy. Ethel led Eleanor down to the front seat where they were joined by the four who had made the journey from Llanhyfryd. The scene was set for Barney's big occasion.

In the vestry the scrum of clergy sorted itself out after the rural dean had mumbled a prayer with the Vicar of Cwmffordd, acting as bishop's chaplain. The organist made a brave attempt at 'Praise my soul' and the service was under way.

What followed was more of a circus than a service with the churchwardens, holding their staves as if they were weapons rather than badges of office, colliding with each other as they were about to march up to lead the clerical procession round the little church. One of Ethel Webster's vases of flowers at the foot of the font was knocked over by the archdeacon. The bell refused to function when Barney was called upon to toll it, to let the parish know that he was now the new incumbent. After several pulls on the rope, eventually he manufactured a couple of clangs. At each stop in the procession there was a tangle of humanity, clerical and lay. Add to that the mangled verses of 'We love the place of God' provided by the post-office lady at the harmonium and the off-key bellowing of the congregation and it became a severe test of my composure. As usual the bishop seemed unaware of the confusion as he sat in his chair in the sanctuary, apparently examining the roof of the chancel.

When Barney had been installed in his prayer desk, the bishop delivered his address, which was an exhortation to the congregation of Llangelli to welcome the new vicar and his wife and to co-operate with the vicar in establishing God's kingdom in that part of the world. He reminded them that the Reverend Barnabas Webster had a rural background and would be able to understand all their problems.

After the bishop's address, Barney announced the services for next Sunday and informed his people that he would be saying Matins every morning in the week at eight o'clock if they cared to join him. Then he invited everybody 'to partake of the refreshments of a light kind which are available in the vicarage. Our visitors will find the vicarage half a mile up the road.'

It was fortunate that the rain had stopped by the time the service was over because we came out into pitch darkness. It was fortunate, too, that the locals, like the Wise Virgins, had brought their torches and were able to lead their visitors to the road.

When Eleanor and I reached the privacy of her car, we were able to indulge in unseemly mirth at the antics in the service. 'Did you notice the bishop?' I said. 'He spent all his time with his eyes turned towards the chancel roof.' She laughed.

'Perhaps he was looking for the death-watch beetle which

would go with the woodworm in the pews. Then once Barney gets going, there will be dry rot in the pulpit.'

'Eleanor Secombe, you are very unkind, not to mention corny, but I love you, all the same.'

The cavalcade of motors plus bus wound its way up the pot-holed drive to the large frontage space available outside the vicarage. It would have been an advantage if the surface had been gravelled or tarmacked. As it was, we emerged from our vehicles into a sea of mud. Never had so many feet been wiped upon one small doormat.

Inside Ethel had gone to town once more with her floral decorations. She had turned the large drawing room into a veritable bower. Refreshments were laid out on two trestle tables which had been set up at one end of the room. The ubiquitous lady from the post office appeared with a tray of cups of tea, together with Ethel similarly laden.

'Help yourselves!' commanded the hostess in her best county voice.

The Pontywen contingent had not waited to be invited and were tucking into the liberal number of sandwiches available. Bertie Owen made a beeline for the bishop when he appeared. 'Nice service, your Lordship. Nice church as well.' His lordship smiled politely and moved towards Eleanor and myself. 'Well, Vicar,' he said, 'I shall be in your parish very shortly, shan't I? How are the preparations going for your big occasion?'

'They are going quite well, my Lord. I think you will be pleased with the splendid way in which the men have decorated the parish church, not to mention St Padarn's. The pageant is behind hand in its schedule of rehearsal but I am sure it will be all right on the night, as they say.'

'I think you told me that Mr Wentworth-Baxter was responsible for the production. That speaks volumes.'

'In fairness, I must say that over the past few weeks he has been working very hard.'

'Let's hope it continues,' replied the bishop and went over to join Barney who had now entered the room.

'By the look of it,' said Eleanor, 'the female complement in this parish is confined to two. Before long it will consist of one, judging by the way the organ was played. Then

Llangelli church will become Barney and Ethel incorporated.'

After the new incumbent had finished his conversation with the bishop, he came over to join us.

'Thank you, Vicar, for your kind words when the archdeacon started laying down the law in the vestry.'

'That's OK, Barney. You have quite a big job ahead of you. It is co-operation you want not something which will put their backs up. Perhaps before long you will get your people to see to the boiler instead of you, and lend a hand in decorating the church.'

'I hope so. When that bell goes every morning at eight o'clock they will know that I am at work as well as them on their farms. It may be that one day some of them will join me. Otherwise it will be a case of the bell calls but nobody answers.'

When we were driving home, Eleanor remarked, 'It will take him some time to fix the bell to call before anybody can answer, especially when Ethel gets into full flow. By that time even on a Sunday it will be a case of just thee and me; solos by Barney, featuring Ethel at the organ.'

'I am afraid I feel sorry for him,' I replied. 'I can see him going to seed rapidly.'

'Never, Fred. He has enough reserves of self-importance to survive in Llangelli indefinitely.'

Next morning after Matins Charles was waxing enthusiastic about the progress he was making with the pageant. He had been only too happy to avoid attending Barney's induction since he had a funeral service to take that afternoon. The two men had a strong mutual dislike of each other.

'I have been down to the colliery to see the manager and he has promised to get some of the men to turn up in their work clothes, with head lamps, etc. They will be there for the opening scene when the foundation stone is laid.'

'It would have been wiser if you had gone to the Union Secretary, Dai Price, first. With the mood the men are in at the moment, I don't think they would take kindly to being ordered to turn up in church for a pageant.'

'Don't shoot the pianist, Fred, he's doing his best. I expect it will be all right, anyway. Another thing, I have arranged with Aneurin Williams to have the first rehearsal of the Gilbert and Sullivan concert next Wednesday at St Padarn's. He will contact all the girls in school and I am sending out notes to all the men this afternoon. Rehearsals with the script are going very well. Iorwerth Ellis is making a splendid Septimus Jones, the first vicar, and so is Moelwyn Howells as Sir Robert Jones-Williams. I must confess he has surprised me. I didn't realize my landlord was so gifted histrionically.'

'Charles, you amaze me. You have done more in the last few days than you have in the last two years. If you maintain this work rate, between us we shall put Pontywen at the top of the diocesan league of activity in no time. Well done, that man!'

'In that case will you be my best man next Easter?'

'Hold on, I thought you were getting married here in my church.'

'Well, if you don't mind, I wondered if my father could take the wedding – that is, of course, if you are willing. You are the only one I could ask to be my best man. I haven't any brothers and I haven't any close friends, apart from you. Bronwen and I have talked it over and she thought it would be a good idea.'

'You must admit, Charles, that it is a little unusual to have the vicar acting as his curate's best man, especially when the marriage is in his own church. Still, you have always been an unusual curate. I accept your invitation on one condition.'

'Marvellous, Fred; what is the condition?'

'That you keep up this work rate. Any flagging and you can look for another best man.'

When I told Eleanor at lunch that he had called me a brick, she replied that he was well acquainted with bricks since he had dropped so many. 'As for his promise,' she said, 'the past two years have been littered with broken pie crusts left by Charles, apart from his dropped bricks. To further mix the metaphors, you had better make hay while the sun shines.'

For the next week I accepted my wife's advice and made Charles work at a pace which left him breathless. Never had he been so assiduous in visiting the sick. I gave him the responsibility for the junior confirmation class, in readiness for the Confirmation next July. He took the Mothers' Union service without a murmur of complaint and all this in addition to his efforts with the pageant and the Gilbert and Sullivan Society.

Then it happened. There was no curate in his stall for Matins the morning after his day off. By lunch time there was still no sign of him. 'He is suffering from exhaustion,' said Eleanor. 'His frail body is unable to take the strain of something called work and he is probably still in bed.'

She was right, as usual. When I called at his digs in the afternoon, Myfanwy Howells, his landlady, met me at the door. 'It's back to normal,' she said. 'He is in bed, feeling sorry for himself, reading a thriller and wondering whether he will be able to meet Bronwen when she comes off duty tonight.'

'What does he say is wrong with him?' I asked.

'According to him he has a terrible headache. It doesn't stop him reading and it hasn't affected his appetite. He has eaten a plateful of fish and chips and a pile of pieces of bread and butter. You had better go upstairs and see if you can get him up.'

When I knocked on his door, a feeble voice invited me to come in. His thriller had been cast aside and his head had almost disappeared under the bedclothes.

'Bored with the who dunnit are we?' I said.

'I can't read any more. My headache is too bad for that. Sorry I wasn't in church this morning. I didn't sleep a wink last night. I know I have been overdoing things this last week or so.'

'Come off it, Charles. Myfanwy tells me you have had a big meal and that you have been sitting up, reading. I shouldn't be surprised if a miracle happens and you will be restored to health in time to meet Bronwen this evening. Don't tell me you have been overdoing things. Hard work never kills anybody. Any more sudden headaches and you will have to look for another best man. I tell you what, if this headache persists, I shall get Eleanor to ask Dr Hughes to see you.'

The bedclothes were pulled back and he sat up.

'There's no need for that. I'll ask Myfanwy to give me some more aspirins. I shouldn't be surprised if they will do the trick. With a bit of luck you will see me in church tomorrow.'

'It is not luck that you need. It is the will to work. You had better recover it.'

I slammed the door behind us.

When I came downstairs, Myfanwy said, 'I expect that slamming of the door will help to cure his headache. He needs some drastic treatment. I think Bronwen will give him that when they are married, or rather if they get married.'

'They will get married all right. Bronwen loves him too much to back out but I don't think he realizes what lies ahead of him. It will be a rude awakening. For the time being he has just had one of those and you can expect him to be up and about before long.'

On my way back to the vicarage I met Full Back Jones who stopped me, waving one of the leaflets containing details of the Centenary Celebration events. Unshaven and toothless, in his mac and wellingtons, battered trilby reposing just above his eyebrows, his face was split in a beam of delight. 'Great,' he lisped. 'You've got a grand dance in the church 'all, I see.'

'We have indeed,' I said. 'Why?'

'I'll be there for that. I enjoy a dance. 'Aven't 'ad one since before the War. Great! Is Doctor Secombe coming? I'll 'ave to grab 'er for the waltz.'

'Oh! She'll be there, Full Back. I shall tell her that you have booked her for a dance.'

Eleanor was greatly amused when I told her about the gravedigger's intention.

'I shall look forward to that. I only hope that he does not come in his wellingtons. I don't fancy being trodden on by them. Well, what has happened to your curate?'

'He has been suffering from a severe headache, which did not prevent him from having a good dinner and reading a thriller. After I had threatened him with having to find a new best man, and with a visit from Dr Hughes, there was an instant improvement in his condition.'

'Talking about Dr Hughes, there is something going on in his mind which I can't quite fathom.'

'What do you mean, love?'

'He seems to have lost all interest in the practice. For example, he has asked me to do all the ordering to replenish our stock of medical requirements. He has always insisted on doing that himself. Then this afternoon he has given me some of his patients to look after, including ones whom he has been caring for over a long period of time. He has not said a word about retiring. All I know is that my work load has been increasing by the week. I think I must do a Charles and develop a dreadful headache, that is, on condition that you feed me well and provide me with thrillers.'

'Eleanor, my sweet, I would do that with pleasure but I can't see you doing a Charles under any circumstances. More to the point, what is Dr Hughes up to?'

'I wish I knew,' she replied. 'Perhaps he has somebody else in mind with more experience than myself to come in and be the senior partner. In which case the sooner he does that the better – both for me and the practice.'

# 15

'What a smug, self-satisfied, pompous front row you are going to have this evening,' remarked Eleanor, as she glanced at the list on my desk. C day had arrived, 17 October, a landmark in Pontywen's history, the 'centenarian anniversary' of St Mary's Church, as 'Dai Tonsorial' put it. She read aloud the names of the notabilities.

'"Mr Gwnfor Williams MP and Mrs Alice Williams; the Mayor, Councillor David Thomas and the Mayoress, Mrs Rhoda Thomas; Councillor David Waters" (alias "Dai Spout"),' she added, '"and Mrs Blodwen Waters." It's a good thing that the bishop doesn't look at his congregation. An eyeful of that lot at the beginning of his sermon and he would never recover.'

'I tell you what,' I replied, 'I would rather look at them than the Pontywen Athletic front row. At least the church front row would not frighten the life out of anybody. In any case, you will have to cope with them, when they come back here after the service.'

'They will be so busy talking to each other and tucking into the food that they will not need me to entertain them. It is the bishop that will be isolated. You know how shy he is. I shall use up all my womanly charm on him.'

'You will be wasting your sweetness on the desert air, my dear. He will be quite happy to remain in splendid isolation. He will not be staying long, if he is true to form. It is a pity that Sir David is away in London. At least those two are well acquainted.'

'Well, they will be meeting each other here after the pageant grand finale. And will I be glad when that comes! I think I shall ask my senior partner for a week off, after all this. Being a doctor, housewife and vicaress is more than my frail body can stand.'

'I prescribe a week's holiday in a certain honeymoon hotel in Newquay, guaranteed to put life back into any exhausted frail body.'

'Frederick, you can prescribe for me anytime. Once everything is over, I shall have a word in Hughes's "shell-like" and we can book a week in Newquay.'

She hugged me and kissed me.

'Now then, back to earth,' she said. 'Are you going to get the drinks for tonight or me?'

It had been a hectic few weeks of preparation. Charles had recovered from his temporary loss of energy; the pageant was well advanced in rehearsals; while the Gilbert and Sullivan Society had come together again and were brimming with enthusiasm for their concert. Arthur the Co-op, our gardener, had recruited the local Chrysanthemum Society to help with the flower festival in St Mary's. Tickets were selling well for the various events. All was set for the centenary programme to swing into action.

Since the bishop was the preacher at the opening service, it was not so much a swing as a gentle sway which began the proceedings. An erudite description of the building of Solomon's temple, which was based on the first verse of the third chapter of the second Book of Chronicles, was not the kind of oratory to inspire the large congregation. It was noticeable that Dai Spout's eyelids were drooping before the bishop had finished reading his text. The mayor seemed to be more interested in searching for the next hymn than in the sermon, until a nudge from his spouse ended the quest. The Member of Parliament was sprawled in his pew and scratching himself in typical parliamentary fashion. Indeed, the front row provided a most unedifying spectacle. As Charles said afterwards, it was 'the embodiment of disinterest'. At least the bulk of the congregation displayed a pretence of attention to the bishop's words, and after the service expressed their appreciation of his lordship's scholarship. 'They gaz'd and still the wonder grew that one small head could carry all he knew.'

I was buttonholed by Mrs Dai Spout during the light refreshments in the vicarage. 'When are you having your confirmation classes, Vicar? I would like our Aneurin to join. He is fourteen now so it's time he was done. I was done when I was thirteen, myself.'

'I remember you asking me about classes for your son a year or so ago when I visited you in hospital, Mrs Waters.'

'So I did; doesn't time fly? I forget what happened that he couldn't come then.'

'As it happens, Mr Wentworth-Baxter is just beginning classes in the church hall in a fortnight, every Wednesday at six thirty p.m. So he will be very welcome. Perhaps you can bring him with you to Holy Communion to give him some experience of the service.'

'To be honest, Vicar, I haven't been to Communion for years now. My husband is Baptist, you see. Not that he goes. He is busy with his council work and with his party meetings. They are always on Sunday mornings. One of these days I'll turn up. I'll see that Aneurin comes every Wednesday, don't worry. As I think I told you when I was in hospital, I'd like him confirmed because its always good to put it in a reference when he is after a job. Employers want young men of good character, don't they?'

'I'm sure they do, Mrs Waters, but they will also want to know if he is a regular worshipper. Here's my curate now. Have a word with him.'

As Charles entered the sitting room I went over to him. 'You have an important confirmation candidate – Dai Spout junior. Mrs Waters would like to speak to you about him.'

'Thanks, Fred,' he murmured. 'That will round off my evening nicely.' Already he had made a mess of acting as bishop's chaplain, handing him his mitre back-to-front and placing his crozier insecurely against the sanctuary wall so that it fell to the floor with a resounding crash during the sermon. It was the only exciting moment in the thirty-minute address.

A minor Labour Party conference was going on in a corner of the room between the MP, the mayor and the councillor, while the two ladies were enjoying the food and the wine. Eleanor was engaging his lordship in what appeared to be a one-sided conversation when there was a scream from the kitchen. Eleanor and I excused ourselves and dashed out to investigate. I opened the kitchen door to find Mrs Watkins with her body pinned against the pantry door, her face ashen with fright.

'It – it's in there,' she breathed.

'What's in there?' asked Eleanor.

'A rat. I opened the back door to put something in the bin and it shot past me into the pantry. So I shut the door straight away.'

'You can come away from the door,' said my wife, 'it can't turn the knob. We shall have to leave it there for the time being. Carry on with making the coffee. Fred, get Mrs Watkins some whisky – while I stay with her for a moment or two.'

When I went back into the sitting room there was a deathly hush as I entered and all eyes were turned on me. 'I am afraid that Mrs Watkins was – er – frightened by a rat, which she has now trapped in the pantry.'

'Is that all?' said the mayor. 'Leave it to me. Is there a light in the pantry?'

'Oh, yes,' I replied.

'Right. Where's the kitchen?'

I led him down the passage, his mayoral chain bouncing off him as he strode. He flung open the door to the astonishment of the two females.

'Where is the pantry, doctor?'

Eleanor pointed to the door.

'If you don't mind, would the three of you get out of the kitchen?'

'I'll go and get Mrs Watkins some whisky,' said my wife and disappeared up the passage, followed by our daily. I stayed outside the kitchen door.

Suddenly from inside there came sounds of violent activity followed by a shout.

'Got you, you bugger!'

'Is it all right for me to come in?' I inquired.

'Of course, Vicar,' said the mayor.

I shall never forget the sight that met me. The first citizen of Pontywen, plus mayoral chain, was standing outside the pantry door, holding the rat by its back legs, like photographs I had seen in the local newspaper of anglers with their prize catch.

'A big one, isn't he?' he said proudly. 'I've killed bigger ones underground but he's not a bad size for a vicarage.'

'How did you do it, Mr Mayor?' I asked.

'The same way as we always do underground, by stamping on them when you have got them cornered. He had no room for any manoeuvre in the pantry. It was such a small space.'

'You had better come and join Mrs Watkins in a whisky,' I said.

'Let me put this thing in your bin first and wash my hands in your sink. Just in case.'

By now Eleanor had joined us.

'Ugh!' she shivered. 'When you have put the body in the bin, you had better go upstairs to the bathroom and use some disinfectant, Mr Mayor. I'll show you where everything is – and thank you very much, by the way. I hope that's the one and only time we get invaded like that.'

'You know what to do now, if it happens again. Just stamp on the thing.'

'I shall leave that to my husband,' she replied and led him upstairs.

The next events in the centenary fiesta went off without incident. There was an excellent concert by the Pontywen Silver Band and a not so excellent performance by the Fol-de-Rols, who seemed to enjoy their performance more than the audience did. The Flower Festival was a revelation to the people of Pontywen. Aided by the Chrysanthemum Society and the Art mistress from Pontywen Grammar school, Eleanor created a floral picture of the town's history, with the Big Wheel of the colliery, the chimney stacks of the steelworks, the parish church, and even the corrugated-iron church of St Padarn.

Then came the grand dance in the church hall, entrance by ticket only, 'to keep out the riff raff' explained Bertie Owen. This was the only event in which he had been let loose because he claimed to be one of the best ballroom dancers in Pontywen. It was he who had booked the Red

Coats dance band and it was he who decided that he would be the MC for the evening. As chairman of the Social Committee, Eleanor was only too pleased to delegate all authority to Bertie for this occasion. 'Since he is running it,' she said, 'he will pester half the population to buy tickets. They will buy them just to get rid of him.' By the day of the dance he had sold two hundred tickets. 'I could have sold more but I had to put a stop to it somewhere. They know a good MC when they see one.'

Since that Thursday was the last rehearsal night for the Gilbert and Sullivan Society before their concert on the Friday, Eleanor and I had an excuse to miss the first hour or so of Bertie's big night. However, we thought we had better call in at the hall to wish him well before the dance. He was busily occupied, sprinkling a profusion of French chalk on the battered floorboards when we entered. Dressed in a dinner suit and sporting a red bow tie he was at his most self-important.

'It's about time the band was here to set up their equipment. I've sent my two men on the door to get the raffle drum from the British Legion. The refreshments are in the kitchen. Mrs Collier's in charge of that, as you know. She was down earlier on. It's just the band now.'

'There's still an hour before the start,' said Eleanor.

'You know me, doctor. I like to get things well prepared; no last minute rush.'

At that moment there was the sound of a vehicle pulling up outside the church hall.

'That's their van. I can tell that clapped-out engine anywhere. I used to drive it myself as a hobble for Lewis the Builder years ago.' After he had rushed out to meet them, I said to Eleanor. 'What's a hobble?'

'Fred, my dear, I am amazed you have not heard that word before. It's a Valley expression for a job on the side – something you do in addition to your normal employment. No income tax involved, cash in the pocket.'

That was the cue for the entry of the minstrels – six of them. They were all elderly gentlemen, clad in red jackets which had seen better days.

''Aven't been 'ere since before the War, 'Arry. Remember

those monthly flannel dances they used to 'ave. I 'ope the piano's been tuned since then. It used to be bloody awful.'

The speaker, a little man, with a stoop and a few copies of music in his hand, turned round to speak to his friend who was following him and carrying a saxophone. As he turned, he saw Eleanor and myself. His face turned the same colour as his jacket.

'Good evening, Vicar,' he stammered. 'Looking forward to the dance?'

'Very much so,' I said, 'but I am afraid my wife and I will be missing the first part of the evening. It's the final rehearsal for our society's concert tomorrow night. By the way, I had the piano tuned last week, ready for the centenary events.'

'Thank you, Vicar. That'll be a great 'elp, won't it, 'Arry?'

Harry nodded his head and made his way towards the stage with its five chairs and a piano stool. There he was joined by the rest of the Red Coats, carrying their various instruments.

'Want any help with the microphone?' asked Bertie, an expert with that piece of equipment, having presided there at open-air events in Pontywen on a number of occasions.

'It's all right, Bertie,' said the band's vocalist, 'I'll get it now in a minute once I've been to the gents. Then you can test it for your announcing.'

'With their red coats,' whispered Eleanor, 'they look more like the Chelsea Pensioners than a dance band. It is going to be a very interesting evening.'

All the talk at the Gilbert and Sullivan rehearsals was about the next production once the centenary programme had ended. The singing of the excerpts from *The Pirates of Penzance* was most satisfactory and the enthusiasm of chorus and cast was unbounded. Aneurin Williams, schoolmaster and musical director, was keen to go ahead as soon as possible. Eleanor insisted that unless she had more time off from her medical commitments she would be unable to take the soprano lead. We decided that we would meet in a month's time and begin rehearsals for *The Gondoliers*, hoping that by then my wife would be able to take part.

As we walked back to the church hall for the grand

dance, she insisted that unless there was a reduction in her working hours, somebody else would have to play Gianetta and I vowed (equally firmly) I would not play Marco unless it was opposite her.

'Let's forget Gilbert and Sullivan for the time being and enjoy the next couple of hours in the company of Bertie and the Red Coats,' she suggested.

The hall was bulging at the seams. Apparently, as Eleanor forecast, half the population of Pontywen had been dragooned into coming to the Bertie Owen extravaganza. Every inch of the dance floor was occupied with partners doing the foxtrot to the vocal accompaniment of the white-haired soloist who late in life had aspirations to become a second Bing Crosby. The first dancer to catch my eye was Full Back Jones, who had undergone a startling transformation. Wearing his best suit, his hair plastered with Brylcreem and parted in the middle, he was flashing his false teeth in a permanent grin. It was only the second time I had seen his dentures, which appeared to be far too large for his small mouth. To add to my bewilderment, he proved to be a diminutive Victor Sylvester, a polished performer *par excellence*.

When the dance ended, Bertie came to the microphone. 'Let's give our vicar and his lady a hearty welcome and ask them to start our next dance. This will be most appropriate as far as the church is concerned, as it were: the Anniversary Waltz. Put your hands together and give them a good clap.'

'Do you realize that this is the first time we have danced together?' said Eleanor. 'Can you do a waltz?'

'Come off it, Dr Secombe, of course I can do a waltz and a foxtrot and a quickstep.'

'A waltz will do for the time being and watch my feet, there's a dear. They don't like being trodden on.'

The saxophonist launched into a rendering of the Anniversary Waltz and we took the floor to some desultory applause.

We had only achieved a couple of turns when half a dozen young gentlemen burst into the hall and on to the dance floor.

'Carry on dancing,' I said to Eleanor, 'it will take some of the attention away from these young roughs.'

John Rees and George Thomas, the two doormen, were trying to move the invaders off the floor as my wife and I were now joined by the other dancers who had to dance around them.

'There's only one answer to this and that's Will Book and Pencil. Excuse me, love.' So saying I escorted Eleanor to the side of the hall and made my way to the exit. The police station was only five doors away from the church hall. I rang the front-door bell and to my great relief PC Will Davies answered.

'What can I do for you, Vicar?' inquired the large constable who was in his shirt sleeves.

'There's trouble at the dance in the church hall. About six youngsters have gatecrashed the proceedings and are refusing to leave the dance floor.'

'Come on in for a minute while I put my uniform on and I'll be with you right away.'

'I have not seen them before, Constable,' I said as we walked to the hall.

'They could be some boyos from up the valley, feeling their feet. Anyway they will feel my feet up their backsides if they are not careful.'

As soon as the burly figure of the local bobby appeared on the scene, the little group of troublemakers moved off the dance floor in the direction of the exit.

'Hold on,' said PC Davies, catching one of them by the coat collar. 'If I find any of you lot causing trouble again in this town, you won't know what's hit you. People have come here to enjoy themselves not to be bothered by the likes of you. Now hop it before I take your names and addresses.'

Hop it they did, and the dancing continued untroubled for the rest of the evening. Full Back Jones invited Eleanor to waltz with him. When she came back after the dance, she said, 'You ought to go to him for lessons. I think he is the best dancer I have ever had as a partner. He puts Bertie Owen in the shade, believe me.'

Bertie Owen came up to us at the end of the evening. 'We have made forty-five pounds, eleven shillings and sixpence, after paying the band. I think everybody enjoyed themselves.

A pity about those youngsters barging in like that. I was coming down to sort them out when Will Book and Pencil arrived, so I thought I would leave it to him. After all, it's his job, isn't it?'

'Very true, Bertie. Thank you for all your hard work and for being such a splendid MC.' I gave him a pat on the back and left him glowing with pride. It was not often that I had patted him on the back.

The Gilbert and Sullivan concert took place in a full hall, like the grand dance, and was equally as successful. Now there was only the pageant to come the next day. I had stayed away from the rehearsals since Charles wanted this to be his own effort, his first *tour de force* in Pontywen.

He was early for Matins on Saturday morning; I found him in his stall in the chancel, deep in prayer. I thought I had better not disturb him but went into the vestry, robed and took my place. Apparently he had not heard me come in. When I said, 'Charles, shall we start?' his head jerked up, like a puppet on a string.

'Oh, of course, Fred. Do you want me to read the lessons?'

'No, just relax. I'll do everything this morning.'

In the prayers I prayed for the success of the pageant and particularly for him as the director and producer. 'Thank you, Fred,' he said as we left the church, 'I am sure that those prayers will help me this evening. We are having a dress rehearsal this afternoon. The six miners have promised to be there. That will be their first appearance. The children were quite excited at the last rehearsal. I expect they will be over the top today but Bertie Owen has promised to keep them under control.'

'I must say, Charles, you are an optimist if you think Bertie can do that.'

'There's always Ezekiel Evans. Because he is playing the Bishop of Llandaff, perhaps he can use his episcopal authority to put them down. This will be the highlight of his career, his ambition fulfilled. From lay reader to bishop in one fell swoop. By the way, I have hired the robes from that costume company you used for *Pirates*. I hope you don't mind. They were quite reasonable. That is the only expense as far as costumes are concerned. The parents have seen to the children's costumes. They have been marvellous.'

'Well done, that boy. You really have excelled yourself. I shall keep out of the way this afternoon. Eleanor and I are going to Cardiff to do some shopping ready for the post-pageant party.'

When my wife came back from surgery she looked exhausted. 'I think you had better do the driving this afternoon, love, and I suggest we do the minimum of traipsing around Cardiff. I can't wait for that holiday to come. My partner was not in this morning so I had to do his patients as well as mine. It is a bit much. Thank heavens for Mrs Watkins. She has been a gem. All we have to do is to provide the filling for the sandwiches. Those cakes she made yesterday are delicious.'

By the time we arrived home from Cardiff the dress rehearsal was over and only the producer-cum-director-cum-narrator was left in the church. He looked pleased with himself. 'If it goes as well as that tonight, I shan't complain,' he said.

The bishop's car drew up in the vicarage drive at seven o'clock prompt. He had decided to drive himself since it was Saturday evening and the chauffeur's day off. Almost immediately afterwards came Sir David Jones-Williams' Bentley. He was always his own chauffeur. The two men were enjoying a glass of sherry in the sitting room, prior to the performance when I joined them. 'No rats this evening, I trust, Vicar,' said the bishop with a rare attempt at humour.

'I hope not. I am afraid the mayor will not be here to act as rat catcher,' I replied.

When the remark was explained to the squire he suggested that perhaps his worship would care to come up to the mansion, where there were several in the old barn.

At twenty-five past seven the bishop, the squire, Eleanor, Bronwen and I took our seats in the front pew in a church which was buzzing with excitement. Mr Greenfield at the organ was fidgeting nervously on the stool, playing with the organ stops. The noises off from the children indicated that the combined effects of Bertie Owen and Ezekiel Evans were to no avail. Suddenly there was a shout from Charles: 'Shut up!'

'I never knew he had it in him,' whispered Eleanor to me.

The next minute, clad in his cassock, he appeared centre-stage in the chancel.

'Tonight we unfold the story of a hundred years of Christian witness in Pontywen, through four wars: the Crimean War, marked in our town by Sebastopol Street and Balaclava Street; the Boer War marked by Mafeking Avenue; the First World War, marked by Jellicoe Street and Beatty Road; and last of all, the Second World War, just ended.

'He has run out of streets,' murmured my wife.

'This wasn't in the original script,' I said. 'It sounds more like a Barney Webster sermon rather than a prologue.'

'Shall be begin this pageant by singing a hymn which reminds us of the only true foundation, "The Church's one foundation is Jesus Christ Our Lord"; the hymn sung at the first service in this church.'

When the hymn ended, we were told that there would be a procession down the aisle which would represent all those present at the great day in 1847. First came the school-children, the boys in their Eton collars and their knicker-bocker suits, the girls in their long dresses, leg-of-mutton sleeves and mob-caps. They were led by a boy and girl carrying a banner. When they turned round to face the congregation, the words 'Church and Queen' were seen. Next came the builders and the workmen, with someone representing the architect and carrying on a velvet cushion the silver trowel, lent by Sir David, who stroked his moustache in proud remembrance of the generosity of his ancestors.

Then came the miners in their working clothes with their faces blackened and their helmets and lamps. When the six reached the chancel, two of them stepped forward and un-rolled a banner on which was printed in large letters 'Built by the exploitation of the Miners.'

There was a gasp from the congregation and a loud snort from Sir David Jones-Williams. 'Bloody impertinence,' he roared and made an angry exit up the aisle, colliding with the first Vicar of Pontywen, the Bishop of Llandaff and his great-grandfather.

The rest of the pageant was an anticlimax, with the words of the participants drowned by the chatter of the congregation. Charles went through his script like a zombie, as did the rest of his cast, while the miners never stopped grinning in the background. The bishop was most sympathetic towards my curate in the vicarage afterwards. 'I suppose there must be resentment among those whose lives have been impaired by pneumonoconiosis or unnecessary accidents underground, but it is a pity that they chose what should have been a time of rejoicing to make their protest.'

When I went to the telephone table to make my apologies to Sir David, I found an envelope there addressed to Eleanor. As I brought it into the sitting room, Mrs Watkins met me coming out with a tray of empty plates. 'I found that on the mat when you were in church,' she said.

Eleanor was in deep conversation with Bronwen when I handed her the letter. 'It's from Elias Hughes,' she murmured with a frown.

She opened it and as she read, her face turned pale. When she had finished it, she passed it to me. The letter said:

My dear Eleanor,
I am deeply sorry to have to burden you with the care of so many patients but I am afraid I cannot carry on any longer. As you know I have not been happily married and, as you also know, I have a deep attachment to Miss Hannah Jones. We have decided that we cannot wait any longer to enjoy what few years happiness remain. So we have gone away tonight to an undisclosed destination. Later on I shall make all the legal arrangements necessary to leave the practice in your hands entirely. Once again, my sincerest apologies for putting you in this situation. I trust you can find a suitable person to join you in the practice as soon as possible.
   Elias Hughes

'The Grand Finale,' said my wife, 'to a perfect day!'

# A Comedy of
# Clerical Errors

To the vanished valleys species –
the South Wales miner

'May the blessing of God Almighty, the Father, the Son and the Holy Ghost be upon you and remain with you from this day forth and for evermore,' intoned the parson in a quavery voice. The dewdrop on his red nose glinted in the morning sunshine. It had been there throughout the marriage service. Its owner was loath to part with it either by the use of a handkerchief or even a sniff. The embarrassed bridegroom had tried to draw the officiant's attention to it by sign language during the opening hymn, only to be met with an uncomprehending stare. What compounded the embarrassment was the fact that the dewdrop belonged to his father and furthermore that the best man was his vicar.

Charles Wentworth-Baxter was my curate and apparently friendless since he had asked me to be his best man for the ceremony which was taking place in my own church. His father, Canon Septimus Wentworth-Baxter, recently retired, had come down from Yorkshire to preside at the nuptials of his son and his bride, Nurse Bronwen Williams, a newly qualified SRN. After the blessing the canon plus his dewdrop proceeded into the vestry, to be followed by the wedding party. The bridal retinue was in keeping with the bride's profession, consisting of Eleanor, my wife, the local doctor, and matron of honour for the occasion, together with the two bridesmaids, also newly qualified SRNs. Mr and Mrs Amos Williams, proud parents of the bride, brought up the rear.

The bridegroom, who wore a clerical dress-suit borrowed from his father and two sizes too large for him, spent the first few minutes in the vestry in a passionate embrace with his beloved while the rest of us talked among ourselves. It was a cough from the canon which ended the love scene.

'Back to earth, Charles,' he commanded, and produced a large handkerchief from his pocket to remove the dewdrop with a trumpeting blow. This relaxed the bride who then had to endure six more embraces of much shorter duration while her husband was signing the register.

'Beautiful wedding!' said Mrs Olive Williams to my wife. 'Our Bronwen looks lovely, doesn't she? My sister-in-law made the dress (she's a tailoress, you see). Cost us most of our coupons, I can tell you – but it's worth it, isn't it?'

It was Easter Monday, 1948 and clothing coupons were not in plentiful supply.

Before my wife could reply, the bride's mother carried on with her monologue. 'Mind, I'd always hoped she would have been married in Tabernacle with the Reverend Josiah Jones-Evans doing the service. Strict Baptist we are, as you know. Still, the Reverend Jones-Evans is down here for the wedding and we've asked him to say a few words at the reception. It's very kind of your husband to let us have the church hall for the meal. We wouldn't dream of going to a hotel for it where they serve strong drink, and fancy Charles's friends with that Gilbert Society offering to serve at the tables and put everything ready beforehand. They've been a great help, I must say, and didn't they sing that sacred song nicely at the end?'

There was a look of desperation on Eleanor's face

which prompted Bronwen to intervene. 'Mam, would you like to hold my bouquet while I sign the register?' As Mrs Williams went to the bride to collect the bouquet, my wife moved swiftly to join the two bridesmaids who were in animated conversation in one corner of the vestry.

'Shall we have the bride now, please? Or may I say, my daughter-in-law?' The canon motioned Bronwen to the desk on which reposed the marriage register. Before she sat in the chair which the bridegroom had vacated, the old clergyman embraced her warmly. He turned to his son and said, 'I hope you realize, Charles, that you are a very lucky young man.' Bronwen blushed and took her seat. Charles was buttonholed by his mother-in-law.

I remained firmly anchored with Amos Williams who was proving to be a surprisingly rounded person for a 'Strict Baptist'. He was very knowledgeable about Welsh male-voice choirs and even about radio programmes like *Itma*, displaying a keen sense of humour. Evidently the fervour for the Baptist cause was confined to Mrs Williams. At one time it had infected her daughter who decided to become a medical missionary only to be turned down by the Society for lack of qualifications. Instead she was persuaded by Charles that she could serve God just as well in Pontywen, as a curate's wife. They were going to live in the curate's house largely furnished with furniture provided by the bridegroom's father, a widower who had retired from his large old vicarage to live in a cottage in the Yorkshire countryside.

With the ceremonial details duly recorded, the procession formed up to leave the vestry. Since Charles was motherless, I suggested that Mr and Mrs Williams should form one couple, Eleanor and I the next, with the two bridesmaids following the bride and groom. Canon Wentworth-Baxter had said that he would rather not join the parade but would leave by the back door of the vestry and meet us outside the church for the photographs. The signal was given to Mr Greenfield the organist who launched into an inaccurate rendering of Mendelssohn's *Wedding March*. Through its discordances my wife murmured to me that she intended to avoid Mrs Williams for the rest of the proceedings if she could.

Outside the church, Humphries the Snap, the local photographer, was waiting to 'record the happy event for future posterity', to use his favourite phrase, repeated at every wedding he attended. He was wearing his long grey overcoat despite the warm sunshine. The coat was as ancient and as indispensable as his big box camera, resting on a tripod together with its voluminous cloth under which he would disappear like a stage magician.

A large crowd of spectators had gathered to witness the proceedings, much to the disgust of Mr Humphries who had to 'carve his way through a wall of human flesh', to quote W. C. Fields. 'Bloody ghouls!' he said to himself as I drew near. 'Beg your pardon, Vicar,' he added as he breathed a whisky-laden aroma in my direction. 'Look at 'em, trampling over your gravestones and dropping confetti everywhere, watching another man going to his doom.'

'You had better be careful with your language, Mr Humphries,' I said to him. 'There's a bus-load of strict Baptists here from further up the valley, the bride's parents and friends.'

'That's all I need to know,' he replied. 'No glass of sherry at the reception in that case. Well, let's get on with it.' He pushed his way to the steps outside the church porch. 'Let's have a snap of the happy couple on their own first, shall we?'

Charles was carrying his father's top hat. He could not wear it because it was several sizes too large for him. When he tried it on in the vicarage, he was engulfed and resembled the illustration of the Mad Hatter in *Alice in Wonderland*.

When it came to the bride's family group, Mrs Williams was calling for the Reverend Josiah Jones-Evans to be included. A dapper little man, with a black trilby to match his black suit, appeared from the throng. Large horn-rimmed spectacles were perched on his beaky nose and evidently he had disdained to wear the obligatory white carnation which was available for guests of the family. By the sour look on his face, perhaps, the flower would have withered in his buttonhole. While everybody else attempted a 'cheese' smile, Josiah stood in splendid isolation, like death's head at the feast, obviously lamenting the desertion of one of his pet lambs to the Anglican fold.

As yet I had not met him. I pushed my way through the chaos to reach him as he stepped down from the family group.

'Mr Jones-Evans,' I gasped, 'I am Fred Secombe, the bridegroom's vicar.'

'Pleased to meet you,' he replied, without a trace of pleasure on his countenance. He deposited a limp right hand in my outstretched hand, withdrawing it in an instant as if he were fearful of being contaminated by the contact with an Anglican priest.

'Bronwen looks delightful, doesn't she?' I said. Small, dark-haired with large dark brown eyes, she reminded me of my wife on our wedding day. She had the same ready smile. 'We shall do our best to help her settle down to her new life. It will be a big change for her but with her good Christian background I am sure she will cope with her changed circumstances.'

'Changed circumstances!' exploded the Reverend Josiah, unable to contain himself any longer. 'With her dedication to her Saviour, the change in her circumstances should have meant her serving Him in a mission hospital in Africa, not wasting her life here in the valleys. She's too good to be spending her time drinking cups of tea with the Mothers' Union and darning the curate's socks. That child had a call, a real call, which has been deafened by the cotton-wool of an easy existence under the guise of serving the Lord in the comfort of a parsonage or a vicarage.'

The vehemence of this onslaught by the little man took my breath away. It was obvious that he must be a charismatic figure in his strict Baptist pulpit. It was also obvious that 'a few words' from the minister at the wedding reception would be disastrous.

'Well, Mr Jones-Evans,' I replied. 'I would have thought that it is only Bronwen who can judge whether a call is a real call or not. As far as I am concerned, I shall leave that judgement to her and her alone. If you will excuse me, I have to get to the hall to see that everything is ready for the reception.'

Before I left the church I had a brief word with my wife who was due to travel the short distance to the church hall in the same wedding car as the bridesmaids. I explained what had happened in my encounter with the minister. 'Why not ask him to say grace,' she suggested, 'and limit the speeches to the best man, the bride's father and yourself. If Mrs Williams doesn't like that, it is just too bad.'

When I arrived in the hall, the church Gilbert and Sullivan Society members were in a state of last-minute confusion, colliding with each other as they raced to place bread rolls on the plates and the condiments on the table, not to mention the delivery of wine glasses to contain the Wincarnis tonic wine for the toasts. The Society was one which I had created in my curate days in Pontywen. It was a benevolent dictatorship in which I acted as producer, director, tenor lead and policy-maker. Charles was the accompanist and my wife was the soprano lead. The musical director, Aneurin, had rehearsed an anthem with the members, Schubert's 'Ave Maria', which the *ad hoc* choir had sung impressively during the signing of the register. Now the choristers had become waiters and waitresses for the occasion.

'Vicar!' called Idris the Milk, churchwarden at St Padarn's, the daughter church in the parish, and a stalwart of the Society. 'Could I have a word with you, please?'

He took me by the arm and led me into the kitchen. 'We've got the bar in here if you want a drink – everything from whisky to a small barrel of beer. So if there's anybody who's allergic to Wincarnis, tell them to come into the kitchen and we'll put them right. How about a spot of scotch now before they all come in – build you up for your job as best man? By the look of that bus-load, you'll need it.'

'Thank you, Idris. I'll accept your offer but for heaven's sake don't let those Baptists see that you are serving strong drink. If they found that out, they would get up and walk out en masse.'

By the time I had swallowed a few mouthfuls of whisky, the guests were beginning to arrive. 'Here's a couple of peppermints, Vicar. Guaranteed to camouflage strong drink at a distance of inches. Suck those and you can look them in the eye without giving yourself away.' Idris produced a packet of mint humbugs from his pocket. 'Here you are! Keep the lot. Your need is greater than mine.'

I took two from the packet and stuffed the rest in my pocket. Sucking hard on the sweets, I went to meet Charles and Bronwen who had just made an appearance, followed closely by Bronwen's parents and the Reverend Josiah. I decided to take the bull by the horns. Taking the minister aside, I said to him, 'Would you like to say grace before the meal? I thought it would be appropriate if you had some part in the proceedings.'

He glared at me. 'Mrs Williams asked me if I would say a few words at the reception.'

'By saying grace, Mr Jones-Evans, you would be saying a few words. I could have asked the bridegroom's father or I could have said grace myself since I am the vicar. However, I am inviting you to say grace.'

His face reddened and he drew in his breath. He was silent for a few seconds. 'Very well,' he replied.

In the meanwhile Charles and Bronwen, with Mr and Mrs Williams plus a weary-looking Canon Wentworth-Baxter, were receiving their guests as they entered the hall. Eleanor and the two bridesmaids were engaged in earnest conversation near the table on which the wedding cake reposed as Humphries the Snap made his way towards me, carrying his photographic apparatus.

'Do you think I could have a snap of the bride and groom with the wedding cake before you all sit down for this meal?' he asked. 'I have another wedding at two o'clock and I'd like to get away if possible.'

'I'm sure you can,' I replied. 'By the way, if you go into

the kitchen, you'll find something much stronger than Wincarnis.'

I was sorry the moment I said it. I have never seen an old man move more quickly. He was in the kitchen before I could draw another breath. In the ten minutes or so that it took for the guests to be received, Mr Humphries had half emptied the whisky bottle, according to Idris. His abandoned tripod and camera stood forlornly in front of the wedding cake.

'Before we sit down for the meal, would you mind having your photograph taken, pretending to cut the wedding cake?' I said to Charles and Bronwen.

'Where is he?' asked Bronwen.

'I think he is in the kitchen. I'll go and get him. He'll be glad to get away.' He was not glad to get away.

'Can't they hold on for a minute or two, Vicar?'

'I think you had better come straight away. It was you who wanted to leave as quickly as possible. If you don't mind my saying so, you'll be in no fit condition to get to your next wedding unless you stop swigging that whisky.'

'Vicar! You insult me. I can always hold my liquor and my – er – speech is never shlurred.'

He poured half a tumbler of scotch down his throat and moved unsteadily into the hall.

The bride and groom were standing behind the three-tiered wedding cake, looking into each other's eyes.

'Would you mind standing at the side, please? I don't want to have a snap of the cake with a couple of heads peeping over the top.' He hiccuped and had difficulty getting under the cloth to take the photograph. It seemed that at any minute tripod camera and Mr Humphries would collapse on the church hall floor. Miraculously that disaster was averted, perhaps by the fervency of my prayer.

'Would you please stop moving about?' ordered the hidden photographer. Since Charles and Bronwen were standing perfectly still, holding the knife between them, they were somewhat bewildered by the remark. 'As far as I can tell, we are not moving at all,' said Charles.

'Right, that's fine. Now stay still.' A muffled hiccup was followed by the emergence from under his cover of Mr Humphries, whose tousled grey locks and bleary eyes, combined with his purple nose, would have made him an ideal subject for a comic postcard.

'Smile, please. Look at me, then. Come on. Let's shee your choppers.'

The bride and groom obliged with a display of their teeth more appropriate for a dental inspection than as an expression of happiness.

The camera shutter came down and their ordeal was over. The photographer made his unsteady way out of the hall, as I breathed a sigh of relief. I went over to Charles who was standing gazing into space while Bronwen was talking to her bridesmaid friends.

'That was a near squeak,' I said to him.

'What do you mean, Fred?' His childlike innocence was a constant source of amazement to me.

'Couldn't you see that he was squiffy, several sheets to the wind?'

He stared at me.

'Drunk, Charles. It's my fault. I told him that if he was allergic to Wincarnis he could get something stronger in the kitchen. I didn't realize that he could put away half a bottle of whisky in a matter of minutes.'

'You don't mean to say that they have drinks in the kitchen? What will that crowd of Baptists say?'

'That crowd of Baptists will not be invited into the kitchen, believe me. You did not expect the Gilbert and Sullivan crowd to go without the social lubricant on Easter Monday, did you? – Lent finished on Saturday. It is not an all-the-year-round exercise for us, even if it may be for them. What is more, I have a shrewd idea that if I invited your father-in-law into the kitchen he would come like a shot were it not for your mother-in-law. If you need a stiffener, I suggest you pop in there now before the proceedings begin.'

'I don't need anything of the sort. For heaven's sake, Fred, tell them in the kitchen to be careful. What if some of the Tabernacle lot go in there for a cup of tea or something and they find that they are boozing?'

'They won't find anything of the sort. I am positive that Idris the Milk who is in charge of the bar is far too discreet to let them know that Wincarnis and tea are not the only liquid available. I suggest that you collect

Bronwen and make your way to the top table. I am going to announce that the wedding breakfast is about to be served.'

I went into the kitchen where the girls were ready to move to the tables with plates of cold ham, tomatoes, lettuce and boiled potatoes. Idris was standing in a corner by the beer barrel. 'Before I borrow a spoon to bang on the table,' I said to him, 'Charles is desperate to let you know that he does not want any of the Tabernacle load to discover that there is illicit liquor on the premises. I told him that you would be the soul of discretion.'

'You know me, Vicar. I can guarantee that as far as this kitchen is concerned, the Baptists will think it is worthy of the Band of Hope.' With a nod and a wink, he handed me a large tablespoon. By now all the guests were seated. Mrs Williams was pouring out her soul to Canon Wentworth-Baxter, while Eleanor was engaged in animated conversation with Mr Williams. I banged loudly on the table and announced that the Reverend Josiah Jones-Evans would say grace. The little man was seated at the end of the top table.

'Will you all rise for the blessing on the food we are about to eat?' he ordered in a powerful pulpit voice. Chairs were noisily pushed backwards as the guests rose for the blessing. He waited for complete silence before launching into the longest grace I have ever heard.

'O Lord,' he began, 'we beseech you in your infinite wisdom and loving mercy to look down with your favour upon your children gathered around these tables and especially upon the two who have plighted their troth to each other. You know, all-seeing God, the secrets of our hearts and therefore why it is that Bronwen, your faithful servant, has chosen to turn from a dedicated life in the jungles of Africa to serve the sick in Pontywen and to share the life of a man of God in this town. May he realize the sacrifice of her dreams she has made for him and may he be worthy of that sacrifice. May God's blessing rest upon them and may that blessing also be upon his gracious gifts of food to be set before us. We ask this in the name of our Saviour, Jesus Christ.'

It was a *tour de force* which cast a blight upon the wedding feast. For the first few minutes afterwards there was an embarrassed silence, aggravated by a loud comment from Bertie Owen in the kitchen: 'That wasn't a grace. That was a sermon, and a rotten one too.' Bertie, former people's warden in St Padarn's until the people voted him out, was 'born to trouble as the sparks fly upward'.

'Shut up, Bertie,' hissed Idris the Milk.

'Only he could do that,' I whispered to Eleanor who was seated between me and Amos Williams. 'It's a wonder he didn't come out into the hall and confront Josiah.'

Bronwen was doing her best to comfort Charles whose face was scarlet throughout the meal. Her father concentrated on his food, looking to neither left nor right. Her mother tried to engage the canon in conversation but with little success. Meanwhile, the cause of the embarrassment was tucking into God's gifts with relish, content that he had used the grace to say his 'few words'.

Eventually, when the apple tart and custard had been consumed and the wine glasses were filled with the nonalcoholic wine, I read out the few telegrams and cards containing the best wishes for the happy couple.

That done, I turned to Mr Williams. 'Are you ready for your speech?' I asked.

'More than ready,' he muttered.

After he had been introduced, he sprang to his feet. 'Bride and groom, ladies and gentlemen. This should be a happy occasion. Our only child, my daughter Bronwen whom I love very dearly, is marrying the man she loves. What's more, I can see that he loves her just as deeply as she does him. She is not sacrificing any dream. I thank God that she is not out in a jungle in Africa, or anywhere else like that. There is plenty of good she can do here in the valleys and if she can do that, married to the man she loves, so much the better. She has been a joy to bring up, a pleasure to have in the house. I am sure that they both will be very happy now and in the years to come. Will you rise with me and drink a toast to the bride and groom? Charles and Bronwen.'

There was a smile on the faces of the happy couple for the first time since the meal began. There was a scowl on the face of the Reverend Josiah. As Amos Williams sat down, he said to me, 'I wish it could have been something stronger than Wincarnis.'

'Mr Williams,' I said, 'when the proceedings come to an end, I will take you to the kitchen where there is a stronger brew, more fitted to the occasion. After all, there was another wedding reception when water was turned into wine of the best quality. I think Charles and Bronwen are worthy of a toast in the best drink available.'

'Hear, hear,' he replied. 'In that case, hurry up and get the speeches over so that we can go and indulge – but for heaven's sake keep my missus out of the kitchen.'

When I called on Charles to reply to the toast, he whispered to me that he was going to cut it short. 'Thank you, father-in-law, for that splendid speech, and thank you both for producing such a wonderful daughter. I can assure you that I will love and cherish her as I promised in the marriage service. I can also assure the Reverend Josiah Jones-Evans that she is already giving dedicated service to the patients in Pontywen Hospital who need her loving care as much as any patients in Africa or wherever.' His voice was raised in anger as he spoke those words. He paused to recover his self-control. 'I should like to thank Mr and Mrs Williams for this reception and, of course, my friends in the Gilbert and Sullivan Society for all their kind help and also for the lovely anthem in the service. Will you please join me in a toast to the lovely bridesmaids and to the equally lovely matron of honour?'

A loud burst of applause came from the kitchen staff when Charles sat down to be greeted by a kiss from his bride. The Reverend Josiah's head was bowed as he examined his empty plate.

As I rose to speak, I felt that it would be unwise to add to the minister's discomfort. 'On behalf of the lovely bridesmaids and of course the delicious matron of honour' (Eleanor gave me one of her remonstrative looks) 'I should like to thank the bridegroom for his compliments and the brevity of his eloquence. I shall be equally brief. It is some three years more or less since Charles first came to this parish as my fellow curate. I can say in all honesty that he has been a good friend and is now developing into a good parish priest. He is full of the unexpected. Bronwen will find that life with him will never be boring – the secret of a good marriage. He is fortunate to have such a good Christian girl as Bronwen as his partner. She will grace any parsonage or vicarage which will come their way in the future. May God bless them both and may they always be as happy as they are today.'

After I had announced that no more speeches were to be given, I invited Amos Williams to follow me into the kitchen. 'What would you like? A scotch or a beer?' I asked.

'A large scotch would be more than welcome,' he replied.

When Idris the Milk had handed the bride's father a generous helping of whisky, I whispered to the bar-tender, 'Keep an eye open for Mrs Williams. If she finds him imbibing, there will be trouble.'

'Turn around, Vicar. It looks as if there is trouble coming from a different quarter. Here comes Will Book and Pencil,' said Idris.

I looked out through the kitchen window to see PC Will Davies standing at the back of the hall. His excessive devotion to duty had earned him his nickname and a reputation of being unbearably officious.

I left the kitchen and went across to the constable who was making his way into the middle of the hall.

'Well, PC Davies,' I said. 'What can we do for you?'

'You realize, Vicar, that you cannot serve intoxicating drinks in your hall without a licence?' He gave me his best magisterial stare.

'I am afraid, Constable, that you have come on a fruitless mission if you think that the guests have been served any strong drink. Since the bride's parents are Baptist and most of the wedding party are Baptists, the wine glasses were filled with Wincarnis tonic wine for the toasts. If you care to inspect the glasses, you can see for yourself.'

His face was a picture of thwarted authority.

'I take your word for it, Vicar, as a man of the cloth. I wouldn't have come here but for the fact that I found Mr

Hubert Humphries, the photographer, sitting on a wall near Pontywen Methodist Church, drunk and incapable with his apparatus. He said he was on his way to take photographs at a wedding in that church and that he had just come from a reception in your church hall. They have had to take photographs with their own cameras at the Methodists'. He must have called in somewhere on his way, I suppose. Sorry to have troubled you.'

'Before you go, PC Davies,' I said, 'I think you will find that we could have served intoxicating liquor in this church hall, as long as no one purchased it. I suggest that next time you intrude upon an occasion such as this you read up the relevant legislation beforehand. It will save you and others a lot of trouble.'

'What you call the biter bit,' remarked Idris, as the embarrassed policeman left the hall. 'Well done, Vicar. Come and join Mr Williams for a spot of the hard stuff. That was something worth celebrating.'

'Too late, Idris, by the look of it. Mrs Williams has just invaded the kitchen. I think Mr Williams will have other things on his mind.'

## 2

'I have some very interesting news for you, Vicar,' announced my wife when she returned from her surgery at lunch-time. 'Your curate is due to become a father at the end of the year.' It was some two months or so after the eventful wedding.

'Bronwen presented herself for examination this morning. Without a shadow of a doubt she is well and truly preggers. It must be a honeymoon child. If so, they are certainly paying for their pleasure. At least, the blushing bride thinks so.'

'You mean she doesn't want the child?'

'Oh, she wants to have a child, but not so soon. She will be washing nappies before she has time to get the confetti out of her hair. Apparently she has not told Charles yet.'

'Obviously not. He was his new carefree self this morning at Matins. I wonder what his reaction will be. I can't imagine him as a father. I know one thing. When she has labour pains he will be having them with her and his pains will be greater than hers. I can see the doctor having two patients on his hands in the maternity hospital.'

'She wants to have the baby at home and she wants me to deliver it. In that case you will have to be his doctor. I shall be far too preoccupied with Bronwen to bother with him.'

He needed my patient care the very next morning at

Matins when he arrived at church looking as if he was in imminent danger of a nervous collapse. There were dark circles under his eyes as if he had not slept all night.

'Has Eleanor told you the news?' he said as soon as he came into the vestry. He spoke as if he had been visited by the Black Death. 'Who would have thought it?'

'Congratulations, Charles. You must be a very proud man. You have beaten me to it and by several lengths at that.'

He stared at me as if I were someone bereft of his senses. 'It's not fair,' he moaned. 'We have hardly had any time together and now there will be three of us in the house. It means that Bronwen will have to give up her job at the hospital and we shall have to manage on my stipend. There's no need to tell you how much that is.'

'There are just two things to say in answer to that. I suppose you know what causes babies. If you don't, Bronwen certainly does. If you didn't want to have a family just yet, there are precautions you could have taken to ensure that the increase in your family could have waited a while. Secondly, Charles, you are about to become a father, one of the greatest privileges life can offer. You will find you will be able to manage financially until Bronwen is ready to go back to her nursing. For heaven's sake, man, cheer up. This is not the end of the world. It is the beginning of a new one.'

'Don't get me wrong, Fred. Of course I shall be proud to be a father and especially since Bronwen will be the mother of my child. It's just that she isn't all that strong and I don't want anything to go wrong with the birth.'

'That's a fine thing to say to the husband of the doctor who is going to take care of your wife. As far as I can find out from Eleanor, she is perfectly well and will be in good condition to deliver a child. In any case, if anything appears to be amiss, then I am sure that my wife will see that she goes into hospital and has the expert attention of a consultant. Now, is there anything else you want to say to justify your totally unreasonable attitude to the birth of your child? Bronwen will need all the support that you can give her. I hope you greeted the news from her with enthusiasm, even if you had to manufacture it.'

'I'm sorry, Fred. I'm afraid I was not over-enthusiastic. If it comes to that, neither was she. I promise that I will give her all the support she needs.'

'My dear Charles, as the weeks go by, the truth will dawn on you that you have been blessed, not cursed. You will find that as the time draws near for the birth of the baby, you will get more and more excited. Now, come on, let's go in and say our prayers. That will help you to a true perspective.'

As we went into the church to say our prayers, I felt I had to pray fervently for Bronwen who would have two children by the end of the year. The one with the nappy would be easier to manage than the other.

When I told Eleanor later in the day of his reaction, she said, 'I am not at all surprised. Charles is a very selfish person and he can see that the baby will be a rival for the affection of his beloved Bronwen. What is more, it means that she will have less time to prepare his meals and to iron his shirts and trousers. All we can do is to give them both as much help as possible.'

'By the way,' I replied, 'he said that Bronwen is not all that strong and he did not want anything to go wrong with the birth.'

'Let me tell you this, Frederick. That girl is much stronger than he is. She may be small but physically she will be able to bear a child without any trouble at all. Make no mistake about that. If he were in her position he would not be able to produce a mouse, let alone a child. He would have died of fright when the pains came on. As for anything going wrong with the birth, if there were the slightest indication I should make sure that the best available consultant would be on hand.'

'Those were my exact words, my love, when he mentioned it. I know one thing, he will be suffering from nervous headaches and stomach-aches for the next seven months.'

They began the very next day when he failed to appear at Matins. There had been a complete transformation in his daily pattern after his engagement to Bronwen. He was punctual for all the services and active in the parish. Now I would be hearing one of his favourite phrases, 'Sorry for the lapse, Fred,' repeated several times in the course of the coming months.

All thoughts of Charles and his fatherhood future were quickly dispelled when I returned to the vicarage after morning service. Standing on the doorstep was Councillor David Waters, known to the Pontywen populace as 'Dai Spout'. Resplendent in his black suit, trilby and his shining black boots, he presented a picture of pomposity writ large.

'Good morning, Vicar,' he proclaimed in his best oratorical tones. 'I thought I would catch you when you returned from your service. I wonder if you could spare me some of your precious time.'

'By all means, Councillor Waters. Come on in. I have to take a sick communion at half past ten but I am free until then. Perhaps you would like a cup of tea or a cup of coffee.'

'A cup of tea would suit me nicely. The people's drink.'

'As you please, Councillor. I suppose it depends upon who the people are.'

'Very funny, Vicar,' he said, and followed me into the vicarage.

I decided to take him into the study where I could sit behind my big desk. I wondered why he was being obsequious in his approach to me. Perhaps a little show of power complex on my part would not go amiss. I ushered him into the leather armchair in front of the desk and went into the kitchen to make the tea. When I returned, he was standing up, examining the contents of my bookshelves.

'I see you've got books by William Temple here. You know he was President of the Workers' Educational Association at one time? Great man, great socialist. Pity he died so soon after becoming Archbishop of Canterbury.'

'A great pity. He was a wonderful man.'

I was not going to rise to the bait and declare my political preferences. I felt that I should not make public my allegiance to any party.

'Milk and sugar, Councillor?' I said.

'Not much milk and two spoonfuls, thank you. Nice study you've got here, Vicar. The last time I was in it was when we came to put the banns in for our wedding. Chapel I am, but the wife is Church, as you know. I'm glad my son is getting confirmed next month. I'm all for the youngsters getting a good grounding in Christianity. My trouble is I've had too busy a time with the party on Sundays to be able to go to church. We have all our committee meetings on Sunday mornings. Anyway, I haven't come here to waste your time. So I'll come straight to the point, as it were. I don't know whether you've heard or not but the council has done me the honour of asking me to be mayor at the end of next month. I should have asked you some time ago, but what with one thing and another ... you know how it is. Anyway, I would be very pleased if you would agree to be my chaplain for my year of office.'

As he swallowed his first mouthful of tea, I sat back in my chair and examined the desk, trying to come to terms with the unexpected. Before I could reply, the councillor launched into a job description of the chaplain's duties.

'Let me explain what is involved, Vicar. There would be a civic service here in St Mary's when you would preach the sermon. This would come after the mayor-making at which you would be present. Then the chaplain has to say prayers before each monthly meeting of the Council. Occasionally you would accompany me to various functions – and that's about it. Your good lady wife, Dr Secombe, would be invited to these of course, if she is able to be present. I know what a busy life she has and if she could not attend some of the functions, we would understand. Well, there it is in a nutshell, as it were.'

'It is quite a big nutshell, Councillor Waters, I must say. Thank you very much for inviting me to be your chaplain. It is an honour which I accept. I am afraid that my wife will have to miss some of the functions because of her duties. However, she will be having a partner to join her in the practice next week and accordingly she will have more free time available.'

He stood up and extended his right hand.

'Thank you, Vicar, for accepting this office for the coming year.' He shook my hand warmly. 'I shall look forward to your company. My wife will be very pleased. Well, I had better be off now. I have to get all the arrangements made for my installation, as it were. Perhaps you will let me know what hymns and readings you will be having in the civic service so that we can get everything in hand at the printers. I'll get the mayor's secretary to send you a copy of last year's service to give you some idea of what is involved, as it were.'

As we strolled down the vicarage drive, I wondered how many 'as it were's' I would hear over the next twelve months.

Half an hour later, after a protracted, one-sided conversation with our loquacious daily help, Mrs Watkins, who had arrived just after Dai Spout had left, I made my way to Miss Agnew to bring her the sacrament. Florence Agnew was an elderly spinster whose father had been an archdeacon in Mid Wales. She was a tall, thin lady who spent her waking hours wandering about the ground floor of her large red-brick house, The Knoll, clad in her nightdress and dressing-gown. Her fingers were all bound in sticking plaster and she reeked of brandy. My monthly communion visit to her entailed a quarter of an hour's service and a minimum of an hour's conversation, equally as one-sided as that with Mrs Watkins, but decidedly more interesting. Miss Agnew was a much-travelled lady with tales to tell from the days of the Raj to the heyday of the Kaiser's Germany, with picture albums and illustrations. Eleanor informed me that the sticking plaster on the fingers was quite unnecessary but was one of the badges of her eccentricity.

I had to wait the usual few minutes in the porch after ringing the doorbell. The grass in Miss Agnew's front garden was as high as an elephant's eye and there had been an invasion of thistles into cracks in the concrete path to the front door. When the door was opened, the bouquet of her brandy caressed my nostrils as Miss Agnew bade me good morning. Her long, straggling white hair was cascaded over the shoulders of her navy-blue dressing-gown.

'Come on in, Vicar,' she croaked, and swayed gently ahead of me into the spacious drawing-room where on a table in the bay window reposed a wooden cross in the centre of a spotless white cloth. 'I've got everything ready for you.' She cleared her throat. 'I'm afraid my voice is a little husky this morning. It must be this dry weather. I am trying to keep my throat moist. You must excuse me if my participation in the service is somewhat muffled.'

'Not to worry, Miss Agnew. I'm sure the Lord will hear your every word.'

She eased herself into an armchair at the side of the table and opened the prayer-book which lay on its arm. 'It is the first Sunday after Trinity, this week's Epistle and Gospel, isn't it?'

'It is indeed.'

'I love the Epistle with its message that God is love. When I was a child that was the text which used to be above my bed. It was beautifully embroidered, I wonder where it went. After my father's death when my mother had to move out of the rectory, she disposed of so much because she had to move into a smaller house. That was one of the things that went.'

By now I was ready to begin the service. Every time I came to The Knoll she provided me with a memory recall as an accompaniment to my robing and the preparation of the elements – it was part of the ritual.

The service over, she remained silent in her armchair,

her head bowed, as I cleansed the vessels of my pocket communion set which she had given me when I first came to give her communion.

'Haven't you your own little set like Canon Llewellyn and Father Whittaker?' she had asked. They were my predecessors and had spent many more years in the ministry than I. When I came next to give her communion, there was a parcel on the table with its white cloth and its wooden cross. Inside was an expensive pocket communion set and a card bearing the inscription: 'May we celebrate together the Lord's Supper many more times in the future, Florence Agnew'.

As I took off my surplice and stole, she looked up at me from her armchair, with a wicked glint in her eye, after receiving the holy sacrament.

'Now then, Vicar, would you care for a small brandy and a coffee while we have our tête-à-tête?' It was always the same question. It was always the same reply.

'If you will allow me to make the coffee, Miss Agnew, while you pour the brandy, I shall be delighted.'

The coffee percolator was bubbling merrily when I went into the kitchen. Two coffee cups were waiting to be filled. On the tray, together with the delicate china and sugar bowl, was a plate of cream biscuits.

When I entered the drawing-room bearing the refreshments, the 'small brandy' on a little side-table by the armchair I was to occupy, was half-way up a large brandy glass.

For an hour I listened to Miss Agnew's description of Bavaria in the first decade of the twentieth century. She had a great love of Nuremberg and had made some excellent charcoal sketches of the medieval square below the Kaiser, the imperial castle which dominates the town.

There was Albrecht Dürer's house and an impressive portrayal of the west front of the famous Frauenkirche with its mechanical clock. 'And to think that this lovely city was defiled by that perverted little Austrian for his dreadful rallies in the thirties,' she said bitterly. 'Next time you come I must show you drawings I made of the Passion Play at Oberammergau and of the town of Augsburg.'

As I came down from the hillside where Miss Agnew's house was perched overlooking the town, Nuremberg and its splendour were forgotten when I came back to the reality of 1948 in Pontywen in the person of Bertie Owen who had been a thorn in my flesh ever since I had come to Pontywen. He had been people's warden at St Padarn's for many years until he was voted out of office at the Easter Vestry a year ago. A shop steward at the steelworks, he had carried his imperious attitude into his church activities, only to alienate the bulk of the congregation.

He crossed the road in Balaclava Street, and stood in my path. 'Vicar, just the man I want to see.'

Bertie was the last man I wanted to see.

'What can I do for you, Bertie?' I should have said that I was in a hurry and had to get back to the vicarage. It would have saved me five minutes and a great deal of the unnecessary worry that followed.

'I don't want to be talking like this to you in the street, but it's about Albert Williams.'

'What about Albert Williams, Bertie?'

He looked around the empty street as if it were full of eavesdroppers. Then he came close up to me and spoke in hushed tones. 'He's getting far too friendly with the choir-boys at St Padarn's, some of them have been going round to his house in the evenings.'

Albert Williams was a bachelor who had become the organist at the daughter church, some six months previously. He was a pleasant young man, who worked in the local bank having been excused National Service because he suffered from a mild form of epilepsy called 'petit mal'. Albert had done wonders for the music of St Padarn's and had recruited several boys whom he was training to a high standard of vocal ability. In so doing he had aroused jealousy among the middle-aged and elderly ladies of the choir who felt that they were being pushed into the background. Foremost among them was Agnes Collier, widow of the former organist, and leading soprano soloist for the past thirty years. Somewhat effeminate, Albert was the butt of many remarks from the entire female complement about the 'pansy's' lack of manliness.

'Do you realize, Bertie, that you are making serious allegations without a shred of evidence? At least, I assume that's the case. Has any choir-boy said that anything untoward has happened at his house? In any case, it is not his house, as you know. It is his mother's house and I am sure that would be sufficient guarantee that the boys were there for one purpose only and that is to have their voices trained – something Albert is doing to great effect.'

Bertie's ruddy countenance deepened in colour.

'All I know, Vicar, is that Agnes Collier happened to be passing his place the other night and saw through the window that he had his arm around young David Morris.'

'Agnes Collier had better keep her suspicions to herself. If that is the only evidence she can provide for a very nasty slur on Albert's reputation, she should be ashamed of herself. So should you, Bertie, for passing on such poisonous gossip.'

He began to bluster. 'I was just doing my duty. I thought you should know what was being said. You are the vicar of the parish, after all.'

'Well, as vicar of the parish, I warn you that if I hear any more of this poisonous gossip I shall have to report it to Albert Williams, giving him the names of those responsible for it. Then if he wants to take action against them he can do so. If you will excuse me, Bertie, I have to get back to the vicarage, otherwise I shall be late for lunch.'

When I arrived at the vicarage, Eleanor was back from her rounds and was about to put a parcel of fish and chips in the oven.

'Just in time, love. Fresh from Cascarini's. Two hake cutlets and sixpenn'orth of chips.' As she bent down to put our meal in the oven I gave her a pat on her posterior.

'You naughty vicar,' she said. 'What's that for?'

'Miss Agnew's brandy has inflamed my passions, I am afraid.'

'Don't be afraid, Frederick, but keep them bottled up until this evening for a more convenient time.'

'By the way, my sweet. I have news for you that will make a lunch of fish and chips look very infra dig. Soon we shall be invited to three-course luncheons with wine to wash them down and to the occasional five-course dinner in the evening with even more exotic refreshments.'

'Explain yourself, please. Whence come the invitations to these shindigs?'

'Well, this morning Dai Spout appeared on the doorstep when I came back from Matins, which was curateless, as we expected.'

'Never mind about that! Come to the point, Secombe.'

'"In a nutshell, as it were", to quote the worthy Councillor, he has asked me to be his chaplain for his year of office which begins next month.'

'That's very short notice, Fred. Perhaps he has asked somebody else who has turned him down.'

'It is the end of next month and apparently he had been thinking of asking me but kept putting it off. Most likely because he had a conscience about his non church-going.'

'More than likely. Congratulations, but you realize that it puts an end to our Gilbert and Sullivan participation for the next twelve months.'

'I realize that. The only thing I can do is to have a word with Aneurin. Apparently the English teacher who produces the school play is an accomplished stage director. As for our roles as Marco and Gianetta I am sure we can find replacements. Iorweth Ellis will be only too pleased to take over my part. He will be able to sing it but the stage director will have his work cut out to turn him into an actor. Perhaps Aneurin knows of some experienced soprano who will "do" Gianetta.'

'I suppose it is just as well. What with my new National Health Service commitments and coping with a new partner in the practice, I think I shall have enough on my plate. There will be occasions when I shall not find it possible to come to some of those luncheons you talked about. I shall make sure I manage the dinners.'

As we were eating our fish and chips I mentioned my confrontation with Bertie about Albert Williams.

'That is typical of Agnes Collier. No wonder her best friends address her as "Ag". The trouble about that kind of talk is the comment it draws from the ignorant that "There's no smoke unless there's fire." Do you think you should have a word with Albert about it? Perhaps it would be better if he confined his voice training to the Church chancel. He is such an effeminate young man that anything he does with young boys will give rise to gossip, for the slightest reason.'

'Perhaps I'll do that but it will have to be a passing reference in the vestry or at the organ. If I pay a visit to his home it will make him think that he is the centre of talk in the church. That would mean his resignation and we shall have lost a very good organist and choir-master.'

After lunch I decided to call on Charles – not only to find out why he was not at service that morning but to check whether he had heard the rumour that Bertie Owen had passed on to me. Bronwen opened the door to me when I rang the doorbell. She seemed surprised to see me.

'Charles left here about half an hour ago to see you at the vicarage. I was on early shift at the hospital and left him in bed. Apparently he overslept. He came to the vicarage later on but you were not in. I have given him a good talking-to about slipping back into his old ways. Whether it will do any good or not, I really don't know.'

'Thank you for your support, Bronwen. I shall reinforce what you said to him when I see him. I think I had better do some hospital visiting now. Perhaps you would ask him to come and see me about six o'clock before Eleanor and I have our meal, that is, if it doesn't clash with your arrangements.'

'Certainly not. We shall be eating at five o'clock. I shall see that he is fed and watered by six.'

Promptly at six o'clock Charles was on my doorstep, looking suitably chastened, with his puppy-dog look much in evidence.

'Sorry for the lapse, Fred. I have been here twice to

apologize. First this morning, then this afternoon. I would have been here earlier and would have caught you before you went out but I was held up on my way here. As a matter of fact I would like a few words with you about that.'

'Come on in, you reprobate. I thought the leopard had got rid of his spots. Evidently I was wrong.'

We went into my study as the appetizing odour of Eleanor's cooking began to percolate through the open door of the kitchen.

Before I could sit down in my favourite chair behind my desk, he launched into an elaborate apology, blaming his sleepless night for his late rising and assuring me that it was a one-off hiccup in his regeneration.

'All right, Charles, I am willing to accept the apology, but let me emphasize that if it is the beginning of a slide into your former habits you will have to start looking elsewhere for another curacy. Now then, what about the few words about being held up on your way here?'

'I had got as far as Mafeking Street when I met Mrs Morris – you know, David Morris's mother – the choir-boy in St Padarn's.'

My heart began to sink.

'It seems that young David has been going round to Albert Williams' home for some voice-training. She doesn't mind that – but the last couple of times he has been there he has been coming home at half past nine to ten o'clock. When she asks David why he has been so late, he says that they have been listening to classical music on his radiogram. She says if it happens again, she will have to take David out of the choir.'

'And I thought it was just Agnes Collier,' I said.

## 3

Albert Williams was a rosy-cheeked, bespectacled young man, immaculately dressed, who gave the impression that he had not yet begun to shave, even at the age of twenty-two. His mother, a widow, had been the school nurse until she retired in 1939. Albert was her only child, born to her when she was in her early forties. Her husband Reginald had been a clerk in the rates office and was known locally as Reg the Spats because of his penchant for that item of dress. He had died at the outbreak of the war, only weeks before Henrietta's retirement. Since then Albert had been the victim of what old Canon Llewellyn had termed 'smother love'. He had no school-friends and his leisure time was devoted to the piano and his Raleigh bicycle on which he was accompanied by his mother on the machine which had taken her around the schools in the Pontywen area. At weekends they would be seen riding out into the rural scenery which lay beyond the town.

They lived in a small semi-detached house in Ashburnham Close, one of the few non-terraced streets in Pontywen. Nurse Williams, as she was known to the local inhabitants, was a regular attendant at the parish church, and Albert had been a member of the choir since his early boyhood. After the sudden death of Mr Collier, the organist at St Padarn's Church, there was a hiatus which a volunteer organist, Miss Usher, filled inadequately. Albert had been practising on the organ at the parish church for some years and acted as a very accomplished deputy to Mr Greenfield, the regular organist. After some weeks of Miss Usher, I felt that the congregation at St Padarn's deserved better than her thud and blunder. Accordingly I invited Albert to take over as organist and choirmaster in the daughter church. In a few weeks there was a marked improvement in the quality of the music and in no time at all there were six extra choir-boys. It was a success story bitterly resented by Mrs Agnes Collier, who could see her soloist status of thirty years' standing being usurped by young David Morris, the leading choir-boy.

After Charles's encounter with Mrs Morris I decided to abandon my idea of a casual remark in the vestry or the chancel and instead to have a word with Albert at his home. 'The sooner the better in that case,' suggested Eleanor. 'Otherwise you have the making of a scandal which will damage St Padarn's much more than Miss Usher's dreadful organ-playing. Why not go this evening after dinner?'

As I entered Ashburnham Close, there was the sound of lawn-mowers at work in the dying sunshine. Expensive cars were parked in the drives. At the end of the cul-de-sac was the little three-up and three-down house with its neighbour, the only 'semis' in a small road of detached residences housing the elite of Pontywen from the manager of the steelworks to the owner of the local bus company. I pushed open the green wooden gate which bore the name 'Chatsworth' on the metal plate nailed to its top. The little lawn was immaculately mown and in its centre was a flower-bed featuring three standard rose trees with buds ready to burst into bloom. From inside the house piano music could be faintly heard.

By the time I had rung the doorbell, I was beginning to regret my instant decision to confront Albert. The appearance of his stern-faced mother at the door did little to help my rapidly diminishing self-confidence. She had always been a martinet in the clinics and was even more so at home.

'Good evening, Vicar!' she said, showing no sign of pleasure at my appearance. 'What brings you here at this time of night?' Considering that it was only half past eight, it was not an auspicious start to my errand.

'I have come to have a chat with Albert about the – er – music in St Padarn's.'

'There's nothing wrong with it, I hope,' she snapped.

'Not at all. On the contrary, it is very good, excellent, in fact.'

On hearing that, she invited me in. Albert was in the middle of a loud passage in a Chopin sonata and she had to tap twice on the door of the front room before he heard her knock. He stopped playing and shouted, 'What is it, Mother? Am I playing too loudly?'

'The vicar is here to see you.' With that she opened the door and ushered me in.

'Vicar! What an unexpected pleasure,' said the young man. 'Take a pew, as you might say.'

'I'll leave you two then to your business.' So saying, his mother disappeared into the back part of the house.

I sat down in an armchair near the window. He left the piano stool and sat opposite me in the other armchair.

'Sorry to interrupt your Chopin, Albert. I suppose it was Chopin, by the way?'

'Oh yes, it was Chopin. One of his polonaises, no. 53. I enjoy playing those compositions. A lot of his patriotism went into them.'

'Very interesting.' I said. 'I was somewhat wary about identifying the composer, having learned a lesson from the warden of my college. Two students would be invited for coffee with that important gentleman every Sunday evening to listen to a weekly music recital on the wireless. My friend and I were his guests on one occasion. He turned on the set just after the piano music had begun. A few minutes later, in a break between the movements, he said to us, "I do love Chopin." A quarter of an hour later, as the performance ended, the announcer informed us that the composer was Beethoven. The warden didn't turn a hair. "Now then," he said, "shall we have some coffee after that beautiful Beethoven?" I am afraid I could never do that. I should want to find the nearest hole to bury myself. That is why I could never become warden of a college, amongst other drawbacks on my part.'

'You mentioned coffee, Vicar. Would you care for a cup of coffee?'

'No, thank you. I have just come from drinking two cupfuls at the vicarage. In any case I don't want to interrupt your enjoyment of the polonaises for too long. I have just popped in to have a word about young David Morris.'

His face paled.

'It seems that his mother told Mr Wentworth-Baxter that unless he comes home earlier from his voice training with you, she will have to take him from the choir. I thought you ought to know, especially since he is such a gifted boy soprano.'

The colour began to return to his countenance.

'He is a very promising lad and his voice is of cathedral quality. It would be a tragedy to lose him. I suppose it is my fault – I have been encouraging a love of music in him by playing classical stuff, orchestral and vocal, on the radiogram and that has made him rather late leaving here. You can tell Mrs Morris that I shall see he is home early from now on.'

'If you don't mind me saying so, it would be wiser if you confined your voice training to the chancel. In that way there would be no come-back from Mrs Morris or anybody else.'

'What do you mean by "anybody else", Vicar? I hope no one has been suggesting that there has been something going on in my relationship with David Morris or any other choir-boy, come to that. If that is so I had better resign and finish with it.'

'Now, calm down, Albert, and stop talking about resigning. That would make it appear that something had been "going on", as you put it. You are doing a splendid job with the choir. It would be a great pity if that came to a stop. I am simply saying that choir practice is best carried on in the church, including individual tuition or whatever.'

He was silent for a while. Then he turned around and faced me.

'I suppose you are right, Vicar. I know very well what some of those old dears in the choir are like. From now on, I shall keep to the church premises for all my practices and voice training – then nobody can say anything.'

'Very wise, Albert. Now I'll leave you to get on with your Chopin.' We shook hands and he saw me to the door.

As I was about to close the gate, I looked up and saw his mother peering out of the bedroom window from behind a curtain. I wondered whether I should have told him to say nothing to her about the purpose of my visit.

I mentioned this to Eleanor when I returned to the vicarage. 'You can't very well tell a son to keep confidences from his mother, Fred. I expect she was straight down the stairs as soon as you had left to find out what happened. By the way, I find it strange that she knocked on the door of the front room to get permission to enter. It is not at all like her to do that. I'm sure it is just as well that you have ended this front-room session with David Morris in view of that. Perhaps young Albert is not as much under his mother's thumb as we had thought.'

Next morning I had a visit from Mr Victor Thomas, the diocesan secretary of the Church of England Men's Society. He was a bombastic gentleman, short, rotund, with dark hair, plastered with brilliantine and parted down the middle. He wore large horn-rimmed spectacles and sported a carefully manicured slimline moustache. A pair of spats adorned the top of his shiny black shoes beneath his immaculate black pin-stripe suit. He carried his Anthony Eden trilby in his hand.

'Ah, Vicar. I hoped I might catch you in. I should have made an appointment, I know, but I happened to be in the vicinity and took a chance. I wonder if I might have a word with you about the CEMS. I shall only keep you a few minutes.' I had heard about Victor's 'five minutes', which could over-run by half an hour at least.

'Come on in, Mr Thomas, I can only give you a few minutes anyway. I have to go to an important meeting at the town hall.' The important meeting was simply to hand in the order of service I had compiled to the mayor's secretary.

Mr Thomas was suitably impressed. 'Of course, you are to be the new mayor's chaplain, aren't you? Quite an honour, Vicar.'

'I don't know about that. The one thing I do know is that the next twelve months will be very busy for me.'

He made himself comfortable in the armchair opposite the desk in my study, as if he was fully prepared to multiply 'the few minutes'.

'Well,' he said, making an expansive gesture with his left hand, 'I suppose you could call this an important meeting. I have been looking up the records and I find that you had a branch of CEMS in this parish some twenty years ago, until it was closed down by the late Canon Llewellyn. With all the men returning from the Forces, our committee is planning a big drive to attract them to the Church – just the right time to revive the branch in your parish.'

His whole attitude and appearance riled me. 'And what are to be the attractions to bring men hardened by the war into the Church?' The tone of my voice opened his eyes wide behind his horn-rimmed glasses. He began to stammer a reply.

'Oh – er, we are putting together a list of speakers on interesting topics. For example, we have just persuaded the headmaster of one of the grammar schools to join our panel. He is going to talk about the origin of place-names in South Wales. We've got an ornithologist to give an illustrated lecture on rare birds, and so on. Then, of course, we have our big rally at the Cathedral once a year.'

'I am told, Mr Thomas, that you always manage to arrange it on Cup Final day when most men will be glued to their wireless sets.'

'You've got to have a sense of priority, Vicar. A rally at the Cathedral is much more important than the Cup Final.'

'I am sorry, but I shall certainly not "revive" the branch in this parish. If it had been a live one, Canon Llewellyn would not have closed it down. On the other hand I am thinking of organizing a men's club, with their own club tie. It will meet in the back room of a pub where they can listen to a speaker on some really interesting topic with a pint in their hands instead of a lukewarm cup of tea in a draughty church hall. We could arrange club outings and an occasional cricket match. I think that will be a better way to attract men into the church in Pontywen than your way of doing it.'

He lay back in the armchair with his mouth open, apparently searching for words which refused to come out. After a brief pause he recovered his wits and launched into an attack upon me. 'Well, Vicar, I must say your attitude shocks me. Yes, "shock" is the word. To think of substituting the public house for the church hall. Well, I must say. Whatever next! I suppose before long you will be advocating church services in public houses. I can only hope that none of the other younger clergy follow your example. It will be God help our churches if they do. Good morning, Vicar.'

Mr Victor Thomas spat the word 'Vicar' and was out of the study before I could show him to the door. As he strode up the drive, I noticed his trilby by the armchair. Opening the study window, I shouted, 'Mr Thomas, you have forgotten your hat.' He came to a halt as quickly as a Welsh guardsman on parade and stood facing the vicarage gate. I picked up his hat and dashed to the front door which he had left open, to find him still standing, but now in an about-turn position, waiting to receive his precious trilby. He glared at me and snapped a 'thank you'. I caught hold of his arm. 'Shall we at least shake hands, Mr Thomas?' I asked. 'I'm sorry if I offended you but at least you know where I stand now.' I offered him my right hand which he seemed to regard with suspicion. After a pause he put a limp hand into mine and then withdrew it as quickly as possible. He said no more but turned on his heels, rammed his hat on his head and disappeared into Church Street. I was never troubled with him again, unlike most of my fellow incumbents.

When I returned to the study, I sat at my desk, thinking over the idea of a men's club. The name is going to be important, I said to myself, something snappy and easily remembered. We had not long finished celebrating the centenary of St Mary's Church. Why not something connected with that? It could hardly be called the Centenary Club, but what about – the Centurion's Club? The more I thought about it, the more attractive it sounded.

By the time Mrs Watkins, our daily, had prepared lunch, I had formulated a programme of activities, and decided on a suitable venue, the Prince of Wales on the outskirts of Pontywen. The landlord, Jim Pritchard, was a nominal churchman and moreover the pub had a large meeting room at the back which was used for rehearsals by the Pontywen Silver Band. When Eleanor arrived after her stint of home visits, I was all set to launch into details of the new club, but the look of distress on her face as she came in the house put an end to that.

'What's the matter, love?' I asked. 'You look as if you have had some kind of a shock.'

'I suppose you could say that. Let's get in the house and I'll tell you all about it. I think a snort of whisky is called for.'

We went into the sitting-room where I poured her a large scotch with one for myself. 'This one is just to keep you company,' I said.

Her face relaxed for a moment. 'Aren't you glad I needed a stimulant, Frederick?' She collapsed into an armchair. 'Well,' she went on, 'you will be surprised to know that my intended partner in the practice has written to me at the surgery to say that he will not be joining me next week or any other week. He has been offered a much more lucrative post in the posh part of Cardiff. It came out of the blue, he says. He apologizes for letting me down but hopes that I shall soon find somebody else to fill the gap. What am I going to do, Fred? Now that the National Health Service has started, we have been snowed under with patients wanting to join the practice, as you know. The paperwork alone is mountainous. What am I to do?'

'I think the first thing you have to do is to give your father a ring,' I said firmly. Eleanor's father was a doctor in practice further up the Valley in delightfully rural surroundings, and serving a prosperous little market town. An ex-miner, he adored his daughter, an only child, of whom he was inordinately proud, unlike his wife who came from a middle-class background and had resented Eleanor's marriage to a clergyman of humble origin.

'The first thing to do is to tuck into Mrs Watkins' shepherd's pie, and then I shall feel fortified to have a word with my father.'

'Perhaps he will come back to Pontywen and work in partnership with you,' I suggested.

'You must be joking. Can you imagine my mother coming back to the smoke and the common people of this town? She hated every minute of their time here in this place. She certainly will not exchange her social life with the hunting and shooting set for incarceration in

Pontywen. My only hope is that Daddy will know some-body somewhere who will be able to help.'

Half an hour later she was on the telephone to her father while I eavesdropped through the open door of my study, pretending to tidy up the chaos of papers on my desk. After ten minutes or so the tone of her voice changed from solicitude to reassurance. 'I'll wait to hear from you then,' she said, and put the phone down. Her face was transformed when she came into the study.

'Thank God for fathers,' I commented.

'Fred, my love, I say "Amen" to that. He said that only this morning he heard from a friend of his that his son was coming out of the Army and was looking for work as a locum. He is going to get in touch with him later today and will let me have the son's address and home number this evening.' She caught hold of me and hugged me so tightly that I thought my rib-cage was going to crack.

'Put me down, you monster,' I commanded. 'You don't know your own strength, a little girl like you. You should be ashamed of yourself.'

'His name is Gareth Andrews, and he trained at Bart's. Daddy said that he met him when he was on leave a few years ago and that he seems an agreeable bloke, as he put it so charmingly. So let's keep our fingers crossed.'

'I should put your hands together as well. I shall certainly do so.'

'By all means, Frederick. I'll stand on my head as well, if necessary.'

What with hands together and fingers crossed, that evening the post in the Pontywen practice was filled. Eleanor phoned Gareth Andrews at his officers' mess in Aldershot and he agreed to the terms she offered him. He was due to be 'demobbed' in a month's time and was looking forward to coming out into the civilian world. He was engaged to be married to a Cardiff girl and until they could find a house in the vicinity he would stay with her parents in Cardiff, travelling up the Valley each day.

To celebrate the occasion, Eleanor and I went out to dinner at the Tudor Arms, where we had had our wedding breakfast-cum-lunch. It was a mock Tudor building erected in the thirties to cater for the elite of the Valleys. This was our first visit there since that milestone in our lives. We were shown to a table for two in an alcove. As we were studying the menu, I heard the loud and unmistakable tones of the rural dean, the Reverend Daniel Thomas, BA, RD. as his notepaper described him.

'Oh, no!' I exclaimed.

'Just keep our heads down and they might not see us,' suggested Eleanor.

'Hello, Vicar!' bellowed the dignitary. 'Fancy seeing you and your good lady! Would you care to join us?'

There was no escape. The waiter showed us to a table for four. Mrs Rural Dean was a fresh-faced, comfortably figured lady with a pleasant smile. Her spouse was a squat little man with a grey, lined face surmounted by a few straggling hairs on his bald head. His beady little eyes were protected by eyebrows which had more hairs than the total of those above.

'Well, well! Fancy meeting you two here. Is it a special occasion or do you come here often?'

I was tempted to say 'Only in the mating season' but I restrained myself.

Eleanor spoke up. 'We have something to celebrate too. I have been without a partner in my very busy practice for the past six months and this evening I have found someone who will be joining me in a month's time.'

'Isn't that good?' said the rural dean to his wife. 'Doctor Seaborne has been doing some very fine work in Pontywen, so I hear – like her husband. Well done, both of you.'

The waiter was hovering behind us. 'Would you care to order some wine?' he asked.

'Let's have some champagne to mark the occasion,' Eleanor suggested.

The rural dean looked at the wine list and his grey face went white.

'Well, we don't drink champagne, only wine. I'm wondering if it will be too strong for driving home afterwards.'

'It's not all that strong,' replied my wife. 'Please allow us to treat you to some. It's not often that we have something like this to celebrate.'

The rural dean's visage returned to its normal grey colour and his beady eyes shone in anticipation of a rare indulgence. 'That's very kind of you, I must say. I think the last time we had champagne was at the wedding of Lord and Lady Llangennith's daughter. She got married in our church in 1935.'

'1936,' corrected his wife with a little smile.

'Was it? I could have sworn it was the year that our sweet peas took first prize at the Abergavenny Flower Show.'

'That was 1937, dear. The same year as the Coronation. Don't you remember our roses came out just in time to decorate the tables in the church hall for the celebration tea? Then, later on, the sweet peas came on in leaps and bounds in time for the show. It was our best year in the garden.'

'I don't know about that. I think 1942 was easily the best. We had that lovely summer after that very cold winter. The flowers may not have been at their best but the vegetables were magnificent. Remember those cauliflowers? One of those would have been enough to feed a family, just on its own, done with some cheese, Doctor Seaton.'

'And do you know why that was the case? The septic tank at the bottom of the garden had overflowed and as the cauliflowers were planted next to it, they had manuring good enough to grow giant plants.'

By this time the wine waiter had arrived with the champagne and the horticultural discussion came to a timely end. Throughout the meal the Reverend Daniel Thomas and his wife continued the duologue, to the quiet amusement of Eleanor and myself. It was a cabaret show *par excellence*.

'Well, thank you both,' said the rural dean as we went into the car park after the meal. 'I hope I shall be able to drive straight after that champagne.'

'It's the corners you've got to watch, Dan, isn't it, Vicar? Any fool can drive straight.'

This remark from Mrs Thomas, delivered with a smile, did not amuse her husband as he struggled with the lock on his car door.

Once inside his precious Morris Oxford which he cherished even more than his garden, he switched on the ignition, to be met with a deathly rattle. After several attempts to start the car while Eleanor and I watched from her new Morris Minor, he dismounted and opened up the bonnet. He stared at the interior in the fading light and then fiddled with the plugs. Back in the car, he tried to arouse the sleeping engine. To no avail.

'Look at your hands, Dan,' said his spouse. 'They are filthy. You'll be having that muck all over your best suit if you're not careful.'

'Never mind my suit, woman,' shouted the dignitary. 'How are we going to get back home?'

'I think the time has come', suggested Eleanor, 'to make ourselves useful.'

'What do you mean?' I asked. 'I don't know one plug from another.'

'Calm down, Frederick. What I am proposing is a tow of their car back to Pentwyn Vicarage. Perhaps the hotel can lend us a rope of some kind. If the rural dean doesn't fancy guiding his car behind ours, you can guide it while I drive.'

'Thank you very much, Eleanor. Let him try a few more times to get the thing started.'

After a few more times the battery surrendered and a deathly silence prevailed.

'You had better come with me to the hotel,' I said to my wife. 'Your female charms will be more effective than my dog collar.'

I went across to the despairing rural dean who was slumped over the wheel of his car, looking into space. 'We are going to see if the hotel can lend us a rope to tow you back home,' I announced.

'Isn't that kind?' said Mrs Thomas. Her husband grunted.

The manager responded to the plaintive appeal of my beloved immediately and produced a tow-rope from a garage at the back of the hotel.

With the help of one of the menials the rope was attached between the two cars.

'Would you like me to guide the car or would you prefer to do it yourself?' I asked the Reverend Daniel Thomas.

'You know what your sight is like, Dan,' said his wife. 'And there is no light coming from your head-lamps. I think you ought to let the vicar take over.'

He offered no objection and moved into the back of the car with Mrs Thomas as if resigned to his fate.

Eleanor switched on the head-lamps of her car with Mrs Thomas as the rural dean's car slithered across the car park.

'You've still got the hand-brake on!' he shouted.

'Sorry, Mr Rural Dean,' I murmured. I fumbled with the brake. By now Eleanor was out of her car and was banging on the window.

'What are you doing?' she demanded.

'I'm afraid I still had the hand-brake on.'

'Then take it off,' she ordered.

'I've done it,' I said.

'Pull the window down. I can't hear you.'

I pulled the window down. 'I've done it, I said.'

'Well, don't shout. We'll move off now and for God's sake keep your eyes on my rear lights! Sorry, Mr Rural Dean,' she added.

As she moved off, I stared as if mesmerized by the lights in front of me. In fairness to Eleanor she drove slowly, but in spite of that, there were bumps in the road where the rural dean's car seemed to disagree with what was happening in front.

Half an hour later Eleanor approached the entrance to Pentwyn Vicarage. It was on a sharp right-hand bend. There was a loud crunch as the car I was steering came in contact with the vicarage gate-post.

'Stop!' I shouted, but the car in front proceeded down the drive. Another clang and the vicarage car broke free of its restraint, making for its home base. As we pulled up outside the haven where it would be, the Reverend Daniel Thomas leaped out of the car with an agility which belied his years.

He dashed into the vicarage porch, frantically putting the key in the front door and then switching on the outside light.

'Look at my car,' he moaned. 'The whole of that door is bashed in. It will never be the same again.'

'I'm sure it will,' said my wife reassuringly. 'Your insurance will cover all the repair to the damage. In a month or so, it will be as good as new.'

'There you are, Dan. The doctor knows. So don't worry!' Mrs Thomas spoke as if there had been a medical check-up.

As we drove away, I said to my wife, 'I don't know what I would do without you.'

'You can say that again,' she replied. 'How else would you escape the consequences of your clerical errors?'

# 4

'First of all, have you brought with you a card or a sheet of paper with your Christian name printed in big block letters?' The candidates assembled in the nave of St Mary's for the rehearsal of the confirmation looked blankly at me when I asked the question. As each confirmee knelt before the bishop, it had been the custom for the clergymen presenting them to announce the Christian name to the dignitary which he would then repeat before laying his hands upon the head of the candidate. Apparently some of the clergy had not been audible on occasions, causing the bishop embarrassment by having to ask again for the name. There were instances when the candidate was given a name by the bishop which he or she did not possess. In order to avoid further trouble of this nature, we were instructed that the clergyman responsible for the presentation should hold up a card or sheet of paper with the name printed in large capital letters.

Charles Wentworth-Baxter broke the silence with a cough.'I'm sorry, Vicar,' he mumbled, 'but I'm afraid it slipped my mind to tell them.' I had given him responsibility for the preparation of the thirty candidates who had been in his charge for six months of weekly classes in the church hall. The rehearsal was being held on the Friday before the Sunday evening when the service was due to take place.

'In that case,' I said to them, 'it is just as well that we are having this run through the service tonight. You can cut out a piece of cardboard or a piece of paper about twice the size of a postcard and print the Christian name by which you are known in big thick letters – just the one Christian name.'

One boy put up his hand. 'Please, sir, what if you have a long Christian name but everybody calls you by a short name?'

'That's all right, Monty. Just put Monty, it would take a big piece of card to spell Montgomery. Anyway, everybody calls Field Marshal Montgomery "Monty", don't they?' Monty Jones blushed with pride at being identified with the great war hero.

Another boy raised his hand. It was Llewellyn Waters. 'I'm not shortening my name, Vicar. My mother says that Llewellyn is the name I was given, not Llew which sounds common in any case.' I was beginning to regret my acceptance of the chaplaincy to his father already. The boy's priggish statement was ironic in view of the fact that his father was known throughout Pontywen as Dai Spout.

'Very well, Llewellyn. That's enough about names. Now let's get down to the service. I am going to pretend that I am the bishop, and Mr Wentworth-Baxter will bring each one of you to kneel in front of me on the chancel step where this kneeler is placed. Remember to bow to the bishop before you kneel down. Don't forget to kneel upright. Then when you have been confirmed get up and bow to the bishop once more. Then go back to your pew and say your prayers, thanking God for what he has done for you. By the way, girls, you may curtsey to the bishop if you wish, rather than bow. Boys will come forward first, the boy on the end moving back into the aisle so that the furthest in is the first in each pew to come forward to be confirmed. The same thing with the girls.'

Only Charles could turn this simple procedure into a farce. It began when he proceeded to go to the last row of boys instead of the front row. Having been told to go to the front row, he propelled the boy at the end of the row forward for confirmation, despite a remonstration from the candidate that he was supposed to move back, not forward. 'Jimmy is quite right, Mr Wentworth-Baxter. The boys come out in reverse order, remember.'

'Of course, Vicar, my apologies.' When it came to the rehearsal ritual of confirmation, the curate was so anxious to keep the momentum of candidates coming forward that he was causing the waiting boy to collide with the boy who had just arisen, forgetting that he had to bow to His Lordship before going back to his place.

I decided to avoid any unseemly confusion of this sort on Sunday by announcing that I would shepherd the candidates from the pews and that the curate would present them to the bishop since he was responsible for preparing them for confirmation.

'There's one other thing,' I said when the rehearsal was over. 'I understand that the bishop these days will question you about the catechism. I am sure that Mr Wentworth-Baxter has given you a good grounding in that over the past six months. So don't be afraid to speak up when the time comes.'

Mr Wentworth-Baxter's face dropped at the news. As soon as the candidates had gone, he came up to me. 'I didn't know that the bishop was going to catechize them. If I had been aware of that I would have given them a refresher course over the past few weeks. Is he going to ask questions of them as a group or is he going to pick on one individual?'

'I have no idea, Charles. Anyway, you know His Lordship. If he does ask a question of an individual he will do so kindly, I am positive. I shouldn't lose any sleep over it, if I were you. All you have to do is to hold the cards the right way up and to check that they have brought them with them in the first place. If they haven't, you had better have some material ready for last-minute printing. I suppose you have seen Miss Wright about the veils for the girls.'

Miss Wright was an elderly lady who had been responsible for the confirmation veils for the girls and ladies for many years.

'I'm afraid I haven't, Fred. In any case she will have them ready. She knows the service is on Sunday.'

'That is not the point, Charles. Miss Wright is the kind of person who loves to be visited by the clergy, whether it is just a pastoral call or simply to show interest in what she is doing for the church. Just pop in sometime tomorrow, please.' It was a very disgruntled curate who left the church that evening.

When I told Eleanor about the disgruntlement, she suggested that we should invite Charles and Bronwen to tea with the bishop. It was the custom in Pontywen to have refreshments in the church hall after the service when the bishop would sign the little devotional manuals presented to the candidates. It was also the custom for the vicar to have the company of His Lordship at tea before the service in the evening.

'Perhaps that will appease him. Besides, it will give Bronwen a break from the house. I think her morning sickness has been getting her down, though she would be the last to admit it. She is a tough little girl.'

'She needs to be, my love, with Charles as her husband. If he had a quarter of her quality, I would be happy.'

'Well, Frederick, he hasn't, and it is pointless wishing it were otherwise. Now then, what about you? Have you been to Protheroe the butcher to collect the tongue for his holy highness's sandwiches?'

'Sorry, love. I'll be there first thing tomorrow after Matins, I promise you.'

'I don't know how you have the nerve to persecute your poor downtrodden curate about not doing his duty when you can't carry out promises yourself, you tyrant.'

Next morning I was standing at the back of an impatient queue in the butcher's shop while Jack Protheroe and his wife endeavoured to cope with serving meat and cutting the necessary coupons out of the ration books as quickly as they could. To my dismay I was joined by Agnes Collier who pounced upon me with as much relish as a hungry hawk finding its prey.

'Vicar! Just the man I wanted to see.' She spoke in quiet, confidential tones which boded ill. 'Perhaps we could have a word once we have been served. I can't discuss it here with you in the shop. How is Dr Secombe? I very rarely see her these days now that you are at the vicarage. She must be very busy with this new National Health starting.' Before I could reply to her question about Eleanor's state of health she continued her one-sided conversation. 'Confirmation tomorrow, isn't it? Only seven from St Padarn's. Things are going downhill fast. It was fifteen last time but that was when you were curate. It used to be even more than that before the war. Still, everything was different then. No coupons, no queues.'

By now I was resigned to a half-hour's verbal battering with a possible load of trouble awaiting me once we left the shop. Suddenly deliverance came, the butcher had noticed me at the tail-end of the queue. He produced a parcel of meat from the refrigerator. 'You'd better have this now, Vicar. It will save you waiting.'

There were loud comments from the irate customers. 'It's all right for some.' 'Where's his coupons?'

'Now then, ladies,' shouted Jack Protheroe. 'Fair's fair. The vicar ordered this two days ago and the coupons have been seen to.'

I made my way through the throng and was waylaid by Mrs Collier as I was about to leave the shop. 'What about that talk I wanted with you?' she asked.

'Come and see me at the vicarage on Monday morning.' I thought it wiser to have the encounter on my territory rather than hers.

'In that case, you'll have to give me time to finish my washing, Vicar.'

'Is twelve o'clock convenient for you?'

'I think I can manage it by then. If I can't you'll have to allow me to be a bit late.'

'Not to worry, Mrs Collier.' The later, the better, I said to myself. Then there will be less time to have to listen to whatever she is trying to stir up. For the time being it would be enough to cope with the confirmation service and the visit of the bishop.

Charles had been delighted at the invitation to tea with the bishop. 'It will be a chance for Bronwen to meet His Lordship. Perhaps it will help to change her mind about confirmation.' So far she had been unwilling to take the step. Her allegiance to the Baptist Church had been very strong and her non-attendance at Holy Communion had been the source of much comment at St Padarn's. Her church-going so far had been limited to Evensong.

Sunday morning had dawned warm and sultry. As the

day went on it became hot, and the one o'clock news on the wireless was punctuated by thunder crackles. By the time Mrs Watkins arrived at three o'clock to help with preparation for the tea-party, the sky had turned an inky blue and the first rumbles had began to roll around the hills. 'It do look as if we're in for one of those tropical storms they are forecasting,' she said. 'You should see the lightning further down the valley.'

The next minute there was a blinding flash and a crash of thunder which shook the house. Then the heavens opened and emptied themselves upon Pontywen. For the next half-hour the storm raged, punctuated by fearful forked lightning and a barrage of thunder-claps. A river of water streamed down the vicarage drive.

'It reminds me of Father Whittaker's famous fête,' I said to Eleanor. My predecessor had organized a fête on the vicarage lawn only to be confronted with a similar 'tropical' storm.

'More to the point,' answered my wife, 'it reminds me that one of us had better get down to 13 Mount Pleasant View and bring Charles and Bronwen. A few steps outside the door and they would be soaked to the skin.'

'I'll go. You will need to be here with Mrs Watkins to get the tea ready. The bishop will be here before long, that is, if his car has not been swept off the road by the floods.'

The streets of Pontywen were awash with rainwater as I drove down to the curate's house. Not a soul was to be seen. I pressed on the horn when I arrived. Charles appeared at the front-room window and gave me the thumbs-up sign. A cascade was pouring down the steps when the couple came out huddled under Charles's big umbrella. Inevitably my hapless curate was unable to close the umbrella after Bronwen had been seated in the car.

'Get in, Charles,' I ordered, 'and leave it on the pavement.' Then I made a quick dash from my driving seat, seized it and attempted to close the thing as the rain fell in torrents. I failed to do so. By now exasperated, I told Charles to open his window and hold the extended top as close as possible to the window as he could. I drove off to the vicarage with the umbrella like some large excrescence clinging to the side of the car. We were greeted by Eleanor standing on the doorstep with a look of bewilderment on her face.

'What on earth are you doing, Charles?' she asked. 'The car doesn't need the umbrella. It's meant for you.'

'Let's get in first, then we'll explain,' I said before Charles could answer. He got out holding the umbrella under which Bronwen sheltered. Then I dashed through the downpour to join them.

'Don't close it,' said Eleanor, 'leave it open in the porch for the rain to drain off it.'

'Leaving it open is the easy option,' I replied. 'You try closing it.'

No sooner had we entered the house than the telephone rang. It was the bishop phoning from a call-box. 'I'm afraid I shall be late arriving. There has been severe flooding in the lower part of the valley and the police have advised me to come to you via a circuitous route which will bring me to Pontywen from the top end. Don't worry, Vicar. I am sure I shall be able to make it in time for the service. This deluge can't last much longer.'

'It never rains but it pours,' remarked my wife when I passed on the news.

By six o'clock the storm had passed and the sun shone

once more, but there was no sign of the bishop. We had decided to hold our tea-party without him, leaving him a generous helping of tongue sandwiches and Mrs Watkins' home-made cake for whenever he arrived. The service was due to take place at half past six. So as soon as the rain stopped we made our way across to the church, skirting the pools on the drive.

Already the vestry was full of excited girls who had come to have their veils fixed by Miss Wright. She was involved in an altercation with one of them, Desiree Jones, who was holding a veil, on the verge of tears. 'She wants to wear that thing,' snapped the elderly veil supervisor. 'Show it to the vicar, girl.' Desiree held up the 'thing', a headdress much more suited to a bride than a candidate for confirmation. 'My mother bought it for me specially,' she said, her lower lip quivering. 'Miss Wright says it's to show off but it isn't, Vicar, honest. It's my mother's present for my confirmation.'

'I tell you what, Desiree, we'll ask the bishop when he comes if he minds you wearing it.' Knowing His Lordship, I was certain that by passing the buck to him she would be allowed to wear her mother's present and I would not incur Miss Wright's wrath for granting her permission to be different from the other girls.

A few minutes later a harassed bishop arrived, escorted by David Vaughan-Jenkins, the churchwarden who carried the episcopal case. 'What an afternoon!' exclaimed the dignitary. 'At one time I thought I would be stranded in a patch of water when it seemed to engulf the bottom half of the car. Fortunately the engine kept going and I made it to the outside. The next thing that happened was that I was unable to apply the brakes and had to wait for them to dry out. However, here I am, all in one piece but more than a little weary. I am afraid I shall not be able to stay long after the service, if you will excuse me.'

'Of course, my lord. We are only too pleased that you were able to get here under the circumstances.' As he was about to open his case on the vestry table, I motioned to Desiree to come forward. All the other girls had gone to their places in the nave. 'I wonder if you could spare a moment to look at this young lady's veil, my lord. Her mother bought it as a present for her, not realizing that the veils were supplied by the church. I'm afraid it is rather ornate and very different from those that the rest of the candidates are wearing.'

He turned around, looked at the veil and then looked at Desiree. 'My dear, if it is your mother's present, you wear it.'

Her face was transformed. A smile of delight spread across her features. There was a transformation too in Miss Wright, who was standing by with the standard veil in her hand. She flung it into the open box and stalked out of the vestry.

'Can I put it on myself?' inquired the candidate. 'I have tried it on at home.'

'Of course,' I said. 'Use that mirror in the corner.' A minute later a happy young lady left to join her friends, prepared like a bride adorned for her husband.

'I hope you don't mind, my lord, but I have asked Ezekiel Evans, the lay reader, to act as your chaplain, while I marshal the candidates and Charles Wentworth-Baxter presents them. He has been responsible for the preparation.'

'Not at all, Vicar. I am sure Mr Evans will make an adequate chaplain.'

A tap on my vestry door at that moment heralded the

arrival of the self-important chaplain, bursting with pride at the honour bestowed upon him. 'Hi 'ope, hi ham not h'intruding,' said the face which had appeared around the door. The momentous occasion was producing a plethora of misplaced aspirates.

'Come on in, Mr Evans,' I said. 'The bishop will be glad of your assistance. Perhaps you will excuse me, my lord, while I check that all the candidates have arrived and have settled down in the nave.'

'By all means,' replied His Lordship. 'Mr Evans, I should be pleased if you would help me with my robes.' Ezekiel's cup was overflowing.

I went out to join Charles who was hovering around the chancel steps where the chair had been placed in readiness for the bishop. 'Do you think I have put it too near the edge?' he asked.

'Of course not,' I replied. 'If you put it any further back he would need arms like a gorilla to reach the heads of the candidates. More importantly, have you checked that they have all brought cards with their names on them?'

'Yes, they have all done that except that some of them have used fancy block capitals more appropriate for scrolls than anything else, but I think the bishop will be able to read them.'

As I surveyed the boys with their scrubbed faces and their neatly parted hair I noticed that Llewellyn Waters had plastered his hair with Brylcreem or some such hair oil. 'If His Lordship puts his hands on his head, then on the heads of the girls in their veils, it will take Miss Wright weeks to get the grease out. She is already in high dudgeon. You had better make him the first to be confirmed, Charles, and by the time the bishop has finished with the other boys, most of the grease will have come off on their nice clean hair.'

The son and heir of the future mayor was removed from the back row of the candidates and transferred to the front pew whose occupants had to be removed to accommodate him in the furthermost place. Evidently he thought the move was due to his important status. He stood up and looked around at his mother and father with as much pride as Ezekiel Evans had shown in the vestry. Llewellyn Waters was to be in number one position.

This elevation went to his head in the bishop's address. The first few questions on the catechism had produced silence in the candidates. The bishop tried again. 'What is the outward visible sign or form in baptism?' Llewellyn's hand shot up. 'Yes?' inquired His Lordship. 'The baby,' said Llewellyn triumphantly. An unseemly burst of laughter erupted from the congregation to the great embarrassment of Councillor and Mrs Waters whose heads were bent as if in prayer that they should be swallowed up and removed from the nave of St Mary's Church, Pontywen.

After that response from the candidate, the bishop abandoned any further attempts to catechize and suggested that it might be well if the newly confirmed continued to go to classes for another six months, when they might learn something to their advantage. Charles tried to hide himself in his stall by turning his back to the congregation and burying his face in a prayer-book.

When the bishop had finished his address and the second hymn had begun, Ezekiel Evans stepped forward to begin his chaplaincy duties. In so doing he engaged in a *pas de deux* with the curate who had vacated his stall to begin his presentation duty. After they had sorted themselves out Ezekiel was handed a large card by the bishop on which the service was printed in large letters. This had to be held in front of him by the chaplain. In the meanwhile Charles had taken up his place on the right hand of His Lordship, ready to present his under-prepared charges.

First the bishop asked the candidates to stand, then motioned to Ezekiel Evans to hold up the service card. The lay reader must have been under the impression that the prelate was shortsighted. He made an elaborate bow and advanced upon His Lordship with the apparent intent of rubbing his nose in the print. After his sight line had been adjusted the bishop read the opening prayer and then asked the confirmed if they would renew the prom-ises made at their baptism. Instead of the loud response we had practised at the rehearsal, he received a barely audible 'I do'. One more prayer and the moment of the laying-on of hands had arrived.

I went down to the front pew to organize the shepherd-ing of the candidates. The five boys moved out in order to allow Llewellyn Waters to be the first to kneel in front of the bishop. Ezekiel's bow paled into insignificance compared with that of the councillor's son who then forgot to hand Charles his card with his printed name. As the boy was in the process of kneeling, the curate darted forward and seized the card which he held up for scrutiny.

The Bishop stared at it uncomprehendingly. 'His name,' he snapped uncharacteristically.

'Er, Llewellyn,' said the curate nervously, looking at the card he had held up and realizing too late that it was upside-down.

Apart from some fumbling of the cards, the rest of the

candidates were confirmed without any hitch. When the service was over the bishop took Charles aside in the vestry and gave him a gentle lecture. 'I know it is not easy to prepare these young people nowadays, what with the wireless and the cinema and all the other distractions to take their minds off more serious matters, but it is your duty to see that they are ready for confirmation. They should know their catechism and not only know it but understand it. If I were you, I should see to it that they meet for a few months at least to receive further instruction. Some bishops might have refused to confirm the candidates if they had had the response your young people gave me.'

It was a very tired dignitary who sat down in the church hall to consume the tongue sandwiches and the home-made cake. 'This has been a long day, Vicar, and if you don't mind, once I have signed the manuals I must go.'

When the bishop had satisfied his hunger he came out from the side room in which he had been closeted and was confronted with the hubbub of the crowded hall, a scrum of the newly confirmed fighting to be first in the queue to have their little books signed. Despite his fatigue, he had a word with each of the confirmed while their parents looked on with pride at their offspring.

One of the last to produce his manual for signing was Llewellyn Waters, watched by his father and mother who had now recovered their composure. As the Bishop handed the boy his signed copy, Dai Spout announced that he was to be mayor next month and that the vicar was to be his chaplain.

'I hope you have a happy term of office, councillor,' said the bishop. 'You have a very competent chaplain, I can assure you.'

As the bishop left, the mayor-elect said to me, 'What a nice man! You could see that he understood what Llewellyn meant when he said that the baby was the visible part of baptism. That is a logical statement after all, as it were.'

## 5

'What a fiasco!' said my curate. 'Those stupid kids, sitting like mummies, apart, of course, from Dai Spout junior whose intelligence is minimal but whose mouth is as big as his father's. It would have been far better if he had kept it shut, like the rest.'

'If you don't mind me saying so,' I replied, 'you really have a nerve to talk about a fiasco. Whose fault was that? Had those "kids", as you call them, been adequately instructed in the catechism, all would have been well. As for Llewellyn Waters and his father, don't forget that I shall have to spend many hours in Councillor Waters' company during the next twelve months. It doesn't help to hear you taking him apart like that. There is something to be said for young Waters. At least he did speak up. Anyway, as a result of the fiasco you will have to keep to the bishop's instruction and hold classes for the newly confirmed over the next six months or so.'

'Fred! You don't mean that. Bronwen is going to need me very much over these next six months. I didn't think it was an instruction from His Lordship. It was more in the nature of a suggestion.'

'Charles, you may have considered it as a suggestion but as far as I am concerned it is an instruction. Half an hour a week is hardly going to take you away from your wife's side a great amount. I hope you don't think that Bronwen's pregnancy gives you *carte blanche* to evade your duties. I'm sure she will not expect you to do so.

Perhaps next time you are supposed to prepare candidates for confirmation you will give them the thorough grounding to which they are entitled.'

So ended the post mortem on the previous evening's events. As we drank our coffee in my study Charles maintained a sulky silence until his departure. An hour later a ring on the doorbell announced the arrival of Mrs Agnes Collier, still flushed with the exertions of her Monday morning laundry, coupled with her brisk walk to the vicarage, indicated by her breathlessness.

'Come on in, Mrs Collier,' I said with a show of feigned bonhomie. She simulated a smile and stalked into the study. As she seated herself in the armchair she gave the impression that like Eliza she had come to stay.

'Now, what can I do for you?' I asked.

'I don't know how to put this, Vicar. It's a very delicate matter but I thought you should know about it before it becomes serious – that is, if it isn't already, if you know what I mean.'

'Well, Mrs Collier, since you haven't told me anything so far, how can I know what you mean?'

Agnes leaned forward confidentially. 'It's – er – about the organist and one of the choir-boys.' She stopped speaking and looked at me to see if I was shocked.

'What about the organist and the choir-boy?' My matter-of-fact tone of voice disconcerted her. She fiddled with her handbag.

'I suppose I had better begin at the beginning, Vicar. I know he's a good organist. Not as good as my late husband, of course, but he does know how to play the organ. I'll give him that. Still, that's beside the point.' She paused for breath.

'Before you go any further, Mrs Collier,' I interrupted.

'I have heard the allegation about Albert Williams and young David Morris which you passed on to other people who passed them on to me. Unless you have something specific to say about the relationship, I would advise you to keep quiet on the subject. Otherwise you may find yourself the subject of a slander action which would be bad for you and for St Padarn's.'

Her eyes had the glazed look of a boxer who had been caught with a knockout punch. She sat silent and stared into space. Then she stood up abruptly and turned her gaze on me. It was a remarkable transformation. Now her face was red with indignation, her eyes burning into mine.

'It isn't a slander case against me you've got to worry about, Vicar. It will be a very nasty case against Albert Williams. I've seen the way he looks at young David and if it comes to that, the way the boy looks at him. There's something going on there, believe me, and if you are going to shut your eyes to it, you'll have to take the consequences. As far as St Padarn's is concerned, the last thing we want is a scandal, it's bad enough now with Mr Wentworth-Baxter in charge. The congregation is going down every Sunday. Get a scandal and the place will be empty. Well, you can't say I haven't warned you. Good morning, Vicar!' So saying, she picked up her handbag from the chair and made an exit worthy of Dame Sybil Thorndike at her magisterial best.

'I wish to heaven I had never appointed Albert Williams as organist,' I said to Eleanor when she came in from her rounds. 'It has meant nothing but trouble ever since he started. As old Canon Llewellyn used to say, wherever there is a choir there is the devil.'

'In that case, Frederick,' she replied, 'perhaps you had better do some exorcism and remove the devil.'

'If I get rid of Albert, it looks as if I am being ruled by Agnes Collier and Co., and I have no desire to give that impression.'

'Well, my love. Sooner or later you will have to do something, it would seem.'

As it turned out, it was sooner rather than later, that very afternoon. As I was about to leave the vicarage to do some hospital visiting, I had a phone call from Evan Jones, the churchwarden at Llanhyfryd. Evan had a large farm on the outskirts of the parish. He had been a troublemaker when I first came to Pontywen as a curate, but ever since his wife had been treated successfully by Eleanor for a long-standing complaint in her legs, he had ceased to be a thorn in my flesh. His affliction was a painful stammer from which he had suffered since childhood.

'V-Vicar, c-could you c-come round s-sometime t-today? I c-can't talk about it on the ph-phone. It is a b-bit p-personal, like.'

'By all means, Mr Jones. I have to visit the hospital first and then I'll come and see you afterwards.'

'Th-thank you, Vicar. I think you sh-should know about it straight away.'

There were only three patients I had to see at the hospital: one, an elderly lady who loved a gossip, was asleep, whilst the other two patients were less inclined to detain me. As a result, after half an hour I was on my way to Blaenycwm Farm, wondering what the churchwarden's mysterious call signified.

It was a lovely afternoon, and once I was out of the smoke which affected Pontywen the sun shone gloriously over the patterned hills of Llanhyfryd. I dawdled my way, feasting on the scenery through the open window of my old Morris Minor and forgetting for the moment the purpose of my visit to Evan Jones. All too soon I had to turn off the main road and crawl up the cart-track that led to Blaenycwm. As I pulled up outside the farmhouse, Del, the black and white sheepdog, announced my presence with a series of barks. On my first visit to the farm he had bitten me on the leg. Since that painful meeting for both of us, when I had retaliated with a kick in his ribs, he had treated me circumspectly. As I got out of the car, he recognized me and kept his distance, content just to glance at me.

Before I could knock on the door the old churchwarden opened it and invited me in with an expansive gesture. 'You d-don't mind coming through to the k-kitchen, Vicar? Mrs Jones is having her af-afternoon n-nap in the f-front room – that's if D-del hasn't w-woken her up.' He pulled out a kitchen chair by the long scrubbed table. 'S-sit yourself down. W-would you l-like a g-glass of cider?' Evan Jones's scrumpy was very potent.

'Just one glass, Mr Jones. I want to drive home straight.'

'R-right you are, Vicar.' He went to the cupboard and produced a large tankard which he proceeded to fill from a stone jar. 'I w-won't join you, if you don't m-mind. I had m-mine with my m-meal earlier on.'

He sat down beside me. 'I w-was going to ring on S-Saturday night but then I thought it b-better to g-get the S-Sunday out of the w-way first. It's a v-very delicate m-matter and I th-thought you should know about it as soon as p-possible.'

It was plain that he was very embarrassed about what he had to say. 'Well, l-last Saturday afternoon, I w-went d-down to the h-hay field to s-see if it w-was ready for

c-cutting. W-When I opened the g-gate I found two b-bicycles l-lying against the h-hedge. Then I n-noticed that s-somebody had b-been walking into the field. A c-couple I thought trampling d-down my hay. S-so I followed the t-track they had made and sh-shouted, "C-come out of there" – b-but it wasn't a c-couple. It was a m-man and a b-boy. They were d-doing up their t-trousers. "Get out of here b-before I c-call the p-police," I said. They were out l-like a shot on their b-bikes and d-down that lane like b-bats out of hell. The t-trouble is, Vicar, I think the man was the one who is the or-organist you've p-put in St Padarn's, the one with the g-glasses who used to h-help in the p-parish church. I m-may be wrong b-but I'm willing to b-bet it was him.'

'Thank you, Mr Jones, for telling me this. Have you mentioned it to anybody else?'

'N-no. It's n-not the kind of thing you t-talk about. I

s-suppose the p-police should know. Anyway I l-leave it to you. You know b-best. S-something will have to be d-done about it, th-that's for sure.'

'Let me think this over. Whatever is done, will have to be done for the best. There's the boy's future to be considered. If the case comes to the courts, he will have to give evidence and he will be the centre of gossip as much as the man. I shall let you know what happens and in the meantime I would be obliged if you say nothing to anybody.'

'I'll d-do that, Vicar. I h-haven't even told my wife. Now then, Vicar, c-come on, drink up that cider. I'll g-go and see if my w-wife is awake. I expect she'll like to s-see you before you l-leave.'

As he went down the corridor, I took a deep drink of the ice-cool cider and wondered why on earth I had wanted to become a vicar so soon. If I were still a curate I could pass on the responsibility for action to my boss whose years of experience as a pastor would make him better qualified to deal with this messy situation.

The sun still shone gloriously as I drove back to Pontywen, but it failed to penetrate the gloom which had enveloped me. David Morris was a good-looking twelve-year-old. Tall for his age, he had blond curly hair and vividly blue eyes. An intelligent child, he had passed his eleven-plus and was doing well in Pontywen Grammar School. An only child, he was adored by his parents who kept a newspaper and confectionery shop on the council housing estate. His father, Glyn Morris, was a burly man, notoriously short-tempered. If he found out that his son had been seduced, Albert Williams would go in danger of his life. It was a prospect which sent shivers down my spine.

When I arrived back at the vicarage, Eleanor had not yet left for her early evening surgery. She looked at my face as I entered the kitchen. 'You're as pale as a ghost,' she commented. 'What has old Jones told you?'

'Can you spare a few minutes?' I asked.

'By all means,' she replied. 'Longer if you like. It's obvious that you have had a shock. Let's sit down in the lounge.'

She sat beside me on the settee and held my hand.

'Well, I can hardly describe it as a shock since it was something I had expected.'

'Don't tell me, love. It's Albert Williams, isn't it?'

'Right, first time. Last Saturday afternoon, Evan went down to inspect his hayfield to decide whether it was ready for harvest and he found Albert Williams and young David either after the act or just before the act – anyway, they were "doing up their trousers", as he put it. He threatened to call the police and they were off down the lane as fast as their bikes could take them. He has not told anybody about it, not even his wife. He thought the police should know about it but has left it to me to decide what to do. As far as I am concerned, the last thing I want to happen is to have the police involved. That would give Pontywen something to gossip about for the next twelve months, apart from the effect on young David and his family.'

'Well, as far as the police are concerned, there is no evidence to convict Albert Williams. They were not caught "*in flagrante delicto*". So that doesn't arise. On the other hand Albert Williams must go from St Padarn's immediately.'

'I know that, love. What worries me is whether I should have a word with David or not. He is a very sensitive child and if he knows that I am aware that he has been involved in something which is an offence he will have a guilt complex which could cripple him psychologically, possibly for the rest of his life. Whatever happens, his parents mustn't know what has happened. His father would throttle Albert.'

'That's something we can talk about later tonight. In some ways, I'm glad this has happened. It means that you will be able to remove the seat of the trouble – Albert Williams. If a surgical operation can remove the cause of the cancer, that is sometimes all that matters. Everything else is of secondary importance.'

As soon as we had finished dinner that evening I said to Eleanor, 'If you don't mind, we can leave our discussion about David Morris till later. I feel I have to remove the cancer, as you put it, forthwith. I hope Albert is in, I don't want to leave it until tomorrow, if I can possibly help it. My cup of anger is running over at the moment. The hotter I can make it for that young man the better.'

'Go to it, Secombe,' replied my wife. 'Frighten the life out of him.'

With my foot firmly on the accelerator I shot through the streets of Pontywen and pulled up outside the Williamses' house with a screech of tyres worthy of a police car in a raid. As I walked up the path, I could hear the piano being played. He was in. My heart beat faster as I contemplated the tirade I intended to inflict upon him. I pressed hard upon the button of the doorbell. There was no response from inside. The piano music continued. I pressed harder this time, the music stopped abruptly. A door was opened and closed with a bang as if Albert was annoyed at the interruption. He flung open the front door. The frown vanished from his face when he saw me, to be replaced by a look of apprehension as he contemplated my angry visage.

'Sorry to keep you waiting, Vicar. I'm afraid I was engrossed by my music. My mother is out at my aunt's. Please come in.' He led me into the front room. 'Take a seat, Vicar.' He pointed to an armchair.

'I won't sit down if you don't mind, Albert. What I have to say is best said standing.' His rosy complexion flushed into a purple. 'Where were you last Saturday afternoon and who was your companion?'

He began to bluster. 'What's all this about, Vicar? What I do outside the church is nothing to do with you.'

'On the contrary,' I shouted, 'it has a great deal to do with me when it concerns any of the choir-boys from my parish, especially when you are discovered in an extremely compromising situation, lying down hidden away in a hay-field.'

'What do you mean by compromising situation? David and I were just out for a ride on our bicycles and as it was such a lovely afternoon, we rested in a field.'

'Come off it, Albert. The farmer discovered you and the boy doing up your trousers hidden away amongst the hay. You are very lucky that he did not contact the police. Otherwise you would have been having a visit from PC Davies instead of me, with a holiday in Cardiff Jail to follow. I warned you not to have any contact with that boy, except in the context of choir practice. This is the end of your connection with St Padarn's. Under no circumstances will you have anything more to do with the organ and certainly not with the choir-boys. Think of the effect you have had on young David and what his parents would do if they knew.'

He collapsed into an armchair and began to weep. 'I

love that boy. He is a delightful boy, in his way I think he loves me. I didn't want to corrupt him. What happened last Saturday afternoon was just a natural expression of our love for each other. It was the first time, I promise you. Now I know that it's the last time.' His sobs became uncontrollable. I waited until they had died down. He pulled out his handkerchief, wiped his eyes and blew his nose. Suddenly I felt sorry for him. It was obvious that his homosexuality was going to bedevil him for the rest of his life.

I sat down in the armchair opposite him. 'Look, Albert. I realize that your sexual inclinations draw you to those of the same sex as yourself. If you indulge them you are going to come into conflict with the law of the land. For your own sake and especially for the sake of those to whom you are attracted, like young David Morris, you must learn to sublimate these feelings in some way or another. You have outstanding musical gifts. Pour your heart into them. Let them suck up your emotions. Don't go looking for another David. That's the road to ruin. I think I had better go now. I'll see myself out. You had better compose yourself before your mother comes back.'

He sat with his head bowed as I left the room and made my way down the garden path to my car. As I drove, I wondered what reason he would give to his mother for his departure from St Padarn's and what reason I would give to the congregation. There would be one person who would guess why he had gone and who would rejoice at his going. Agnes Collier would be convinced that her warning to me was responsible for it.

When I gave Eleanor the account of what had happened she said, 'I feel sorry for him, trapped inside his own nature. I expect he will shed more tears tonight in the privacy of his bedroom. I wonder if David will do the same when he discovers that the affair has ended or whether he will have forgotten all about it in no time, and no tears shed.'

'Which brings me to what I should do about the boy. If he will have forgotten about it as quickly as that then there will be no point in me saying anything to him. However, if this relationship has become a deep one, then I think I owe it to him to have a talk about it. David is a very sensitive lad. I should imagine that the experience is not one which he will shrug off easily.'

'You know him better than I, love. If that is your impression, by all means have a talk with him. He will not be able to turn to his parents for help and guidance, that's certain.'

'It's going to be a much tougher assignment than tearing a strip off Albert Williams. I can't go and see him at his house for obvious reasons. It will be awkward to get any privacy in the vestry. The best plan, I think, will be to meet him outside school tomorrow afternoon and have a word with him in the car.'

The following afternoon I parked the car near the gates of Pontywen Grammar School and waited for the eruption of pupils when school-time had ended. Promptly at four o'clock the exodus began with some of the sixth formers strolling through the yard, followed a few minutes later by a rush of first and second formers, some of them swinging their satchels in combat with each other. Bringing up the rear, in school cap and blazer and with his satchel slung over his back, was David Morris.

I alighted from the car and met him as he was coming through the gates. 'David,' I said. 'Just the boy I want to see.' He looked at me quizzically. 'I should like to have a little talk with you, if I may. My car is just across the road.'

As he sat in the front seat alongside me, I felt angry again that this likable and innocent boy had been led into such a situation. I fumbled in my mind to find a suitable way to broach the subject. It would have been easier if I could have indulged in trivial remarks to lead up to it but my anger with Albert Williams made such an approach impossible. We sat in silence for a short time while the boy's bewilderment gave way to a mixture of embarrassment and trepidation.

'I don't know how to put this, David, but I must tell you that I know about your relationship with Albert Williams, and especially about the incident in a hayfield last Saturday afternoon.'

His face lost all its colour. 'You're not going to tell my parents, are you, sir? My father would kill me if he knew. I told them I was going out for a ride with my friend down the road.'

'Is that the first and only time that you have done that with him?'

'Yes, sir. I swear it is. It won't happen again, sir, honest.'

'You realize that you broke the law when you did it and that Albert Williams could go to prison if it was reported to the police? Mr Evan Jones, the farmer, told me that he had thought of telling PC Davies but, instead, he came to me with the story. You have been a very lucky boy, David, that it hasn't gone any further.'

'I'm sorry, sir, very sorry. Perhaps I should give up the choir to keep away from Albert.'

'You won't have to do that. I have been to see him and told him that he has got to leave St Padarn's and that he must not have anything more to do with you.'

'Thank you, sir. Can I go now? My parents will be wondering why I'm late coming home.'

'I'll drive you as far as Inkerman Street and you can walk from there. You won't be all that late then.'

As we drove off, he said, 'Thank you, Vicar, for not telling my mother and father, I promise I won't ever do anything like that again. I knew it was wrong when he did it to me but he said it wasn't wrong because he loved me and it was his way of showing it.'

I pulled up on the corner of Inkerman Street. 'There's my friend, sir,' he said. 'I'll catch him up. He won't half be jealous when I tell him I've had a ride in your car.'

'So much for my worry that David Morris would be deeply affected by his experience with Albert Williams,' I said to Eleanor later that evening. 'He was much more concerned that I would tell his parents than anything else. It is obvious that Albert's claim that the boy reciprocated his affection was a self-manufactured delusion. There were no tears from David – just relief that the whole episode was over.'

'Thank God for that. I am afraid it is going to be vastly different for Albert – it is all very well you telling him to sublimate his feelings by burying himself in his music. For one thing, you have taken him away from the organ and the choir. Secondly, if he still had that outlet, it would not prevent him from giving way to his inclinations.'

'Well, that is what we were taught in the theological college in a lecture on how to deal with homosexuals. Sympathy for their plight and sublimation as the remedy for their condition.'

'What superficial bilge! His inclinations, as you call them, will never go away. It may be that Albert will try to sublimate them with an overdose of tablets now that he has been found out. I would have thought that a better idea would be for him to get a transfer from the bank in Pontywen to a big city. He could settle down away from his mother and make his friendships with men of his own age where his inclinations would not be noticed as they are in a small town like Pontywen.'

'But that would be condoning a grave sin, if I advised him to do that.'

'For God's sake, Fred, why don't you grow up?' she exploded. 'All you have done with your so-called advice is push him deeper into the mire.'

'I resent that. I did what I thought was right. I can't do any more than that.'

'Sometimes you are pathetic. If you don't mind, I'm going to bed. I've got a busy day ahead of me tomorrow. Goodnight.' She closed the door with a bang.

It was our first real quarrel. I stayed downstairs and listened to the wireless until they played the National Anthem to end the programme for the day. I spent a restless night on the edge of the bed, manufacturing arguments to justify myself which I could use in the morning.

When the alarm clock went off, I was in a deep sleep, exhausted by my mental effort. I put my hand out and turned it off. The next thing I knew I was being kissed on the cheek by my wife, who was in her dressing-gown. 'Wake up, sleeping beauty. There's a cup of tea on the bedside cabinet. I'm off for my bath.'

I never used the arguments, being only too happy that yesterday had gone and that today was a new day with peace restored. It was some weeks later that they told me at the bank that Albert had been transferred to a branch in West London.

## 6

'We've reserved a seat for you, Dr Secombe, in the front row of the gallery. You'll have a beautiful view of all the proceedings from up by there. Our Llewellyn will be sitting next to you, so you'll have company. I've told him he's got to behave himself. So he won't be any trouble to you.'

Blodwen Waters had pinned us in a corner of the mayor's parlour prior to the mayor-making ceremony. The first time I had met her was when she was in a bed in Pontywen Hospital. It was my initial sick visit in the parish as a raw beginner. I had learnt two important lessons from that encounter – never to ask a female patient what was wrong with her and never to ask to say prayers with someone who rarely attends church. The first question elicited a blush and the single word 'internal', and the second a panicky 'No, thank you. Have they told you something I don't know?'

On that occasion some three years previously Blodwen's hair was dyed a colour which was a messy compromise between pink and red with dark roots in attendance. Today she displayed a glorious, unadulterated scarlet head, evidently intended to match the colour of her mayoral robes. With her beaky nose and pointed chin, she would look like a bird of paradise later that afternoon.

The Mayor's Parlour was as dingy as the rest of Abergwynlais Town Hall. The building was a red-brick monstrosity erected in the early years of the century when industry flourished in the Valley. It was a monument to coal, steel, sweated labour and bad taste. The neglect of the thirties and the war years combined to give it the appearance of a municipal slum, with its peeling paint and accumulation of grime. Three potted palm plants which appeared to be languishing for the sun were the only adornments in the room, apart from an enlarged photograph of the Prince of Wales (in his bowler hat and long coat) visiting the Valleys in the depression of the thirties when he uttered the famous remark, 'Something must be done.'

Councillor David Waters was engaged in earnest conversation with the outgoing mayor, Councillor David Thomas, who was clad in his roles of office for the last time. The mayoress, Mrs Rhoda Thomas, a large, comfortably padded lady, was similarly clad and enjoying a joke with the mayor's secretary, Mr Frank James, a little bespectacled man in a black pin-striped suit, as much a badge of office as the mayoral robes.

Just as Eleanor was beginning to wilt under the endless stream of trivialities pouring forth from Blodwen Waters, Frank James came to her rescue and suggested that the time had come to escort her and Llewellyn to their places in the gallery. The Mayor's Parlour led directly into the Council Chamber and as the secretary opened the door a loud hubbub of conversation emerged. To my great relief Blodwen transferred her attention to Rhoda.

'I'm going to get swamped in that robe, Rhoda, and as for that hat it's going to be murder for my hair. They spent hours in the hairdresser's yesterday doing me up.'

'I can see that,' said her counterpart drily. 'You'll soon get used to wearing it. You can use hairpins to clip it to your head, if you want to. That's what I do, anyway.'

'Come over here, Vicar, and join us,' said David Thomas. 'You don't want to get caught up with women's talk over by there. They've laid on a nice reception for us in the banqueting 'all, you'll be pleased to know. Dai here has seen to that, 'aven't you, Dai?'

'Well, let's put it this way, as it were. Within the limits of these frugal times, as it were, there's quite a good little spread waiting, sit-down, not standing-up buffet. I thought it would give a fine kick-off to my year of office.'

'I like that phrase "frugal times", Dai. It makes a change from "austerity". That word has just about been done to death. I should use "frugal times" in some of your speeches. Well, "frugal times" or not, Vicar. I am sure you will enjoy being Mayor's Chaplain. I know my little man did, Minister of Aberdulais Cong, Elfed Rees Williams. Have you met him?'

'No, Mr Mayor. I'm afraid I haven't. Is he here today?'

'Had to take a funeral of one of the deacons. Business before pleasure, that's it, isn't it, Vicar?'

At this stage in the conversation Frank James re-entered with a request that we get ready to proceed into the Chamber. 'You go first, Mr Chaplain. Stand by the chair far right, Councillor and Mrs Waters to the chairs on either side of the mayor and mayoress. Are you all ready?' Mrs Waters patted her hair and took a deep breath.

The mayor's secretary flung open the door and shouted, 'Will you all be upstanding, please, for your mayor and mayoress, the mayor-elect and the mayoress-elect and their chaplain.' For a little man he had a tremendous voice, one which any boxing MC would envy. 'Right, off you go, Vicar,' he whispered.

I moved forward and tripped as I caught my foot in the

bottom of my cassock, a favourite trick of mine. I saved myself from falling headlong by grabbing the curtain which was used to exclude the draught. Unfortunately the force I applied to the grab was sufficient to pull down the pole to which it was attached. The chaplain-elect, the mayor-elect and the mayoress-elect were enveloped in the musty folds, to the great amusement of the incumbent mayor and mayoress and to those in the Chamber who could see the incident. By the time we had disentangled ourselves, Blodwen Waters' face was as scarlet as her disarranged hair.

'What a bloody start!' she exclaimed. 'Sorry, Vicar, but look at my hair. It looks as if I've been pulled through an 'edge backwards. I'll 'ave to comb it before I can go in there. Excuse me.' She disappeared and went into the toilet which was in the corridor outside the Mayor's Parlour.

In the meanwhile the occupants of the Council

Chamber were still on their feet. Frank James went back out and shouted, 'Will you all take your seats for a minute or two?' 'Another cover-up is it?' shouted a wag. The mayor's secretary closed the door. I pulled up my cassock and adjusted my belt.

'It's a pity you hadn't done that earlier,' said the mayor-elect. 'Then we wouldn't have had all this mess.'

'Don't shoot the pianist,' interjected the mayor. 'He's doing his best. In any case, you'll have to watch yourself, Dai. It's very easy to trip over these robes, believe me. That's right, isn't it, Rhoda?'

'Oh yes, it is. I've tripped over a few times this last year. Your Blodwen will have to watch it because she's a lot thinner and smaller than me. Perhaps it's a good thing it's happened now. So that you can watch out yourselves every time you dress up.'

How I wished I had been their chaplain.

It must have been at least ten minutes before Blodwen returned, her hair once more immaculate but with a face like thunder.

'I was telling Dai that you will have to watch your robes, Blodwen, in case you trip over them. It's easily done,' said the mayoress.

'I can look after them very well, Rhoda, thank you. Once bitten, twice shy.'

'Well done, Blodwen, but remember the other proverb, pride goes before a fall.' The mayor received one of Blodwen's special dagger-looks for this remark.

'Now, then. Shall we line up again?' requested the mayor's secretary. 'The same order as before. I'll put the curtain back up while you're in the Chamber.'

Once again he opened the door and shouted his announcement.

This time with my cassock tucked up so far that I had a large bulge above the belt and a large expanse of trousers visible, I led the procession on to the platform. When I reached my chair at the far end and turned to face the assembly, I looked up to see my beloved in the front row of the gallery with a large grin upon her countenance as if she were enjoying some hilarious pantomime. Most of the audience seemed to be sharing the same amusement.

When the mayoral entourage was in position, the mayor in his capacity as chairman asked the councillors and the guests to be seated. Below us on the right hand side was the town clerk, bewigged and gowned. Unlike the mayor's secretary, Daniel Harries-Jones was a tall, broad-shouldered individual, a tyrant to his underlings. He had been described to me once by the Vicar of Abergwynlais as a balloon of pomposity. 'Why a balloon?' I had asked. 'According to the dictionary a balloon is anything which is hollow and inflated,' was the reply.

'Before I ask the town clerk to swear in my successor,' said the mayor, 'I must say my few words and I promise you they will be few. I've always used this recipe for public speaking: "Stand up, speak up and shut up."' As he made this remark he turned to Dai Spout at his side who may have known how to speak up but who certainly never knew how to shut up. The observation was not lost on his listeners.

'I have enjoyed my year of office tremendously. It is good to see how we are settling down in the Valley after the last war. There are problems, for example we have got to build more council houses for the men who have done their bit in the Forces and indeed those who have worked so hard at the coal-face. I know all about that, being a miner myself. We've made a start these last twelve months and I'm sure the new mayor will do all he can to build on it.

'David Waters has served this council for many years faithfully and is now the senior councillor. He has earned the right to this office and I am sure he will be worthy of it. I extend my best wishes to him and his good lady and hope he will enjoy his year as mayor as much as I have done.'

Then he called on the town clerk to administer the swearing-in ceremony. Daniel Harries-Jones made a great show of standing up and smoothing down his gown. He mounted the platform and handed the councillor a bible. Holding it with a shaking hand, the mayor-elect promised that he would be an impartial chairman and a faithful servant of the community. After this he signed the document on a small desk at the side of the platform.

As the audience applauded the mayoral chain of office and the mayoral robes were placed on the new mayor by his predecessor and likewise on the new mayoress by her predecessor. Once enveloped in his scarlet robes, the Mayor of Abergwynlais stepped forward to deliver his mayoral address.

'Thank you, Councillor Thomas, for your kind words, much appreciated. Well, here we are gathered together on this auspicious occasion, representing, as it were, the hopes and aspirations of the borough of Abergwynlais. There's so much to say. I have not written a speech. I speak from the heart, as it were, not from a piece of paper.'

The next quarter of an hour dragged by as the audience must have wished he had confined himself to a piece of paper – many heads were nodding by the time he had finished his peroration. Then he turned to me and announced, 'I have appointed as my chaplain the Reverend Frederick Secombe, Vicar of Pontywen, and I will now ask him to say a few prayers.'

To say that this request was a great shock to me would be an understatement. I had not been given any advance notice that I was to lead the council members and guests in prayer. Furthermore, I was not trained in the art of extempore prayer. Unlike the new mayor, I needed 'a piece of paper' to read if I was to pray publicly. 'Will you all please stand?' I found myself saying, my mouth dry, my tongue cleaving to my gums. There was a long pause. 'Shall we say together the Lord's Prayer?' While my mouth was repeating the familiar words, my mind was racing frantically to find something to say afterwards. By the time the 'Amen' had arrived there was still a void waiting to be filled. A much longer pause ensued. Beads of sweat anointed my forehead. My heart was pumping fast.

Suddenly there came into my head the opening words of the marriage psalm, 'God be merciful unto us and bless us'. Then I added, 'Especially us in the borough of Abergwynlais and thy servant David. Show him the light of thy countenance and be merciful unto him during his year of office through Jesus Christ Our Lord.' There followed the blessing from the communion service, which I knew by heart, and the 'prayers' were over.

Back in the Mayor's Parlour, David Thomas said to me, 'You are going to be a great asset and example to the mayor, short and straight to the point. I liked "thy servant David". It sounded very biblical. My chap never said that.'

In no time, the room was full of councillors and guests.

Eleanor cornered me. 'Trust you to put on a show. What should have been "ring up the curtain" became "ring down" the curtain before anything had started. By the way, there was a mistake in your few words to the Almighty. You should have said, "Be merciful to us during his year of office".'

The new mayor and mayoress were receiving congratulations from all and sundry while their offspring was raiding a plate of biscuits he had discovered on a side table. Eleanor and I were now trapped by the town clerk who was delivering a monologue on the importance of his office. Relief came when the mayor banged the desk with an empty ink pot.

'I'm pleased to tell you that for the first time since the war there is a sit-down meal awaiting you in the banqueting hall. You will find your names at your places and there is a table plan by the door as you come in. There will be glasses of sherry served to you down there and there will be wine with the meal. For this piece of resistance, as it were, in these frugal times I am grateful to an anonymous donor.'

'Anonymous. Bloody funny,' said a voice behind us. 'That's Evans and Watkins. They've just been given the contract to build the new school in Llandenis. I shouldn't be surprised if that isn't all that they have been given.'

I turned around to see Councillor Bill Owen, the only Communist member of the council, known locally as Bill Moscow, a little man whose face was decorated with a few blue scars, the miner's trademark.

'If I were you,' warned the town clerk, 'I should keep comments like that to yourself. Otherwise you could find yourself in trouble, Councillor Owen.'

Bill Owen winked at me and then looked up at the

figure towering above him. 'A Daniel come to judgment, is it?' Daniel Harries-Jones glared at the ex-miner. 'I tell you what, Mr Town Clerk, don't you threaten me, I've eaten bigger men than you for breakfast.' Faced by this challenge, the chief municipal officer moved away quickly to join the throng who were pressing towards the exit like the excited crowds in Cardiff Arms Park after a Welsh victory and anticipating a drink to celebrate.

'Look at them, Vicar,' said Bill Owen. 'As Karl Marx said, "A man is what he eats", and that just about describes them, or as your lot describes them in the Bible, like the Gadarene swine.'

'I must say,' remarked my wife, 'you seem to be very well read.'

'Don't patronize me,' retorted the councillor. 'I've probably read more books than you have, love. I tell you what, the Miners' Welfare has had a much bigger library than the council one, and a better selection of books too. It's a pity that it's getting run down these days, but there you are, the miners today aren't the men they used to be. They are more concerned with the amount of beer they pour down their bellies at the club than what could go into their minds at the Miners' Welfare.'

'Excuse me,' Eleanor replied, 'my father was a miner and I know what the Miners' Welfare did for him. But he didn't want to waste the rest of his life underground and like you he read a great deal. In the end he qualified as a doctor and is still using his knowledge and experience to help others. I can only hope that you are using your knowledge for the benefit of the community as much as he has done.'

The councillor looked at her and then at me. 'I suppose this is your missus. I tell you what, boyo, you've got a good one here. I'm sorry to have been so rude, madam, but from your remark I thought you were one of those who came from a different background, of privilege and of holier and better than thou. I can see that it isn't the case and all I can say is that the vicar here is lucky to have you as his wife.'

I thought the time had come for me to intervene. 'Believe me, Councillor Owen, I know how lucky I am to have Eleanor as my wife. Perhaps I should explain that like her father she is a doctor and is using her knowledge to benefit the community.'

By now the room was empty. 'See what I mean,' said the councillor. 'They have evacuated this place quicker than if there had been an air-raid warning. Well, Doctor, I am sure that you will be a great benefit to the community. I'm not so sure about your husband who is paid to sell the idea that there's pie in the sky when you die. Anyway, I tell you one thing, it's good for Abergwynlais that they've got you two for the next twelve months.'

The Banqueting Hall was a pretentious name for an unadorned large room not much bigger than the church hall in Pontywen. At the far end was the top table and at either end of it two long tables were placed where most of the guests were already seated. A solitary waitress stood by the side of the board and easel which contained the table plan. On her tray there were a few glasses of British sweet sherry. 'All the other's gone,' she said, when we asked for the dry variety.

We made our way down to the top table where we found our places at one end. The mayor's secretary appeared behind me when we sat down. 'The mayor would like you to say grace,' she said.

'With pleasure,' I replied. 'By the way, I wish he had

told me that I was to say a few prayers in the Council Chamber. I would have brought my prayer-book with me in that case.'

'Don't worry, Vicar. You did very well as it was. Perhaps he thought you would know you had to do it, but there you are. I'm afraid he's like that, I should always keep a prayer-book handy if I were you. He's very unpredictable.'

'How exciting,' said my wife when he had gone. 'I would have thought that Dai Spout was extremely predictable, hardly the sort of person of whom you would say, "You never know what he's going to do next."'

'Well, at least next Sunday at the civic service that won't apply,' I remarked. 'The service is printed and I shall be in charge.'

'Wait and see,' replied my wife.

When we arrived back at the vicarage after the reception we found a car parked in the drive and a well-dressed, middle-aged man inspecting the flower border around the lawn.

'Good afternoon, Vicar,' he said. 'I have been trying to get into the church but I found all the doors locked. My name is Powell and I am the parks superintendent for the borough. I must say you have your lawns and borders in good shape. It is a tribute to you.'

'That's due to our excellent gardener, not to me,' I replied. 'What can I do for you?'

'The mayor has asked me to bring some flowers and plants to decorate the church for the civic service on Sunday. This is the first time I have had to do this. So obviously I shall have to look at the interior to work out a colour scheme and where the plants can be seen to best advantage.'

Eleanor looked at me, scarcely able to control her mirth.

'This is news to me, Mr Powell. The mayor has not mentioned it to me, and the lady on the flower rota has probably ordered her flowers for the Sunday.'

'All I can say, Vicar, is that it was news to me this morning when he asked me to make these arrangements. Apparently they used to do it before the war. I think the mayoress is very keen on the idea.'

'I'll go and get the keys for you, dear,' said my wife. She ran around to the back door before she could disgrace herself with unseemly laughter.

'How did the mayor-making go?' inquired Mr Powell. 'I understand there was a sit-down reception this year.'

'There was indeed,' I replied, 'and wine with the dinner, to paraphrase the Duke of Plaza Toro.'

The parks superintendent stared at me. 'Excuse me, Vicar, but who was the Duke of Plaza Toro?'

'A character in *The Gondoliers*, Mr Powell. I am afraid I am a Gilbert and Sullivan addict and I find myself quoting lines from their operas from time to time. We have a church Gilbert and Sullivan Society here in Pontywen, and they are going to perform *The Gondoliers* next year.'

'My wife likes Gilbert and Sullivan, Vicar. She's a bit of a singer, contralto. Mind, she has never done one of their operas, but she has taken part in the musicals in Abergwynlais before the war.'

'That's very interesting,' I replied, 'because Myfanwy Howells, one of our cast, has to back out of our next production because of various other commitments. She is our leading contralto and she would have been playing the Duchess of Plaza Toro – I wonder if your wife would be interested.'

'I am sure she would. She is doing nothing at the moment. I think she would jump at the chance.'

At this stage Eleanor arrived with the keys, smiling broadly.

'Mr Powell has just been telling me that his wife is a contralto who likes Gilbert and Sullivan but never had a chance of performing in one of their operas since her society did other musicals. He thinks she might be interested in doing the Duchess of Plaza Toro, now that Myfanwy Howells has had to withdraw from our show.'

'Marvellous,' said my wife. 'I'll have a word with Aneurin Williams on the phone while you and Mr Powell look round the church. By the time you come back I should be able to give you a message to pass on to your wife, Mr Powell. We rehearse on Thursdays, by the way. Isn't life so unpredictable? You come here at the mayor's request to survey the church and end up by getting your wife a part in *The Gondoliers*.'

As we went up the path to the church, a human scarecrow emerged from behind the gravestones, wearing a battered old trilby, filthy raincoat and even filthier wellington boots. It was 'Full Back' Jones, the gravedigger, whose cadaverous face, unshaven and toothless, could not have been more appropriate for his trade. He coughed loudly to draw attention to himself. The parks superintendent turned around to be confronted with this gruesome sight.

'Sorry to interrupt you, boss,' it lisped, 'but Matthews the Undertaker 'ave been looking for you. It's a re-opening and they wants the funeral as soon as possible. He'll be down to see you tonight but I've got to 'ave a look at the grave plan in the vestry so that I can get on with the job. Walters, the name is, Balaclava Street, 'e says you know the person. You used to bring 'er communion when you was in St Padarn's.'

'Poor old Granny Walters,' I said. 'Of course I knew her. Mr Wentworth-Baxter has been taking her communion since I moved to St Mary's. All right, Full Back, if you go around to the vestry door, I'll open it for you from the inside.'

As he disappeared up the side path, a bewildered Mr Powell inquired, 'Why is he called Full Back?'

'He used to play at full back for Pontywen rugby team many years ago. Apparently he wasn't much good and only played a few games for them but he has never stopped boasting about his brief career. So everybody in Pontywen knows him as Full Back Jones. I am afraid his grave-digging is about as effective as his rugby was.'

Once inside the church, the parks superintendent began to make notes. 'I must say the church is in very good condition, recently redecorated, by the look of it.'

'Yes, we had our centenary last year and the men of the church sacrificed their spare time to celebrate the occasion by giving it a face lift.'

'And a good job they have made of it, Vicar, quite professional. I hope we can do just as good a job with our floral decortications. The mayoress suggested a colour scheme of red and yellow, the Labour Party colours. They should stand out beautifully against the white walls.'

As we moved up into the chancel the vestry door opened and a trilby-hatted gargoyle of a face peered around the door post. 'Boss, I've put the book back.' With that announcement the door was closed.

'I have never seen him without his trilby hat,' I said. 'It is rumoured that he wears it to bed. In that case when he dies it will have to be prised from his head.'

'He is what you would call a character. Life would be all the poorer without them. Well, Vicar, I think I have seen all I want to see. If you don't mind, we shall come here on Saturday afternoon about three o'clock to do our work. I hope you will be happy with it.'

'I am sure I shall be, Mr Powell. I'll have a word with the lady on the flower rota. Don't forget to ask your wife about the part of the Duchess of Plaza Toro. If she is interested we shall be pleased to see her next Thursday evening.'

After I had seen him off, I went into the vicarage to be met by my wife in the hallway. 'You have two visitors in the study. By the expressions on their faces I think it spells trouble. They are large gentlemen. If you need any help, just call for me. I shall be practising my jujitsu in the kitchen. What an exciting day we are having.'

I took a deep breath and opened the study door. Seated in the two armchairs facing my desk were Albert and Arthur Walters, already wearing black armbands to match their black looks.

'I am very sorry to hear about your mother's death,' I said. 'Was it sudden?'

'Sudden,' growled Albert, 'I should think not. She's been on her death-bed for the last three months and nobody has bothered to visit her.'

'Hasn't Mr Wentworth-Baxter been bringing her communion?'

'The last one who brought her communion was you and that was when you were at St Padarn's. Since then nobody has bothered to visit her.'

'I am very sorry about this, Mr Walters. As far as I knew, she was being cared for by the church.'

'The funeral is two o'clock next Friday, if that's suitable for you, Vicar. We don't want nobody else. I'm sure our mother wouldn't either. Mr Matthews said he'll be seeing you later tonight. We'd like to have a service here in St Mary's, if you don't mind. I know she used to go to St Padarn's years ago but since nobody from there has come to see her, we'd rather she was brought into St Mary's.'

'By all means. I shall be able to take the service and perhaps later on you will let me know what hymns you want.'

'I can tell you that now,' intervened Arthur. '"The Lord's my Shepherd" and "Abide with Me". They were her favourites. Whenever they came on the wireless she would be singing them. She knew all the words too.'

They stood up to leave. As I shook hands with Arthur I apologized once again for the church's neglect of their mother. 'Don't worry, Vicar. It's not your fault, we all know that.'

When they had gone, I went into the scullery where Eleanor was doing some ironing. 'You didn't need me then?' she asked.

'Not at all, love. It is Charles's blood they are after. He was supposed to be taking her monthly communion after I moved here and he has not been near her for the whole of that time. Wait till I see him tomorrow.'

'Be careful not to spill blood on our newly cleaned carpet, Frederick. What did Mr Powell have to say?'

'He thinks he will be able to make a fine display of floral decoration in the colours the mayoress has asked for – red and yellow.'

'I see,' said my wife. 'Scarlet to match her hair and yellow to match her teeth.'

'How these women love each other,' I replied.

'You've got it wrong, dear. It's how these Christians love each other.' She giggled and then attacked my pyjama trousers with the iron.

## 7

'Honestly, Charles, you are incredible. Your sins of omission would fill enough books to stock a library. Ever since you have been in Pontywen you have been more of a liability to the church than an asset. I thought when you married Bronwen that you had changed your ways. This poor old lady was on her death-bed for weeks, completely neglected by the priest who had been given the responsibility to care for her. She died without the last rites of the Church, to which she was entitled. It was fortunate for you that the family has insisted that I take the funeral. Had it been you who had to officiate you would have felt the lash of their tongues.'

He sat with his head bowed, a familiar sight which had been repeated in the vicarage study several times over the past three years – that and the usual wounded spaniel expression on his face when he did raise his head.

'Sorry, Fred. What happened was this: I had forgotten all about Mrs Walters for some reason or another and then when I did remember a few weeks ago, I felt too embarrassed to call there after such a gap.'

'That makes matters even worse. It was not just amnesia but a bout of cowardice as well. As an act of penance you will have to play the organ at the service in St Mary's. Eric Greenfield can't get away from work to play at the funeral. I should keep a low profile if I were you, otherwise there might be a gap in your teeth. Those big men in the Walters family are very handy with their fists, so I hear.' The colour drained from his face.

The old lady's husband had died in an accident at the Pontywen Colliery in 1919, leaving her with a family of five boys and three girls to bring up on the pitifully small compensation she was given, plus her widow's pension. In the small terraced house in Balaclava Street she reared her children to adulthood in a way which earned her the respect of her neighbours as well as that of her family. She was a supreme example of the Welsh matriarch. She made sure that none of her sons would have to work underground. Four of them were employed in the steel-works and the youngest joined the army when he was seventeen. The eight children worshipped their mother who was nursed through her illness by her eldest daughter, the only one of the family who still lived in the house where they had all been born.

Friday turned out to be a hot summer's day. 'Gentlemen only at the church and graveside' read the announcements in the evening paper. When I arrived at 11 Balaclava Street for the service in the house, I was ushered into the middle room by Albert Walters. 'Have a drop of something before you start, Vicar.' He handed me a tumbler which was half-filled with whisky.

Already the house was crammed with mourners. The smell of mothballs and cheap perfume mingled with the body odour of sweating humanity, whilst from the open door of the front room which had sheltered the death-bed of the old lady emanated distinct evidence of disinfectant. It was a powerful concoction which combined with the whisky to make my head spin by the time I was ready to take the service in the front room. Everybody had to stand. There was no room for chairs.

'Anybody want to see Mrs Walters before we screw the coffin down?' bellowed the undertaker, Mr Matthews, from upstairs. For someone in his profession he was singularly devoid of any sensitivity. He was at his best as a carpenter. No one wished to take advantage of his offer. In any case it would have been extremely difficult for anyone to squeeze through the scrum of humanity to make the journey upstairs to view the mortal remains.

'We shall begin our service with a reading from the seventh chapter of the Book of Revelation. "After this I beheld and lo, a great multitude which no man could number."' The first vocal signs of grief were heard. By the time I came to the last verse of the lesson: 'And God shall wipe away tears from their eyes', there was a torrent of tears from all the daughters and the daughters-in-law which continued throughout Psalm 23. I was seized in the grip of a violent attack of claustrophobia. 'Shall we say together the Lord's Prayer?' I found myself saying. Breathing was becoming difficult for me. I felt as if I was about to faint.

'Two quick prayers,' I said to myself while everybody else was saying the Lord's Prayer. 'O Lord, we pray for those whom we love but see no longer.' A loud wail arose from Meg, the eldest daughter. I competed with her for audibility throughout the prayer, a competition which she won with ease as I found myself gasping for breath. 'I've got to finish now,' I ordered myself. 'The blessing of God Almighty be with us all, now and always,' I paraphrased. I closed my eyes for a few seconds. When I opened them the room appeared to be going around in circles. 'Would you excuse me,' I said to Meg, 'but I have to get back to the church to see that everything is ready for the service. I'll see you next week.'

A path was made for me among the mourners. As I emerged from the throng in the doorway I had never known the polluted air of Pontywen to be as welcome. I stood and took gulps of air as if I were drinking the best champagne. One of the drivers opened the front door of an ancient limousine for me. 'No, thank you.' I said. 'I shall walk on. By the time you leave here, I shall be in the church.'

When I arrived at St Mary's, I was met by the strains of 'Crimond' being played by Charles at the organ. As an organist he was a splendid pianist. He had no idea of how to use the foot pedals but he made up for that deficiency by playing the keyboard accurately and using the organ stops judiciously.

'You can stop that, Charles,' I said, tapping him on the shoulder and causing him to crash into a discord from fright. 'I didn't hear you come in,' he gasped.

'You could have put hymn-books and prayer-books out in the pews before you started on the organ. And before you say "Sorry" for the thousandth time you had better get cracking now before the mourners arrive. I don't think the Walters crowd want to see you.'

He was off the organ seat and down the aisle as if his life depended on it. Then, gathering up armfuls of books, he was running towards the front pews and dropping several as he went. By the time he had finished, he was sweating profusely and panting like an overweight prop forward after a run across the field.

'Just in time,' I said, as I walked down towards the door at the west end. 'I can hear the hearse drawing up.'

A few minutes later the cortege, led by myself reciting the burial verses in the Book of Common Prayer, made its way down the aisle to the foot of the chancel where I had placed the trestles to await the arrival of the coffin. Charles was featuring the vox angelica organ stop in a quiet, tremulous rendering of Mendelssohn's 'O Rest in the Lord' while the undertaker's sergeant-major tones barked out instructions to the four Walters brothers who were acting as bearers. 'Careful now. Mind what you're doing. Thank you, gentlemen.' At the back of the church friends and neighbours of the male gender filed into the pews while Mr Matthews loudly directed the family into the front pews.

I waited for the master of ceremonies to retire to the west end of the church before announcing the first hymn, 'The Lord's my Shepherd', played somewhat tentatively by the nervous curate but sung with fervour by the scratch male voice choir. When that ended I announced that we would say Psalm 90 in alternate verses. It turned out to be a solo recitation by the vicar because Charles was too frightened to make his voice heard at the organ and the congregation were reluctant to join in. However, they were prepared to co-operate in the saying of the Lord's Prayer and in a rousing rendition of 'Guide Me, O Thou Great Redeemer' to the tune of 'Cwm Rhondda', something they had often sung in pubs, bus outings and twice a year at Cardiff Arms Park.

At the end of the service we had to wait for some more military manoeuvres with the coffin supervised by RSM Matthews before we emerged from the church into the afternoon sunlight. My head had cleared and I felt at peace with the world. I was leading the coffin containing the body of a servant of God to its last resting-place. In the distance I could see the familiar sight of Full Back Jones standing by the newly dug grave, ready to sprinkle the earth over the coffin when it was laid in the ground.

The only sound to be heard was the crunch of gravel made by the feet of the bearers and the mourners. We came to a halt opposite the waiting grave-digger.

Suddenly the silence was shattered by a shout – 'This is the wrong grave.' It was Albert Walters, one of the two leading bearers who were standing with their mother's coffin weighing heavily on their shoulders. 'Put the coffin down,' ordered the undertaker. By now the air was filled with a hubbub of voices as loud as any when last orders were called at the Workingmen's Club.

'Where is the right one, then?' demanded Mr Matthews.

'Over by there, next to that headstone,' replied Albert. 'I used to come here with my mother when I was a kid. It had a wooden cross on it then but that's gone ages ago. We were going to 'ave it replaced but never got round to it.'

'The first thing to do is to go to the vestry to check the grave number,' I said. 'It's not like Full Back to make a mistake like this.'

'Well, according to the register, boss, the grave is F8,' interjected the grave-digger, 'double depth.'

'There's only one way to find out. Mr Matthews and Mr Walters, will you come with me to the vestry, please?' I asked, 'And will everyone else please stay where you are for the time being?' When we arrived at the vestry I opened the register with trembling fingers to find the page with the all-important number. Eventually I turned the entry for 17 January 1918, 'Albert Joseph Walters, age 37', and alongside in the margin 'F6'. It could have been mistaken for F8 because the curl at the end of the six at the top almost reached the bottom half of the figure, but there was no doubt that Full Back Jones had dug the wrong grave.

'What did I tell you?' said Albert. 'Now what do we do? We've got all the refreshments and that in the house. We can't ask everybody to come back tomorrow.'

'I'm afraid that is exactly what you will have to do. In no way will the grave-digger be able to open up the grave ready for burial today. I'm terribly sorry that this has happened. As you can see, it was a mistake which anybody could have made. If there had been a headstone or wooden cross on the grave this would never happened.'

'I tell you what, Vicar. After the way my mother was treated when she was alive and now when she's dead, the church 'as 'ad it, as far as I'm concerned, and I'm sure that will go for the rest of the family, I can tell you.'

Since none of the Walters family ever came to church it would have made no difference to the attendance figures whatsoever.

'It will have to be at three-thirty, Vicar,' said the undertaker. 'We've got a two o'clock at Moriah churchyard and you know how long they go on. So we'll meet you at the church then. What about the coffin? Do you want us to take it back to the house?'

'Not at all,' I replied, 'let the body rest in peace in the church. That will compensate for all the mayhem this afternoon. I suppose that's all right with you, Mr Walters. I'm sure it would upset your sisters and your wives if your mother's body came back to the house.'

'You're telling me, Vicar. It will be bad enough as it is without having my mother going back and fore like a yo-yo. I think it's disgraceful in any case. I tell you what, you haven't heard the last of this. I'll be writing to the paper for a start.'

'You do what you like, Mr Walters, but I'm sure your mother would not want a big fuss made about what has happened. She was a very dear lady who never said an unkind word about anybody. In the meanwhile I suggest that we go back and inform everybody about the new arrangement. The sooner your mother's mortal remains are taken back into the peace of the church the better.'

I closed the register and ushered the two men out of the vestry, apprehensive about the reaction of the waiting mourners. Albert raced back with the news that he was right about the grave. By the time I arrived at the wrongly dug grave, I was faced with an angry mob who minutes ago were the silent mourners. For the first time in my life I appreciated what Daniel must have felt in his predicament in the lions' den. In the meanwhile Full Back Jones had retreated behind a large gravestone, prepared to stay out of sight until the coast was clear.

'Gentlemen!' I shouted. 'I must apologize for this unfortunate happening. Since the grave was unmarked, the Sexton had to consult the register in the vestry. The grave number at first sight looked like F8 and that is the grave which he opened. However, when we examined the number a few minutes ago, it transpired that the number was F6.'

'Why couldn't it have transpired to Full Back that it was F6?' demanded Arthur Walters.

'Your brother will tell you, Mr Walters, that it was very difficult to tell the difference. Anyway, under the circumstances, I have to inform you that we shall meet at the church tomorrow at three-thirty when the burial will take place in the correct grave. In the meanwhile the body of the late Mrs Walters will lie at rest in the church until then. Once again I apologize for all the inconvenience involved and I hope that you all will be able to meet here tomorrow afternoon to pay your last respects to someone who was a true Christian in every meaning of that word. We shall say a few prayers in the church and then go to the graveside.'

My words seemed to have stilled the storm of protest. The Walters brothers once again carried the coffin on their shoulders into the church, only to find that my curate, in an unusual display of zeal, had taken the trestles back into the vestry. By now the bearers were showing signs of exhaustion. It had been a long walk from the grave. The undertaker had offered the services of his trolley for the funeral, but the men had insisted they wanted to carry their mother's body.

As Mr Matthews and I made our way to retrieve the missing support for the coffin, he said to me, 'I'll bring my trolley tomorrow. I bet they'll be glad of it. They'll have sore shoulders for a week after this.' When we entered the vestry there was no sign of the trestles in the alcove where they were kept. I opened the curtains which covered the cassocks and surplices but the stands were not there. Charles had struck again.

'Perhaps you had better go back into the church and suggest that they rest the coffin on top of the front pews, Mr Matthews, otherwise they will be in no fit state to attend the burial tomorrow.' The undertaker disappeared immediately. As I surveyed the vestry, I racked my brains for a solution to the mystery of the missing trestles. Then the vestry door opened. It was Full Back Jones.

'I thought you wanted them trestles in the church again. So what are they doing outside the door? I was coming back for my wheelbarrow from the boiler-'ouse when I saw them. I'm sorry for the mess-up about the graves, boss, but I could 'ave swore that was number eight. I'll 'ave to work like the clappers now to get that grave done for tomorrow.'

'That's all right, Full Back. You get back to that new grave and I'll get these trestles back where they are needed.' The thought of Full Back Jones working 'like the clappers' was as unlikely as Charles Wentworth-Baxter doing the same in his parochial duties. They were like 'two lovely berries moulded on one stem' in that respect, but certainly in no other.

Carrying the trestles on either arm, I staggered into the chancel to be met with glares from the Walters contingent. The undertaker managed to meet me and to take one of the trestles. 'You should have called me, Vicar,' he said.

When the trestles were in place, the brothers lowered the coffin to its resting place and then departed quickly from the scene, relieved from their burden and anxious to return to the house and the refreshments. In the meanwhile, the driver of the hearse began to bring the wreaths and cut flowers into the chancel. It was then that I remembered the church was to be invaded by the Parks Department at about the same time that the mourners would be entering the church for the few prayers. A dozen dire scenarios flooded into my mind. The mayoress, who was coming to inspect the decorations, would take it that the coffin in the midst of her red and yellow flowers was a bad omen for her year of office. The Walters family would resent the intrusion of the council workmen into the solemnity of their mother's funeral, and make another protest. Mourners would be colliding with the decorators who would be rushing to get the Saturday chore over as soon as possible.

I went back to the vicarage and sat in the armchair in my study, hunched up in despair. At this late stage I could hardly expect the parks superintendent to change his arrangements. On the other hand, to change the time of the funeral would be to invite a shower of coals of fire on my head from the Walters family. I realized the agony that Mr Hobson felt when he had to make his choice. The sound of Eleanor's car coming down the drive roused me from my melancholy. Thank God for Henry the Eighth and the marriage of the clergy he brought about, I said to myself, even if he had more than his fair share of wives. I arose from the armchair and went to meet her at the door, greeting her with a kiss.

'What's that all about?' she inquired. 'If it's cupboard love, I am afraid you will have to wait quite a while. I am expecting a full surgery at five o'clock. If it is not cupboard love, then by the look on your face it is a tale of woe and you have just a quarter of an hour to tell Eleanor.'

We moved into the sitting-room where she sat down on the settee and patted the cushion beside her. 'I am sitting comfortably,' she said, quoting the presenters' words on the new children's programme on the wireless. 'So you can begin, but cut it short, there's a dear.'

By the time I had finished my account of the afternoon's events she was convulsed with laughter. 'It's no laughing matter, love. It's a whole series of catastrophes. There's poor old Granny Walters who should be resting in her grave in peace, hanging about in the chancel and holding up the preparations for the civic service, not to mention her family who are in militant mood, to say the least.'

'Fred, my love,' replied my wife, 'poor old Granny Walters is looking down from above and feeling very important at being able to feature in the Dai Spout saga just before his moment of glory. She could never have had such prominence if she were still confined to her bed in Balaclava Street. I don't see why you can't ring up the parks superintendent and ask him if he could either come earlier with his workmen or later, as the case may be. It is just one of those things that happen. Go and ring him now. He should still be in his office. If he is not, then you can get someone there to ask him to ring you as soon as possible.'

I went into my study, found the Parks Department number and dialled it nervously. There was an instant reply. 'Can I speak to the superintendent, please?' I asked. 'Speaking,' said the voice.

'This is Fred Secombe. I am afraid that there has been an unexpected hitch in the arrangements for the decoration of the church tomorrow afternoon. You see, at the time when you are due to start your activities, there is a body in the church and there will be mourners there for a short service a little later.'

'I see,' said the voice, 'but why didn't you tell me this when we arranged the time?'

'Well, the funeral should have taken place this afternoon, but unfortunately it has had to be postponed until tomorrow and the undertaker cannot come earlier because he has already arranged a funeral at Moriah Chapel earlier in the afternoon. The – er – truth is that the gravedigger dug the wrong grave.'

There was a long pause and a bout of coughing at the other end of the phone.

'I am sorry about that, Vicar. I shall contact my men immediately and arrange for them to begin earlier tomorrow morning. We shall be in the church at 11 a.m, if that suits you.'

'That is fine by me. I hope the coffin on its stand and the flowers placed around it will not interfere with your preparations.'

'Not at all, Vicar. Its presence will help to keep the noise down while they work. There won't be much shouting tomorrow, I can tell you. I shall let the mayoress know of the change in time. If she can't make it, I'm afraid that's just too bad. By the way, how did the grave-digger come to dig the wrong grave?'

'It's a long story, I'm afraid, and is best summed up by saying he didn't know a six from an eight.'

'Well, having had a glimpse of him I am not at all surprised. He looks as if he doesn't know what soap and water is, either.'

When I went into the sitting-room, my beloved said, 'By the look on your face, it would seem that all is well. What would you do without me, your acting unpaid assistant? Talking of which, isn't it great that I shall be having my acting paid assistant with me on Monday? No more unreliable locums and more time to spend with you, love.' She jumped up, kissed me lightly on the lips and waltzed out of the room. In no time at all, her car was on its way up the drive.

Next morning Charles and I were joined by Granny Walters for our service. 'It's a bit eerie having the coffin up here in the chancel with us,' said my curate.

'The only reply to that is that at least she is having your company in death, if she didn't have it in life, and don't forget to remember her in the prayers after the third collect.'

Before we could reach that point, there was a loud banging on the vestry door. 'Hold on, Charles,' I said. 'I expect that is Full Back. Only he could be making enough noise to wake the dead.' I went into the vestry and opened the door.

'Boss, I've put the blessed pick through my foot.' He

pointed down to the instep of his filthy wellington boot. Blood was oozing through a hole.

'Stay there,' I said. 'I'll bring my wife along straight-away. Charles, get a chair for him.'

I ran back to the vicarage. Eleanor was in her dressing-gown in the kitchen, making a cup of tea.

'What on earth is the matter?' she said.

'Full Back has put a pick through his foot,' I gasped.

'Get the car out of the garage while I do a quick change,' she ordered. By the time I had manoeuvred the car to the front of the house, she was dressed and was carrying her medical bag with her.

'Heaven knows what infection has got into that foot, knowing his unwashed state,' she said. 'Obviously he will have to be taken to the hospital and given penicillin as soon as possible.'

When we arrived outside the vestry, Charles was look-ing paler than the patient whose face was so dirty that it was difficult to tell the state of his complexion. 'Sorry about this, boss,' said Full Back. 'What's going to 'appen with the grave?'

'Never mind about the grave, let's get that wellington off so that the doctor can have a look at your foot.'

'I'll get the boot off,' said my wife. When she removed it, the sight of the blood streaming from the wound combined with the smell of his unwashed foot turned my stomach. Charles had disappeared into the vestry, unable to cope with the unveiling of Full Back's injury.

In no time at all Eleanor had placed a piece of lint and a piece of cotton-wool on the foot and bound them tightly with a roll of bandage. She took me aside into the vestry where my curate was sitting at my desk with a vacant expression on his face, obviously overwhelmed by

the occasion. 'Stage one,' she said. 'The next thing is to get him to the vicarage and bathe the wound. Fred, you had better phone the hospital casualty ward and prepare them for the emergency treatment. I think he has broken the bone but the most important thing at the moment is to kill the infection. Otherwise it will not be a broken bone to worry about but septicaemia and the prospect of him losing his leg. Charles, you and Fred get on either side of him. Then, when I have turned the car around, get him into the back with his leg on the seat.'

I had never been in such close proximity to the grave-digger, whose lack of personal hygiene generated enough aroma to rival anything the local pig farm could supply. Charles's complexion had now progressed from white to green. In the meanwhile Full Back Jones was suffering so much pain that his language in my presence knew no restraint. 'Blessed' had become 'bloody', and his foot was hurting like 'buggery' instead of like 'blazes'.

When Eleanor had ministered to his immediate needs in the vicarage she drove off in her car with him to the hospital, leaving me to find someone to dig the grave for the afternoon's burial. As far as I could see, the only hope I had was to contact Tom Cadwallader, the sexton at Llanhyfryd Church. Tom was a giant of a man and would be able to do the job in the short time available. However, his humble cottage was devoid of a telephone, as it was of electricity and other modern conveniences.

My ancient Morris Minor made the journey to Llanhyfryd at a speed which cut at least ten minutes off my average for the three-mile run. When I arrived at the cottage, his wife was on the gate in earnest conversation with Miss Owen who presided at the harmonium in the parish church. 'You're in a hurry, Vicar,' said Mrs Cadwallader, startled by the screech of brakes and my rapid emergence from the vehicle.

'Where's Tom?' I asked.

'He's down in the bottom of the garden getting some of his compost heap for his kidney beans,' she replied.

'I've got to see him at once,' I said. She took a few steps down the path and shouted, 'Tom!' It was loud enough to be heard back in Pontywen. To my intense relief the burly figure of her husband ambled up the path.

'You're up here early, Vicar.' The very slowness of his speech had a calming influence on the turbulence in my head.

'Can you do a job for me urgently? In fact, straight-away.'

He looked at one quizzically.

'What job is that, Vicar?'

'Digging a grave in Pontywen Churchyard ready for a burial this afternoon.' There was a long pause while his brain came to terms with my request.

'Where's Full Back Jones, then?'

'He's been taken to hospital. He put a pick through his foot.'

'Nasty,' he said. Tom was a man of few words. 'You want me to come now, then?'

'Yes, please.'

'What about his dinner?' asked Mrs Cadwallader.

'I'll see he gets something to eat at the vicarage. I'll bring him back as soon as he has filled the grave in. I'm afraid it won't be until about five o'clock.'

'Well, that's his Saturday gone,' she said crossly.

'I was only going to be in the garden, woman,' said her husband. That was the longest sentence he spoke for the rest of the time he was in my presence that day.

## 8

'He's a lucky man,' said Eleanor. 'The X-ray shows no break in the bone but there is severe bruising. The doctor thinks his wellingtons were thick enough to prevent any further injury.'

I met her as she was on her way out to take her surgery. Tom Cadwallader was now busily engaged opening up the grave, only too happy that Pontywen Churchyard was free of the rock which was to be found in parts of Llanhyfryd Churchyard. There had been one famous occasion not long after my arrival in the parish when he used dynamite as a last resort to open up a grave. Unfortunately it had been when the mourners were already in church for the service. The loud blast which ensued was like the Last Trump and coincided with my reading of the burial lesson. 'The trumpet shall sound and the dead shall arise.' There has never been a more startled congregation than that one, not to mention the clergyman. I was unable to continue the lesson for quite a while.

'Mrs Cadwallader is worried that her husband will be without food. So I have told her that we shall give him something to eat, forgetting that Mrs Watkins will not be here today because it's Saturday, I hope you don't mind.'

'Fear not, Frederick, and all will be well. I shall pick up some fish and chips on my way back from my visits. All you have to do is to put the oven on at about a quarter to one. I would suggest that you get a bottle of beer for Tom. He is bound to be very thirsty, excavating in this warm weather. Perhaps a barrel would be more appropriate by the look of his girth. By the way, there's one good thing about Full Back's stay in hospital. He will come out so clean that people in Pontywen won't know him.'

'Give him a month back home and he will soon be recognizable. Anyway, he will be anxious to be up and about as soon as possible. He will not want Tom Cadwallader to be invading his patch if he can help it.'

'I must be off, love. I'm late for my surgery as it is. You can get on with your epic for tomorrow. Don't forget you have the whole of the council at your mercy. So sock it to 'em, kid.'

'Very elegant encouragement, I must say, from a vicar's wife.'

'Oh, shut up! Give us a kiss and let me go to my duties.'

I granted her request and watched her shoot up the drive like a latter-day Malcolm Campbell.

As I went back into the house, I thought over what she had said. I had intended to preach an innocuous sermon based on the parable of the Good Samaritan, stressing that councillors had to be good neighbours to all the citizens whom they represented. However, since the little conversation with Bill Moscow and his hint of corruption in the town hall I had felt more than a little disturbed. Occasionally I had heard tales of school-teachers bribing councillors to secure a headmaster's job for them but I had regarded such rumours as tittle-tattle. The Communist's words indicated that bribes were not confined to the sphere of education but extended to building contracts as well.

In the study, I began to thumb through the Epistles to find a suitable text and in no time at all I found what I wanted. It was as if I had been led by the Spirit to find it, St Paul's Epistle to the Romans, the thirteenth verse of the thirteenth chapter: 'Let us walk honestly as in the day.' Although I was unaccustomed to praying in public without the use of a prayer-book, my sermons were always preached without notes. I had thought of writing out my civic service sermon, but now I felt that I could best achieve my objective by my usual method of looking at the congregation and addressing them face to face, without the impediment of being tied to 'a piece of paper', as Dai Spout had put it.

After an hour of reading through commentaries on the Epistle and some essays on Church and State, I subsided into an armchair to sort out my thoughts. My musings were interrupted by a ring on the doorbell. It was the parks superintendent.

'Excuse me, Vicar. I should like your advice on the decoration of the end of the church where you have the altar. I know you won't like it too cluttered up because of your communion service in the morning. I hope I have not interrupted you in your work, but we have finished in the body of the church and I would like to let the men get away for what's left of their Saturday. They weren't overjoyed when they knew they had to work today, I can tell you.'

'I'm sure they weren't. I'm in the middle of preparing my sermon for tomorrow. Still, a break will do me a power of good. Has the mayoress been to see the decorations?'

'She was going to come for a few minutes to inspect the work when it was done. Then when she heard that there was a coffin in the church, she changed her mind. She said it would be a bad omen for her to see it.'

'I thought it might have that effect on her. Well, the old lady inside it would be the last to put a curse on anyone. To talk of much lighter things, Mr Powell, is your good lady looking forward to joining us for *The Gondoliers*?'

'By the way, Vicar, my name is Hugh. Yes, Rhoda is quite excited about it. She says it's the only chance she will ever have of becoming a Duchess. So she may as well make the most of it.'

When we entered the church, it was like a visit to the Chelsea Flower Show. The window-sills, the ends of the pews and the font were ablaze with red and yellow flowers. At the foot of the lectern were pots of red geraniums. The only clash of colour was in the chancel where Granny Walters' coffin lay surmounted by a massive wreath forming the word 'Mam' in white carnations and surrounded by wreaths in colours of all kinds.

'I thought we had better leave the choir stalls alone because of the coffin and the wreaths. So we ought to have a splash of colour on the altar and on either side of it. I've got some red and yellow roses for the vases on the altar and I wondered whether I might put a few pots of geraniums at the back where they would not be in your way at the communion service tomorrow morning.'

'That will be fine, Hugh. My name is Fred. So please drop the "Vicar" bit from now on. Yes, I think you have done the church proud. I doubt if it will ever look as splendid as it is now. The congregation at tomorrow morning's service are in for a delightful surprise.'

'We'll remove the pots of flowers on Monday morning but the cut flowers are yours until they fade away. It's up to you, Fred, to do what you like with them.'

'There's only one answer to that. On Sunday evening we shall bunch them up and take them to the housebound members of the congregation who will be thrilled to have them.'

I left Hugh Powell in the church supervising the adornment of the sanctuary and went into the churchyard to see how the stand-in grave-digger was progressing with his labours. To my amazement there were now two large mounds of earth on either side of the opening and the only indication of Tom's presence was the loud grunt which accompanied each spadeful of soil. When I reached the grave, he was several feet down.

'Nearly finished, Vicar,' he said.

'Well done!' I replied. 'It takes Full Back half a day just to dig a few feet down. Would you like me to drive you home now, and pick you up later to fill in the grave?'

'No, thanks. Better stay here now. Do a bit of tidying up that long grass.'

'In that case, you can have some fish and chips at one o'clock and a bottle of beer to go with it.' He wiped away the sweat which was streaming down his ruddy countenance and almost smiled. The thought of being apart from Mrs Cadwallader for the next four or five hours and being fed and adequately watered had made his day.

As I was emerging from the jug and bottle department of the Lamb and Fly, with a carrier bag laden with half a dozen small bottles of the local brew, I was confronted by Bertie Owen, a militant shop steward in matters ecclesiastical as well as industrial. 'Why haven't any of the sidesmen from St Padarn's been invited to help at the civic service in St Mary's? After all, it's something that concerns the whole parish, not just the favoured few up there. I tell you what, if I had still been churchwarden you would have known about it by now.'

'I'm sure I would have, Bertie, but as you are not churchwarden I don't see that it's any business of yours. Obviously you don't know it, but I have asked both the wardens from St Padarn's to come and help at the service. Since we only need six sidesmen at most to hand out the service forms, it is pointless having any more present. They would be falling over each other. You will be very welcome to attend the service even if your help isn't needed.'

'Then, what about this business of Mrs Walters going to be buried in the wrong grave and the curate not coming to see her?'

'Bertie, you really are an old applewoman. If you think anything of your church, you had better stop going around and stirring up trouble. It's small wonder that the congregation replaced you at the last Easter Vestry.'

'That's all you can say after everything I've done for St Padarn's. Well!' He turned on his heels and strode off.

When Eleanor came in with the fish and chips from Cascarni's, I told her about the encounter with Bertie. 'What did you expect, love?' she said. 'Obviously the Walters family are going to broadcast their grievances as much as possible, and who better to do their broadcasting for them than Bertie Owen? As for the sidesmen required for the service tomorrow, only he could make a fuss about that. He's just frustrated that he can't be there bossing everybody about. You had better go across and get Tom to come for his victuals. Far better to have his silent fellowship than Bertie's backchat.'

I found him in a corner of the churchyard, wielding a scythe in the heat of the day. 'This could do with sharpening, Vicar,' he commented.

'I don't doubt that, Tom. Full Back very rarely used it. He is only too pleased to have Jones Blaenycwm's sheep in here to keep the grass down.'

'I'll take it home and sharpen it.'

'Never mind about that for the time being. Come and have some food and drink.'

As Eleanor forecast, we did all the talking while Tom concentrated on eating and drinking. By the time the meal was over he had emptied four bottles of best bitter. It was a happy man who went back to the grass-cutting.

We were in the sitting-room enjoying a gin and tonic when an MG two-seater pre-war model made a noisy entrance down the drive. In it was a young man in a sports jacket and open-necked shirt, plus cravat, and a young lady in a bright summery dress. They were out of the car in a trice as if on urgent business.

I went to the door and opened it just as the young man was about to press the button.

'Don't tell me, Vicar. You saw us come down the drive.'

'To be more exact, I heard you come down the drive and then I saw you.'

'It is rather noisy, I must admit. I am Gareth Andrews and this is my fiancée, Heather Francis. My apologies for intruding upon you but it was such a nice day that I thought it would be a good idea to bring Heather with me to see the place where I shall be working.'

By now, Eleanor had joined me on the doorstep. 'Welcome, partner, or should I say "pard", and welcome, too, to the pardess.'

There was much hand-shaking all round. Gareth Andrews was at least some five inches taller than my five foot seven, whilst Heather was about the same height as

Eleanor in the five foot region. He was dark-haired and sported a luxuriant black moustache whilst his fiancée was a platinum blonde. They made a handsome couple.

'Please come in. We are just enjoying a gin and tonic. I am about to take a funeral in an hour or so's time and the gin is the only strong drink which will not taint my breath. Would you care to join us?'

'By all means,' said Heather. 'It is my one and only drink. That doesn't go for Gareth but he's omnivorous, anyway.'

In no time at all, we were a happy and congenial quartet. I was very glad for my wife who had been coping with a burgeoning practice, completely reliant on a mixed bag of locums for help, some of whom were not as competent as they might have been. I filled their glasses and suggested a toast. 'To the new era in the Pontywen medical history and long may it prosper.'

'Come off it, boss,' said my beloved. 'I should be doing that, not you. You can do that for your next change of curate, whenever that may be. Anyway, I second what he has said.'

We raised our glasses and drank, not as deeply as Tom Cadwallader but just as satisfactorily.

Time went by very quickly. Gareth and Heather talked about their wedding plans and their need to find a home in Pontywen. Eleanor gave Gareth a rough picture of what was involved in the practice with its preponderance of lung complaints. I looked at my watch. The funeral was due in quarter of an hour's time.

'I'm afraid I have to go now,' I said, 'but I should be back in half an hour or so. There are just a few prayers to be said in church and then the committal.'

Gareth stood up. 'Do you mind if I come across to the

317

church with you? My uncle is an incumbent in the Hereford diocese and I have spent many happy hours at his rectory. I'd like to have a look at your church since I shall be worshipping there before long. In any case it will give the two girls an opportunity for a natter.'

As we walked up the church path I suggested to him that he could have a look inside the church while I went to see Tom Cadwallader to check if everything was ready for the burial. There was no sign of his burly figure anywhere. I went up to the far end of the churchyard where he had been wielding the scythe. There was neither sight nor sound of any activity. On the way back to the grave, I heard a sound, a sound of inactivity. It came from behind a large gravestone, a loud snore. The Llanhyfryd sexton was sprawled out in careless abandon, with the blade of the scythe in perilous proximity to his scarlet moon of a face. Like Granny Walters, he was at peace with the world, but unlike her he was soon to awake to the harsh reality of life. Carefully I removed the scythe from its place, then I caught hold of him and shouted, 'Wake up, Tom.' There was not even a flicker of an eyelid. The snores grew louder. It was evident that the four bottles of beer and the heat of the sun had anaesthetized him as effectively as any patient in the operating theatre of Pontywen Hospital.

I ran rather than walked to the church. Gareth was standing in the nave surrounded by the red and yellow flowers, admiring the east window of the church installed in 1925 in memory of Sir David Jones-Williams' father. It depicted the manger scene at Bethlehem, where the three kings with their gifts were supplemented by three miners with helmeted head-lamps, apparently brought there by courtesy of the colliery owner who had exploited them.

'Gareth!' I gasped. 'I'm in trouble. The grave-digger who should be at the interment sprinkling the earth on the coffin and, more importantly, filling in the grave afterwards is lying behind a grave dead drunk.'

'That's terrible,' he said. 'You'll have to sack him. He can't come to do his job in that state, it's unbelievable.'

'It's believable, all right,' I replied, 'because I gave him the four bottles of beer which caused it. My main concern at the moment is the funeral which is due any minute now.'

He looked at me as if I were as drunk as Tom Cadwallader.

'I'll explain later,' I went on, 'but how can I get him round?'

'My dear Vicar, you can't get him round immediately to say the least. Why don't I divest myself of this jacket and leave it in the vestry? I'll get the handfuls of earth and do the sprinkling. If we can't bring him round to normality, I'll fill in the grave. I know what to do. I've seen it done often enough during the war. As for the sprinkling that comes with the earth to earth, ashes to ashes, dust to dust bit, leave it to me.'

By the time I had robed, the funeral cortege was arriving at the churchyard gates. I went out to meet them. The undertaker came up to me. 'Straight out into the churchyard, Vicar?'

'A few prayers in church first, Mr Matthews.'

'As you say, Vicar. I just thought that as we've already had the service, there was no need for anything else.'

The drivers opened the car doors for the mourners to alight. There was obvious hostility on the faces of the mourners who felt that they were in some kind of unnecessary replay with no worthwhile jamboree to compensate for it afterwards.

I went on ahead into the church and took my place in my stall ready to read the prayers. Opposite me, out of sight of the mourners, Gareth stood at the side of the organ, now minus his jacket but not his cravat. He gave me the thumbs-up sign, presumably for my encouragement. I felt as if I were in some kind of bizarre pantomime, rather than at Granny Walters' funeral.

One by one the mourners shuffled down the aisle and into the pews where they surveyed the floral decorations with some bewilderment. When they were all seated I stood up to address them. 'I am very sorry that you have had to come back here for the second time. I understand fully the distress you must feel as a result. We shall say a few prayers for the repose of the soul of Elizabeth Walters and then proceed to the graveside for the burial. Let us pray.'

The mourners slumped forward in the pews in what has been described as 'the shampoo position' and mumbled the Lord's Prayer. After the reading of the prayers, I moved down the nave and waited to lead the cortege out into the churchyard. Mr Matthews removed the wreaths from around the coffin and then in his sergeant-major voice gave instructions to the Walters brothers for the carrying of the coffin. After a number of manoeuvres they began to bear their mother's body down the aisle. As we came out of the church and walked down the central path of the churchyard, I could see Gareth in the distance, his shirt-sleeves rolled up, obviously ready for business. When we reached the graveside he was standing behind a neighbouring gravestone, keeping a watch on the proceedings. 'Man that is born of woman has but a short time to live,' I intoned, as we moved from the path to the grave which had been dug deeper and far more neatly than anything Full Back had done since I was in Pontywen. I motioned to Gareth to come forward before I said the words of committal. When his tall figure appeared beside me clad in expensively cut trousers and a silk cravat adorning his open-necked shirt, carrying a handful of earth, the undertaker and the bearers stopped in their tracks, paralysed by astonishment. There could not have been a greater contrast between the filthy appearance of the bearer of the earth yesterday and what they witnessed now.

Mr Matthews recovered his composure: 'Thread the webbing through the 'andles, gentlemen. Right. Now when you stand on the plank, wait for me to say "lower" before you start and don't forget to lower gently. Hang on to the webbing after you've lowered, don't forget. Then leave the ends on the planks.' When the brothers had complied with his instructions and the coffin lay in its place, I began the words of the committal. 'For as much as it hath pleased Almighty God of his great mercy to take unto himself the soul of our dear sister here departed, we therefore commit her body to the ground.' I nodded to Gareth who stepped forward smartly and collided with Albert Walters who would have joined his mother had it not been for the intervention of Arthur, who pulled him back from the brink.

'Sorry, old man,' said the volunteer sexton, as the two brothers glared at him.

'Earth to earth,' I went on, and a shower of small stones and clay thudded on the coffin. 'Ashes to ashes', and another fusillade followed. 'Dust to dust', and by now Gareth had run out of ammunition and an anticlimax of a small plop resulted. 'You can move back now,' I whispered to him. 'Apologies for running out of earth,' he whispered in reply.

'In sure and certain hope of the Resurrection to Eternal Life,' I continued, uninterrupted for the rest of the service. By the time the prayers ended, Gareth had disappeared. I shook hands with mourners who then spent five minutes looking at the wreaths that the two drivers had brought from the church. In the meanwhile I was approached by the undertaker who was anxious to discover the identity of Mr X and what had happened to Full Back. 'Excuse me for asking,' he asked, 'but who dug that grave? It wasn't Jones, that's for sure. It's almost professional. What's more, who's that toff who threw the earth, not to mention the stones, on the coffin?'

When he had heard all the details, minus any information about Tom Cadwallader's drunken incapacity, he wandered off back to the mourners nearby to tell the story about Full Back's injury. I had told him that Gareth Andrews was standing in for Tom because the grave-digger had 'been taken short'. Mr Matthews was most impressed that the new doctor had volunteered his services. 'Sounds like a good man,' he said.

I went back to the scene of the Cadwallader siesta to find Gareth kneeling alongside the recumbent figure. 'He is still in the arms of Morpheus, I'm afraid. He won't be in any fit state to fill in that grave today. I would suggest that we leave him here for the time being. If you can provide me with a spade, I shall do my best to fill in the grave.' We went back to the boiler-house where the grave-digging implements were kept. He looked at the pick. 'That's a nasty-looking tool,' he said. 'I tell you what, if old Tom had been using it he would have pinned his foot to the floor. It's a good thing that your Full Back is such a half-hearted worker who wouldn't use up much energy in his work. He probably gave it a gentle prod.' He put the spade over his shoulder and began to sing the dwarfs' chorus from Disney's *Snow White*: 'Heigh ho, heigh ho, as off to work we go.'

In no time at all, spadefuls of earth were raining down into the grave. Granny Walters' coffin disappeared very quickly. It took Gareth under an hour to fill in the earth and level it off.

'If ever you lose your job,' I said, 'I'll take you on here for a reasonable wage. Excellent. Thank you very much indeed.' The sweat was streaming down his face and his cravat had been stuffed into his trouser-pocket. His hair was straggling over his forehead. He had tucked his trousers into his socks to prevent any soiling of them, but his once-polished shoes were now bedaubed with top-quality Pontywen mud.

As we went back to the vestry to collect his jacket, we were met by Eleanor and Heather who showed the same reaction as the undertaker and the mourners at the sight of Gareth. 'What on earth have you been doing?' demanded Heather. 'Look at the state of you!'

'It's my fault,' I said.

'I might have known,' remarked my wife.

'No, it's not his fault at all,' Gareth interrupted her as she was about to elaborate on various incidents in my past. 'I volunteered to fill in a grave.' The two girls stared at him as if he had taken leave of his senses.

'I should have said it's our fault, love,' I explained. 'Tom Cadwallader is lying behind a gravestone, paralytically inebriate. Since we supplied him with the means to achieve that state and it was you who suggested we give him beer with his fish and chips, I suppose it is our fault.' The explanation was followed by a stunned silence. 'I think more to the point at the moment, is how we are to bring him back from the Land of Nod and how I am going to explain to Mrs Cadwallader, pillar of the Mothers' Union in Llanhyfryd, that the vicar rendered her husband drunk and incapable.'

'The first thing is to get him to the vicarage and fill him with black coffee,' said Eleanor. 'Let me get my jacket from the vestry first,' suggested Gareth, 'then Fred and I can pick him up between us and propel him in the direction of the vicarage.'

'In that case,' my wife replied, 'Heather and I will get back there as quickly as possible and get the coffee brewing.'

By the time Gareth and I returned to the gravestone behind which Tom Cadwallader had collapsed into inertia, there were signs that the giant was coming back to life. His snoring had ceased and his attitude of careless abandon had given way to a knees-up position with his back against the stone.

'Are you awake, Tom?' I shouted. He shook his head as if the noise of my voice was more than he could bear. A frown wrinkled his smooth forehead and one eye opened in an attempt to focus on me.

'Vicar,' he murmured, 'where am I?'

'You're in the churchyard, Tom, and we are going to help you up and get you back to the vicarage. Then we shall take you home to Llanhyfryd.'

Slowly, very slowly, his senses returned. 'What about the funeral, Vicar? Have they come yet?'

'They have come and gone. Now we want you to come with us.'

Gareth looked over the grave-digger's head at me and winked. 'Now then, old man,' he said, 'we are going to put our arms around you to help you up. One, two, three.' It was like trying to lift a recalcitrant elephant. Any more attempts like that and I was in danger of incurring a hernia.

'What about the grave?' slurred Tom.

'Don't worry about that. This gentleman has filled it in.'

He stared at Gareth. 'He has?'

'Yes, it has all been seen to.' Tom shook his head slowly in disbelief. He still showed no inclination to leave his tombstone.

'Come on, Tom. Mrs Cadwallader will be wondering where you have got to.'

The mention of his wife's name acted like an alarm-bell. He swivelled his bottom around and used his long arms to catch hold of the stone to haul himself up. He remained draped over the memorial to Thomas Arthur Davies and his family for a minute or two.

I began to wonder if the bulk of his weight would make the gravestone keel over. 'Ready to move now?' I inquired. 'We'll come on either side of you to steady you.'

He left his anchorage and attempted to stand. It was fortunate that he listed towards Gareth who was strong enough to withstand the pressure. Had it been towards me, we would have been in a heap, with myself the flattened middle of a sandwich between Tom and Pontywen Churchyard.

Slowly our trio began to move towards the vicarage like a human inchworm. By the time we reached the church gates, Tom's head was beginning to clear and his legs showed a degree of co-ordination. As we came down the vicarage drive, we had an interested audience watching us through the sitting-room window.

Eleanor and Heather came out to meet us, showing unseemly signs of merriment to the extent of wiping tears from their eyes. 'Come round the side to the kitchen,' said Eleanor. 'I've got a jug of black coffee ready.'

Once inside the kitchen, Tom slumped into a chair. 'Here you are, Tom, a mug of nice black coffee. That will put you right in no time.' She placed the mug firmly into his hands.

'Don't drink coffee,' he said.

'You try this coffee. It's a special brand. You'll love it,' coaxed my wife.

He put the receptacle to his mouth and took a deep gulp. Then he shuddered. It reminded me of the way my father drank whisky – a shudder with every mouthful. Tom wiped his hand across his mouth and took another large swallow, then another. He finished the jug of coffee as quickly as he had consumed the beer earlier.

'Better get back,' he announced, and stood up as steadily as if he had never been in contact with the demon drink. I heaved a sigh of relief.

When we arrived at his cottage, Mrs Cadwallader was at the gate, in a state of high dudgeon. 'I thought you would have been back long before now, Vicar. His dinner has dried up in the oven.'

'For a number of reasons, it took longer than I thought, I'm afraid. Anyway, I have paid Tom overtime, as it were. So he got two pounds ten instead of two pounds. I hope that will compensate for the inconvenience.'

This news had its desired effect. The scowl vanished from Mrs Cadwallader's face and her beloved was welcomed, not with open arms, but with considerably less hostility than otherwise.

That night, when Gareth and Heather had gone, my wife and I were relaxing in the sitting-room before retiring. 'Well, love,' she said. 'Granny Walters is up there, absolutely delighted. She has been lying in state in the Parish church, surrounded by flowers provided by the mayor and corporation. It has taken two grave-diggers to dig her grave, but the final accolade is the best of all, the grave has been filled in by the new doctor in Pontywen. Her cup must be running over.'

# 9

The clouds were queueing up to empty themselves on Pontywen the next morning, after a week of unbroken sunshine. 'Do you think the Almighty is trying to tell Dai Spout something, as a non-attending Baptist who switched his allegiance to the Church for the sake of prestige? Then there is his wife, a non-attending Anglican who has seen to it that her objectionable young son has been confirmed in order to give weight to his testimonial when he applies for a job. What a pair! No wonder a deep depression has rushed in from the west.' Eleanor was looking out through our bedroom window on a typical rainswept Valley scene.

'He sendeth the rain on the just and the unjust, according to the Sermon on the Mount,' I replied, 'and like it or not, I am the mayor's chaplain for the next twelve months, so we had better make the most of it.'

'Come on, Frederick, where's your sense of humour? You sound just as pompous as Dai Spout himself. If being mayor's chaplain has this effect on you, you'll be unbearable by this time next year. When you say, we had better make the most of it, surely that means we can have plenty of laughs out of the experience.'

'OK, love. You win. Perhaps I am treating the whole business too seriously. What about rejoining the Gilbert and Sullivan Society? After all, you now have a partner in your practice. So your workload will be much lighter and Aneurin still has not found a leading soprano. It means, too, that I shall have to persuade Iorweth Ellis that he is at his best as a chorus-leader. Then I can take over the tenor lead again and play Marco to your Gianetta.'

'You Machiavellian vicar, you! Then, of course, you will tell Aneurin not to bother about asking his colleague to take over the production and you will be in full charge once again. You are not only Machiavellian, you are Pooh Bah as well.'

'I acknowledge my transgressions and my pride is ever before me. Yes, you are dead right. I should love to take over the production once again. It will certainly be a busy time but the G & S will be the perfect antidote to a year with Mr and Mrs Dai Spout. With the help of *The Gondoliers* I shall be able to survive.'

'With the help of a quick bath and shave, you will be able to take the eight o'clock service. You had better get a move on, love. The godly few will have an unforgettable experience awaiting them, a quiet communion with the Almighty in Kew Gardens. They will not appreciate a breathless arrival of the vicar into their midst, I can assure you.'

It was ten to eight when I slipped into the vestry by the side door to be greeted by David Vaughan-Jenkins, the vicar's warden, who made a point of being in the church for the early communion at least a quarter of an hour before the service was due to commence. 'Very impressive, Vicar,' he said. 'I have never seen the church look so lovely, though I must confess I should have preferred a colour scheme of blue and white rather than red and yellow. Still, beggars can't be choosers.' He had once been an unsuccessful Conservative candidate in a by-election in the Valleys, with a five per cent share of the vote. 'I still bear the scars,' he had told me.

'Everything is ready, Vicar,' said Gwyn Evans as he came into the vestry from the sanctuary. He was a pleasant sixteen-year-old who acted as server at that service and who was as punctual as the churchwarden. 'The place is ponging like a – a lady's boudoir. I nearly fell over a pot of geraniums when I was putting out the bread and wine.' He grinned like a Cheshire cat and proceeded to put on his surplice to hide his blushes.

I went out into the heavily scented air of the chancel, accompanied by the server, to commence the service for the regular dozen who attended because they did not wish to be distracted by the singing and the sermon which were an essential part of the eleven o'clock Eucharist, twelve individuals who each had their private line to the source of their being.

All was proceeding according to the usual pattern of this service until it reached the administration of the bread and wine. One by one the worshippers came out of their pews slowly as if loath to reach the altar rails. Then it happened. Miss Doris Williams, an elderly spinster, a devout lady with a large nose and spectacles which seemed to have difficulty in surmounting it, collapsed as the queue was forming in the chancel. I was standing with a wafer poised between my thumb and forefinger when the worshippers formed a scrum around the unconscious Miss Williams who had been caught in his arms by David Vaughan-Jenkins as she fell.

Since Doris Williams was scarcely more than six or seven stone in weight, the churchwarden was able to carry her into the vestry as if she were a babe-in-arms. As they disappeared the rest of the worshippers recovered their composure and the service continued. When I had given the blessing, Gwyn and I proceeded into the vestry to find Miss Williams sitting up in my chair with a complexion like a whited sepulchre. 'I'm so sorry, Vicar,' she breathed. 'I must have fainted. I always fast before my communion, as you know. It may be that the strong scent of those lovely flowers affected my empty stomach. I have never passed out like this before. It was providential that Mr Vaughan-Jenkins was behind me to catch me as I fell.' She gave him one of her special smiles. He reciprocated with a faint glimpse of his teeth.

As he counted the collection, he informed her that he would take her home in his car once his duties in church were over. He was rewarded with one of her extra-special smiles.

When they had gone, Gwyn said to me as he was leaving, 'It's a good thing Mrs Vaughan-Jenkins wasn't here. Otherwise he'd be in trouble, wouldn't he?'

'Go on home, you naughty boy,' I told him. 'Otherwise you will be in trouble.'

'How did the eight o'clock contingent like the decorations?' inquired Eleanor when I returned to the vicarage.

'At least one of them regarded it as a knock-out,' I replied. 'Miss Williams, Sebastopol Street, fainted as she approached the altar rails and blamed it on the strong scent of the flowers. She left me stranded with the wafer in my hand while everybody else turned their attention on her. However, David, the warden, caught her as she fell and carried her into the vestry.'

'That must be the one and only romantic moment in her life,' said my wife. 'I should not be surprised if she contrives one or two more collapses if David happens to be behind her in the godly queue.'

'You're as bad as young Gwyn Evans, Eleanor. He suggested that the warden would have been in trouble if his wife had been there.'

'I don't think Elvira Vaughan-Jenkins, president of the WI and valued customer of Pontywen's only ladies' hairdressing salon would consider Doris Williams a rival for her husband's affections. She would be much more concerned if her husband's head was turned by some of the ladies who will be present at the social event of the year this afternoon.'

'It is not a social event, love. It is just a civic service. The mayor-making was the social event, not a wet afternoon in St Mary's.'

'As far as Elvira is concerned, this afternoon is what matters. She was not invited to the mayor-making. So today's service will be her only contact with the VIPs of the borough. I can guarantee you will find her hovering around the back of the church as the distinguished company arrives ready to impress in a new outfit which cost a bomb and most of her clothing coupons.'

She was right, as usual. When I entered the church through the drenching rain, the first person I met in the porch was Mrs Vaughan-Jenkins who was standing in the open doorway, arrayed in an expensively cut two-piece and looking like the lady of the manor waiting to receive her guests at a dinner-party.

'What a terrible day, Vicar,' she breathed. 'Isn't the church looking lovely? Such a profusion of flowers. A little gaudy, perhaps, and such a preponderance of red and yellow. The mayoress's choice, I gather. It's a good thing I am wearing pea-green. It will help to reduce the monotony of colour. David insisted on coming early to supervise everything, so of course I had to come with him. I thought I might while away the time making our visitors feel at home while the men are giving out the service leaflets, etcetera. A woman's touch is always helpful, isn't it, Vicar?'

'It all depends on the time and the place, I suppose, Mrs Vaughan-Jenkins. I expect your husband will be glad of your help.' So saying, I moved on into the church where David was giving instructions to Idris the Milk and Charlie Hughes about their part in the proceedings. Harold Jones, the people's warden, was placing 'reserved' cards in the front pew to the accompaniment of Mr Greenfield at the organ where he was attempting to play Jeremiah Clark's 'Trumpet Voluntary'. The air was filled with the overpowering scent of the floral decorations to such an extent that any member of the congregation who suffered from hay fever would not be able to survive the service without severe damage to the nasal passages.

Half an hour later, the church was full of chattering guests and the porch was full of steaming mackintoshes. The mayoral party had not arrived, with only five minutes left before the service was due to commence. In the vestry there was an excited hubbub as members of St Padarn's choir who had been invited to augment the parish church contingent were being placed in line for the ceremonial procession into the nave by Mr Greenfield prior to his rapid departure to the organ stool for Jeremiah Clark's masterpiece.

'Now, calm down, everybody,' I shouted. The noise diminished. 'Remember where you are. This is God's house, not Pontywen Square on a Saturday. It's OK, Mr Greenfield, you had better get back to the organ now.'

He turned to go out and was almost bowled over by Bertie Owen coming post-haste into the vestry.

'The mayor's car is blocked by some cars outside the church, Vicar.'

'Aren't the wardens seeing to that, Bertie?'

'Yes, they're out there getting soaking wet, but I thought you ought to know.'

'Did they ask you to come and tell me?'

'Not exactly.'

'I am sure they did not. They have arranged for someone to come and tell me when the mayor is in the church
porch. Why do you have to poke your nose in, Bertie?
Would you mind joining the congregation while I wait
for the message that the mayor and mayoress have
arrived.'

This conversation was heard with great amusement by
the choir as if it were a double act in a music hall. A
minute or two later Harold Jones came to inform me that
the mayoral party were in the porch. 'They are very upset
at being obstructed by the cars outside, Vicar, so that
they couldn't park outside the church doors. We got
umbrellas to shelter them but you know what the wind is
like. I'm afraid they're a bit wet.'

They were very upset indeed by the time I had gone to

the door to receive them and lead them down the aisle. The mayoress was distraught. 'Look at my hair,' she moaned, 'let alone my new suit. Everything is going wrong. First of all, you pulled the curtain down on us at the reception. Then you had somebody dead in here when they were doing the flowers and now this.'

'I am very sorry, Mayoress. I may have pulled the curtain down on you but I am not responsible for the rain.'

'But you are responsible for keeping a space outside the door for us, Vicar.' said the mayor. 'It's an understood thing, as it were. Anyway, let's get on with it.' I gave the signal to Mr Greenfield to begin the 'Trumpet Voluntary'.

We moved down the aisle to the tentative rendering of the ceremonial music as the congregation stood to receive the chief citizens of the borough and their entourage. After I had ushered them into their places, I went to the vestry to say the opening prayer with the choir before they moved into the church. When I opened the door, I was greeted by a noise several decibels greater than before. I closed the door with a bang. 'Quiet,' I yelled. There was a deathly hush. 'It's a good thing Mr Greenfield has all the stops out on the organ, otherwise all the council would have heard the commotion here. Let's have good behaviour in church as well as good singing. Now, let us pray.'

As a safety precaution, I had made sure Charles was not involved in the service by asking him to take charge of a joint Sunday school in the parish hall that afternoon. I had not bargained for the mayor's contribution to the service. He had been asked to read the second lesson, St Paul's Epistle to the Romans – Chapter 13, verse 10 to the end. Dai Spout came to the lectern after the hymn had finished. I had tried to catch his attention during the singing to alert him. He buried his face in the hymn-book, making any visual signal to him impossible. Fortunately the pages had been made ready for him by Ezekiel Evans who had read the first lesson complete with dropped aitches and a full quota of misplaced ones.

The mayor adjusted his spectacles and cleared his throat. He read slowly, with a faint touch of the Welsh *hwyl* in his voice. When he came to the end of the chapter, I stood up to begin the next part of the service. To my consternation, he carried on reading the next chapter. By the time he came to verse 6 – 'He that eateth, eateth to the Lord, for he giveth God thanks and he that eateth not to the Lord, to the Lord he eateth not' – I decided to end the suffering of a bemused congregation. I came out from my stall and tapped him on the shoulder. He reacted like a startled fawn.

'The lesson should have finished at the end of the chapter,' I whispered.

'I'm sorry, Vicar, I thought it meant that I had to read on to the end of the Epistle.' Since that would have entailed another three chapters, it was obvious that he was prepared to stay at the lectern for most of the afternoon. He was not nicknamed Dai Spout for nothing. As he returned to his pew he was greeted by a glare from his spouse. In stark contrast was the sense of relief evident on the faces of the congregation.

I began my sermon with the words, 'My text is taken from the lesson read so ably by the mayor, "Let us walk honestly as in the day."' The chief citizen smirked with self-satisfaction. It was a smirk which disappeared as the sermon developed.

'The keystone of local government must be honesty. Everything out in the open. Walk honestly as in the day, not skulk under the cover of night. There must be no deals behind closed doors. There must be no place for bribes to secure headships or to gain lucrative contracts for building firms. When citizens pay their taxes they expect their money to be used in fair administration, not to line the packets of a few.'

It was one of those rare occasions when it could be said that the silence was such that you could hear a pin drop. 'I am speaking generally, of course,' I went on. 'I am sure that in this borough there is the probity of honest men who have been elected to serve their fellow citizens. To be a councillor involves a great deal of self-sacrifice, the loss of one's spare time and putting up with innumerable inconveniences. In other words it is only the dedicated who can accept the challenge of being a councillor. They have come to church today because they need our prayers as much as they need your votes. Above all we pray today for your new mayor. May he walk tall and honestly as in the day and may his lady mayoress be enabled to be his mainstay throughout the next twelve months.'

As I passed the front pew on my way to the sanctuary, from the corner of my eye I could see six frowning faces engaged in singing 'O happy band of pilgrims', in a tight-lipped rendition which boded ill for the farewell at the end of the service. When I had given the blessing, I proceeded down the chancel to the front pew to escort them down the aisle. I felt as if I were leading a party of mourners at the funeral of a loved one. When we reached the porch I turned to shake hands with them. 'Look!' I said, 'The sun is coming out.'

'That is the only bright spot of the afternoon,' growled the mayor. 'What did you mean by raking up all those old lies about corruption in the Council? The pulpit isn't the place for that kind of thing, as it were.'

'Neither is the church porch the place to start a discussion on the matter, Mr Mayor,' I replied. 'I did not accuse any councillor in this borough of such behaviour. I was speaking generally, as I pointed out. Perhaps we could have a talk about this at a more convenient time and place.'

'We'll do nothing of the sort, Vicar. I appointed you to be my chaplain, not my political adviser, as it were,' he said. 'My husband is quite right,' added the mayoress. 'I'm sorry in my heart now that I ever pushed him into asking you to be his chaplain. It's been a proper disaster, that's all I can say. We'd better be going, Dai.'

They went without a handshake, as did most of the councillors, who seemed to be in a hurry to escape. However, there were members of the congregation only too eager to shake my hand and congratulate me on saying something which ought to have been said publicly long ago. When they had all gone, David Vaughan-Jenkins was fulsome in his praise of the sermon. 'As an ex-Conservative candidate in this constituency, I think you did a great job in the pulpit today. I could tell you of many cases of bribery and corruption, but as a bank manager my lips are sealed. What you did took courage, young man.'

'Perhaps it was foolhardiness rather than courage,' I replied. 'Judging by the reception I had from the council members as they left the church, it would appear that I have blotted my copy book. I have a shrewd suspicion that I shall not be invited to many functions in this mayoral year.'

'Well, I do not think you will have missed much,' suggested Elvira who had come to join us. 'Did you see some of those outfits? Those councillors' wives have as much dress sense as the gypsies on Pontywen Common, I don't know why I bothered to get a new outfit for the occasion. I thought at least there would be some of the more important people of the borough present like the captains of industry and their wives. You would have thought that at least Sir David Jones-Williams and Lady Jones-Williams would have been invited, for example. As it was, it was more like a Trades Union outing.'

'I must admit, Mrs Vaughan-Jenkins, I did not expect a fashion display this afternoon, unlike my wife who thought, as you did, that there would be an element of high society mingling with the riff-raff. Perhaps the mayor was influenced by his wife in his selection of invited guests, in case she suffered from competition. In any case, as far as I am concerned I am sure there is corruption in high-society circles and if I had to preach to a convention of captains of industry, as you call them, I would preach the same sermon.'

When I went back to the vicarage, my wife greeted me with open arms. 'Well done, you lovely man! That was a sermon straight from the shoulder, as they say. You should have seen Dai Spout's face and that of his missus, if it comes to that, as they followed you down the aisle at the end of the service. I tell you one thing, they will never forgive you for that.'

'You are quite right, my love. I received a ticking-off after which they departed without shaking hands. Dear Elvira applauded my effort afterwards but for the wrong reasons. She thought I was putting the lower orders in their place and bewailed the absence of the captains of industry and their wives among the guests. I told her that if I had been preaching to the said captains I would have preached the same sermon on the assumption that there was just as much corruption amongst them as there is in the Council Chamber.'

'Frederick, you really are developing into a firebrand. I tell you something, you will be making headline news in the local paper. I saw a reporter there this afternoon. He was scribbling like mad when you came to the juicier part of your sermon. You may have started a first-class row. I bet the correspondence column will be full of letters on the subject.'

Next morning, after Matins, Charles was eager to hear more about the sermon. 'Idris the Milk said it was one of the best sermons he had ever heard and that Dai Spout looked absolutely murderous as he left the church. They were all talking about it at evensong. Even Mrs Collier said it was good.'

'Look, Charles, I have preached much better sermons than that, I hope. They are only making such a fuss about it because I chanced to say something which everybody talks about privately but never in public. I thought that yesterday's service was the occasion to bring out the matter of local government bribery and corruption into the open. I felt strongly about it after hearing one or two things after the mayor-making ceremony. Anyway, let's forget all about it. I am more concerned today to find out how Eleanor's new partner is doing in his debut at the surgery. She is keeping her fingers crossed that she has picked a winner. If she has, it will make life a lot easier for her.'

When she came home at lunchtime, she had a large smile on her face. 'What a difference!' she exclaimed.

'Normally on a Monday morning the waiting-room is still full at eleven o'clock. Today by eleven there wasn't a sound of a cough or a sight of a patient. It was gloriously empty. Not only that, but according to the dragon, when the patients came out of Gareth Andrews' room they were all more than satisfied with their treatment.'

The dragon was Miss Philpott, the receptionist, who had been in the surgery since before Eleanor was born. Even if the patients were satisfied with the new doctor it would be a long time before she gave her approval.

'What's more, he was very keen to do his share of house visits after surgery,' Eleanor said. 'He said he wanted to find his way about Pontywen as soon as possible. I feel as if a tremendous weight has been lifted off my shoulders. We should be able to have that holiday we have promised ourselves for so long. Cornwall, here we come.' She caught hold of me and gave me a bear-hug.

'I tell you what, my love,' I breathed, 'now that tremendous weight has been lifted off your shoulders they aren't half strong.'

That afternoon I had to attend the quarterly meeting of the deanery clergy in the back room of the Bull Inn at Tremadoc. There was the usual quota of ancient clerics sunk into the armchairs and the two settees. It was my turn to read a chapter of the chosen study book, *The Minor Prophets in the Twentieth Century*.

The minutes were read by the drawling Obadiah Morris, the chapter clerk, whose voice had such a soporific effect that by the time he had finished, not only was the Reverend Thomas Hughes, Rector of Llansantffraidd with Pentwyn, aged eighty-six years and the Rip Van Winkle of the deanery, sound asleep, but at least three others were looking at me through half-lidded eyes. It was not an encouraging sight for any speaker.

I thought I would enliven the proceedings by telling a weak joke I had been told about Malachi, the last of the minor prophets, the subject of the chapter. 'A long-winded preacher had been boring his congregation with a complete tour through the books of the minor Prophets. "And now," he said, "we come at last to Malachi: 'Where shall we put Malachi?'" The squire, who had been sitting in the front pew, sat up. "You can put him here," he said, "I have had enough," and stalked out.'

Far from enlivening the proceedings, I found I had succeeded in closing the three pairs of half-lidded eyes completely. I was left with the rural dean, the chapter clerk and the Reverend Williams-Evans, the deanery's liaison officer with the religious bookshop in Cardiff. By the time I had dealt with the argument for a possible date of authorship as 460 BC or even a later date nearer 315 BC, their eyes had again reached the half-lidded state. I read through the rest of the chapter as loudly and as quickly as I could to prevent being the only one awake in a comatose gathering. Valiantly, those three pairs of half-closed eyes had striven to keep the lids apart. As I finished, the rural dean stretched himself in his armchair and with his arms extended above his head, announced, 'Now then, let's have some tea.' The word 'tea' was sufficient to rouse two of the sleepers but not to wake Rip Van Winkle, who was still in the Land of Nod when I left.

As I drove back to Pontywen I wondered if my sermon had made the headlines in the evening paper. When my car pulled up outside the vicarage door, I was greeted by an excited Eleanor waving the early edition of the

*Monmouthshire Post*. I jumped out of the car and ran up the steps. 'You have reached stardom, Frederick – the front page of the paper, with a photograph of you taken on the day of your induction. I tell you what, it is the first time a parson's words have taken precedence over those of the local MP or the Trades Union bosses, not to mention the captains of industry.'

She handed me the newspaper. There on the front page was emblazoned in big block capitals, 'MAYOR'S CHAPLAIN ATTACKS TOWN HALL CORRUPTION'. Underneath was a verbatim report of my sermon, but omitting the words 'I am speaking generally' and giving the impression that I was referring to my own borough. 'That, my love,' said my wife, 'will really put the cat amongst the pigeons.'

It was not long before there was a considerable fluttering in the dovecote. Inevitably the first sign of panic came from the mayor. He was on the telephone before we sat down for our evening meal. It was no exaggeration to say that for a man noted for his flow of words he was extremely incoherent. From what I could gather he was telling me that I had opened a whole can of worms and that God knows where they were going to crawl, as it were. Furthermore he suggested that if I wanted to be a politician I should use a soap-box not a pulpit.

Not long afterwards the town clerk rang up to say that my insinuations would have to be substantiated and if not there would be grave legal consequences for me. He was followed by the leader of the council, noted for his itching palm. He was trying desperately to find if I had any substance for my accusations and sounded very relieved to know that I had not.

'Perhaps now we can have some peace for our dinner,'

said my wife, when I had put the phone down. 'It is a surprise treat to celebrate the new partnership. Mrs Thomas, Cwmdulais Farm, gave us that trout when I was there earlier this afternoon – a thank-you for easing her arthritis.'

As she said this, the telephone rang yet again. 'The Vicar of Pontywen speaking,' I said.

'This is the *Daily Mail* here,' the voice replied.

## 10

'For heaven's sake, Iorwerth, try to *look* happy when you sing "We're happy as happy can be"' and, by the way, tripping to the right does not mean giving an imitation of a cart horse.'

Iorwerth Ellis, tenor, with aspirations to take the tenor lead, looked at me with a decidedly sour expression on his face. When some months previously I had signified my intention of opting out of the production of *The Gondoliers*, he had been convinced that stardom had arrived for him, despite his complete lack of any histrionic ability. Now that I had come back as tenor lead and producer, he had to be content with the minor role of Antonio with one small solo and no lines to speak. His cup of bitterness was overflowing.

It was now four months since the civic service. My sermon had been a nine days' wonder, but not in the mind of the mayor who confined my duties to the saying of prayers at the monthly council meetings. This meant that I was free to indulge my passion for Gilbert and Sullivan, and to play opposite Eleanor whose burden of work had been made so much lighter now that she had an excellent partner in her practice. Gereth and Heather had married and were living in Ashburnam Close, the elite cul-de-sac in Pontywen.

One of the fringe benefits of the marriage was Heather's mezzo soprano voice and her amateur stage experience. She was given the part of Tessa, joining

Eleanor's Gianetta in an attractive blonde and brunette combination. The only fringe benefit from my chaplaincy was the advent of Rhoda Powell, the parks superintendent's wife. She was an Amazon with a powerful contralto voice perfectly suited to the Duchess of Plaza Toro, whose consort was a little weed of a man, Trevor Willis, a comic actor *par excellence*.

Bronwen's pregnancy was at the visible stage and she had given up her nursing at the hospital. This meant that Charles was always on time at Matins, with a wife to push him out of bed. She had undertaken to come and help Gwen Shoemaker, wife of Idris the Milk, in making tea for the cast during the break in rehearsal and giving moral support to her husband at the piano.

The musical director, Aneurin Williams, teacher of music at Pontywen Grammar School, provided the female chorus from his senior pupils and this year had recruited some of the young men from the Sixth Form, including Malcolm Evans, the head prefect, whose young tenor voice and appearance made him a natural for the role of Luiz, the Duke's attendant. As Aneurin said, after one rehearsal, 'You are lucky, Vicar, to have so much youth in your chorus. It is a refreshing change from the other societies in the Valleys whose female complement would be better employed at home knitting matinee coats for their grandchildren.'

We were still rehearsing in St Padarn's Church, a corrugated iron edifice, with the pews and chairs pushed to one side to make a playing arena, and chalk marks indicating the size of the stage in the Grammar School hall where the production would take place. After an hour of strenuous chorus exertion involved in the opening of *The Gondoliers*, I called a halt for the tea-break.

Heather, Eleanor and myself were joined by Gareth who was paying his first visit to the Society. 'I must say I am most impressed by your chorus, especially the girls. They are obviously quite young but blessed with good voices as well as good looks. Where did you find them?'

'He did not find them,' said my wife. 'They are almost all of them pupils of the musical director, as I was myself once. It was fortunate for my husband that he married someone who recruited his MD, who in turn recruited his chorus. I am beginning to wonder if that was the reason why he married me.'

Before I could reply the church door was flung open and the burly figure of Will Book and Pencil strode towards us. 'Excuse me for interrupting, but it is an emergency. There has been a roof fall down at the pit. I tried to get you at the vicarage. Then I went to Ezekiel Evans and he said you were here. I didn't think you were here as well, Dr Andrews. That's what you call prudential, isn't it?'

In no time at all, Eleanor and Gareth had driven to the surgery in his car to pick up their Gladstone bags, leaving behind alarm, where only minutes previously there had been happiness and excitement at the first stage rehearsal.

'Charlie Thomas and Harry Williams are on the two-till-ten shift,' said Bertie Owen. 'That's why they had to miss tonight's practice.'

'My father's on that shift too,' added Malcolm Evans.

'And mine,' said two of the girls.

'There's no point in carrying on tonight,' I announced. 'Perhaps it is not as bad as it sounds and no one has been badly injured. In any case the three of you had better get home as quickly as possible. Your mothers will need all the support you can give them at a time like this. See you all next Thursday when I hope all things will be back to normal and nothing drastic has happened.'

The three young people hurried out into the October night while the rest of the cast began to leave in a hubbub of concern and speculation. 'Will they have to go underground?' asked Heather in tones of great perturbation.

'I don't know whether they both will have to do that. Perhaps one will have to stay at the pit-head to tend to the men who have been brought up in an injured condition. It all depends on what has happened, how bad a fall it is and how many are trapped.'

'Can I be of any use?' inquired Bronwen. 'I should think a trained nurse would be of great help at the pit-head.'

'You're not going down there,' ordered Charles. 'You've got our child to think of and in any case by now they will have alerted the hospital. So there should be plenty of trained nurses available.'

'You can never have enough trained nurses if it is a really big accident,' persisted his wife.

'I tell you what,' I said, 'let's all go down there, the four of us, and see what is involved. I am sure that I will be needed as a priest and so will you, Charles, if there is anything of a serious nature. So let's go round to the vicarage and pick up the car. Then we can see for ourselves what is needed.'

As we walked to the vicarage, we could hear the warning bell of an ambulance on its way to the colliery. There was a sense of menace in the air as the sound of one bell died away and another distant bell broke the brief silence. Conversation was minimal. Our minds were too full of foreboding to speculate on the extent of the accident. Pontywen Colliery had always had a good safety record. Apart from the occasional death of an individual, there had never been a major incident, but this one boded ill.

It seemed that every street through which we drove was fearful of what had happened under the ground on which the terraces were built. Little knots of people were gathered around open doorways. All the euphoria which had come from the nationalization of the mines on 1 January 1947 was evaporating with the realization two years later that coal not only provided the community's way of life but paid for it at the cost of human sacrifice.

When we reached the colliery, there was a large crowd of anxious relatives outside, waiting for news of their loved ones. The constables stood in front of the closed gates. I parked the car further up the street. 'Stay here,' I said to my passengers, 'I'll have a word with the police to find out what the situation is and to see whether we'll be needed inside the gates.'

One of the constables recognized me at first sight. 'Hello, Vicar. Nasty business, isn't it? Eight of them trapped by the fall. Most of the shift had gone on ahead, fortunately, when the roof collapsed on their mates behind them. They are down there helping but it must have been an extensive fall. I should think there'll be quite a few dead and a lot of casualties.'

'Can I be of any use?' I asked. 'I have my curate with me and his wife who is a trained nurse. My wife is a doctor and she is already here with her partner.'

'I think the best thing is if you will go inside and find out. I know Dr Secombe is here. She and the other doctor were the first on the scene. They are underground, as far as I know. Anyway, go and see for yourself what is needed of you. Go to the manager's office, they'll be able to tell you.'

After I had run back to the car to keep the others informed, I made my way to the manager's office, following the directions given me by the constable. As I did so, I could see stretchers being unloaded into a fleet of waiting ambulances. Inside the office there was total confusion, the telephone was ringing constantly, clerks were running about, colliding with each other in the process. A police superintendent was engaged in earnest conversation with the manager, Haydn Price Williams, a former rugby international. As I hovered in their vicinity, I caught the eye of Mr Price Williams. 'Can I help in any way,' I asked, 'underground or at the pit-head?'

'They won't want you underground, you would be in the way. You could be of help when the injured come up by offering comfort of some kind. At the moment, the less cluttering up there is the better.' If the situation at the pit-head was as chaotic as that in the office, I could see his point.

I decided that I had better get back to the car first to let my passengers know that they were surplus to requirement. Charles was much relieved but Heather was worried about her husband being underground. 'How do you think I feel about Eleanor?' I told her. 'The best thing you can do, the three of you, is to get back home. As soon as I know anything about Gareth, I'll let you know.' I gave her the car keys with instructions to drive the Wentworth-Baxters' home and to leave my car at her place in Ashburnam Close until I phoned her with further news.

By the time I reached the pit-head, there were a half-dozen ambulances queuing up to ferry the injured to hospital. As I rushed towards the pit-shaft, I strained my eyes to see if there was any sign of my wife, but to no avail. Then I recognized a nurse from Pontywen Hospital who was about to get into an ambulance with one of the stretcher cases. The miner lay with his eyes closed, sweat dribbling white streaks on the black canvas of his face. As the two stretcher-bearers lifted him carefully into the vehicle, I suddenly realized it was Charlie Thomas, one of the Gilbert and Sullivan chorus who was on that shift. 'Charlie,' I shouted.

He opened his eyes and focused on me. 'I tell you what, Vicar, your missus is doing wonders down there. See you soon.' Then he went back into oblivion.

'I doubt it,' said the nurse, 'but what he said is true. They say that Dr Secombe and Dr Andrews have both been crawling through the debris to inject the trapped men with painkillers to ease them, apart from seeing to those who have been injured on the other side of the fall.'

Ambulances came and went with the dead and injured. The hours went by and the pit-cages came up with tired rescuers, but there was still no sign of Eleanor and Gareth. Then, to my intense relief, two doctors from the Casualty Department at Pontywen Hospital arrived. They told me that they had come to take over from Eleanor and Gareth. By now the overpowering smell of coal dust was clogging my lungs and biting into my soul. I wondered how men could endure such afflictions to earn a living, even if they had rid themselves of the coal owners who had exploited them over the past 160 years or so. I had tried to comfort the injured as they arrived at the surface. It was a pointless exercise. They had looked death in the face. All I had to offer came from a life untroubled by constant physical danger and cocooned in a clerical collar.

I shall never forget the moment when the pit-cage rattled to the top and a little figure in coal-blackened overalls with a miner's helmet on her head emerged amongst another contingent of rescuers. I ran to meet her and picked her up, hugging her as if she were a long-lost relative. 'If I were you, my love,' she said, 'I would put me down unless you want a veneer of anthracite on your best clerical suit. Not only that, but my bones are aching and they can't stand a bear-hug.'

'Where's Gareth?' I asked. 'Heather is beside herself with worry.'

'He's fine but very tired, like me. He is coming up with the next load of helpers from below. I'll tell you something, Fred, I shall never want to go through anything like that again. How those men can spend their lives on their backs in that narrow claustrophobic environment I shall never know, but I tell you what, they are brave men, believe me. It hasn't hit me yet but it will by tomorrow. You will have to cosset me for a few days, I'm afraid.'

'As many days as you like, love. I suppose you saw Charlie Thomas. I had a word with him when he was put in the ambulance.'

'I'm afraid that poor old Charlie has not long to live. His spine has been crushed. It is a miracle that he is still breathing. He told me that Harry Williams is trapped behind that wall of coal with about eighty others. How on earth they are going to get through to them without causing further falls, I don't know. Apparently there is a danger of a fire-damp explosion as well. Already there must be a dozen men who have been killed outright. It was not a pretty sight, Fred.' She caught hold of my arm tightly. 'I had better get to the changing-room and get this gear off. I must wash my face, too, before the grime gets embedded in my wrinkles. You'd better stay here and wait for Gareth to come up.'

While I waited for her colleague to appear, I wondered what had happened to Malcolm Evans' father and to the fathers of Marilyn Owen and Shirley Jones, the two school-girl members of the chorus. Were they among the dead or the living? I thought of Charlie Thomas puffing on his pipe, giving his famous impression of the *Queen Mary* coming up the channel, and then of his wife, a 'plump and pleasing person' who was so proud that at the age of fifty he was a member of the Gilbert and Sullivan chorus. As I waited, a bus-load of men from Abergwynfi Colliery arrived to supplement the rescue team.

Then once again the pit-cage rattled to the top and among its occupants was the tall figure of Gareth Andrews, his shoulders bent and his head down, as if the weight of the world was bearing down upon his jaunty self. I went across to him as he joined the others on the way to the changing-room. He appeared to have more coal on his face than any of the others. It was a complete mask, more appropriate to Man Friday than the newly arrived Doctor Andrews, recently of the RAMC and the handsome occupant of Room 2 in the Pontywen surgery.

'Gareth,' I said as I drew near to him.

He lifted his head and looked at me out of half-lidded eyes. 'Fred, I am absolutely devastated. I was only in at the last stage of the war, long after the Normandy landings, but I tell you what, I never want to be in another do like this. The suffocating atmosphere, the carnage that coal can create, it has been an eye-opener to me. Your wife has been a revelation too. She has been squeezing through the smallest of gaps to try to reach those who are trapped, to administer medical aid. I take my hat off to her.'

'I join you in that,' I replied. 'Heather will be greatly relieved to know that you are OK. She has taken my car to your place and I've told her that I would phone her once I had news of you. Eleanor has gone to wash and get out of her protective clothing. So perhaps you would phone Heather from here to let her know you're OK and I'll wait for Eleanor and you to give me a lift back to your place. Then I think I had better go to see Charlie Thomas's wife and Harry Williams' wife, too, if it comes to that. It's difficult to know where to begin to carry out my job.'

'If you do that half as well as your wife has done hers, Fred, you can rest content. See you very shortly.' He hurried towards the changing-room. By now it was almost one o'clock in the morning and the crowd outside the gates was bigger than ever, eerily silent. About ten minutes later Gareth and Eleanor met me, and the three of us made our way to Gareth's car, which was parked not far from the gates. He had sold his sports model and had invested in a Triumph saloon which he felt was more in keeping with his GP image.

I sat in the front with him, while Eleanor lounged on the back seat, exhausted by her efforts underground. 'I don't know whether I should go to see Charlie's wife or Harry Williams' wife once I have brought you both to the vicarage, love.'

'You will do neither,' commanded my wife. 'It is far too late to be doing that. Why don't you go first thing in the morning after service? By then things may have sorted themselves out. Perhaps the rescue teams will have got through to Harry and his pals. As far as Charlie is concerned, I should think his wife will be at his bedside in the hospital. You will be of far more use to her once you have had a sleep and come to your senses. It's pointless darting around like a scalded cat this time of the night.'

'She's right,' said Gareth. 'I should think it requires a calm state of mind to comfort the nearest and dearest, to use a hackneyed phrase. Far be it from me to teach his grandmother how to suck eggs, I speak only from a medical point of view. As far as I am concerned I shall be only too glad to hit that pillow and shut out the last four or five hours.'

'Hear, hear!' came my wife's voice from the back of the car. So it was that once we had left Ashburnam Close, we retired for the night.

Neither of us slept well. I woke to discover that the

time was only twenty past two and Eleanor was weeping quietly. I could feel her shoulders shaking as she lay with her back to me. I turned towards her and put my right arm around her. I said nothing but just held her close to me. Gradually the tears ceased and her body relaxed. Two hours later we were both awake again. 'I think I'll make a cup of tea,' I said, 'and while I'm up, I'll ring the colliery to find out what the situation is.'

'They've enough to do, Fred, without us adding to their workload. You go downstairs and make the tea, there's a love. Take a couple of aspirins and bring some for me, please. They'll do instead of sleeping pills.' Soon we were asleep once more.

I had set the alarm for seven o'clock but by six o'clock I was wide awake. Eleanor was still asleep. I put on my dressing-gown and went down to the study to telephone the colliery, only to get the engaged signal. I made myself another cup of tea while I waited to phone again. This time the line was free but I had to wait minutes for a reply. A tired voice announced, 'Pontywen Colliery.'

'This is the Vicar of Pontywen speaking,' I replied. 'Sorry to bother you at a time like this, but could you tell me if you have been able to get through to the trapped miners yet? Some of them are my parishioners.'

'I am afraid not, Vicar. The rescue teams are having to go very carefully in case they cause another fall. They are going to be relieved at seven o'clock by men from the Cwmdulais pit, that's all I can say at the moment.'

My next call was to the hospital to inquire about Charlie Thomas. 'He passed away at four o'clock this morning,' said the ward sister. 'He had been in a lot of pain for the few hours he was alive. All I can say is that it was a merciful release, Vicar. Mrs Thomas was with him when he died. She has taken it very well so far but that's because she is still in a state of shock. I think she will need your help badly when the shock wears off.'

Rosie Thomas was childless and had built her life around Charlie, whereas Harry Williams was blessed with a good wife and a large family. If anything were to happen to Harry there would be any amount of support for Dilys Williams. I lit the fire under the boiler so that Eleanor could have a bath to wash away any traces of the coal dust which had clung to her. I could still smell Pontywen Colliery on her as she lay by my side in bed. There was no doubt that if there was a further fall she would have to be underground once again. For her sake as well as for the trapped men, I prayed fervently that there would be no such happening.

At seven o'clock I went to our bedroom with a cup of tea for Eleanor. She was sitting up in bed staring into space. 'I feel as if I haven't been to bed for weeks,' she said. 'My body is still aching after crawling on my belly. How those men work in a space of three or four feet wide day in day out, I don't know. It's a nightmare existence.'

'I rang the colliery at six o'clock. The men are still trapped behind the fall but a fresh team of rescuers has come. Let's hope they will be able to get through to them. I rang the hospital, too. Poor old Charlie died at four o'clock this morning. Rosie was with him. I'll get along to see her first thing after service. By the way, I have lit the boiler. So you can have a bath and relax before going to surgery. I should have another hour in bed, if I were you, and then enjoy a nice breakfast of bacon and egg, cooked by your favourite chef, once you have had your soak in the bathroom.'

'My favourite chef! I didn't know Mrs Watkins was coming in early this morning. Sorry, love, only kidding. Believe me, I can't tell you how much I want those eighty men to be rescued, if it's only for my sake. I don't think I could face another stint in that hell-hole. I'll take your advice and have that extra hour. So hop it, Frederick, and wake me when the time is up.'

To my amazement, when I went to the church to open up for Matins there were some dozen or so parishioners waiting outside. It was the first time since I had been in Pontywen that there had been a congregation for the early morning service. I announced every Sunday that a daily service would be held at nine o'clock but not a single person had ever turned up. Dilys Williams was there with three of her daughters. Even young Malcolm Evans was present. It was only recently that he had begun to attend church after joining the Gilbert and Sullivan Society.

As we robed in the vestry, Charles expressed his great surprise on finding parishioners joining us for our normal duologue. 'This always happens where there is big trouble, I suppose. I remember people turning up in our parish church at home for the National Day of Prayer when the last war was looming. They had never put their foot inside there before nor did they afterwards – it's just one big cry for help, Charles.'

During the service we spent a few minutes in silent prayer for the trapped men. The rest of the service meant little to the worshippers, who knew nothing about Jehosaphat's war with Ahab or the intricate arguments of a chapter in St Paul's Epistle to the Romans. They were in church for one reason only, and in that silence there was an intensity of supplication that no words could express.

I encountered a different kind of silence a little later that morning. When the service was over I made my way to Balaclava Street to see Rosie Thomas. I could feel my heart beating faster, and my throat was dry. How am I going to comfort someone, the centre of whose life has been taken away in an instant? I said to myself. I dreaded facing her in her misery. I stood outside number eleven for quite a while before I could summon up enough courage to knock on the door. It was opened by Gwen Shoemaker. 'Come on in, Vicar,' she whispered. 'We'd better go into the front room for a minute. She's sitting in the kitchen by the fire. The shock has made her feel cold.'

We went into the little parlour. The blinds were drawn but the morning sunshine filtered through sufficiently to illuminate the room without Gwen having to switch on the light. 'Her sister is coming down from Coventry this afternoon. Her husband went up from here to look for work in the depression. He's got a good job now with the car firm. Own house and phone and that sort of thing. So I was able to go to the phone box and ring them for her. She's getting into Newport at 2.47 this afternoon. Will I be glad! I haven't had a word out of her all the time I've been here.'

She led me into the kitchen where Rosie was sitting in a rocking-chair, looking into the fire. 'It's the Vicar, Rosie,' she said. Rosie never looked up but kept staring into the flames as if mesmerized by them. I took a kitchen chair and brought it alongside her. When I caught hold of her hand, it was ice-cold. 'I'll make a cup of tea,' said Gwen, and disappeared into the scullery.

I held on to Rosie's hand, which was lifeless. Words refused to pass her lips. I looked at her face which was drained of colour and resembled a death-mask. The only sound was of Gwen taking the lid off the kettle and filling it and replacing the lid, followed by the rattle of cups in the kitchen sink. Its very ordinariness relieved the tension in me. I felt my fingers loosening the vice-like grip which I had unwittingly inflicted on Rosie's hand. Now we both stared into the fire and a strange peace came upon me. I knew that the only comfort I could give her was by sitting quietly by her side and mutely witnessing her grief. It was not something I could even begin to share but it was something for which I could show my sympathy by simply holding her hand.

I stayed there for at least an hour, never saying a word. Then, suddenly, there was the sound of the hooter from the colliery. My blood ran cold. It was the sound we had missed in the noise and excitement of our first stage rehearsal the night before – one which I had prayed earnestly not to hear again. Rose was unmoved. I left her still staring into the fire.

I went into the parlour where Gwen had closeted herself. She came to meet me as I opened the door. 'It sounds like more trouble, Vicar, doesn't it?' she said. 'As if there's not been enough.'

'All I hope is that it doesn't mean my wife has got to go underground again, Gwen. It is a selfish thing to say, I know, but she had more than she could stand last night without another dose. So if you don't mind I shall be off to the vicarage to phone up and find out what has happened. I'll be back later today, I expect.'

As I walked home there were little groups of people out on the streets anxiously wondering what had happened. Then, as I turned the corner into Vicarage Road, a woman came out of her house with a large smile on her face. 'They've got them out,' she shouted. 'I've just heard it on the wireless.' She went next door and banged on the door. By the time I had reached the vicarage gates, the whole street was ringing with excited voices, rejoicing in a great deliverance.

I strode down the drive and rushed to the phone to let Eleanor know the good news. Before I could speak, she said, 'It's all right, I know. Isn't it wonderful? I rang the colliery when I heard the hooter. My heart was in my mouth. When they told me the hooter was a celebration, not an alarm, I felt a great weight lift off my shoulders. Bed early tonight, love.'

## 11

'Hail, Poetry, thou heav'n born maid! Thou gildest e'en the Pirate's trade. Hail, flowing fount of sentiment. All hail! All hail! Divine Emollient.' The last time the Gilbert and Sullivan Society had given a full-throated rendering of this unaccompanied chorus from *The Pirates of Penzance* was on the last night of the performance of the opera in the Pontywen Grammar School hall. Now it was being sung with even greater fervour in the unusual setting of St Mary's Church.

Charlie Thomas loved it. 'Let's have "Hail, Poetry",' he would demand at any impromptu concert in the Lamb and Flag after rehearsal, or in the bus taking the Society for its summer outing. His untrained, rich bass voice would be unleashed with an intensity which made the other members of the bass section surplus to requirement. He would have been proud to hear how they responded to the challenge to make up for his absence.

The church was so full for the service that the attendance reached the peak of 'standing room only', something that even the Harvest Festivals throughout the years had never reached. It was a fitting testimony to a man whose sense of humour and kindliness had made him much loved by the community from which he had been snatched in a moment of time. In the front pew sat Rosie, her sister and her husband. It was the only pew with any space left. The widow sat with her head bowed throughout the service. She did not look up once. She did not shed a tear. It was as if she had died with Charlie. All that was left of him was in the coffin. All that was left of her was a living shell. She died less than a year after him, another victim of the colliery disaster.

In the meanwhile the mayor was organizing a civic service to commemorate the twelve miners who had been killed. He had not consulted me but had gone to the Reverend Elias Evans, the Minister of Tabernacle Baptist Church. 'It's the biggest place of worship in Pontywen, as it were, Vicar. There'll be far too many people wanting to come if we had it in your church. He said he would take the service, if you will say the few words, as it were, since you are my chaplain. I had suggested that you would do the prayers, as it were, but he said that if you are not accustomed to spontaneous prayer it would be better if you did something else.' He made it sound as if I were second-rate.

When I told Eleanor she said, 'After what happened at the last civic service I would have thought that the last place he would have wanted you to occupy was the pulpit. I expect he thinks that you would hardly be controversial in a memorial service, or would you, love?' She looked at me as if she were daring me to be controversial.

'Since I am more used to spontaneous sermons than to spontaneous prayer, I shouldn't like to say. It depends upon what happens between now and the service, I suppose. I can tell you one thing, my sweetheart, it will come as much from my heart as Elias Evans' prayers. I can tell you one other thing, I expect he will have as shrewd an idea of what he is going to say in his spontaneity, as I shall have in my few words off the cuff, "as it were".'

Pontywen was slowly recovering from the unwelcome prominence thrust upon it by the disaster. News reporters from the national press and even the Pathe Gazette film crew had visited the town and interviewed survivors. As the days went by and the funerals of the twelve were over, the little town settled down to semi-normality. It would be a long time, if ever, before life became the same as in the pre-disaster years.

The two-monthly Parochial Church Council meeting provided me with an opportunity to shift the focus of attention from the pit disaster to the innovation I had been considering for a while, namely, the formation of a men's club. When I suggested to the council that it should meet in a pub, there was instant opposition from Ezekiel Evans who was on his feet before I could enlarge further on what I had in mind.

'Vicar, h'I can't believe what h'I'm 'earing. Public 'ouses are for the consumption of beer, not for church meetings. Think what the Temperance Society will say, let alone the Nonconformist ministers. Their pulpits will 'ave a field day h'at the church's expense. Beer and the Bible don't mix, h'I can h'assure you.'

'Mr Evans, if you will sit down and allow me to continue, you will have a clear idea of what I am suggesting. The "Prince of Wales" has a large room at the back of the premises where the Pontywen Silver Band rehearse. There is an entrance to it from the outside. If you do not wish to visit the bar, Mr Evans, all you have to do is to stay in the room. I am sure we can come to some arrangement with the landlord whereby he can provide us with light refreshments. Those who wish to drink a pint of beer with their sandwiches may do so and those who are abstainers can have their cup of tea or a glass of lemonade. One other thing, Mr Evans, don't forget that the Deanery Chapter of Clergy always have their meeting in the back room of the "Bull" public house, Tremadoc. I feel it will be much more congenial to enjoy a drink and listen to a talk or have a discussion away from the confines of the church hall.'

'Hear, hear!' chorused a number of voices.

David Vaughan-Jenkins, the people's warden, rose to speak. 'May I congratulate you, Vicar, on a splendid idea. If we are to increase the number of men in our congregation, there is much more likelihood of that happening when we meet in what has been a social centre in the community for generations, the inn or the tavern or the pub, call it what you will. Don't forget, Mr Evans, that in the Middle Ages, many a church had its own ale house. By the way, Vicar, have you any thoughts on a name for the club? Something short and snappy, unlike a title like "The Pontywen Church Gilbert and Sullivan Society", if you will pardon the reference.'

'I take your point about our G&S group, Mr Vaughan-Jenkins, but I am afraid we are stuck with that now. As for the new club, I had thought we could connect it with the centenary and call it the Centurion Club.'

'If you don't mind my saying so, Vicar, that sounds more appropriate for a Roman Legion Club. We already have the British Legion Club in Pontywen.' The warden looked disappointed that his witticism was received with dead-pan faces.

'Before we talk about a name for a club, let's decide if we are going to have one.' Bertie Owen stood up and surveyed his audience in his best shop-steward manner. 'What's wrong with the old Church of England Men's Society that we had years ago, before Canon Llewellyn put the kybosh on it? The diocesan organization needs more recruits, so the Secretary tells me. There is strength in numbers, not in splitting up into little tin-pot groups. I demand that first of all, Vicar, you put your proposition to the vote. Let's have a democratic procedure.'

'By all means, Mr Owen,' I said. 'Canon Llewellyn closed down the branch because he felt that there was as much strength in the diocesan organization, as you call it, as there was in the cups of weak tea which were drunk at the meetings. It is pointless expecting the men of Ponty-wen to be attracted to the church by a handful of men sitting around in a classroom in the church hall and contemplating their navels. Would someone like to propose that we form a men's club which will meet at the Prince of Wales?'

'As people's warden,' said David Vaughan-Jenkins, 'I have great pleasure in proposing that we form a men's club and that they hold their meetings in the back room of the Prince of Wales.'

'As Vicar's warden,' said Harold Thomas, 'I second that.'

'All those in favour?' I asked. All but two hands shot up. 'All those against?' Ezekiel Evans and Bertie Owen raised their hands and looked around defiantly. They reminded me of the song I used to sing as a child in the Band of Hope. 'Dare to be a Daniel. Dare to stand alone. Dare to pass the Public House and leave the beer alone.'

'I've got a good name for the club,' said Idris the Milk, 'what about "The Saints"? Some of us are from St Padarn's, some from St Mary's and some from St Illtyd's. The one thing we've got in common is "Saint". I know that none of us are anywhere near being saints, but we all stand for the saints whose names are in our churches.'

So it was that the Saints Club was founded in Ponty-wen, to the great amusement of the populace, some of whom suggested that 'Sinners' would have been more appropriate. It was decided by the Parochial Church Council that the vicar would approach Mr Jim Pritchard, the landlord of the 'Prince of Wales', about the use of his back room, and that the first meeting of the club would elect officers and committee.

The next morning I made my way to the 'Prince of Wales', arriving there an hour before opening time. Mrs Pritchard opened the door to me. She was a little sparrow of a woman in her fifties, dowdily dressed for a publican's wife, with an accent familiar in the streets of Manchester rather than those of Pontywen. Ruby Pritchard had been transferred to South Wales when her husband's playing days were over. Jim Pritchard had played rugby for some of the top clubs in South Wales, until he went north and signed on for one of the leading clubs in the Rugby League circuit. A massive man, with an impressive beer belly, he had been landlord of the 'Prince of Wales' since the immediate pre-war years. Red-faced and bespectacled, he moved with a lightness of step at odds with his size. In his heyday, he must have been an awesome sight looming down on an outside half.

'This is an unexpected pleasure, Vicar,' Mrs Pritchard said. 'I don't think we have had a parson inside these doors since we came to Pontywen.' She led me into the saloon bar where Jim was checking the levels of the upturned bottles of whisky.

'Jim, it's the Vicar.' He turned around sharply to make sure that he had heard his wife correctly. 'Good God!' he exclaimed. 'I beg your pardon, Vicar. You are the last one I thought to see. Not that I am a bad lad, but the church and the pub are in two different leagues in this part of the world. It certainly wasn't like that up north. The vicar of the parish up there used to have a Harvest Thanksgiving in the public bar – but down here, it's not respectable. The pub is beyond the pale.'

'Well, as far as I am concerned, Mr Pritchard, the pub is not beyond the pale. As a matter of fact, I want the pub to be to be very much inside the pale. I wonder if we could have a chat about something I have in mind, if you are willing to co-operate.'

'Certainly, Vicar. Would you care to come upstairs to the sitting-room? Would you like a drop of something before we go up?'

'No, thank you, it is a bit early to indulge just yet. Perhaps after we have had our chat, if you don't mind.'

'Not at all,' he said. 'Only too willing to oblige a parson.'

The sitting-room was large and comfortably furnished with an expensive three-piece suite. Its windows looked out on the coal tips which adjoined the hill above Pontywen. On the walls were photographs of Jim in his heyday, both in Rugby Union and in Rugby League, sometimes solo and sometimes seated among his team-mates.

'I must say, Mr Pritchard, you look a tough proposition in those pictures,' I commented.

'I suppose I was in those days. Since then I have put on a lot around my middle and lost a lot of what was on my head. I doubt if I could walk around the field nowadays, let alone run around it, believe me.'

'If it came to a competition between you and me, I bet you would leave me standing. You are still light on your feet. That's something I have never been. Anyway, that's not what I have come to talk about. Last night our

Parochial Church Council decided that we want to form a men's club and that we should like to meet in your back room, if it is possible and if you are willing. We should like to have some sandwiches with our drinks, if you could provide them. We should be meeting every month on a Friday throughout the winter.'

He looked at me wide-eyed. 'All I can say, Vicar, is that I've not been so stunned since a Wigan forward laid me out for half an hour. Yes, of course. The Pontywen Band rehearse every week there on a Wednesday but apart from that, the room is very rarely used. We shall be delighted to have you if it's only to give the pub a good name. As far as the sandwiches are concerned, you let us know how many are coming a few days before and that will be fine. I'll give you a price per person later this week if you want it by then. Now then, I know we haven't been chatting very long, but what would you say to a little drop of scotch, to seal the deal?'

That little drop turned out to be half a tumblerful, sufficient to curtail my visits for the rest of the morning.

A fortnight later on a Sunday afternoon at three o'clock, the memorial service to the miners who had been killed in the colliery disaster took place at the Tabernacle Baptist Church, a large building constructed from locally quarried stone and resembling a town hall rather than a church. It was filled to capacity. When I took my seat in the deacons' sanctum at the foot of the pulpit, it was an awesome sight. The Pontywen Male Voice Choir occupied the front of the gallery, resplendent in their dark blue blazers, proud of their recent near-success in the National Eisteddfod where they had come third in the main choral event. Behind them and around them a mass of humanity was squeezed into the available pews. At ground-floor level, the local dignitaries were seated at the front. The mayor and the councillors rubbed shoulders with Sir David Jones-Williams and other former colliery owners who were joined by the steelworks masters, the industrial giants of the district. Behind them were the relatives of the dead miners. Every available space elsewhere was filled.

I sat next to the Reverend Godfrey Thomas, Minister of Moriah Congregational Church, a friend of mine since my curate days in the parish. 'Doesn't it make you feel sick', he whispered to me, 'to see these big-wigs up in the front and those who have suffered the most in mind and spirit stuck behind them?'

'I couldn't agree more,' I replied. 'It doesn't make me feel sick but it does make me feel very angry, especially when we had all that bowing and scraping from Elias Evans when the VIPs came in.'

'Talk of the devil,' said Godfrey. 'Here he comes.' The minister swept up the steps into the big pulpit to begin the service.

After a flowery tribute to the 'leaders of the community present' and a less eloquent acknowledgement of the bereaved, he announced the hymn, reading every word of the first verse which was already known by heart by every member of the congregation: 'Guide Me, O Thou Great Redeemer'. It was sung with a fervour only to be found in Wales. Then came the first prayer addressed to 'Our great compassionate God in whose hands it lies to give and to take away'. This was followed by the lesson taken from the seventh chapter of the Book of Revelation, ending with the words 'For the Lamb which is in the midst of the throne shall feed them and shall lead them unto living fountains of waters' and 'God shall wipe away all tears from their eyes'. This was read without any attempt at dramatic effect by Godfrey Thomas but with a sincerity which spoke to the hearts of those who had cried copious tears. Then the Male Voice Choir sang 'The Lord's my Shepherd' to a setting of the tune 'Crimond'. By now a wave of emotion had swept over the whole congregation.

Now came the second part of Elias Evans' 'spontaneous' prayers. Unashamedly he played upon the feelings of those who had lost their loved ones, sometimes mentioning by name one of those who had been killed, drawing loud sobs of distress from that particular family. As I listened to the cries of those whose hearts had been broken by the tragedy which had invaded that love, I felt a wave of great anger sweep over me that he should milk the occasion for his own satisfaction while those who had exploited the killed in the past sat crowned with honour in the front pew.

As the minister announced that the Vicar of Pontywen would give the address at the end of the next hymn, 'Jesu, Lover of my Soul', I knew that I should have to abandon what I had intended to say and speak my mind. When I stepped up into the pulpit, it appeared to me that I was on a stage. It was so much bigger than the enclosed space of the pulpits in St Mary's and St Padarn's. Not only that, but because it was central and not to one side, it seemed that the congregation was mine to command. Before I began to speak, I felt I had a power complex.

'And God shall wipe away all tears from their eyes,' I announced as my text. 'Many are the tears which have flowed in Pontywen, making a river of sorrow over these past weeks. Men we have known and loved have been swept away from our midst and our hearts go out to those who have lost their loved ones. Fathers, husbands, brothers have been sacrificed to King Coal. His altar has accumulated many victims over the past hundred years or so, and now in our own town it has claimed more than a fair share.

'This community owes its existence to coal. In the middle of the last century men came from the countryside in England as well as Wales in search of work. The colliery owners provided them with the terraced houses which straddle our hillsides, paid them a pittance and took their money in the truck shops. Instead of gold dust the miners found coal dust which clogged their lungs and shortened their lives. It is true that they found fellowship, fine fellowship bonded by adversity, something that no other industry has known. It is this fellowship which will enable the people of Pontywen to cope with the calamity which has hit the town.

'We meet in the presence of God whose love for us was so great that he gave His Son to die for us. He raised Him from the dead as a pledge to us that beyond this vale of tears is another life where pain and suffering are banished. Into this life our twelve brothers have been taken by the one who alone can wipe away all tears. We commend them into His hands and pray that He will grant them rest eternal. Amen.'

As I looked down from the pulpit when I had ended my 'few words' I could see that Sir David Jones-Williams' countenance was suffused with a deep purple, as if he were about to explode in a fit of apoplexy. The mayor and mayoress had their heads together, obviously bewailing their misfortune in appointing me as chaplain. When I joined Godfrey Thomas in the deacons' enclosure he whispered to me, 'You've certainly put the cat among the pigeons, boyo. Good for you, but I shouldn't turn your back in the presence of the mayor unless you've got chain-mail protection.'

I decided to stay within the safety of my confines while the Reverend Elias Evans was escorting the honoured guests out of the chapel. However, Sir David chose to break ranks and headed for me with grim intent. 'Vicar,' he spluttered, 'by what right did you use that pulpit to preach socialist claptrap instead of the word of God? If it had not been for my forefathers, those men who came to work here would have starved to death in their hovels in the countryside. I must tell you that I shall never again set foot in St Mary's Church as long as you are the vicar there.' He turned on his heel and stalked out, bumping into one of the bereaved in the process.

'What did I tell you?' said Godfrey. 'It will be the mayor's turn next. They'll be calling you "Red Fred" from now on.'

No sooner had I entered the vicarage than the telephone rang. 'You've done it again, haven't you?' shouted the mayor. 'It was a black day when I was stupid enough to ask you to be my chaplain, my one big mistake, as it were.' With that he slammed down the receiver.

Eleanor came out from the kitchen where she was preparing our tea. 'Don't tell me,' she said, 'it was His Worship Dai Spout. Well done, love.' She kissed me lightly on my cheek.

'That's not all, love,' I replied. 'Sir David Jones-Williams, Baronet, of this parish, has informed me that he will no longer set foot in St Mary's Church as long as I am vicar here. He accused me of preaching "socialist claptrap" instead of the word of God.'

'It took guts to say your piece this afternoon. What

you said was perfectly true and it came from your heart, that was plain for all to see. Don't bother about Sir David up there in his Ivory Tower. He is not exactly a great contributor to the church, anyway. As for Dai Spout and his missus, they don't come to church but wanted to exploit it for their own glory. Well, it hasn't happened. The ordinary people of Pontywen appreciated what you said. You should have heard them outside the chapel afterwards. They are the people that count, not those pompous people in the front row. Good for you, kid. Come into the kitchen with your most devoted fan and have a cup of tea. That will put the smile back on your face, "as it were".'

Some three weeks later, the Saints were holding their first meeting in the 'Prince of Wales' to elect their officers and committee for the coming year. Greatly daring, I had invited the bishop to be their first speaker. Since I had given him such short notice, I didn't expect him to come, especially since the venue was a public house. To my amazement he had said that he was free and that he would be pleased to attend the inaugural meeting.

When Ezekiel Evans and Bertie Owen learned that the bishop was to speak at the opening of the new club, they decided that they would withdraw any objections they had to its formation. In the meanwhile the churchwardens at the three churches arranged that all the men in their congregations would be circularized about the event. Since the local press had got wind of what was to happen, there was no lack of publicity. 'Vicar turns to drink' was one headline in the *Monmouthshire Post*.

The back room of the 'Prince of Wales' was a bleak rectangle, its walls painted in a drab yellow and showing signs of urgent need of redecoration. There were some thirty or so chairs arranged in rows facing a table which was covered with a dirty green cloth and behind which were three chairs. On the walls were five photographs of the Pontywen Silver Band, taken at various stages in their history of forty years. At the other end of the room was a large table, resplendent with a spotless white tablecloth and with the refreshments laid out on the brewery-stamped plates.

A quarter of an hour before the meeting was due to start there were already forty men present, most of whom were in the saloon bar ordering their drinks. I had asked Charles to stay outside in the car park to meet the bishop and bring him round to the back-door entrance. At twenty-five past seven big Jim Pritchard heaved his way through the scrum in the doorway to the bar, escorting the bishop. 'I've rescued His Holiness from the crush in there,' he said. 'It's worse than Cardiff Arms Park. I'll bring him his gin and tonic in a minute. That's on the house, Your Holiness. Could you get a few of your men to bring more chairs in, Vicar? All I hope is the refreshments will be enough to go round.'

'My apologies, my lord, I had asked Charles Wentworth-Baxter to meet you and bring you to the back entrance.' The bishop smiled at my embarrassment. 'If genius lies in the heart of delegation, Vicar, then I am afraid you will not come into that category as long as you rely on that young man. May I say how good it is to see so many men coming to the first meeting of the new organization. The church needs to find new ways to reach the men who are on its fringe and even beyond that. I think your experiment is worthy of encouragement and that is why I am here this evening. Not just for the gin and tonic,' he added.

It seemed a long time since an extremely shy bishop had interviewed me as a young ordinand and was unable to look up from a scrutiny of his desk as I sat in front of him. As someone who had been closeted in a college up until his elevation to the episcopacy, his eight years on the bishop's bench had broadened his outlook and even given him a sense of humour.

There was still no sign of Charles by the time that everybody had been seated. He had come with me in my car not long after seven o'clock and had gone out into the car park almost immediately after arriving. Some of the men said they had seen him hanging around when they came in, but the latecomers had not encountered him. I decided to begin the meeting without him.

It was a most auspicious launch for the Saints Club. There were fifty-two men present, some of whom had to be seated on two benches which had been brought in at the back. The bishop and I sat behind the table, leaving one chair empty. I had asked His Lordship to say the opening prayers, but he insisted that I should do that as the incumbent of the parish.

'Would you all stand, please, and after a moment of silence I shall say a few short prayers.' No sooner had the moment of silence begun that it was broken by a series of muffled shouts and bangings from behind the inner wall of the room. 'Will you all be seated for the time being?' I said. 'Mr Vaughan-Jenkins and Mr Harold Thomas, would you please investigate the cause of the noise?' By now the sounds were becoming frantic.

'Your missing curate, I think, Vicar, if I am not mistaken,' murmured the bishop.

He was not mistaken. Very soon the commotion ceased. A few minutes later, the two churchwardens ushered a red-faced Charles Wentworth-Baxter into the room, to suppressed laughter from the Saints. I motioned him into the empty chair. He began to explain his absence.

'You can tell me what happened later,' I hissed. 'Now, shall we stand again and compose our thoughts before our prayers?'

It must have taken me at least a minute before I could compose my own thoughts sufficiently before opening my mouth to address the Almighty. I was engaged in a hard-fought struggle to subdue my antipathy towards my assistant, a struggle I had fought frequently on other occasions.

Ten minutes later David Vaughan-Jenkins as elected chairman had taken my seat by the bishop, and Idris Shoemaker, alias Idris the Milk, was on the other chair as secretary. A committee of four had been chosen and the Saints Club had become a reality. Suggestions for talks and activities followed in abundance. The formation of a cricket team was decided as a summer venture. Outings to places of interest, especially cathedrals, as proposed by Ezekiel Evans, were envisaged. It was left to the committee to make arrangements which would turn the proposals into a coherent programme.

When the chairman called on the bishop to address the meeting it was evident that the members of the new club were becoming thirsty. 'There will be plenty of time, gentlemen, to place your orders at the bar, after we have heard what the bishop has to say to us.'

'Thank you, Mr Chairman,' said the speaker. 'I have no wish to keep you from your liquid refreshment longer than is necessary. First of all, I wish to say how encouraged I am to see so many men at this inaugural meeting. I can only hope that the numbers will not decrease but, I trust, multiply as the years go by. Secondly, I must emphasize to you that Christianity is not all beer and skittles but involves regular worship at your parish church and not just a monthly visit to the "Prince of Wales". Thirdly and lastly, you will be pleased to know, I hope you will give your vicar all the support that his leadership deserves. He is a young man with a fresh outlook on the work of a parish priest. Don't let him down. Now, if you will stand, I shall give you my blessing.'

Later, when the refreshments had been eaten, the bishop had departed and last orders were being called at the bar, I asked Charles what had happened to him. 'Well, Fred, when you asked me to go to the car park to meet the bishop, I began to develop a stomach-ache – perhaps it was the liver and onions we had before I came out. Anyway, I had to dash to the lavatory. In my hurry and not looking where I was going, I went into the ladies instead of the gents. Then, to my horror when I had finished, I found I couldn't open the door. I had banged it shut in my desperation to get in there. I shouted and shouted and banged the door.'

'So we heard, as we were about to pray,' I said.

'Sorry about that, Fred. Well, anyway, Jim Pritchard came with a ladder and got me out. He said I had jammed the lock. He told me to use the gents next time, otherwise people may get the wrong idea about me.'

## 12

'What are Duck Apple and Apple and Candle?' chorused the schoolgirl members of the G. & S. at the *Gondoliers* rehearsal. The 'Saints' club committee had arranged to have a Hallowe'en party when their programme was first planned. A fortnight before the event, I suggested to them that they might ask the Gilbert and Sullivan Society to join them for the occasion. This was received with enthusiasm, possibly because it meant the presence of the nubile young ladies of the chorus. When Hubert Evans, who was known to be tied to his wife's apron strings, proposed that spouses should be invited also, the proposition was turned down because there would be too many at the party.

'Duck Apple', I explained, required a large tin bath of water on which were floating a number of apples. Three competitors from either side, kneeling outside the bath with their hands behind their backs, had to catch an apple in their mouths. The first three to achieve the feat won that particular round. After the final of 'Duck Apple' came 'Apple and Candle' which involved a candle and an apple suspended on the end of two pieces of string. The participants were blindfolded and given a stipulated amount of time to catch an apple. Once again their hands had to be behind their backs, with the added disadvantage that a mouthful of wax was less agreeable than a mouthful of water.

The invitation was greeted with even greater eagerness

by the *Gondoliers* contingent, especially by the younger element, who were intrigued by the thought of the Hallowe'en games. A joint committee to organize the evening was set up, chaired by Idris the Milk since he was a member of both organizations. Another person on the committee was Bronwen Wentworth-Baxter, assistant tea lady at the G. & S. rehearsals. (Bronwen was now well advanced in her pregnancy, with the baby due in two months' time.)

Whilst she was the embodiment of serenity, Charles was the epitome of anxiety. The prospective father appeared at the daily morning service, looking more and more haggard as each day passed. 'If you don't relax,' I told him, 'your wife will be less troubled by labour pains than the phantom ones which you will experience.'

'I can't help it,' he replied. 'Bronwen is forever telling me not to be so concerned, but she's such a petite little thing, isn't she? She is not like Harold Thomas's wife for example, big and strong. Somebody was telling me the other day that she used to have babies like shelling peas – all over in an hour at most, sometimes before the midwife could get there. Bronwen is a different proposition, say what you like. I know she is in the best of hands, with Eleanor looking after her, but she means so much to me and if anything went wrong, I don't know what I would do, I can tell you.'

'Forget the "buts", Charles, and try to be positive. Eleanor says that everything seems in line for a straightforward delivery of a healthy baby. You should be encouraging your wife, not annoying her by sticking a chair behind her bottom at every hour of the day, to make her take the weight off her feet. She is not an invalid. Bronwen is simply in the process of bringing a child into the world, which is why God made her and gave her the means to do it, with your help, of course. That is why she needs your help as much *now*, as when you started the process last March. You owe that to her, believe me. Today I'll give you something to get you away from underneath her feet. You can do the communions at the hospital this morning and then visit the faithful in Sebastopol and Inkerman Street this afternoon.'

It was the day before the Hallowe'en party.

'I promised I would get the balloons for the party this morning and some other things that she wants. Then this afternoon I was going to blow up the balloons.' He looked like a child who had been deprived of a treat for a misdemeanour.

'Look, Charles, you can get those things this morning after the communion. As for you blowing up the balloons this afternoon, you can do it tomorrow. In any case, I doubt if you could achieve that feat. By the time you had blown up one of them, I wouldn't mind betting that you would have shrivelled it up seconds later, by failing to tie a knot at its top. I am sure that Bronwen will do a much better job of that than you can. You will be doing something much more worthwhile by visiting those two streets, and please don't just knock once gently at a door and then walk away quickly, writing "out" in your visiting book.'

When I returned to the Vicarage from the service, Mrs Watkins, our daily, informed me that Dewi Jones, the retired missionary from China who had taken charge of Llanhyfryd, had telephoned. "E said 'e would ring again later this morning. Dr Secombe told me to tell you that she've 'ad to go to the 'ospital after she've done 'er visits, so she won't be 'ere for lunch. She've asked me to make you some sandwiches before I go. Arthur 'ave brought in some lovely tomatoes from the green'ouse. So that should make you a nice little snack.'

I had seen very little of Dewi lately. His wife's rheumatoid arthritis had reached the stage where she had become housebound. As a result, apart from taking his Sunday services out in the country, he was not much in evidence in Pontywen. They were a delightful couple and, up until Mrs Jones's incarceration, they had been frequent visitors at the Vicarage, regaling us with tales of their time in China.

When Mrs Watkins retired to the kitchen, I went into the study to write my monthly letter for the parish magazine I had originated. Previous to its inception, the only parish news printed was in a deanery publication which came out quarterly. I had been editor of the school magazine and later in college I had been in charge of their publication. Earlier in the year, a recently 'demobbed' regular soldier had set up a small printing works in the town. It was a golden opportunity for me to realize my ambition as the editor of a monthly magazine. The Parochial Church Council had given it its blessing and the sales were sufficient to make a small profit, after I had canvassed all the shops in Pontywen for advertisements. The letter had to be done that day to meet the deadline.

Since I was writing just two days before All Saints Day, I decided I would write a job description for a saint. 'Wanted,' I began. 'A human being, not a plaster saint. Someone who knows his or her own faults and is prepared to do something about them. Must be able to laugh at himself or herself and not at other people but only with them.'

At that moment the telephone rang. I left my desk

thinking that I must arrange for the instrument to be on my desk and not on the hall table. It was Dewi Jones. 'Sorry to disturb you, Fred, but I'm afraid that I have bad news for you. I shall not be able to take the service in Llanhyfryd this Sunday. Rachel's condition has worsened and our doctor feels that perhaps a visit to the hospital in Bath for patients like herself might at least relieve the pain, if nothing else. I shall stay in Bath for the time being. If necessary I shall have to stay for a few weeks. I shall let you know about that in due time. She has told me that she does not need me with her in Bath, and that I would be doing more good in Llanhyfryd. I have told her otherwise. I'm sure you will agree, Fred.'

'Of course, Dewi. I have just began to write the "Dear Friends" letter for the magazine on the subject of Saints. I think Rachel is a prime candidate for selection in that category even though she would deny that most emphatically. Stay in Bath as long as you like. She will need you more than the congregation at St Illtyd's, much as they love you.'

'Bless you, Father. I am sure that our friend the Archdeacon will be able to supply you with a locum for the time being. Once Rachel returns, I shall be only too pleased to resume my care of the little church. I have grown to love it and the people.'

'The feeling is reciprocal, I can assure you; I hope the hospital and its waters will do her a power of good. See you when her treatment is over. Give her our love and tell her that our thoughts and prayers are with her, as always.'

I put the receiver down and then phoned the Archdeacon immediately. The Venerable Griffith Williams was an ambitious cleric, tipped by many as the next bishop of the diocese, a forecast shared by himself. As I waited for him to answer, I compared him with Rachel Jones and decided that he would be a non-runner in the saintliness stakes. The last thing he would ever do would be to laugh at himself, or if it came to that, to laugh with other people. Abraham Lincoln is reported to have said that every man over the age of forty is responsible for his face. The Archdeacon's visage wore a perpetual frown and he was fifty-three years of age.

'Archdeacon speaking,' intoned the voice at the other end. He never spoke. He always intoned.

'Fred Secombe, Vicar of Pontywen here, Mr Archdeacon. I wonder if you can help me. The Reverend Dewi Jones has been helping me at Llanhyfryd, as you know. Unfortunately his wife has to go into hospital at Bath for treatment of her rheumatoid arthritis. Dewi is going to stay nearby, to keep her company for the next few weeks at least. If you could find someone to help me, I should be more than grateful.'

'Now let me see. Would you hold on while I consult my list of retired clergy, Vicar?' There was a two-minute silence. 'Hello! Yes, I think I have someone who can help you. I am afraid he is rather old and will need to be picked up to take the services. He is the Reverend William Glossop; William Glossop who lives at number thirty-three, thirty-three Blaenavon Road, Blaenavon Road, Cwmtydfil, Cwmtydfil.' If he carries on like this, I said to myself he will earn himself the nickname of Dai Duplicate or Little Sir-Echo. 'Have you got that, Vicar?'

'I have indeed. Thank you very much, Mr Archdeacon. Is he on the phone?'

'Yes, he is. I am afraid that he is rather deaf. So you will have to speak up. The number is Cwmtydfil 979,

Cwmtydfil 979. Oh! One other thing. Because of his age he suffers from bladder bother. Perhaps you could arrange for a receptacle to be in the vestry. Occasionally he has to slip out during the singing of a hymn.'

Evidently the congregation at St Illtyd's were due for some surprises from their temporary parson, with his sudden departures to the vestry. Perhaps he would drop off to sleep like some of the ancient clergy at the Deanery Chapter meetings.

With these thoughts in mind, I rang Cwmtydfil 979. I waited for what seemed an eternity to get a reply. When I was about to put the receiver down there was a click as the ringing tone ceased. I waited another eternity before a voice quavered, 'Who is speaking, please?'

I expanded my lungs and bawled, 'This is the Vicar of Pontywen.'

'You needn't shout, Vicar. What do you want?'

'The Archdeacon says that you might be willing to take the services for the next few Sundays at Llanhyfryd Parish Church.'

'Where?'

'At Llanhyfryd Parish Church.'

'You're shouting again, Vicar. Did you say Llandovry Parish church?'

'No. Llanhyfryd Parish Church, which is linked with the parish of Pontywen.'

'Oh, you are the young man who has turned to the public house to hold his meetings there. I must tell you that as a lifetime abstainer I don't agree with that.'

'I'm sorry about that, Mr Glossop, but can you take these Sunday services for me?'

'Well, only if you send someone to pick me up. What time are your services?'

'Eleven o'clock and half past six.'

'Yes, I think I shall be able to come. Ask them to be here early and will you arrange for a chamber pot to be in the vestry?'

'Thank you, Mr Glossop. Yes, I shall see that your chauffeur will be with you in plenty of time and that some kind of receptacle will be there for your use in the vestry.'

'Very well, Vicar. Shall I be reimbursed?'

'The churchwardens will pay you two guineas a service.'

'Thank you very much. The old age pension is not much to live on these days. I'm a widower, you see. We managed when my wife was alive but I find it very difficult now I am on my own. It's a lonely life now.'

He was about to expand on the theme of loneliness when I had to apply the guillotine to any further conversation. The magazine was demanding my attention in the study, with its job description of a saint. I decided to add one further qualification to the others I had in mind – patience. I found that, as I became more involved in the various activities of a parish priest, my tolerance level was diminishing rapidly and my ministry was impaired as a result.

I finished my parish letter and added a note about Rachel Jones's visit to hospital with the subsequent arrival of the Reverend William Glossop to replace Dewi Jones for the time being at Llanhyfryd. When I had finished, Mrs Watkins tapped on the study door to let me know that she was leaving and that she had prepared some 'lovely' sandwiches for me on a plate in the kitchen. No sooner had I sat down with *The Times* crossword at my elbow and Mrs Watkins' lunchtime treat-in front of me, than the telephone made its presence known yet again.

'The Vicar of Pontywen speaking,' I snarled.

'What a way to greet your loving wife, Frederick! Have you had a bad morning?'

'Sorry, love. It began with Dewi apologizing for the fact that he can't take services for the next few weeks and it ended with a request for a chamber pot from his stand-in. In between came the nasal strains of the Archdeacon intoning a series of repeats.'

'It all sounds very interesting, my dear. You must fill me in with further details later. I am afraid I have to add to your headaches by informing you that it looks as if I shall not be with you until well after our normal evening meal time. I am speaking from the hospital. The gynaecologist is away for a few days and Matron has asked me to superintend a very tricky delivery case which could even go on until the early hours of the morning. Anyway I'll ring you again later on. I suggest you get yourself some fish and chips. That should be enough to tide you over. I tell you what, I would rather have that than hospital food any day. I'll be in touch.'

When I had finished my meal of Mrs Watkins' sandwiches and completed *The Times* crossword by guessing the answers to two of the clues, I turned my attention to the magazine once more. After enumerating the various qualities required for the job description of saintliness, I strove to finish with a long purple passage. It shrank into a small patch of two sentences after many trials and errors. 'Only those who find that they cannot exist without communion with God, any more than they can exist without breathing, need apply. Only those who do not apply will be considered.' As I sat admiring my punchline it occurred to me that I had been eliminated already since pride was the deadliest of all sins. Any further contemplation was ended by a ring on the doorbell.

It was Idris the Milk, still wearing his apron. 'Sorry to disturb you. I've got Daisy tied up outside before I take her back to the stable. Just a quick word about tomorrow. I've just taken our tin bath down to the "Prince of Wales" on the cart, ready for the Duck Apple. Jim Pritchard is under the impression that he is supposed to be supplying the refreshments as he normally does. Bertie Owen had said that he would let him know that we were doing our own thing just for this once. Gwen and Bronwen have organized everything. Loads of people have promised sandwiches and cakes. I know I'm stupid to let Bertie be responsible for letting Jim know but he was so definite he would do it – I wonder if you could go and have a word with him. He could stop us going there, the mood he's in at the moment, if we don't pay for his food.'

'Thanks, Idris,' I replied. 'What on earth made you allow Bertie to pass on a message? He's as reliable as the Pontywen bus timetable. What do you expect me to do with Jim Pritchard? He's twice my size so I can hardly confront him.'

'I thought maybe you could use diplomacy, Vicar. You're good at that. You know, butter him up a bit. The pub closes at 3 o'clock. When I got there he was busy pulling pints. If you get him after closing time perhaps he'll be more relaxed.'

'I'm glad you said relaxed, Idris. I should think the last person he wants to see when he's putting his feet up is me.'

An hour later I was knocking on the back door of the 'Prince of Wales'. Sabre, the Alsatian guard dog, began to bark in menacing tones. 'Quiet! you stupid bloody dog.' It was difficult to know which of the two sounds was the more threatening. When the door was opened, the landlord eyed me with a mixture of surprise and suspicion. 'Good afternoon, Vicar! Come on in, will you? Do you mind sitting in the saloon bar while I check on the optics and one or two other things?'

So much for the feet-up supposition of Idris, I said to myself. As I sat on the edge of one of the red leather-topped stools I launched into the deep. 'I've just been talking to Idris the Milk, Jim, and he tells me that there has been a mix-up about the catering for tomorrow night's Hallowe'en party. Apparently Bertie Owen should have told you two weeks ago that the Saints Club were being joined for the event by the Gilbert and Sullivan Society, and the two of them would be responsible for the refreshments on that evening. Why on earth Idris relied on him to tell you, I don't know.'

'You can say that again, Vicar. Everybody knows what Bertie's like. The result is that I've ordered everything for the "do" and it's too late to stop it now. I get my stuff from the Co-op and I can't see them agreeing to cancel the food at less than a day's notice. As far as I'm concerned, they'll have to have the two lots of refreshments and that's it.'

'Is it possible for you to sell the refreshments in the saloon bar tomorrow?'

'Look here, Vicar. When the men come in here in the evening, they've had their meal. They're coming to have a drink, not a nibble on a sandwich. As you know, almost all of them are from the pit or the steelworks. If they are going to eat, it's the knife and fork for them and a hot meal, not a couple of sandwiches and cakes. I think you had better tell Idris and his committee, if they're going to come here tomorrow night, they've got to pay for the refreshments we've got for them. If they want to have the use of this room in the future, they either do that or it's back to your church hall.'

'Fair enough, Jim. I should think that by the time they have exhausted their energy in all the games they have arranged, they will be only too willing to have a double dose of sandwiches and cakes.'

By the time I had been refreshed by the use of Jim's optics, I felt fortified enough to call in at number one Hillside Avenue, the abode of Idris and Gwen, to pass on the news of my abysmal failure at the 'Prince of Wales'. Their house resembled Dr Barnardo's, in that their door was always open. 'It's me,' I called out and walked down the passage to the closed living-room door.

'Come on in, Vicar,' Gwen shouted.

When I entered the room I was greeted by the sight of a glowing fire inside the immaculately black leaded grate. Whether it was high summer or deepest winter, there was always that fire blazing away, the focal point. Beside it, Idris dozed in the afternoon when he came home from his work, and around it the family met for meals and conversation. 'We're out here,' she announced. I went into the scullery where I discovered my curate's wife with a bulging pinafore, assisting the milkman's wife. Gwen was rolling out pieces of pastry while Bronwen was using a circular cutter to make the tarts. 'The G & S incorporated!' I said.

'You could say that, but more important, how did you get on with Jim Pritchard? Idris said he had asked you to have a word with him about the refreshments. He's been worried sick since he came back from the "Prince of Wales". It's a bit much to ask people to pay for refreshments after they have given so much food themselves.'

'I'm very sorry, Gwen, but I have to admit I got

nowhere. He said that he had ordered the food from the Co-op and that they would refuse to cancel the order at the last minute. If we didn't pay for the food, there would be no more meetings in the "Prince of Wales". I can see his point of view only too clearly. I thought it was a hopeless exercise before I went there.'

'So did I, to be honest,' she replied. 'I told Idris it was a bit much asking you to go and see him anyway. Let's go into the living room and have a cup of tea. Take the weight off your feet, what do you say, Bronwen?'

Mrs Wentworth-Baxter grimaced. 'Don't say that, please. I get enough of that from my husband. If I listened to him I would have to stay in bed until the baby is born. What would happen to the house and to our meals, I dread to think.'

No sooner had we sat down than Idris appeared. 'Well?' he inquired when he saw me.

'What did you expect? It's pay up or get out. I can't say I blame him. You know where the blame lies.'

The people's churchwarden collapsed into his armchair at the fireside. 'I'll never rely on Bertie Owen ever again.'

'How many times have you said that before?' said Gwen. 'You know what he's like. Let's get the kettle on the fire and have a cuppa. I hope you've learnt your lesson. Do it yourself next time, not leave it to Bertie.'

Half an hour later, Idris was fast asleep, mesmerized by the coal fire. 'I think I had better be off.' I whispered.

'He's so rude, isn't he?' said his wife, also in a whisper. 'I think Bronwen and I had better finish our work.'

Some two hours later I was taking my place in the queue for the fish and chips at Cascarini's Fish Bar in Pontywen Square. There was the usual motley throng of housewives, husbands who had been sent out to get 'two cutlets and six penn'orth' while the table was being laid, and children who brought the order written on a scrap of paper, wrapped around the coins necessary for payment. One of these children was Tommy Harris, the scourge of St Padarn's Sunday school. As I joined the queue he was in the middle of an altercation with another boy in front of him. 'Stop pushing me,' said Tommy's opponent.

'I wasn't pushing you,' came the reply.

'He was, wasn't he, mister?' appealed the boy to a steelworker standing behind Tommy. The man was still wearing the sweat rag around his neck, fresh from his labours at the furnace. 'Don't ask 'im. 'Ow could 'e tell?' said Tommy.

'You keep your mouth shut, young 'Arris. I could see you was pushing 'im.'

'If it comes to that, you was pushing me behind me.'

'Any more lip from you, Tommy, and I'll give you a clip around the ear.'

'You and who else?'

As the steel-worker was about to administer the punishment, 'young 'Arris' noticed me standing behind him. ''Allo, Vicar,' he said brightly and then turned to face the front of the queue. 'Sorry, Vicar,' said the man, 'but 'e's asking for it. Always causing trouble, or spoiling for a fight.'

'You needn't tell me that,' I replied. 'I know him quite well. He comes to our Sunday school at St Padarn's.'

'I know 'im quite well too. 'E lives next door but one to me, a proper little bugger, I can tell you. Perhaps you can teach 'im some manners at your Sunday school. 'Is parents 'aven't been able to do it, that's positive.'

By now the little fracas had become the centre of

attention amongst the customers; Giuseppe Cascarini, whose accent was redolent of the valleys rather than of Naples, his place of origin, was more interested in what was happening in his shop than he was in the state of the chips in the pan. I felt I had to jump to Tommy's defence. 'Well, Mr, er . . . Lewis,' I said. 'Well, Mr Lewis, we are not all saints by any means. I am certainly not one. He's not a bad lad. Tommy has plenty of guts and a keen sense of humour. What's more, he's a very good brother to the two children in his family, so I should remember that, if I were you.'

He glared at me, swallowed hard and kept silence for the rest of the time he was in the shop.

When it came to my turn at the counter I thought I had better order two fish and chips, in case Eleanor came home earlier than expected. 'I must apologize, Vicar, for the bit of a row earlier on,' said Giuseppe. 'You know what it is like when they send the kids. But there you are, one and ten pence, please.'

As I came out from the shop, I was met by Tommy. 'Thank you, Vicar,' he said. 'I didn't 'ear properly what you said, but it shut old 'Arry up, that's more than his missus does, that's for sure.'

'You must learn not to be so cheeky, then you won't get into trouble. You had better run home with those fish and chips otherwise your parents will want to know why they're cold.'

It was a chilly, starry night with a hint that November would bring some early snow to the valleys, when the calendar changed in a day's time. I shivered in the biting north-east wind. The kitchen was warm and welcoming when I came in through the back door. I opened the oven and put the parcel of Cascarini's best, wrapped in the

*Daily Herald*, on the top shelf. Leaving my overcoat on, I filled the kettle, ready for a pot of tea to supplement my meal. No sooner had I turned the tap off than there was a ring on the telephone.

'Get that kettle on,' came the voice at the other end. 'I'll be with you in a quarter of an hour or so.'

'There's more than a cup of tea waiting for you. How do you fancy a cutlet of hake and six penn'orth of chips, fresh from Cascarini's.'

'Wonderful,' said my wife. 'And I wouldn't object to a tot of whisky to start with; I need it, believe me.'

'You don't sound very happy, love.'

'I'll tell you all about it when I get back and that can't be too soon.'

By the time she came home I had laid the table in the dining-room instead of the kitchen. The bunch of chrysanthemums from our garden, picked that afternoon by Arthur, our part-time gardener, now joined the condiments instead of reposing on the window ledge of the sitting-room. With all the bars on the electric fire on full blast, the temperature had moved from the igloo stage to the almost bearable when I heard the car coming down the Vicarage drive. As she opened the door I met her with a half a tumblerful of whisky in my hand. 'How about that for service, love?' I said.

She put her arms round my neck and burst into tears. I led her into the dining room and thrust the whisky into her hand. 'Drink a mouthful of this, there's a dear. Now sit down and let me cuddle you for a minute.' We sat there for quite a while with her head on my shoulder. When her sobbing had subsided she raised her head. 'That poor woman! She went through all that suffering for nothing. It was a dreadful haemorrhage, and the baby was asphyxiated. It was awful. It was a beautiful baby, a little girl. That's the first baby that I have lost. I hope to God it's the last.' She began to weep again. Suddenly she stood up. 'I must pull myself together. This is very unprofessional. What is it that President Truman said? "If you can't stand the heat, get out of the kitchen." There's a lot of truth in that, isn't there?'

'Agreed, my love,' I said. 'Well, you are not in the kitchen, you're in the dining-room. So transfer your bottom to the dining chair and you will be served with fish and chips *à la* Cascarini. Finish off that whisky while the waiter disappears to bring you your main dish, hot from the oven, having been sheltered in the *Daily Herald*. I am afraid they had run out of the *Daily Worker*, otherwise it would have been well and truly red-hot.'

'Fred, that's pathetic. I know you're trying to cheer me up, but that's not worth even one gold star for trying.'

'Excuse me, teacher. I think I deserve five gold stars. You sound as if you are back to normal already. So could you please park yourself while I take charge of the kitchen?'

Later, as we drank our cups of tea, Eleanor began to put the afternoon's tragedy into perspective. 'I suppose I must have delivered dozens of babies safely since I've been in practice. There are countless more children I shall be bringing into the world in the years that lie ahead. I know that is no consolation to the mother who lost her baby today. The only consolation I have is that I could have done nothing to prevent it happening. Perhaps in the not too distant future, technology will develop to such an extent that it will be possible to make the death of a baby at childbirth a rarity.'

'Well, very soon, my sweet, you will be bringing the first of the Wentworth-Baxter brood into this world. The sooner the better, as far as the prospective father is concerned.'

'Thank God, there should be no complications with that delivery. The baby is well placed in the womb and Bronwen is in excellent health. So all should be well.'

'There is only one caveat to that. Have you ever known a Wentworth-Baxter enterprise to be quite straightforward?'

'Secombe, that's a very wicked remark. I can only hope that you won't have to regret making it.'

## 13

Next morning I had a phone call from the Rural Dean. 'I
wonder if I could come and borrow some Ancient and
Modern hymn books from you, Vicar? We have a confirmation service here this evening. There are four other
parishes bringing candidates. There are even two candidates from Trehafod. I am coming down to Pontywen to
pick up some bottles of pickles we have been promised
from Howells the greengrocer. Is eleven o'clock all right
for you?'

'Fine by me, Mr Rural Dean. I'll have them here at the
Vicarage ready for you. Are you all right for veils?'

'They are bringing their own veils with them for the
female candidates. We have a few to spare anyway.'

The mention of Trehafod, a parish of one hundred and
fifty souls, hidden away in the hills, reminded me of a
well-known anecdote about William Rees, its incumbent
for forty-six years who had died recently. It was said that
at one time there had been no confirmation candidates
for more than twenty years. When the Bishop inquired of
the Vicar the reason for this dearth the old man replied,
'Well, my Lord, we are so much out of the way up here
that it would be a long old journey for you. So I have
been doing the few that we have had myself to save you
the trouble.'

I was thinking about this legendary story as I went
across to the church for Matins. Charles met me as I was
coming up the path. 'You are early this morning,' I said.

'Can't sleep,' he replied. 'These are worrying times. It won't be long now before Bronwen's due to have the baby, as you know. I keep waking up every five minutes.'

'For heaven's sake, Charles. Eleanor has told you that you have nothing to worry about. Everything is straightforward, apparently.'

'That's not my only headache, Fred. There's the financial aspect. It's all right for you. You are well away, as an incumbent with a wife who is a doctor. Now that Bronwen has given up work, we have to rely on my curate's stipend and you know how inadequate that is.'

'In that case you will have to look for a living. Trehafod is vacant now that old William Rees has tottered into the arms of his maker. It is the kind of parish that would suit you nicely, the minimum of work, delightful countryside. You could stay there for the next fifty years or so; another William Rees. The parish is in the gift of the Bishop. I shouldn't think there would be a rush of candidates.'

'Many thanks for that vote of confidence. All the same, I think I should write to his lordship today. The sooner I get a living the better, even if it is in the middle of nowhere. It can easily be a stepping-stone to something better when the time is ripe, can't it?'

'I suppose it all depends on what you decide is the ripe time, Charles. Some times take longer than others to ripen and in your case the ripening process could be a protracted one. Anyway, let's go into the church and say our prayers about it.'

As we came into the vestry after service, he said to me, 'I have made up my mind. When I read that verse from the seventh chapter of the Wisdom of Solomon, "God loveth none but him that dwelleth with wisdom", I felt I was being guided to make a wise choice. I shall definitely write to the Bishop today.'

'Better still, Charles,' I suggested, 'why don't you come to the Vicarage now and phone him? There is no time like the present for the man of wisdom and it will save you the money you would spend in a call-box.'

'I don't know about that. Do you think he would mind a curate phoning him without giving him notice? It's a bit of a cheek, don't you think?'

'Not at all. You don't have to give written notice to the Bishop if you want to phone him. If he's busy, he will ask you to call him later. I am sure that he will not regard you as impertinent. Would you like me to make the initial call and say that you wish to speak to him?'

'Thanks, Fred, that would be a great help.'

Ten minutes later, after I had made us both a cup of coffee, we went into the hall from the study, and he stood by my side, his body trembling as I dialled the Bishop's number. His secretary answered and asked me to hold on for a moment.

'What's happening?' inquired Charles.

'That was his secretary. She has asked me to hold on. He has either paid a visit to the lavatory or perhaps he hasn't quite finished his breakfast,' I whispered. Charles began to giggle nervously.

His giggle was cut short when the Bishop's voice was heard loud and clear on the receiver, which I was holding at arm's length. 'This is Fred Secombe, my Lord.'

'Good morning, Vicar. What can I do for you?' He sounded unusually abrupt.

'It's nothing you can do for me. I have Charles Wentworth-Baxter with me who wishes to speak to you. I suggested that he made the call from the Vicarage rather than a public telephone-box. I shall leave him with you, my Lord.'

I handed the receiver to my curate and disappeared into the kitchen where I had heard Mrs Watkins arriving, ready for her morning round of domestic chores. She was rubbing her hands together vigorously. 'There've been quite a few flakes of snow when I was coming down just now,' she said. She lived up on the hillside, in a row of small cottages exposed to the easterly winds.

'There's still some hot water in the kettle, if you'd like a cup of tea. It won't take long to boil up again,' I said.

'Thank you, Vicar, I'd love one if it's only to keep the cold out and that. I can drink tea until the cows come 'ome, I can.'

She sat down at the table, still clad in her coat, and launched into a recital of how many times a day she stopped for a cup of tea. Before she could reveal her evening drinking habits, there was a loud tap on the door. 'Come on in, Charles, and tell us the news.'

My curate's face spoke volumes before he uttered a word. It was split from ear to ear. 'What do you think?' he asked.

'I know. He has told you to pack in the ministry and apply for a job where perhaps you can be useful, if possible.'

'Don't be horrible, Fred. He has offered me the living of Trehafod. He said that I will not be able to move in until well into next year, because of the state of the house after old William Rees had lived there for forty-six years.'

'Congratulations, Charles. You had better get back to Bronwen as quickly as possible to pass on the good news. I expect she will be glad to know your offspring will be breathing the pure air of Trehafod instead of the polluted variety we have to endure in Pontywen. She will be nearer to her mother up there, too.'

'Why did you have to mention that? That is something I hadn't thought of. That is a decided disadvantage. I bet Bronwen thinks so, too. Still, we may not be there very long, you never know. The great thing is I can be my own boss once I am there.'

'Thank you, Charles. You make me sound like an ogre instead of your best friend.'

'You know what I mean. Of course you are my best friend and you have been very good to me, much more than I have deserved, I must admit. The thing is, I have reached a watershed in my life. I am about to become a father. I need now to stand on my own two feet.'

'Well, use those two feet to get home *tout de suite* before the hot news begins to cool. Mrs Watkins says it is beginning to snow.'

Promptly at eleven o'clock the Rural Dean was on my doorstep with an empty carrier bag in his hand. 'Twenty hymn books will be sufficient, Vicar. We've got sixty in the church. If this snow begins to fall properly, we'll be lucky to have eighty for the service. I won't stay, if you don't mind. Too much to do, you see.' As he was putting the books into his carrier bag, I told him that Charles had been offered the living of Trehafod. 'Very good,' he said. 'It will be a change for them to have a young man. It will be nice to have another young vicar at the Chapter meetings too. In any case, old William Rees never came to one for the forty-six years he was in the parish. No wonder the Archdeacon called him Robinson Crusoe.' He began to laugh at this witticism. He was still laughing as he got into his car. 'Robinson Crusoe! Ha! ha!'

Eleanor was not laughing when she came home after

morning surgery and her post-surgery visits. There was a thin layer of snow on the roof and the bonnet of the car. 'The top of the valley is like the Arctic,' she said. 'It won't be long before the snow settles on the roads. Thank heavens I have finished my visits for today.' She sniffed the aroma which was coming from the kitchen. 'And thank heavens Mrs Watkins is the chef for today.' We had decided to have a midday meal because of the Hallowe'en feast at the 'Prince of Wales'.

As we sat down to our bowls of 'cawl', mutton soup with a wide range of vegetables, I told her about the Wentworth-Baxter promotion. 'Well, he has made it, after all,' she commented. 'I never thought he would. All I can say is that he owes it to you. No other vicar would have had your patience to suffer him for so long, believe me.'

'In fairness to him, love, he did admit that I had been very good to him, much more than he had deserved.'

'You can say that again. I am so glad for Bronwen's sake. If they had to try to cope with the baby, on a curate's stipend, it is she who would have suffered. I expect the Bishop felt that the parish of Trehafod was the one place in the diocese where he could do the least harm. That makes two of your curates in splendid isolation, both of whom, I am willing to bet, will remain there indefinitely.' The other curate to whom Eleanor referred, was the Reverend Barnabas Webster, a somewhat elderly late entrant into holy orders who had left his village shop to serve the Lord instead of his customers. I soon discovered that he would have been better employed serving his customers. In an exercise of damage limitation, the Bishop had exiled him to a sparsely populated rural parish where he was happy being his own boss, as Charles wished to be.

'Perhaps now, Frederick, the Bishop will find you an assistant curate who will assist rather than hinder.'

'I don't know about that, love. Curates are not in plentiful supply nowadays. Once the post-war input of candidates gets out of the colleges and into the parishes, things will be different. Another couple of years should see that happening.'

'For your sake, my dear, I hope it is sooner than that. With three churches to look after and just one geriatric with bladder bother to help you, you will be hard put to advance the frontiers of the Kingdom of God in Pontywen.'

Later that afternoon I went down to the garden shed to sort out some apples for the Hallowe'en games. There were now only a few snowflakes in the air and it looked as if the weather would be no hindrance to the success of the evening. Eleanor was busy baking some Welsh cakes on the stove top when I came back into the kitchen with a basketful of apples. 'All is safely gathered in,' I sang, ''ere the winter storms begin.'

'You're a bit late there, Fred. There are still three trees to be plundered and the snow has arrived already. It's probably a memo from the Almighty, that it's time you finished your apple harvest. Arthur asked you weeks ago, whether you wanted him to pick them, but, no, you said, you wanted to do that job. The poor man thinks you don't trust him.'

'He knows perfectly well that I trust him. You can ask him that yourself, if you don't believe me. He'll be there tonight.' Arthur Williamson, retired delivery man for the Co-op Bakery, had been my part-time gardener for the past twelve months, and had transformed the kitchen garden.

'I'm just pulling your leg, Secombe. I know that the only motive you have for picking the apples yourself is pride of possession. All this fruit is mine. I would not want to upset Arthur's evening anyway.'

By the time we arrived at the 'Prince of Wales' the back room was full of excited noise and activity. The female chorus of the Gilbert and Sullivan Society were chasing each other around the bath of water, which occupied the centre of the floor space. All the chairs were lined up against the walls, many of them occupied by the 'saints' with their beer glasses in their hands, enjoying the spectacle of the young maidens besporting themselves. The landlord had brought in the piano from the public bar and placed it next to the table, on which was laid out an impressive array of refreshments. When we came in Charles and Bronwen came to greet us. It must have been the first occasion at a function that Charles had been present before I had arrived. The couple were in such a state of exhilaration that it was obvious to all that their cup was brimming over. To my amazement Bronwen came up to me and kissed me. 'Thank you for getting the Bishop to give Charles his new job. It's going to mean so much to me.' Then she turned to Eleanor and hugged her.

'Be careful with that lump, young lady,' warned my wife. 'It hasn't got that much longer to stay there but I know how you must feel. I'm so glad for you, Bronwen.' Charles stood by, saying nothing but grinning like a Cheshire cat, enjoying the prospect of becoming both father and vicar.

Idris the Milk had been appointed by the joint committee as MC for the evening. 'Will you all fill up your glasses in the next quarter of an hour?' he bellowed. 'After that no one is allowed to sneak out to the bar until the interval. We have got a full programme of games and music. So hurry up and get your liquor or your lemonade. Don't forget, girls. No booze for you: stay in here and don't go into the bar, Gwen will take all your orders in here.'

They crowded around his wife shouting their orders. 'Hold on, girls. Give me a chance,' she pleaded. 'Wait your turn and I'll write down what you want.' She produced a writing pad from her handbag and began to write down their requirements. 'Pay me when you get your drinks. Don't bother me with money at the moment. I want two gentlemen at least to come with me to the bar to carry the trays.' There was a rush of volunteers sufficient to carry enough drinks to slake the thirst of five times the number of girls present. The young ladies had never had such a lot of attention paid them.

'Now settle down, everybody,' shouted Idris, when the procession from the bar had ended. 'Unlike most programmes, we are going to have our piece of resistance first. Vicar, will you float your delicious apples on the water in the bath, please? All these lovely apples have their stems still intact. You can either try to pick them up by the stem, or else if you have a mouth big enough, no names, no pack drill, you can try to turn the apple into a gob-stopper. Whatever happens, you must have your hands behind your back. Anybody trying to use their hands will be disqualified straight away. Now, will the first team from each side step forward and kneel by the bath. G. & S. on my right, "Saints" on my left.'

Inevitably, Bertie Owen had managed to get into the first round, representing the 'Saints', together with Arthur the Co-op, and Harold Thomas. Opposite them were three enthusiastic schoolgirls, Rachel Owen, Sally Jones and Brenda Llewellyn. Rachel was a well-built teenager.

Sally and Brenda were slim and petite. 'Now then, girls, stay where you are and Gwen will put a towel around your necks. We don't want your mothers complaining that you have been drenched. Gentlemen, you can fend for yourselves. When I blow the whistle the battle begins. Get your mouths in shape, everybody. Have you finished, Gwen? Right, off we go.' There was a loud blast on the whistle, and the attack began on the six apples floating in the water.

The first into the fray was Rachel, lunging towards the nearest apple, which had attracted the attention of Arthur as well. Their heads met across the bath with a resounding crack. It was fortunate for Arthur, with his bald head, that Rachel was as well endowed with hair as with the rest of her anatomy. In the meanwhile Bertie Owen, ignoring the MC's remark about big mouths, was attempting to capture the whole of an apple in his wide-open mouth. As he thrust his face towards an apple for the fourth time, giving the impression of a man eating shark, the top part of his set of false teeth fell into the water, to the great hilarity of spectators and competitors alike. Immediately Bertie divested himself of his jacket and began to roll up his shirt-sleeves to recover his missing denture. 'Foul!' bawled Idris. 'Off you go.'

'I'm not leaving here without my teeth,' lisped Bertie, 'foul or no foul.' He plunged his hand into the bath, splashing water over his two fellow competitors, who were unprotected from the deluge.

'We didn't ask for a baptism,' Arthur complained.

'Got em,' shouted Bertie and held aloft the dental plate, as if it were some kind of trophy. The next second, it was back in his mouth.

'That's the cleanest his teeth have been for months,'

commented Llew Jones. Eventually the contest ended with a score of nine apples to the Gilbert and Sullivan Society against three for the 'Saints'. When the game was over there was more water on the floor of the 'Prince of Wales' than there was in the bath.

'And now for a surprise item,' announced Idris. 'A duet between Mabel and Frederick, in other words, the Vicar and Mrs Vicar accompanied by our popular Curate. What you might call a clerical gathering at the piano.' It was indeed a great surprise to Eleanor, and myself, since it was some eighteen months since we had last sung that set piece from *The Pirates of Penzance*. Charles advanced towards us with a score of the operetta.

'It's all right, Charles,' I said. 'We don't need it.'

'Big head!' whispered my wife. 'For that I hope you remember your words as well as the music.'

As the opening notes sounded tinnily from the public bar instrument, the months slipped away and we were once again on stage, at the last night of the performance in the School Hall, the night we became engaged. The libretto called upon us to declare our love for each other 'till we are wed and ever after'.

'Apart from a few hesitances, Frederick, you were word perfect; I must admit I was more hesitant than you,' said Eleanor.

'It never showed,' I replied.

'Always the gentleman,' she murmured.

'The next item is in memory of our dear friend, Charlie Thomas, to be conducted by our splendid conductor, Aneurin Williams. "Hail Poetry" sung by the full chorus,' announced Idris.

'Hang on, Idris. How can we be full? We haven't had our refreshments yet.' This second interruption from

Llew Jones was greeted with groans for its lack of taste, as a prelude to a tribute to a much-loved man. 'We'll ignore that,' said the MC. 'Mr Williams, will you please take over?' Aneurin stepped forward and stood by the piano. 'Do you want a note?' he asked.

'No,' came the reply. He raised his right hand and, as he brought it down, there came a volume of sound, which shook the walls of the back room, as loud as anything produced by the Pontywen Silver Band at their rehearsals. It was one of the most moving experiences of my life. There was a long silence after the music died away; an unspoken prayer for the soul of a dear friend.

When the chorus had returned to their seats, Idris came into the centre of the room. 'There will now be a short interval for refreshments. You can have your grub now, Llew and I hope you enjoy it.' It must have been the least enjoyable meal he had ever eaten. For the next half hour, chaos reigned as the men fought their way into the bar and the volunteer waiters fought their way out of it, with trays laden with soft drinks for the girls. To add to the chaos was the scramble around the refreshment table, where Gwen and Bronwen, plus their helpers, endeavoured to cope with the inroads upon the plentiful supply of sandwiches, pickles and cakes.

Eventually, when calm had been restored, stomachs filled, and thirsts satisfied, Idris introduced the second half of the evening's entertainment. 'The piece of resistance in this second half is once again the first item, "Apple and Candle". At least in this game you won't get wet. Bertie may find his false set stuck in a candle, but at least he won't drown his pals. Gwen and Bronwen will blindfold the competitors who will come forward, one at a time. You will be given one minute to catch an apple.

Once again, it is hands behind your back. This time, one bite out of an apple will earn one point. Nobody has a mouth big enough to get it round an apple as Bertie showed us earlier on, so as soon as you have bitten one piece, not scratched the apple or left a tooth mark on it, but bitten a piece out of it, that gets you a point. If you can get two or more pieces out within two minutes it means extra points.'

The apple and the candle were suspended from an old gas bracket, at the side of the room, the chairs having been cleared away from under it. Once again, Rachel Owen was sent in to bat first for the G. and S. but, whereas she had found it easy to pick up the apple by its stem in the bath of water, she found herself biting pieces of wax rather than apple. On the other hand, the men found it easier to get at the apple by reason of their superior height. The last 'man' in for the G. & S., with two points to win, was Gwen. She had played the game many times before and knew the secret. Not for her the headlong lunge but instead the gentle stroke of her nose against the dangling object, followed by a quick bite when the apple was identified. Her three bites gave her side a clear victory, cheered loudly by the girls who were jumping up and down.

There followed various musical items. Then came the last event of the evening. 'I want all the chorus placed in the middle of the room.' said Idris, 'ready for an old favourite, musical chairs. Our excellent pianist will provide the music. Will you all give him a hand for his efforts throughout the evening?' Charles stood up at the piano and bowed as he received his ovation.

'Now, I want everybody to join in this, no sitting out. All take your place round the chairs, please.' The pianist began to play the Policeman's chorus from *The Pirates of Penzance* as Bronwen decided to join in the fun, despite the handicap of her bulge. After five rounds, when there were only ten competitors left, she was still there, unseen by her husband who had his back to the proceedings. When the music restarted, he speeded up the tempo and then stopped suddenly. Bronwen, who had been behind Arthur, whose little bandy legs had been working overtime, came into a violent collision with my part-time gardener and fell to the floor. There was a breathless hush. Charles turned round to see what was happening, to discover his wife lying on the floor. Before he could reach her, Eleanor had moved to her side. 'I feel terrible,' breathed Bronwen. 'I think something is happening.'

'Phone for an ambulance, Idris.' my wife said, in her best professional manner. 'Now then, let's get you into Jim's sitting room while we wait for the ambulance to come.'

'What on earth made you join in the game?' demanded Charles whose face was paler than that of his wife.

'Shut up, Charles,' ordered my wife, 'and help me to get her out of here.'

I followed the three of them upstairs to the sitting room where Ruby Pritchard was waiting to receive us, having been warned by her husband about what had happened.

'Would you mind if she rested on your bed while I examine her?' asked Eleanor.

'Of course not,' said the landlord's wife. 'Is there anything you want?'

'Some warm water and towels for a start.'

'Is she going to be all right?' inquired Charles, who was shaking in his anxiety.

'Of course she is,' said Eleanor. 'Now be a good boy

and go downstairs out of the way until the ambulance arrives. Get Jim to give you a good dose of whisky. That's all the medicine you need. Fred, ask Idris if he will get the party to break up, and let them know that everything is OK and that nothing terrible has happened. It is all under control.'

Charles went to the bar counter, where Jim Pritchard had prepared a large whisky for him. 'Sit over there, Reverend, in the corner. It's already past closing time so you'll have a bit of peace down here. Come on, gentlemen, drink up and get a move on, please.' The few customers who were left swallowed their beer and made a quick exit. When I went into the back room, only Idris and Gwen were left.

'Is there anything I can do?' asked Gwen.

'No, thank you,' I replied. 'Mrs Pritchard is helping Eleanor and apparently all is well.'

'The ambulance people said they would be here as soon as possible, whenever that is,' said Idris.

'Apart from the, er, incident in the last half hour, it has been a very enjoyable evening, thanks to you and, of course, Gwen, who must have worked very hard. Perhaps by tomorrow morning we shall have some good news for the parish. That will round off the enjoyment nicely.'

'I hope so, Vicar. I don't think I'll be able to sleep tonight, worrying about what has happened. Bronwen has been so happy about the baby coming.'

'I tell you what, Gwen. I'll let you know first thing tomorrow if the baby has arrived and everything is OK.' If they had waited longer they would have had the good news before they left.

When I went into the bar, Charles was taking his

second dose of medicine. 'Would you care to join your curate in a glass of whisky, Vicar?'

'With the greatest of pleasure, Jim, and many thanks.'

'I remember when our first was born up North,' said the landlord. 'The only thing that kept me going while I was waiting for the missus to deliver the goods, like, was the old whisky bottle, good old Doctor Barleycorn.'

As I glanced across at Charles, it was evident that the good old doctor was about to send him into sweet oblivion. His eyelids were almost closed.

The next second his eyes were wide open. There was a cry of a baby upstairs. 'Good God, that was quick!' exclaimed the landlord.

Charles was up on his feet instantly. 'Do you mind if I go upstairs?' he asked excitedly.

'Of course not,' replied Jim.

'Hold on, Charles, I'd better come with you,' I said. 'You can't just dash into the bedroom.'

He went up the stairs two at a time. Mrs Pritchard met us on the landing. 'I were just coming to fetch you, Reverend. You've got a little boy.' Charles began to weep.

'For heaven's sake, Charles, you can't go in to see Bronwen like that. It's time for joy that a man has been born into the world and he's your son.'

'Don't come in just yet, Charles,' shouted Eleanor. 'Everything's wonderful and you have a lovely baby boy.'

It was another quarter of an hour before the ambulance arrived. By then Bronwen was sitting up, in a nightdress borrowed from Ruby Pritchard and holding her son in her arms, watched by a husband who was still in a daze. The ambulance men put a blanket round her shoulders and led her out into the night, accompanied by Charles.

'That was one of the easiest births I have ever witnessed,' said Eleanor as we made our way home in the car. 'And what a place for a son of a parson to come into this life!'

'What do you mean, love? He was born in an inn.'

'True enough, but it was certainly more comfortable than a stable. When our first is born, I shall make sure that he or she is born in a hospital ward.'

'And when will that be, pray?' I asked.

'After tonight, I feel quite broody. In a year's time, shall we say, if not sooner.'

'Sooner, I should say,' I replied. She stopped the car and kissed me.

# The
# Crowning
# Glory

To my grandchildren, Elena, Hannah, Gwyn and Nicholas, in the hope that the post Elizabethan era will produce a better world.

'I don't see any need for this meeting at all.' Bertie Owen, shop steward and deposed churchwarden, was on his feet amidst groans and sighs from his listeners. 'Tabernacle, Bethel, Moriah are doing nothing at all and don't forget that "Tab" give their Sunday School an outing to Porthcawl, not out to the cowfield like we do. They say that their kids will be going to the street parties. Balaclava, Sebastopol, Inkerman have got their celebrations arranged, not to mention Alma and Delhi.'

'Before you run through any more battles, Mr Owen, would you mind sitting down for a moment,'I said, to a chorus of 'Hear! Hear!s' 'I am fully aware of the many street parties which are being organised. There is no earthly reason why our Sunday-school children should not be able to attend them and also take part in whatever we as a Parochial Church Council can provide for them. In any case I hope we shall be able to put on entertainment for the grown-ups as well.'

It was the first meeting of the newly elected Council after the Easter Vestry on Low Sunday 1953. The whole country was agog with excitement at the prospect of the forthcoming coronation of the second Elizabeth on 2 June. Already there was talk of a new Elizabethan age. For too long the nation had been shackled by the austerity of the post-war regime. The chains had been loosened by the Festival of Britain in 1951 but rationing still lingered on and the word 'control' was the most detestable in the current vocabulary.

I had now been Vicar of Pontywen for nearly five years, with a three-year-old son, David, and a six-month-old baby daughter, Elspeth. My wife, Eleanor, the local doctor, was fortunate to have David Andrews as her partner in the practice. He had come to the town after service in the RAMC and had been an immediate success with his ability to diagnose and with the sympathetic manner which accompanied the diagnosis. His wife, Heather, had given birth to their first child, a baby girl on Easter Day. Both mother and child were doing well.

'What I had in mind', I went on, 'is a full programme of events both for the children and the adults. A "go as you please" variety competition in the church hall for young and old. A dance, a whist drive. That sort of thing. Mrs Heather Andrews hopes to be back in harness after the birth of baby Christine by 2 June and says that she would like to give pony rides for the children. I am sure that you all have many more ideas about how we can enjoy ourselves to celebrate this historic day.'

As soon as I sat down, David Vaughan-Jenkins, people's churchwarden at the parish church and local bank manager, took the floor. 'May I say, Vicar, that I am sure your proposals will have our fullest support (Hear! hear!). How kind of Mrs Andrews to offer the use of her pony for rides for the children. I think, perhaps, Vicar, you should have said that she hopes to be back "with harness", rather than "in harness".' He paused to allow for laughter or at least some audible appreciation of his heavy-handed humour. None came. He coughed and proceeded with his peroration. 'Might I suggest that we elect some kind of Coronation Celebrations Committee who will co-ordinate activities after we have had contributions from the meeting suggesting other things that might be done. Mr Bertie Owen has informed us that other places of worship are doing nothing to mark the occasion. I suggest that they join us in our activities on such a committee. One other thing, I shall contact headquarters to see whether the bank may make a donation towards the cost of the festivity. If ever there is a worthy cause, I am sure this is it.' This time his remarks were greeted with hearty applause.

Next on his feet was Idris Shoemaker, alias 'Idris the Milk', people's warden at St Padarn's, the daughter church. 'I would like to second Mr Vaughan-Jenkins's proposition about a committee to organise the events and to support his idea about the Chapels combining with us. Mind, I don't think Moriah Baptist will be too keen on a whist drive or a dance.'

'Before we go h'any further,' intervened Ezekiel Evans, the parochial lay reader. 'Might h'I suggest that we h'invite h'all the other places of worship in Pontywen to join us in an h'act of prayer h'and dedication. Old Canon Williams in h'our cathedral last Sunday said we could be h'embarking on a new h'age of religious revival and denominational 'armony. First things first. Never mind about h'enjoying ourselves and all that.'

'May I echo Mr Evans's words,' I said. The lay reader's face was a picture of self-satisfaction. 'By that I mean – "before we go any further". The purpose of this meeting is to arrange a programme of festivities to celebrate the coronation of our new monarch. It is not to promote a religious revival in Pontywen.' The smile vanished from

Ezekiel's face. 'Quite frankly I see no point whatsoever in asking all the other places of worship, as Mr Evans put it, to join us for a service or for a week of fun and frolic. I doubt if they would agree to a united service on our terms and I am positive that they would not wish to be involved in fun and frolic.

'In any case, by the time we had organised an interdenominational committee and debated what form of service we should have and where it should be held and who would take part etcetera, the coronation would have taken place weeks earlier. As for the fun and frolic aspect, that is a non starter. However, if you wish to go ahead and vote on the proposition before you, please do so.'

As soon as I sat down, David Vaughan-Jenkins was on his feet. As a bank manager, he was a pragmatist. He withdrew his proposition, with the enthusiastic support of his seconder, who realised that the proposer had unwittingly led the meeting up a blind alley. From that moment, the meeting proceeded to manufacture ideas for entertainment at such a speed that Miss Alice Worthington, secretary to the Council and secretary to the Colliery Manager, found her shorthand ability put to the test.

The people's warden at the parish church was on his feet once again. 'I revert to my original proposition, omitting references to other places of worship. In other words, I propose that we the church people of Pontywen elect a committee to organise coronation festivities to mark the occasion. I further suggest that we include the parish of Llanhyfryd and their representatives on that committee.' This was seconded by Idris, who had second thoughts about Moriah and Bethel joining us to arrange a week of pleasurable activity. The motion was carried, with only one vote against, that of a sulking Ezekiel Evans. Even Bertie Owen voted in favour, not wishing to be left out of the picture and hoping that there might be a place for him on the organising committee. However, the eight names of the elected did not include his, bringing the number of those sulking up to two.

An interested spectator of the meeting was Emlyn Howells, my new curate, who had joined me some days previously from a curacy in Aberllynfi, a small market town in the neighbouring diocese. An ex 'Bevin Boy', his health had been seriously affected by his work underground. Part of one lung had been removed, leaving him with breathing difficulties on occasions. He was stoutly built, with a ruddy complexion belying his physical condition. An open-air enthusiast after his mining experience, he was a keen camper. At the interview prior to his appointment he had asked me whether he might form a scout troop in the parish, a suggestion I welcomed gladly since my two previous curates would have found difficulty lighting a camp fire with matches let alone doing so by rubbing two sticks together. It would appear that for the first time since I had become an incumbent I would have an assistant who would assist instead of hindering.

As we left the hall together after the meeting I asked him what he thought of the evening's business. 'I must say that I was most impressed by the way in which everybody produced ideas for the programme of events. If it had been my former parochial church council, the most they would have suggested would have been a tea party, and even that would have been badly organised. I suppose that is the difference between the countryside and the industrial valleys in the pace of life?'

'Very true, Emlyn,' I replied. 'You will see this when you attend a meeting at Llanhyfryd. Yet, even there, you will find plenty of suggestions coming from the members of the council. They have no wish to be outdone by the Pontywen crowd.'

'That is what competition can do for you,' said Emlyn. 'Perhaps they might have been more forthcoming in Aberllynfi if they were linked with another parish – though I doubt that very much.' He stopped abruptly as he was seized with a bout of coughing. 'Excuse me, a nasty tickle. I get that occasionally.

'One more thing, Vicar,' he went on; 'if you don't mind my saying so, it was good to see a chairman who was in command of the meeting and who knew where he was going. My last Vicar, dear man though he may have been, was obsessed with the idea that "we should be all of one mind", as he used to put it at every Church Council meeting. The result was that what should take an hour at the most became two hours or even three. So many liked the sound of their own voices. It's a wonder I never fell asleep.'

'I promise you, Emlyn,' I replied. 'Our PCC meetings will be too short for that to happen. I may be a bit of a closet dictator, in that I know what I want and am prepared to put down the self-important from their seat, but it saves time and it gets things done.'

When I was back at the Vicarage, Eleanor had just finished feeding Elspeth and was engaged in bringing up the baby's wind. She had insisted on breastfeeding the children despite the inconvenience it caused her as a busy GP. 'A mother's milk is much better for the health of a baby than the powdered product from a factory.'

She was bursting with excitement. 'What do you think? Your brother has phoned to say that he is sending us a television set so that we can watch the coronation.'

My brother, Harry, was now a radio celebrity in the 'Goon Show' as well as a stage success with his fine belcanto singing allied to his 'Goon' humour. Before he was called up as a Territorial Army Gunner just before his eighteenth birthday, he had taken part in amateur theatricals. My father, who was similarly involved as a reciter of comic monologues, had dismissed any idea of a stage career for my brother because he was of too nervous a disposition. After six years on active service, most of which was spent entertaining the troops (in between fighting the Germans), he had come home to Swansea, a seasoned performer. In no time at all he was engaged by Vivian Van Damm to do his 'shaving act' at the Windmill Theatre for the princely sum of twenty-five pounds a week. Six years later he was a comparatively wealthy man who could afford to send his brother a television set, a priceless possession in 1953 for someone living in the Valleys.

Later that evening, when the baby had been put in her cot for the night, we discussed the problem of compiling a complement of viewers for the great day. The Vicarage lounge was a big room but certainly not big enough to accommodate all those who would want to see the happenings. It would require the wisdom of Solomon to choose a suitable guest list and even he would have to offend a large number of the congregation.

'The only way to avoid contention', suggested Eleanor, 'is to keep it quiet that we have a television set.'

'That, my love, is impossible,' I replied. 'First of all we shall have to get Jones the Wireless to put it in for us, and you know what an old woman he is. Secondly, can you imagine Mrs Watkins keeping quiet about it. Let alone Marlene.'

Mrs Watkins was our 'daily' who had been indispensable to us since the birth of our children. Marlene Evans was one of the chorus of the church Gilbert and Sullivan society. She had become nursemaid to the children on leaving Pontywen Grammar school with a low-level academic record but with a much higher level of child care.

'In that case,' said my wife, 'our only hope is that one or two other members of the congregation will have installed television sets by the great day, and we can share the list of viewers. Perhaps David Vaughan-Jenkins will get one. Even if he does not want one, I am sure his wife will be asking to have such a mark of prestige. They have enough money, that's positive. What about the Nicholls? I bet they have a set already, the biggest you can buy. As Manager of the steelworks he has the only Rolls Royce in Pontywen. So I am sure that he will have the equivalent in television sets.'

'My dear love, since they come to St Mary's at Christmas and Easter only, I do not think you can class them as members of the congregation. They are twicers not members. Anyway I expect their drawing room will be occupied by golf-club friends and folk of that ilk.'

'I like the "ilk" bit, Fred. Still, I think it is worth a try. At least you will be able to boast that you are in the same league television wise, and that you are prepared to share your good fortune with the peasants. You can promise to provide them with an approved selection of our best behaved worshippers who would not damage their carpets or their furniture.'

'Come off it, Eleanor. Ernest Nicholls is not at all like that. I admit that his wife comes into that category, as does her daughter, married as she is to Brigadier James Morris, Welsh Guards. Anyway I suppose any chance that Ernest would agree to sharing a view of the coronation with some of the St Mary's crowd would be overruled by the petticoat government of the rest of the household.'

'I suppose you are right, but you never know. If you get in now, perhaps you could persuade them that they would be contributing to the new age of Elizabeth the Second, a gesture to the proletariat that under our new Queen we shall be one nation with no divisions of race or class.'

'There's something wrong with your logic, Eleanor. You cannot mention the word proletariat and in the same breath declare that in this new Elizabethan age there will be no distinction of class. In any case I shouldn't think they would want an end to such a division. They are very happy with the difference between them and the working class. However, I shall venture forth tomorrow to Chez Nicholls to see what their reaction will be.'

The next morning I had a telephone call from the Reverend Daniel Thomas, the Rural Dean. 'I'm glad I've found you in, Vicar. It's like this. I'm in a bit of a hole. The Mothers' Union deanery service is going to be held in our church this afternoon. The Archdeacon was down to preach at the service, as you probably know. Well, he has just rung up to say that he has got laryngitis. I could hardly hear him over the phone. So I am sure that the ladies would never be able to hear him in the pulpit. I was wondering whether you would like to take his place. Use one of your old sermons. Don't put yourself out.'

Since I never wrote any sermons, I would have to 'put myself out'. At that moment I wished I had been like the vicar in my home parish. He had a twelve months' supply of written homilies which he would up-end on the last Sunday of the year and begin to preach all over again in the New Year. For example we always knew that on the Seventh Sunday after Trinity he would re-count how he had saved a child from drowning in the river near his home. Then on the thirteenth Sunday after Trinity, when the story of the Good Samaritan was the gospel for the day, we would be given details of the principal features of Jericho, together with a potted history and a geographical survey of the road to Jerusalem.

'It's very flattering of you to ask me to deputise for the Archdeacon, Mr Rural Dean. I shall do my best to be worthy of the honour.' My tongue was firmly in my cheek as I said it.

'That's good of you. There will be a tea afterwards in the church hall. Will Dr Sebohm be coming with you?' After I had been six years in the deanery, he could never get my name right.

'I am afraid she will be out on her rounds in the afternoon, much as she would like to be there.'

'A busy lady, I'm sure. Perhaps one of these days the two of you will come to tea with us and bring your children with you. My wife hasn't seen them yet and I am sure she would love to have them here. Anyway, we'll see you there at the service this afternoon. It is at three o'clock. Thank you once again.'

When I put the phone down I looked at the clock. It was a quarter past eleven. I had a couple of hours at most to compose the sermon. Before I had time to take my Bible commentary from the bookshelf the doorbell rang. There was a young couple on my doorstep. A handsome lad, he looked as if he was in his late teens and was shabbily dressed in trousers and a jacket which had seen better days. His open-necked shirt had not been near a wash tub for some time. His petite companion was even younger and was clad in a tent of a dress which bulged ominously around her waist line. It was she who spoke first. 'We've come to put our banns in, Vicar.' Her voice was firm and devoid of the Valleys intonation. She sounded as if she came from a middle-class background.

'You had better come in,' I said. 'I don't normally deal with banns of marriage at this time of the day but since you are here we might as well go ahead with the arrangements.'

I ushered them into the study where they seated themselves in the two armchairs in front of my desk. 'Mike is working the afternoon shift, you see, Vicar, and so we couldn't come this evening. As it is urgent, anyway, I hope you don't mind the intrusion.'

By now, I was intrigued by this relationship. I wondered what accent would come from the silent partner's lips. 'The first thing I have to ask you is your age. I may be wrong but I should judge by your youthful appearance that you are both under the age of twenty-one. In that case neither of you can be married without your parents' consent.' They bowed their heads. 'How old are you, Mike?'

He addressed the floor and spoke in a thick Valleys accent. 'Nineteen.'

I turned to the girl. 'Now then, my dear, what is your name?'

She raised her head and looked me full in the face. 'Margaret,' she replied.

'And how old are you?'

She dropped her head again and then raised it defiantly. 'Seventeen,' she said, her big blue eyes firmly fixed on mine.

'So then,' I went on. 'The first thing I have to ask is whether you have your parents' consent. Without their written consent I cannot call the banns of marriage. The second thing I have to say concerns you, Margaret. It is quite obvious that you are in an advanced stage of pregnancy. It will take a minimum of three weeks to have your banns called. You realise that? On the other hand, you could have a licence which could mean that it would be days rather than weeks. I am a surrogate and that means I could issue you with a licence.'

''Ow much would that cost?' enquired Mike.

'Three guineas,' I replied. 'However, most important of all at the moment is whether you have your parents' consent. Without that you can't be married.'

This time Mike spoke up. 'My mother and father are willing for us to get married. They've said we can 'ave a room with them until we find somewhere else. It's 'ers that are against it.'

Margaret's head had been bowed for some considerable time. 'Perhaps, my dear,' I said to her, 'you should let me know if your parents are prepared to give their consent to the marriage. If they are not, then there is no possibility whatever of a wedding. That is the law of the land. So do you have their consent or do you not?'

'If my parents are agreed that my child should be a bastard, it's up to them. I hope they will have it on their consciences for the rest of their lives.'

'In other words, Margaret, you have not had their permission.' She shook her head.

'What's more, my father wants to have me go to somewhere where I could have my baby adopted at the moral welfare place for unmarried mothers. I've told him I'm not going to do that.'

'There is one thing that puzzles me more than anything else, my dear, and that is why you want to get married in church rather than the registry office. I have never seen you in church.'

'You haven't seen me in church here, Vicar, because we have always gone to Penglais Parish Church. We moved to Pontywen two years ago, and my parents decided they would keep up the connection. I have been confirmed and have been to Communion regularly except over the past few months. If I am going to be married, then it will have to be in church.'

'Well now, I am afraid I cannot spend any more time with you at the moment. I have some urgent business on hand. Can I have your names and addresses, please? Then I shall contact your parents to see what can be done. First of all you, Mike.'

'Michael John Roberts, 13 Balaclava Street.'

'And you, Margaret?' There was a pause. She took a deep breath.

'Margaret Elaine Price, Raglan House, Ashburnham Close.'

'I shall see you both here on Friday evening at seven o'clock. In the meanwhile I shall be in touch with your parents.'

I watched them as they walked up the Vicarage drive. For young lovers they were strangely apart, no holding hands. Instead he was a stride ahead of her throughout the length of the drive, as wide apart as their addresses.

It took me half an hour to compose my thoughts sufficiently to begin work on my sermon to the Mothers' Union of the deanery, the large majority of whom would be grandmothers. I read through the accounts of the birth of Jesus in St Matthew and St Luke's gospels. St Matthew refers constantly to 'the young child and his mother'. Thinking of Margaret who was only seventeen, it seemed to me that shortly there would be two children in the Price family – a mother and her infant. Then reading through the Bible commentary I was reminded that probably Mary would have been only fourteen, a common age of espousal, three years younger than Margaret.

By the time Marlene came back to the Vicarage with our two children, whom she had taken to the Recreation ground for a fresh-air outing, it was half past twelve. She was followed closely by Eleanor, who had returned from her morning surgery and visits. She had made it a rule that her duties were confined to the morning, with the afternoon free for the children. Occasionally she would do an early-evening surgery, leaving David Andrews to cope single handed for most of the time.

'A nice afternoon for a drive into the country,' she said, as she came through the door.

'In which case you will have to count me out, I'm afraid,' I replied. 'Dear Mr Rural Dean has invited me to preach at the deanery Mothers' Union service because the Archdeacon has lost his voice.'

'His wife and his congregation will be pleased about that, even if you are not, by the look of you. Never mind, love. Think of that bevy of beauty facing you when you get up into the pulpit.'

'Eleanor, you are a wicked woman sometimes, thank God.'

As Marlene was leaving, I asked her if she had known Margaret Price in Pontywen Grammar School.

'I didn't know her very well because she came into our form just a term before I left. She had only just come to live in Pontywen from Penyglais. In any case, she kept herself to herself, didn't want to know us. She used to go to a private school once, so she said. I think her parents had plenty of money and used to spoil her. Her father used to come and pick her up sometimes in a posh car.'

'What was all that about?' Eleanor inquired after our nurserymaid had gone.

Over lunch I told her about the 'marriage interview' and their strange behaviour as they walked up the drive. 'She is certainly not one of my patients,' my wife said. 'I must ask David if she is one of his lot. She might be, especially since her parents live in the same road.'

'Anyway,' I replied, 'I am going to see them tomorrow, so if David can supply some information I shall be grateful.'

Pontywen Church was full for the Mothers' Union service when I arrived there. The banner carriers were outside the porch debating the order in which they were to march down the aisle. Inside the small vestry there was a crush of elderly clergymen already robed. In the middle of this clerical scrum was the Rural Dean looking 'like a fly trapped in a jam jar', to use one of Idris the Milk's favourite expressions.

'Thank goodness, you have come,' he exclaimed. 'I was beginning to think something had happened to you. Now then, gentlemen, if you don't mind, will you let me pass so that I can give the signal to the organist that we are ready? Come out in any order once I have said the vestry prayer, except of course that the preacher and I will be last.' He disappeared for a few seconds and then came back to the doorway. 'Let us pray,' he commanded. The vestry prayer was said at such a rate that it was unintelligible until the last few words, 'through Jesus Christ our Lord'. The organ began to play and the scramble to emerge into the chancel ensued, with the Rural Dean squashed against the vestry wall. I had taken the precaution of hiding behind the robes cupboard to escape injury.

'Come up into the sanctuary with me, Vicar,' said the dignitary. 'I will take the banners from the Mothers and hand them to you to prop up against the wall.' My heart sank. I had contended with these contraptions a year previously at a Mothers' Union festival in Pontywen. They had a habit of sliding on the polished floor as soon as you had turned your back.

During the singing of the hymn the procession moved up the aisle to the altar rails, led by a buxom lady, proudly carrying the banner belonging to the home territory. 'Thank you, Mrs Evans,' said the Rural Dean. 'Would you mind putting this one, Vicar, on that stand in the corner?' That was the easy part of the ceremony. There were six more banners to go. I tried to rest the next one against a memorial tablet to a former Vicar of Pentwyn, hoping to use the same manoeuvre on the other side with the following one. Evidently the late Emmanuel Hopkins felt his dignity impaired by being treated this way. After three attempts to prevent it sliding to the ground, I walked across the sanctuary and stuck it in the opposite corner to the banner of honour.

By now there was only one verse of the hymn to go and still five more banners to be laid against the walls. The Rural Dean was puffing his annoyance like a grampus whale and the strain of holding up the heavy Mothers' Union emblems was telling on their elderly bearers. 'Try to hurry up,' commanded the Reverend Daniel Thomas in the loudest of stage whispers. 'Put them anywhere but hurry up.'

As the singing of the last verse died away there were only two more left to be installed in the sanctuary. There was a space left for two on the north side. I took the first one and rested the pole against the altar rails: miraculously it stayed upright. As the sweat streamed down my forehead and gummed my shirt to my body under my robes, I advanced upon the last remaining empty space. Anxiously watched by a breathless audience of clergy, I laid the banner dedicated to St Mary's Abergwynlais MU against the wall. As I turned to rejoin the Rural Dean, I heard an ominous noise of a sliding pole which attracted the company of its neighbour, the both of them crashing to the floor. 'For heaven's sake, Seabourne, leave them where they are. Let's get on with the service.' I was only too relieved to accept this instruction from the exasperated old man.

It was a subdued preacher who ascended the pulpit for

his sermon. He was even more subdued when he discovered there was no Bible on the pulpit lectern. It would have been no inconvenience to the majority of preachers who have written their sermons with their text adorning the beginning. To someone who prided himself on his ability to preach extempore, it was disastrous.

I had intended to preach on verse 18 of the first chapter of the Gospel according to St Matthew, 'Now the birth of Jesus Christ was on this wise. When as his mother Mary was espoused to Joseph before they came together, she was found with child of the Holy Ghost.'

When the hymn before the sermon ended, I found myself looking at the congregation with a mind which had become blank. I managed to stammer the usual invocation, 'In the name of the Father and of the Son and of the Holy Ghost, Amen.' The congregation subsided into their seats and waited for the peroration. I stared at them in silence, vaguely trying to remember the text. They stared back. The sweat which had besprinkled my brow and drenched my shirt returned in even more copious quantities.

On my way to Pentwyn in my old Morris Minor I had imagined myself rising to great heights of pulpit oratory, destroying the Victorian image of the Blessed Virgin Mary as a mature matron and calling for sympathy for schoolgirl mothers. On my way back I mused on my mumbled *mélange* of pious platitudes which masqueraded as a sermon.

'Well, Bishop,' enquired my wife on my return home, 'how did it go?'

'I don't think I shall be asked to preach at another Mothers' Union deanery service.'

'What a relief for you,' she replied.

## 2

I made my way up the hill to Ashburnham Close the following evening. I was undecided which of the two houses I had to visit should be the first. Neither prospect was pleasing. I was positive that my attempts to persuade the Nicholls household to share their television viewing with a contingent of Pontywen churchgoers would meet with a frosty response. On the other hand I feared an equally frosty attitude from the parents of Margaret Price, who would regard my visit as an embarrassing intrusion into their family affairs. The choice was decided for me as I entered Ashburnham Close. Ernest Nicholls was taking his Alsatian for its evening exercise. 'Hello, Vicar,' he said. 'What brings you to this neck of the woods?' He was a short bespectacled gentleman whose stature made it difficult to determine whether it was he or the dog who was in charge, especially since the hound was dragging its owner along the pavement.

'As a matter of fact, Mr Nicholls,' I replied, 'I have come to see you and Mrs Nicholls, amongst others.'

'In that case, we had better delay Bruno's trial of strength for a short while and return to the "Hawthorns".' I was interested to see who would be the winner in the tug of war that would follow. It was no contest. One sharp word of command from the little man and Bruno came to heel instantly. He was truly a man of authority.

A brand new Rolls Royce with a personalised number plate, ENI, stood in the drive of the mock Tudor house, a product of the late thirties. The immaculately manicured lawn was bordered by rose trees already in full bud, evidently out-of-bounds territory for Bruno. 'Would you mind waiting a moment while I incarcerate the hound? My wife and daughter are out,' he said.

Man and beast disappeared round the side of the house while I surveyed the Price residence which stood opposite, built in the same black-and-white timbered style. Ashburnham Close had six such temples of opulence completed by a speculative builder in the nick of time before Hitler put paid to any further enterprise on his part. I wondered why someone like Margaret could have given herself to a young man so devoid of charisma as Mike. I remembered a saying of Mrs Richards, my landlady when I first came to Pontywen: 'Life is full of liquorice all sorts, isn't it?'

My musings were terminated abruptly by an invitation from Mr Nicholls to enter his domain. He produced an impressive bunch of keys and unerringly selected the one for his front door in a trice. I was ushered into the drawing room, and waved into a spacious armchair. 'May I offer you a drink, Vicar?' he asked.

'You may indeed,' I replied with alacrity.

'Scotch or a G and T?'

'Scotch, please, with just a touch of water.'

'In that case, I suggest you do the touching yourself. I prefer mine intact, or as W.C. Fields would say, untouched by human hand.' This he said with a pathetic attempt at mimicry. He went to the well stocked drinks cabinet and brought out a decanter three quarters full of whisky. The decanter and the glasses were of expensive cut glass, unlike the Vicarage set which were purchased from Roberts the Ironmonger, who was getting rid of pre-war stock.

Once he had settled into the armchair opposite me, he enquired the reason for my visit. I thought it better to launch into the deep immediately since the ladies of the house were not present. In one corner of the room, facing me, was a large television set enclosed in a walnut wood cabinet. I pointed at it and said, 'It's to do with that.'

He looked at me quizzically. 'What about that, Vicar? I can assure you that I have a licence for it. It's for my wife's pleasure more than mine. I am more interested in tinkering around with cars than with sitting passively to fill up my spare time.'

'I expect you will be sitting passively on 2 June, Mr Nicholls,' I replied, 'in common with all those who have a television set. However, I have come to you on behalf of those in the congregation at the parish church who are not fortunate enough to have the chance to see the coronation.'

He stared at me. 'What are you trying to say, dear man? That I should give it away to the poor and needy of the parish.'

'Of course not. I shall be having a television set in a week or so, courtesy of my brother, and I expect one or two others in the congregation will have one in time for the great day. My concern is that as many as possible will be able to see the service in Westminster Abbey. The only way that could happen would be if those who have sets would share their good fortune with others. I am going to invite as many people as I can into the Vicarage to view the proceedings. I am hoping that Mr Vaughan-Jenkins will do likewise in his place. I hope you do not think it an impertinence but I was wondering if you were prepared to do something similar.' There was a silence, as he removed his spectacles and wiped them in his handkerchief after breathing on them. I waited for him to put them back and look at me. There was an encouraging twinkle in his eyes when they focused on me.

'Well, Vicar, I must say that this is an unusual request but I do not think it an impertinence. However, my wife might think so. As far as I am concerned, I would be willing to invite a few people from your members to come and join us. For all I know Mrs Nicholls may be thinking to invite some of her friends along who have no set. All I can do is to have a word with her about this. She and my daughter have gone to Cardiff for the day and I shall be picking them up from the station later this evening. I shall give you a ring sometime during the next few days and let you know the verdict.'

We spent the next half hour talking about the state of Welsh rugby and the shortcomings of the Town Council. After the second tumbler of whisky, I left the 'Hawthorns' in a semi-alcoholic haze and prepared to make my way across the road to meet the parents of the pregnant young lady who had appeared on my doorstep two days previously.

The Price residence was showing signs of wear and tear on its exterior. The black paint had began to part company with the timber and the white plastered walls were several shades darker than their original colour, thanks to the polluted air of Pontywen. Weeds were fighting a winning battle with the gravel on the drive. The lawn was still awaiting its first cut and the flower border its replanting. I could imagine Mrs Nicholls making disparaging remarks about the eyesore opposite.

I searched in my pocket for a packet of Polo mints which I had bought providentially and wondered whether they would be sufficient to conceal the whisky aroma. As I stood at the gate, I recalled an incident at a wedding when the best man put a polo mint on my copy of the marriage service instead of the ring for which I had asked. The momentary giggle I enjoyed at the thought disappeared as I contemplated the interview which was about to take place. I walked up the drive slowly and stopped outside the porch, crunching a mouthful of mints before I felt ready to press the button of the doorbell. I swallowed the breath fresheners and announced my presence with a loud ring which echoed around the hall. A long silence ensued. I was about to write a message on the back of one of my visiting cards when I heard footsteps approaching on the gravel behind me. I turned to see a tall, well-built, grey-haired man and his wife, a short thin lady who was beside him. She was an older version of Margaret with the same brilliant blue eyes.

'Good evening, Vicar,' said Mr Price. 'Margaret has told us you would be calling some time this week.' His face was grim. He opened the door and invited me in. Mrs Price had not said a word but gave the impression that she was timid, fearful, very much subservient to her husband. They were both wearing light raincoats and wellington boots. 'If you will excuse us, we had better discard our walking apparel. Go into the drawing room, please, and make yourself comfortable. Would you care for a cup of tea. I am afraid we haven't anything stronger to offer you.'

'A cup of tea will be most acceptable, thank you,' I replied, still feeling the effect of something stronger. 'Milk and sugar?' enquired Mrs Price. Her voice and her tone were deferential. I was beginning to feel sorry for her.

'No milk and two spoonfuls of sugar, if you can spare it, that is.'

'That's all right, Vicar. We have plenty of sugar.' She disappeared into the kitchen in a flash, as if she was glad to escape. I wondered if she would still be in the kitchen when the time came for a discussion about her daughter's predicament.

As I waited for the tea to arrive I surveyed the contents of the 'drawing room'. A grand piano took up the space in the window. It was a Bechstein, but apparently neglected, by the amount of dust on its surface and the absence of any music copy. The piano stool stood some distance away, alongside the armchair on which I was seated, and served as a stand for a photograph of Mr and Mrs Price and their daughter ensconced in deckchairs at the seaside. The golden letters of the maker's name looked reproachfully from under the upturned lid of the piano.

The rest of the furniture and the pictures on the walls were not in the same exalted category. The three-piece suite was covered in moquette which had seen better days whilst the framed paintings were reproductions which could be seen in any store. There was an occasional table against the wall by the fireplace where the mantelpiece was the repository for two Spanish dancers captured in china and two framed wedding photographs. 'Change and decay in all around, I see,' I said to myself.

Suddenly Mr Price appeared in the doorway, relaxed in a knitted cardigan over an open-necked shirt and grey flannels, his feet reposed in tartan-coloured slippers. He carried a pipe and a tin of tobacco, evidently determined to be at ease. 'I hope you don't mind me smoking,' he said. 'It helps me to unwind at the end of the day. I suppose it is a hangover from babyhood. Then it was a dummy, now it's a pipe. Do you smoke, Vicar?'

'No, Mr Price. I once tried it in college when a friend suggested that cigarette smoke might ease the toothache from which I was suffering. Draw in some smoke and keep it inside your closed mouth, he instructed. My mouth was not closed for long, I began to cough violently. The toothache was worse than ever. It was an experiment which put me off tobacco for good.'

He attempted a smile which died almost as soon as it was born. By the lines on his face it would appear that Mr Price was not of a humorous disposition.

Any further discussion was delayed by the appearance of Mrs Price with tea for two on a tray decorated with a lace-edged cloth. As I thought, the Margaret problem was to be the subject of a *tête-à-tête* between her father and myself. After serving the tea, the lady of the house went back to the kitchen, leaving the two of us to sort things out.

'Well now,' began the master of the house, 'I gather from my daughter that she has come to you to put in banns of marriage. As I am sure you are aware, Vicar, she is under the age of consent. No way am I going to allow her to marry this young layabout who has not the means to support her. She is an intelligent, gifted child. You see that piano. Up until six months or so ago, she would be playing it like a concert artiste. Her piano teacher said that she had the ability to go far. That is why we sacrificed a lot of our money to buy that grand piano. Look at it now. It's a white elephant. Why in God's name should she throw all that away for somebody whose idea of music is a gramophone record of Frank Sinatra and who is quite content to live with her in one room in his parents' miner's cottage.'

All the time he was speaking, the tone and volume of his voice was rising and finished in a crescendo with the words 'miner's cottage'. My head was still spinning as a consequence of Mr Nicholls' hospitality. I strove to find words which could stem the tide of his anger and direct the conversation into a more rational channel. It was a vain exercise. My mind was blank. I sat looking at this man's despair at what he felt the fates had dealt to him and wondered how I could bring God into the impasse. Now I felt as sorry for him as I had felt for his wife earlier on. I had to break the silence.

'Mr Price, I realise how you must feel. May I ask, is Margaret your only child?'

He raised his head. 'We had a son who was run over by a baker's van which was speeding along when he was crossing the road. He was seven years of age. Robin was our first child, Margaret was born three years later. So, yes, she is our only child. All our love and affection was lavished on her. Whatever she wanted we gave her. Until we came to Pontywen she went to a private school in Cardiff, by which time our money was running out. I had lost my job as manager of an insurance company and am now working for a property developer in Newport at a much reduced salary. Life is hard enough without this disaster looming in front of us. I just cannot understand what she is doing.'

'I suppose there is very little logic in the thinking of an adolescent,' I replied. 'There is always that element of rebellion against what their elders expect of them. Please don't misunderstand me, but it may be that you set your sights on a target for her which she found too demanding, too intimidating. As a result she sought consolation in a love affair with a handsome young man whose intellectual gifts were few but whose physical attractions compensated for his lack of academic ability.'

He looked me in the eyes. 'You may be right, Vicar, but that is no answer to the question facing us right now. She was only a few months over the age of consent when the baby was conceived – a mere child. Under no circumstances whatsoever shall I give permission for the marriage. Her mother and I have told her that the best thing she can do is to go to the Moral Welfare home in Cardiff to have her baby. Then she can have it adopted and take up her life without the burden of caring for a child at her age. She had seven O levels last year and is in the lower sixth form at Pontywen Grammar School. Not only that, she has passed all her piano exams with top-level marks and was studying for grade seven when she threw it all up. It's a tragedy, Vicar, that is what it is. There she is, still out at this time of night. I expect she won't be in until ten at the earliest, when she'll go straight to bed.'

The head of the house was on the verge of tears as his voice began to break. He coughed and blew his nose.

'Mr Price,' I said, 'would you like me to have a word with Miss Lloyd Jenkins, the Moral Welfare organiser, before I see the young couple on Friday evening? She is a very kind, middle-aged lady with great experience in this field. When is the baby due?'

'The doctor says she is six months pregnant. As you can see by her size it looks like nine months. Her mother was the same when she was bearing our children. Yes, I would be very grateful if you could use your influence to get Margaret into the maternity ward at that place.'

'I shall do what I can, Mr Price. What's more important at the moment I shall try and persuade Margaret to see sense when she comes to the Vicarage. From what I can gather from her when she came to see me, that is not going to be easy. As you know full well, she is a young lady with a very strong will indeed. Anyway, I shall do what I can.'

He escorted me to the door without bothering to let his wife know that I was leaving. 'Please thank Mrs Price for the tea and biscuits.' He grunted an unintelligible reply as he watched me go down the drive.

It was half past nine when I arrived home. My wife

was stretched out on the settee in the front room, apparently fast asleep. I kissed her gently on the cheek only to get an instant response. 'And where do you think you have been, Prince Charming? While you have been away, I have had to deal with two couples intent on signing their death warrant and most of all with a telephone call from your erstwhile colleague and pain in the neck supreme.'

'You don't mean Charles Wentworth-Baxter, by any chance?' I enquired.

'How did you guess,' she replied, with heavy irony. 'He will be here at ten o'clock tomorrow. He sounded as if he were in his usual distraught state.'

Charles had been a fellow curate with me in Pontywen and after that was my underling when I was appointed Vicar. He must have been the most incompetent cleric ever and was fortunate to be appointed to a living, admittedly the most remote and sparsely populated parish in the diocese, the ecclesiastical equivalent of Siberian exile.

Over breakfast next morning we speculated about the reason for his visit. He and his wife, Bronwen, a former nurse at Pontywen Hospital, were now the proud parents of four children whom they had begotten in the space of five years. As Eleanor said, 'They are living far too close to the rabbit warrens out there. Give them long enough and they will be responsible for half the population of the parish. I suppose there's nothing else to do in the wilderness.'

'Perhaps that is why he wants to see me,' I replied.

'What do you mean, Frederick? To find out what's causing this population explosion?'

'Of course not. After all, his wife was a nurse and knows the facts of life. As far as I can see they must want a large family. In that case he will need a bigger parish with a bigger income – though why he should come to me about that I don't know. He should go to the Bishop.'

'Knowing Charles,' said Eleanor, 'he would be coming to you to find out how to approach his holy highness. If you remember, when he was here he could never do anything without your guidance even to the extent about when he would clean his teeth.'

'Pray, don't exaggerate, woman. Whatever the purpose of his call, we shall soon know.'

Unusually for him, he arrived at ten o'clock precisely. 'It must be important,' observed my wife as his car came down the drive. He remained inside the car for at least a couple of minutes in deep contemplation. 'Yes, very important,' she added. He opened the door slowly and looked inside the interior as he got out, apparently loath to leave his pre-war Austin Big Seven. He closed the door gently and then, staring at the Vicarage doorsteps, languidly ascended them as if in some kind of hypnotic trance. 'Put him out of his misery, love, and open the door before he rings the bell,' said Eleanor. 'Otherwise he might be standing outside on the step for another five minutes.'

When I opened the door, he jumped back like a startled fawn. 'I was just about to ring the bell,' he said. 'You gave me quite a fright.'

'Sorry, Charles, that's the last thing I want to do,' I replied. 'Come on in – it's great to see you. Go into the study and take a pew. Eleanor's got some coffee ready, haven't you, dear?'

She had appeared behind me as I greeted him. 'Freshly

made and guaranteed to please all our customers. How are the children?' she asked.

'Fine and very noisy as usual when I left them,' he said in a flat tone of voice.

'And Bronwen?'

'She's fine too.' If anything his tone of voice was even flatter and devoid of enthusiasm.

After Eleanor had left us to drink our coffee in the privacy of my study, Charles launched into the purpose of his visit immediately. 'Fred, I can't stand the boredom of that parish any more. There is absolutely nothing to do for somebody like me. If I were a country man it would be different. I could keep a few sheep and cows like the Vicar of Aberpengwm or perhaps become an ecclesiastical market gardener; I don't know a turnip from a parsnip. As for shearing a sheep or milking a cow, I would be a disaster. I'm a square peg in a round hole.'

'You are certainly in a hole, the worse hole in the diocese,' I replied, 'but how to get out of it will not be easy with your track record. Let's face it, Charles, you hardly set the Thames on fire in Pontywen, did you? Have you had a word with the Bishop? There are no livings vacant at the moment but he might keep you in mind when a suitable one crops up. Quite a few of the incumbents at this end of the diocese are well past the retiring age.'

'To be honest, Fred, I have approached him a couple of times but on each occasion I have had a polite but dusty answer. The reason why I have come to see you this morning is to ask whether I could help out in Pontywen occasionally – with the Gilbert and Sullivan Society, for example, or if you are going to do another door-to-door visitation of the parish. Anything to get away from those endless fields and the vacant faces when I look down at them from the pulpit, not to mention the tuneless roaring which goes under the heading of hymn singing. If the Bishop knows that I am keen enough to drive down to a town parish to help in any way I can, maybe it will persuade him that I am desperate to move to a populated area. He can't say that I am neglecting my parish when I could visit the entire church congregation in the space of an afternoon.'

I had never seen Charles more animated. Evidently solitary confinement had inspired him far more than his five years in Pontywen had ever succeeded in doing.

'You amaze me,' I replied. 'There was I thinking that the sinecure of your rural backwater would be paradise for you and instead it turns out to be hell. Before accepting your offer of help in this parish there are one or two practical details to be decided. For example, who is going to pay for your petrol for these excursions to Pontywen? Do you intend staying for a couple of days a week? Furthermore don't forget that I now have an excellent curate in Emlyn Howells. How is he going to feel about a former curate appearing on the scene? All these things will have to be worked out, Charles. One other thing, you must ask the Bishop's permission before you embark on this experiment. I suggest you do that first. Then we can talk.'

'Does that mean you will agree that I can come if the Bishop allows it?' he asked eagerly.

'Let's get stage one over first, shall we? Phone him later today. It's better to do that than write to him.'

When he left the Vicarage he was a changed man. He

skipped down the steps and shot into his car, smiling broadly. Once inside, he wound down the window. 'See you soon,' he shouted, and then roared up the drive as fast as his old Austin could manage to take him with its clapped out engine and faulty silencer.

'Well?' said Eleanor, when I came into the hall. 'What transpired to cause such a transformation in the poor worm who crawled out of his limousine on arriving? What magic have you worked?'

'You won't believe this,' I replied.

'I can believe anything about Charles Wentworth-Baxter but, pray, carry on with your explanation, Frederick. I am all ears.'

'He wants to come back to Pontywen to help out in any way he can – with the Gilbert and Sullivan rehearsals, even with another door-to-door survey of the parish – anything to get away from his sojourn in the wilderness.'

'And you said yes? Fred, you must be mad. He is a walking disaster. He will be trouble, not a help.'

'I can't see his lordship giving him *carte blanche* to leave his parish, however small it is, to work somewhere else as a kind of therapeutic hobby. Even if he is given the episcopal blessing, the next hurdle will be the Parochial Church Council. Knowing Charles, they will be very reluctant to provide cash for his petrol and his hospitality.'

Ten minutes later my wife and I had gone our different ways, she to relieve David Andrews at the surgery and myself to visit the home of Michael John Roberts at 13 Balaclava Street. As I made my way through the four streets which lay between the Vicarage and the Roberts abode, it was interesting to see the effect of the Festival of Britain in 1951 on the doors and windows of some of the houses. There was an end to the uniform drab. Blues, reds and even yellows had replaced the obligatory brown of the pre-war years, in a rebellion against the stultifying austerity of the forties. The outside of number 13 Balaclava Street had its woodwork decorated in a daffodil yellow. I raised the black-painted knocker and gently announced my presence in case one or other of the male occupants had been working nights. The curtains of the front window were held to one side as the caller was investigated by a lady whose curling pins were swathed in a large scarf, tied in the manner of a female pirate. As soon as she saw me she disappeared so quickly that it might have been an illusion on my part. I waited for the door to open but waited in vain.

Determined to get an answer, I decided like John Peel in the hunting song to awaken the dead. I banged on the door so loudly that the neighbour appeared from number 14, thinking that it was she who was being summoned. 'Hello, Vicar,' she said. 'I thought it was our door. They are in. Perhaps they are round the back. I'll go and call them for you.'

There was no need. The next instant number 13 had opened its portals. 'I thought I heard some knocking,' mumbled the embarrassed vision of the front window. 'Come on in, Vicar, will you please? Excuse my hair, will you? I've only just washed it. My 'usband and me are going out to a special do at the Miners' Welfare tonight. They've got Tommy Cooper coming. Go in the front room, I'll be with you in a minute.'

I went into the front room, which was furnished with a newly purchased artificial leather suite still smelling of the store room from which it had been removed. On the freshly papered striped wallpaper three flying ducks were *en route* to the ceiling and in front of the immaculately black-leaded hearth lay an imitation Persian rug for which no self respecting native of that country would claim responsibility.

When the lady of the house appeared next, she had discarded the pinafore she wore at my first sight of her and was clad in a red jumper designed to show off the salient points of her upper anatomy complete with a navy blue skirt to match. Apart from her yellow scarf disfigured by the coils of hair erupting underneath, Mrs Roberts was dressed impeccably for a housewife in Balaclava Street.

'Now then, Vicar. I know what you have come about. It's about our Mike and Margaret, isn't it? Well, I've got a surprise for you. They've gone up to Gretna Green to get married.'

## 3

'Mike knew that you was coming here today, but told me to keep it a secret,' said Mrs Roberts. 'Margaret's parents don't know. They went off this morning earlier to catch the train from Cardiff. He said that perhaps they might 'ave to wait three weeks before they can get married. I told 'im what's going to 'appen about your job in the pit. The next thing is you'll be drafted into the army and where will you be then?'

She sat on the settee next to me, clutching and unclutching her hands but completely dry eyed. 'As far as I know, I replied, 'I think the right to get married at the blacksmith's forge at Gretna Green was abolished years ago. In any case, where's the money coming from to keep them while they wait to get married. I am sure Margaret has nothing. I don't suppose Mike has plenty in his pocket.'

'Oh, I think 'e've saved up quite a bit; never been one to throw his money about. In any case I've told them that they can stay with us until the time comes when they will 'ave somewhere of their own to go to. I know what it's like. We was in two rooms for years after we was married until we got this 'ouse, and what a state it was in when we had it. It took us ages to make it really fit to live in. Now, as you can see, it's beautifully furnished and painted.'

'Yes, it is, Mrs Roberts, a tribute to you and your

husband. Coming back to the purpose of my visit, I think I had better see Mr Fitzgerald the Diocesan Registrar. He will be able to tell me whether they can get married without parental consent. After that I feel I must see Mr and Mrs Price to let them know what has happened, whether Mike wants it kept a secret or not. They have a right to know, don't you agree?'

Her face turned the same colour as her jumper, a deep red. 'I suppose so,' she mumbled. 'Mind, if they had treated Margaret better and not wanted to put 'er in that Welfare 'Ome, this wouldn't 'ave 'appened.'

'I shall let you know what Mr Fitzgerald says and I shouldn't be surprised if Mr and Mrs Price come to see you once I have told them about the elopement. They will want to find out as much as they can. After all, she is their only child.'

I stood up and moved towards the door. She remained seated, her head bowed as if suddenly aware for the first time of the gravity of the situation as far as the Prices were concerned.

'Well, I'll be off now, Mrs Roberts,' I said. I moved into the passage which had been freshly papered with a covering of large red and white roses on a black background providing a lurid contrast to the daffodil yellow of the front door. She came quickly out of the front room and pushed past me to open the door into the street.

'Thank you for coming, Vicar,' she said, her eyes brimming with tears. 'I 'ope everything is going to be all right.'

Daniel Fitzgerald was a large, red-faced gentleman whose owlish countenance was decorated with a pair of horn rimmed spectacles. He seemed to spend far more time polishing them than wearing them. His favourite neckwear was a bow tie. A different one appeared each day in a wide variety of colours. His suit never changed, a shiny black serge which grew shinier as the years went by.

Like his suit, his opinions never changed. He was the ultimate diehard. For example, although he was the Diocesan Registrar in a Church in Wales diocese, he never ceased to mourn the passing of the Established Church or the Ecclesia Anglicana, as he called it, from its Welsh territory. There was one occasion when a highly respected Bardic lay reader was giving an address on St David at a lunchtime service in a town church. Daniel was sitting at the back, his arms spread out along the top of his pew. 'The Church in Wales is much older than the Church of England,' said the lay reader. This provoked a noisy banging on the pew with some kind of coin. Encouraged by this reaction the Bard asserted that while St David and the Welsh Saints had established Christianity throughout Wales the heathen English had to wait another century or so to be converted by Rome. By now Mr Fitzgerald was on his feet shouting, 'Nonsense. Don't listen to the man. He's talking balderdash.' Deciding that discretion was the better part of valour, the preacher left the pulpit only to be confronted in the Vestry at the end of the service by the irate Registrar.

The Diocesan Registry cum solicitor's office was in a street near the Cathedral. It was on the first floor of an Edwardian building, the ground floor of which was occupied by a gents' tailor. I went up the rickety stairs, then along the landing to the glass door bearing the name of Daniel T. Fitzgerald, LLB, SOLICITOR, DIOCESAN

REGISTRAR. I tapped gently on the door when a burst of typewriter activity had ended. 'Come in,' barked a contralto voice. The Amazon was seated behind a desk which was dominated by a large, ancient typewriter, probably a vintage model. Miss Muxworthy, bespectacled like her employer, had been in charge of the office since the First World War. I had come to know that her bark was worse than her bite.

'Ah, Vicar,' she said, in a much more friendly tone of voice. 'Mr Fitzgerald is expecting you. Take a seat while I tell him you are here. I think he is on the phone at the moment.' The seat was a leather-covered dining chair which like everything else in the office was showing signs of old age. The secretary was as tall and as large as her boss. On my first acquaintance with her as an ordinand, she towered above my five feet seven inches and so intimidated me that I began to stammer. Now we were the best of friends whenever I came to the office.

She disappeared into the next room and I could hear a conversation going on behind the closed door. As soon as it ended Miss Muxworthy reappeared and informed me that Mr Fitzgerald was now ready to receive me. I was greeted with a beaming smile from the registrar who came forward to shake my hand. 'Good to see you, Vicar,' he boomed. 'And how's your delightful lady wife? Still doctoring, I expect.'

Eleanor held a high place in his esteem ever since she had saved him from choking in a restaurant. It was during my curate days when we were celebrating her promotion to partnership in the practice by a rare night out at the Valley's only luxury dining place. We were seated at a table not far from where he was dining alone and enjoying his chicken supreme when a bone became lodged in his throat. His face had turned purple and he was gasping for breath. She was at his side in an instant and extracted the obstruction in a trice. Ever since that day we were remembered every Christmas with a bottle of best claret and a bouquet.

'Now then, what can I do for you?' he enquired, after asking about our two children and ushering me into another of his dining chairs. He sat back in the chair behind his desk and peered at me through his large spectacles, like a judge focusing his attention on someone in the witness box.

'I should like your advice on an urgent matter concerning some parishioners of mine,' I replied. He took off his spectacles, breathed on them and began to polish them with his handkerchief. 'Carry on, Vicar,' he said.

'Well, without going into too much detail, it appears that a young lady of seventeen who is pregnant and her young man who is nineteen have run off to Gretna Green to get married. The girl's parents have refused to give consent to her marriage in my church. Not only that, at the moment, they do not know she has eloped. My information has come from the young man's mother who lives in a small terraced house and who is prepared to let the couple have a room in which to begin their married life. The girl's parents live in a large detached house in the posh part of my parish. So what I should like to know from you, Mr Fitzgerald, is whether the blacksmith at Gretna Green can perform the ceremony. I have understood that such a marriage is no longer allowed to take place. Am I correct in thinking so?'

Once again he polished his spectacles and then proceeded to put them on again as if they were necessary to make a legal pronouncement.

'You are indeed correct, Vicar. The Marriage Act (Scotland) 1939 ended the blacksmith's shop weddings at Gretna Green. However, if they reside for fifteen days over the border after giving notice to a registrar and no one has objected, they will get away with the wedding. According to the 1949 Marriage Act, such a marriage would be lawful. I would imagine they would very soon find that out and find a district where they can reside and get a licence, that is, if they have the money to do it.' He took off his glasses to indicate that the official business was over.

'Apparently, according to the mother of the young man, who is a miner in Pontywen Colliery, he has saved a fair amount of money. So I think they should be able to support themselves for the fifteen days or so. Now I have the unenviable obligation of telling the girl's parents of the elopement. She has had the benefit of a private school education until her father's demotion brought her to Pontywen and to a state school. Margaret is an intelligent and gifted child with a possible career in music. Mike, her young man, has only his good looks to offer and very little besides.'

'All I can say, Vicar,' replied Mr Fitzgerald examining his spectacles minutely before replacing them, 'is that you have a very difficult pastoral problem. It is not for you to resolve it. You must stay on the sidelines and let the main protagonists sort it out. I agree that you must let the young lady's parents know immediately what is happening. After that it is up to them to decide what to do, whether they want to go chasing up to Scotland to find her or just accept the marriage as a *fait accompli* in a fortnight or so's time. It is up to them. You have done your part by providing the necessary information.'

An hour later I was pressing the button of the Prices' doorbell in Ashburnham Close. It was half past one. I had to ring twice before I had an answer. A flustered Mrs Price opened the door, wearing an apron. 'You must excuse my dress, Vicar. I have been preparing the food for dinner this evening. We have company coming. Do come in, will you? I expect you have news for us after seeing Mike's parents.'

She led me into the lounge and enquired if I would like a cup of tea or coffee. 'No, thank you,' I replied. 'I shan't stop long. I am afraid I have news for you which you will find disturbing. Mike and Margaret have eloped. They have gone to Gretna Green to get married. I have consulted the Diocesan Registrar and he informs me that although the blacksmith's shop is no longer available for weddings, they can get married by residing for a minimum of fifteen days anywhere in Scotland. I only found out earlier this morning from Mike's mother and went immediately to the Registrar to discover what the legal position was.'

Mrs Price's face drained of colour and her bottom lip began to quiver. She collapsed into an armchair. 'I must phone her father straight away. He will be furious. He worships that child. He thinks she is the most wonderful creature on God's earth. It's almost an obsession with him, Vicar. We paid out money for her to go to the private school in Cardiff. We couldn't really afford it but he insisted that she wasn't going to any Valley school. Then we paid out money on that grand piano when there wasn't much in the bank. On top of all that he lost his well-paid job and we had to come down here to a Valley school for her. This will kill him.'

She began to shed tears. In no time at all she was sobbing violently. I went to her and put my arm around her. 'How am I going to tell him?' she wailed. 'He will be so angry, so very angry.' It was obvious that she was in fear of him and his reaction to the news when it was told him.

'Would it be any help,' I said quietly, 'if I phoned him and told him what has happened? It will save you all the aggravation. I shall try to be as diplomatic as I can in letting him know.'

Her convulsive sobbing began to subside. 'I should be most grateful if you would do that,' she replied. 'You don't know how uncontrollable he can be in certain circumstances. You can phone him from here if you like. The sooner he is told the better.'

'I think it would be wiser if I spoke to him from the Vicarage,' I replied. 'It won't take me two minutes to get there. I have the car outside.' I had no intention of talking to the irate Mr Price, with his wife hovering around me. There was also the extra time it would give me to think of the right approach.

She gave me his office telephone number. 'Ask for extension 7,' she said. 'He should be back from lunch by now.'

During the short space of time it took me to drive back to the Vicarage I rehearsed several opening gambits, from 'Mr Price, your daughter has eloped' to an enquiry after his health followed by a gradual imparting of the news in a couple of stages. The net result of this exercise was mental turmoil when I lifted the phone to dial the office number. As I did so, Eleanor's head appeared round the door of the study.

'Where on earth have you been, Fred? Your lunch was ready ages ago. I couldn't wait for you any longer. I have to go to the Maternity Clinic now. You will find your shepherd's pie in a somewhat dried-up condition in the oven. The children are out with Marlene. Next time, phone me, there's a good boy, if you are going to be late for your lunch. See you later.'

Before I could reply she had gone through the front door. By the time I had dialled the Price number, I could hear her car speeding up the drive. I wished I could have had a word with her before making my call.

Extension 7 was engaged. I had to wait several minutes before it was free. While I waited I remembered the words of Daniel Fitzgerald. 'You must stay on the sidelines.' Here I was in the middle of the pitch. My head was in a whirl and my heart was pounding. 'Hello!' said the voice curtly.

'Is that Mr Price?' I asked feebly, knowing full well that it was he.

'Yes, what can I do for you?' There was as much warmth in his tone as you would get from a lighted match in a freeze-up.

'This is the Vicar, Mr Price.'

'I am sorry, Vicar, I didn't recognise your voice. How did you get my number?' Evidently he did not like to be phoned at the office.

'I had it from Mrs Price. You see, I have urgent news for you. It's about Margaret.'

There was a momentary silence at the other end. 'Don't tell me something has happened to her.' He sounded like a different man, panic-stricken, a disintegrated iceberg.

'Nothing has happened to her like an accident, for example. However, I am afraid that she and Mike have eloped to Gretna Green.'

'What!' he bellowed, blasting my eardrums.

'Apparently they went off early this morning, expecting to get married in the blacksmith's forge. They will find that it is no longer a marriage venue. However, I understand that if they reside in a district across the border for fifteen days they will be able to get married. I have been to see the Diocesan Registrar and he assures me that this is the case.'

From the amount of heavy breathing at the other end which accompanied my report on the elopement, I began to fear that he was on the verge of an imminent heart attack. The heavy breathing continued when I had finished speaking. It was obvious that he was incapable of speech, either through incoherent rage or a dangerous medical condition.

'Mr Price,' I said, 'are you there?' There was no reply. 'Mr Price,' I shouted. I heard a muffled noise and then followed a complete silence. I put down the receiver and dialled the office number.

I dialled three times. Each time the line was dead. After a frantic third attempt to contact the office, I realised that I was attempting the impossible. Since the receiver was dangling at the extension 7 end, the phone at the Vicarage was unable to contact the office number.

I put the receiver down and tried to think of the nearest place with a phone. There was a telephone kiosk in the town square but there was always someone in there, with one or two people waiting outside. The thought of the town square reminded me of Howells the greengrocers. Moelwyn and Myfanwy Howells had a phone which Charles Wentworth-Baxter used to call me when he was a lodger there. I ran out to the car and drove off at high speed. There was a parking place outside the shop. I pulled up with a screech of tyres, jumped out of the car, and dashed into the shop to the amazement of three old ladies who were having a gossip on the pavement.

'You're in a hurry, Vicar,' said Moelwyn, who was weighing some tomatoes for a customer.

'May I use your phone?' I gasped. 'It's urgent.'

'I can see that,' he replied. 'You know where it is – on the window ledge in the living room.' *En route* I collided with Myfanwy, who was coming to help in the shop.

'What on earth is the matter, Vicar?' she enquired.

'It's a matter of life and death. I've got to get to the phone. I'll explain later.'

'Oh dear,' she exclaimed.

When I got to the phone, I realised I had not brought the piece of paper with the office number on it.

'Myfanwy!' I shouted. 'Where is the telephone directory?' She came running into the room with the directory.

'Sorry,' she said. 'I took it into the shop this morning to look up a number and forgot to put it back.'

As I thumbed through the pages devoted to the name Morris, my frustration became intense. Every second wasted in finding the number was adding to the possibility that by the time the extension 7 office was reached, it would be too late. At last I discovered W.G. Morris & Co. at the bottom of the column.

'Morris and Company, can I help you?' said the receptionist.

'This is urgent,' I replied. 'Can you get somebody to go to Mr John Price's office at once. I am afraid that he must have been taken ill. He seems to have dropped the receiver and I cannot get any response from him. I am his Vicar and I had to give him some news which might have come as too great a shock for him. Will you please let me know what has happened? This is Pontywen 279.'

While I waited for a reply, I told Myfanwy what had happened.

'I could see by your face that something drastic was going on. Your face is as white as a sheet. I'll get you something to bring the colour back to your cheeks.' She went out and came back with a tumbler of whisky.

The minutes stretched into an eternity.

Then the phone rang. I picked it up, my hands shaking. 'Mr Morris wants to speak to you,' announced the shaky voice of the receptionist.

'I am afraid, Vicar,' said the property developer, 'that I have some bad news for you. John Price has suffered a massive heart attack. The ambulance has just taken him away for examination at the hospital but the expectation is that he will not be able to survive. I wonder if you would be so good as to break the news to Mrs Price. It would be much better coming from you rather than from his place of employment.'

As I drove to Raglan House in Ashburnham Close, I wondered if I had been wise to offer my services to Mrs Price as the herald of bad tidings. Perhaps if she had told her husband, it might have softened the blow somewhat. Now I had to be the bearer of even worse news to a lady who appeared to be frightened of her own shadow. Small wonder I kept crashing my gears.

For the third time in two days I made my way up the drive in trepidation, wondering why on earth I had got myself involved with the young couple instead of sending them away when it was apparent that I could not marry them. There was an instant response when I rang the door bell. Evidently, Mrs Price must have been hovering around the hall waiting for the call from her husband once he had been informed about the runaways.

She was startled to see me. 'Vicar, I didn't expect to see you so soon again. Come in, please. I haven't heard from my husband as yet.'

I waited to speak until we were both seated in the front room. She had been studying my face ever since I had appeared at the door, and I felt that she had a premonition of what I was about to tell her.

'I am afraid I have some bad news for you. Your husband has had a very bad heart attack and has been taken to hospital in Newport. They are going to carry out an examination, of course, but apparently it is extremely serious. I am so sorry to have to be such a merchant of gloom.' I went to her and put my arm round her shoulder. She looked shrivelled up by all that had happened in such a short time to her daughter and now to her husband.

To my amazement she put aside my arm and stood up. 'We must get an SOS message on the wireless to Margaret at once. She means a lot more to him than I do. I was afraid that something like this would happen. How do we do that?'

'I should think that we should have to inform the

police and ask them if it is possible to have it broadcast, or perhaps the hospital can do it. In any case they don't broadcast an SOS until just before they read the news at six o'clock. So there's plenty of time. Would you like me to drive you to the hospital first of all? Then we can ask there how to go about it. More important than that, you will be able to be at your husband's bedside at this critical time in his life. He will need you now more than ever.'

'Vicar,' she replied. 'He has never needed me, apart from supplying him with meals and clean clothes. I doubt if it will make much difference whether I am at his bedside or not. It would be much more comfort to him if Margaret was there. That is why it is so important to try to get her to come back. If anybody could rally him, she could.'

Soon we were on our way to the hospital. The traffic on the Valley roads was very heavy and it took us an hour and a half to get to the hospital. Throughout the journey Mrs Price was completely composed and spoke of her early married life with her husband and how happy it was until Robin her son was killed in an accident.

The hospital car park was full. I took the liberty of parking in one of the places reserved for the consultants. At the information office there was a long queue which we ignored and went to the Matron's office. A cleric's collar is always an open sesame in a hospital and in no time at all we were at the bedside of the unconscious John Price. A consultant, a junior doctor and the nurses were in attendance in the side ward to which he had been taken. 'I am afraid that your husband has had a massive heart attack,' said the consultant. 'He has been X-rayed and it has revealed that his heart is in a very bad state. This collapse could have happened at any time. I am sorry to say that there is nothing we can do for him. He could die today. He may last out a few more days at the most. It must be a great shock for you. If it is any consolation I can assure you that he has been living on borrowed time for a while.'

'Thank you for being so frank,' she replied. 'There is one thing. My daughter is somewhere in Scotland. She is our only child and my husband was very devoted to her. I wonder if it would be possible to send out an SOS for her on the wireless.'

'I should think so,' he said. 'I would suggest that you go to Matron's office. You can say that I have asked that the request should be made. She will then contact the police who will give the necessary information to the BBC.'

'Would you like me to go while you stay with your husband?' I said to her.

'That is very kind of you. By the way, doctor, this is our Vicar. He has been a great help over the past few days. You see, my daughter has eloped to Scotland.'

The consultant came to her and held her hand. 'My dear lady, you have really been through the mill, haven't you?' he murmured.

As I came to the Matron's office door she was advancing towards me from the opposite direction. A tall buxom lady with a military bearing, she was an imposing figure, authority personified. 'Can I help you, Vicar?' she demanded, rather than asked. I felt glad that I was not the hospital chaplain.

'It is rather urgent, Matron. I wonder if I could have a few words with you in the privacy of your office.'

She gave me the kind of look which Mr Bumble would have given to David Copperfield when he asked for a second helping.

'I am afraid it will have to be a few because we are very busy this afternoon. Come on in, will you?'

We went past the secretary at her desk and into the inner sanctuary. 'Take a seat,' she ordered, while she stood towering over me in a most disconcerting fashion. Evidently my words had to be few.

'I have come from the Llewellyn ward where a parishioner of mine has been brought in with a massive heart attack. The consultant has asked me if you could inform the police to contact the BBC with an SOS message. He says that the patient is in imminent danger of death. His only child, a daughter, has eloped to Scotland and her whereabouts there are not known. I should think not very far across the border. By the way, she is six months pregnant.'

She sat down. Her whole attitude changed. 'I take it that the mother is here in the ward,' she said quietly.

'She is indeed. I offered my service as a courier so that she could stay by her husband's bedside.' The Matron produced a sheet of paper from a drawer in the desk. 'Shall we get the details, Vicar, and I shall be in touch with the police immediately.' When she had written the necessary information she stood up and escorted me to the door. 'Will you please tell Mrs Price that I shall be along to see her shortly,' she added as I left.

When I returned to the ward I found the curtains screening the bed. There was no sound of a conversation behind them. I hovered around for a few seconds. 'Mrs Price,' I whispered.

She appeared at once, still as dry-eyed and composed. 'They have gone for the time being,' she said. 'Are they going to send out an SOS for Margaret?'

'The Matron says that she will contact the police immediately. She expects that they will be able to get the message broadcast before the six o'clock news. She said that she will be along to see you soon.'

'Everybody is being very kind. It helps to restore your faith in human nature, I must say. I suppose it takes something like this to happen to make you realise that.'

It amazed me that the frightened wife who spoke the minimum when I first encountered her in the presence of her husband was the self-possessed lady who had chatted to me all the way to Newport, and who now appeared to be completely in charge of the situation. 'Do you want me to stay with you for a while, Mrs Price?' I asked.

'You must be a very busy man, Vicar. I am most grateful for all that you have done as it is. No, thank you. You get on your way. I have a sister in Cardiff. I shall give her a ring later on and let her know what has happened. She and her husband have a car. So they can be here in no time later today.'

'What about Mr Price? Has he any relatives? I can ring them if you want me to. It will be no trouble.'

She caught hold of my arm. 'That is very good of you but there is no need. His only brother died of a heart attack a few years ago. Apparently his father died in the same way. His mother died only recently. So there is no one on that side alive. I shall let you know what has happened and I shan't forget your kindness. Would you like to see him before you go?' She parted the curtains.

There lay her husband, his eyes closed, his mouth wide open and minus his dentures. We stood for a moment in silence. 'How are the mighty fallen,' she said.

# 4

No sooner had I arrived in the Vicarage than the telephone made its presence felt. 'Not again!' expostulated my wife. 'That's the third time in the last ten minutes.' As I picked up the receiver she added, 'And you have a lot of explaining to do for your playing away from home for the past three or four hours. Your children are beginning to think that they are fatherless.'

I put my hand over the mouth of the receiver. 'Be patient, my sweet, and all will be revealed.'

'Ernest Nicholls here,' announced the voice at the other end. 'I have had a word with my wife about sharing our television set with some of the parishioners. You will be pleased to know that she says that we shall be able to entertain four of them but no more than that. Apparently she has already invited a few of her friends but in view of your plea that we should share our good fortune in having a set with those who have none she felt obliged to do something about it. Quite frankly, I am amazed that she has done so.' I was about to express my agreement but controlled myself and said how delighted I was at her generosity. I put the phone down and then put my arms around Eleanor who was standing at my side.

'Don't think you can get around me by doing that,' she said in mock anger. 'Come on, out with it, but before that, what was the call about?'

'That, my dear love, was Mr Nicholls informing me

that his good lady had consented to having four specially picked specimens of the Pontywen proletariat in her drawing room to watch the coronation. He informed me that he was amazed at this condescension.'

'And so say all of us,' exclaimed my wife. 'Now comes the problem of deciding what four persons of virtuous behaviour are to be selected for this great privilege. Perhaps it would be wise to put a number of names into a hat and make a lottery of it.'

'Do you know what,' I replied. 'I think that would be a very good idea. First prize see it with the Nicholls, second prize join Vaughan-Jenkins, third prize view at the Vicarage. Runners-up look through the shop window outside Jones the Wireless.'

'Well, at least we seem to be making some progress towards D-Day,' said Eleanor. 'Next, would you mind explaining your absence from the bosom of your family for most of today? You had better go and see your children after you have done so. They may have forgotten what you look like by now.'

'When you have heard what I have to say, I think you will agree that I have had a very busy and very taxing day.'

By the time I had recounted all that had happened she came to me and kissed me. 'My dear love,' she murmured, 'you have indeed had a very taxing day and evidently it is not over yet. It is not long before the six o'clock news. We must listen for the SOS. I shouldn't be surprised from what you have told me that you will have a call from the hospital to say that Mr Price has died. It will be a miracle if he survives until the time his daughter arrives, that is, of course, if she does arrive.'

There was no miracle. No sooner had we heard the SOS message on the wireless than there was a telephone call from the sister on the ward to say that Mr Price had died and that Mrs Price would like to see me. 'I don't get this,' I said to Eleanor. 'It's only just an hour or so ago that she told me that her sister would be coming to the hospital and that my services were no longer required for the time being. From what she said at her husband's bedside, she is hardly overwhelmed with grief. Strange woman!'

'You can say that again,' my wife replied. 'If I were you, I should not rush back down to Newport. Go and see the children and I'll get you something to eat. She has had more than her fair share of attention from you already.'

It was past eight o'clock when I entered the hospital. Mrs Price was waiting for me in the entrance hall. She smiled when she saw me. 'It is very good of you to come once again after all you have done for me today. I am sorry to have to impose on you once more. Apparently my sister is not at home. Matron advised me that it would be advisable for me to get back home as soon as possible and out of the hospital environment. You are the only one I could think of to take me back. I hope you don't mind, Vicar.' She spoke as if she were requesting a lift after a shopping expedition, not a bereavement.

All the way back to Pontywen she chatted incessantly about everything from the coronation to what needed to be done to the house and garden. She wondered if she would hear from Margaret later that evening and what her daughter's reaction to the news of his death would be. 'It would be wonderful if she gave up the idea of getting married and stayed with me instead, even if it means her bringing up her baby here.' The only time she mentioned her husband was confined to a single sentence almost at the beginning of our journey from the hospital. 'Well, all I can say is that I am glad John did not have to suffer and died without an atom of pain.' Then she went on to talk about making arrangements for the funeral and the refreshments to follow at the house. She hoped Margaret would be there to help with preparing the food. 'She's a good little cook, you know.'

'I suppose you will want to get back to the Vicarage now,' she said, as we stopped in the drive.

'If you don't mind,' I replied. 'But I will come in for a few minutes. Perhaps your sister will be home by now. I'll wait until you have phoned her. Maybe she will come over and stay the night with you.'

'Let me make you a cup of tea,' she said. 'Go into the sitting room and make yourself at home. Once I've put the kettle on I'll go and phone my sister again.' I went to the window and looked out at the overgrown grass on the lawn. Evidently John Price had thrown in the sponge. From the conversation in the car it appeared that Mrs Price was about to remedy the neglect which was apparent inside and outside the house. Far from being a cloud descending upon her, the death of her husband had lifted a cloud which had been hanging over her for many years. It was a time of release.

My musings were interrupted by the ringing of the telephone. There was the sound of hurried footsteps in the passage from the kitchen to the hall. 'Margaret,' exclaimed her mother and then burst into tears for only the second time that day. I came out from the sitting room to see if there was anything I could do. Mrs Price was standing holding the receiver and sobbing uncontrollably. I took the receiver from her hands gently.

'Mother!' repeated a tearful voice at the other end.

'Margaret, this is the Vicar. Your mother is too upset at the moment to speak.'

'How is my father, Vicar?' She sounded desperate. I took a deep breath.

'I am sorry to have to tell you this but he passed away a few hours ago.' She began to cry. I had never felt so helpless in my life, standing between two wailing women, the one in Pontywen and the other somewhere in Scotland. It was Margaret who was first to stifle her grief.

'Can I speak to my mother now, please?' she asked.

'Mrs Price,' I said firmly, 'Margaret wishes to speak to you now, otherwise her money will begin running out in the call box.' Mention of the call box seemed to bring her to her senses.

'I'll get her to reverse the call,' she said. I handed her the receiver and retreated rapidly into the lounge, closing the door behind me. I had no wish to be further involved in the three-way conversation.

Some ten minutes or so later the receiver was replaced and a somewhat shame-faced Mrs Price came into the sitting room. 'I am sorry about that, Vicar. I just couldn't help myself. Anyway the good news is that my daughter will catch the train home first thing in the morning. Even better than that, she says she will stay with me until she has the baby and then later on decide whether to get married or not. I have a feeling that she will not. I can look after the child if she wants to carry on with her education. It will give me a new interest to brighten up my life. What does that old hymn say, "God moves in a mysterious way, His wonders to perform"?' A contented smile spread across her tear-stained face. Evidently John Price had not died in vain.

She assured me that she was in no need of company that night and that she would phone her sister after I had gone. As I opened the door of my car to drive off, she said, 'That reminds me. I must get someone from John's office to bring his car back tomorrow. Perhaps I can get some driving lessons once this is all over and so can Margaret later on. It is pointless having a machine if you can't use it. It will be quite a challenge to be in the driving seat.'

The next morning I had a telephone call from the Bishop. 'Charles Wentworth-Baxter has rung me with a strange request. He wishes to leave his parish for a few days each week to come and assist you in Pontywen. I have told him that since you already have a most capable assistant in Emlyn Howells there is clearly no need of any extra help. In any case, with Wentworth-Baxter's record in your parish I should imagine he would be much more of a hindrance than a help. It is obvious to me that his request springs more from a desire to escape boredom than an eagerness to give of his best in a more populated parish. However, I have not forbidden him from coming but I have informed him that he must have your complete agreement and that this experiment must be for a limited time only, otherwise his parish will feel neglected.'

No sooner had I put the phone down than there was a ring on the doorbell. There was no mistaking that ring, which consisted of two short jabs on the push button followed by a long pressure which would awaken the dead. The above had arrived. Charles stood on the doorstep, grinning at me. 'Reporting for duty, sir,' he said and gave me a sloppy salute.

'There'll be no duty for you today, I can assure you,' I told him. 'There are a lot of things to be sorted out before you can set foot in Pontywen again. Come on in. I have just had the Bishop on the phone and he is not at all over the moon about your "strange request", as he called it. Still, never let it be said that I have stood in your way in your bid for advancement to greater things in the diocese. Go into the study while I make us a cup of coffee. Eleanor is at the surgery.'

The inane grin was still on his face when I came back with a tray of coffee and biscuits. I felt a strong urge to wipe it from his face as we sat sipping the hot coffee. I launched into the offensive. 'Charles,' I said, 'if you are going to come back here you will have to work ten times harder than previously. For example, Emlyn Howells is in the process of setting up a Scout troop in the parish. We shall need someone to inaugurate a Cub pack. That will be one of your first tasks.' The smile vanished and a frown took its place. He stared at me in disbelief. 'Then again, I am thinking of starting some kind of fellowship for the old-age pensioners on a Wednesday afternoon in the church hall. You know the kind of thing. Tea and biscuits, dominoes, whist drives and a sing-song. With your ability at the piano you would be the ideal person to get it off the ground.' The colour was beginning to drain from his face.

'The other project I have in mind is a young people's club with rock and roll records on an amplifier, table tennis tournaments, spelling bees and so on. If you want youngsters to be linked to the church this is one of the best ways. I have been thinking of forming a committee to organise it. You could have the job as chairman.'

By now he seemed to be on the verge of a nervous collapse. 'What about Emlyn Howells?' he stammered. 'Shouldn't he be doing these things? I was thinking I could help out with the Gilbert and Sullivan crowd and with doing some door-to-door visiting. I'll be no use at any of those projects you have mentioned, no use at all.'

'In that case, dear Charles, it is no use you coming to Pontywen at all. As it was in the beginning, is now and ever shall be as far as you are concerned. All you want to do is to escape from your noisy children and your too peaceful rural surroundings for a few days a week. It is not work that you want but an excuse to idle away your time in Pontywen rather than in your parish backwater. Sorry, my friend, but it is not on.'

He sat hunched up in the armchair, a picture of misery. I waited for his reply. There was a two-minute silence. Then to my amazement, he said, 'You are right. I know. I was never energetic in Pontywen. So how could you believe that I would be different if I came back? The truth is I am desperate. Things are chaotic in the house. Bronwen seems to have lost interest. It's like living in a pigsty. I go around in underclothes that have not seen a washtub for ages, not to mention my clerical shirt which is a permanent fixture. I never know when to expect my meals and when I do get them they are not very appetising to say the least. I tell you what, Fred, I am getting to the stage when I will not be able to put up with it any longer. It's as bad as that.'

'When you say that you will not be able to put up with

it any longer, Charles, does that mean you will start helping in the house. With all the time you have on your hands, why can't you do some washing? I am sure you will never be able to do any ironing but I am positive you could wash clothes, and napkins if it comes to that. As far as the meals are concerned, there is no reason why you couldn't do some cooking. From what I can see, it is poor Bronwen who is desperate, much more than you. With four children born within the space of five years I should think it would drive most women to distraction. For God's sake, Charles, stop thinking about yourself. Turn your attention to Bronwen and the children. Your responsibility is to them first and foremost.'

Suddenly the savaged sheep turned into a tiger. He stood up, his eyes blazing. 'And what gives you the right to talk like that?' he shouted. 'Since when did you do any washing or cooking. You've got it made, with an affluent wife who can pay people to do those menial tasks and look after your two children. I came to you because I thought you were the one person that could help me. I had forgotten how holier than thou you could be. I shan't impose on your precious time any longer. Don't bother to see me out.' He strode towards the door, which he flung open in a melodramatic fashion. The front door was closed with a slam that shook the house. That was followed by an equally violent slam of his car door. The starter motor was given similar treatment but it failed to arouse the engine. After a multiplicity of attempts, the battery refused to cooperate any further. A long silence reigned.

I looked out of the window to behold a pathetic figure

spreadeagled over the driving wheel, his nose almost in contact with the dashboard.

From his very first encounter with a steering wheel when he drove the Vicar's car into a ditch Charles had had no luck with cars. The episode in the ditch was his one and only driving lesson in the company of Father James Whittaker. Prior to his move into the wilds, which necessitated the use of a car, he had a course of lessons with Jones the Garage who had promised to supply him with a second-hand car at a reasonable price. At the end of the first twelve lessons, during which he had done irreparable harm to the gear box and had dented the car in several places, Elias Jones suggested that he should use a bicycle to get around his rural parish. Undaunted, Charles went to the driving school which had recently taken over the second-hand furniture shop in Pontywen.

After another twelve lessons the instructor at the 'Safe Drive' establishment decided that his pupil was ready to sit the first of several driving tests. To his amazement Charles was given a licence to drive. Eleanor suggested that his clerical collar must have convinced a gullible examiner that someone who worked for the Almighty would have supernatural power to avoid accidents no matter how incompetent he might be. Idris the Milk insisted that either the examiner had been bribed or he was drunk at the time of the test. Whatever the reason, Charles was now let loose in charge of a car for good or for ill.

The Austin Big Seven was the third car he had bought since he had become Vicar of Penglais. The first one he had was the result of an advertisement in *The Times*. 'Impecunious curate requires car for use in rural parish.

£100 maximum.' He had a reply from a Morris Minor enthusiast who offered a car which had been rebuilt. It was a 1932 Morris Minor. After six months in his new parish, he turned the wheel to enter his ramshackle garage. The wheel was turned to the left and the car went straight on into the wall which bordered the garage. The steering wheel had snapped. At least the Almighty had seen to it that the car was not on the road. Apparently the rod had been involved in an accident and had been rewelded. Since Charles had lost the letters from the vendor, there was nothing he could do to claim compensation.

His next venture was the acquisition of his late father's car. The Reverend Septimus Wentworth-Baxter had been elevated to a place prepared for him in the heavenly establishment as a loyal servant of the Church of England for fifty-two years since his ordination. As a result Charles had been able to fill some of the rooms in his large Vicarage with furniture appropriate to its age. In tune with the furniture was the aged Bentley which consumed more petrol than the twice-weekly bus visiting Penglais to take its inhabitants to market. Fortunately for Charles its engine decided to give up the ghost and join its former owner as no longer part of this mortal world.

So my ex-curate decided to come back to Pontywen to buy a used car from Elias Jones 'at a reasonable price'. It was a car which could be parked outside the Bishop's palace not at all looking out of place, according to the vendor. Since Charles was in urgent need to park his car in that vicinity he agreed to pay Elias £200 for the privilege, a sum which he could ill afford in view of his family commitments. After two breakdowns, at the second of which the family were stranded on top of a bare mountain inhabited by sheep and rarely by human beings, Charles accused Elias of malpractice. The garage owner accused his customer of abusing the machine he had purchased. It was deadlock, neither of the parties having the money or indeed the will to pursue the matter any further.

Now, Charles was faced with the situation of asking Elias Jones to come to his aid or of walking two miles to the next garage. Evidently the decision was one with which his brain was unable to cope. He was in limbo.

Since I was fully acquainted with this void which perpetually bedevilled my former curate, there was only one thing I could do. I went out and opened the car door. I shouted, 'Charles!' He sat up in an instant, like a schoolboy pinpointed by a tyrannical schoolmaster. 'Come on into the study and we'll phone Elias Jones to come and see to it,' I said.

'Over my dead body!' he snarled. 'In any case, it's nothing to do with you. I'll walk down to the Mile End Garage and ask them to come and see what is wrong. It may be Elias Jones's car but they will have a much better idea of what to do with it than he would. That man's a fraud, a twister.'

'Look, Charles,' I said, 'you can phone the Mile End from here. It will take you half an hour to walk there and then you'll have to wait for them to bring you back. I know you must be very upset but, for your own sake, calm down and try to get this car business sorted out. Otherwise you're going to get stranded in Pontywen.'

A few minutes later he was on the phone, pleading

with the proprietor of the 'Mile End' Garage to rescue him. The desperation in his voice was sufficient to bring an instant response. In no time at all a mechanic was attending to the stricken machine. As soon as he opened the bonnet, he exclaimed, 'Oh! My God!' which was followed by an apology for blasphemy in the presence of two men of God. 'When did you last have the car serviced?' he asked.

Charles could not remember. 'In fact,' he said, 'I only take it to the garage when something goes wrong.'

After a cursory examination the mechanic diagnosed a major malfunction which would require a day's work at the very least, that is, if the necessary spare parts were available. He produced a tow rope from the back of the van and 'affixed' it to the Austin Big Seven. 'Hop in, Vicar, and be careful steering. I'll drive slowly in any case, so don't worry.'

This did nothing to assure someone whose steering was suspect even when a tow rope was not involved and whose cup of woe had overflowed so much that he was unable to think straight, let alone drive straight.

'I don't wish to interfere, Charles,' I said, 'but would you like me to steer the car? I have had experience of doing it.' I did not add that it was only on one occasion, and that ended with me steering the Rural Dean's car into the gatepost at the entry to his drive. However, that was on a dark night with only the side-lights on, not in broad daylight, I told myself. Also, I was being towed by my wife and not by a car mechanic, an expert on towing.

He accepted my offer with alacrity. The panic-stricken look disappeared from his face only to be replaced by a furrowed brow as he contemplated the absence of his car for a day or two. 'How am I to get back to Penglais? What's more, how am I going to get down here to pick the car up. There isn't another bus from the village this week.'

'If our friend here will drive us back from the garage, I will run you home. When the car is ready, I will come to your place and drive you back to pick it up. How does that suit you?'

He put his arm round my shoulder. 'Thanks, Fred. You have been a real pal to me once again. I'm sorry for that outburst earlier on but things have really got on top of me. Perhaps something will turn up to change my luck, you never know.'

The journey to the garage was uneventful, unlike the news given by the garage owner. 'I am afraid you will have to pay for a new engine or a reconditioned one. When did you last put oil in this car? There isn't a drop left in it. Charles looked at him blankly. 'I have never put oil in it and I wouldn't know where to put it anyway.'

Ernest Williams, proprietor of the Mile End Garage, raised his eyes to heaven and then brought them down to focus on the cleric opposite him. 'Well, Reverend,' he said, 'I suppose you believe in miracles but even miracles won't work on cars that haven't got oil in them. If I were you, I would get cracking on learning how to look after a car or you'll be needing miracles to pay for a new engine every year.'

When we arrived at the Vicarage, Eleanor's car was parked outside the garage. 'You had better come in, Charles, and have something to drown your sorrows before I take you home. You look as if you need it badly.'

As we came through the front door, my wife came to meet us. 'What has been happening?' she asked. 'I saw the Mile End van bringing the two of you back.'

'I am afraid that Charles has had some bad luck with his car. The engine has packed up and he has to have a new one. So once he has had a drink and some sandwiches, I am driving him back to Penglais. Make yourself comfortable in the sitting room, Charles, and I'll be with you in two ticks.' So saying, I went into the kitchen, where my wife was standing with her hands on her hips.

'Since when have you taken to helping me in the kitchen?' she demanded. 'What's going on?' By the time I had told her about the episode of the Wentworth-Baxter outburst in the study and the subsequent farce of the unoiled engine, Marlene came in with the two children.

'Marlene,' said my wife. 'Could you possibly stay for the next two hours or so? I'll pay you double time if you'll oblige. The Vicar and I have to drive Mr Wentworth-Baxter back to his Vicarage.'

'I don't mind,' replied our baby minder. 'I'm not going out tonight. Come on, kids, let's go up to the nursery.'

After she had gone upstairs with her charges, I turned to Eleanor. 'Now it is my turn to ask what's going on.'

'Well, my dear, from what you have told me, Bronwen is evidently in need of some female support. I know her and it is not like her to go to pieces. Mind, any woman living with Charles for any length of time would have to be a combination of Mother Theresa and Joan of Arc to survive unaffected.'

Half an hour later the three of us were on our way through the countryside, Eleanor and I in front and a glum Charles in the back. He had insisted that he wished to take the back seat. As my wife commented later, it was time that he took that position and stayed there. Evidently, she said, Bronwen and the children had been there long enough.

The evening sun was low in the cloud-streaked sky as we passed the road sign which announced that we were in the village of Penglais. Apart from a few cottages there was nothing else to indicate that we were in a village. Half a mile further on, we turned into the Vicarage drive, a winding weed-afflicted gravelled path, bordered by broken-down fences. As we pulled up outside the porch, a woman with a baby, clad only in a vest, in her arms and surrounded by three unkempt children came to greet us. As she brushed some straggling hair from her fore-head, she said unconvincingly, 'What a nice surprise to see you both.' Were it not for the fact that we were at Penglais Vicarage we would have not recognised this slattern as Bronwen.

Then she asked as an afterthought, 'What has happened to our car? Don't tell me that you have had another accident, Charles?'

'Of course not,' he snapped, as if he had never had one. 'Something has gone wrong with the engine, that's all, and I've got to wait to have it repaired in Pontywen.'

As we got out of the car, the three children ran back into the house, as if they were scared of strangers. 'They are very shy, aren't they?' said Eleanor.

'I suppose they are,' replied Bronwen. 'It's because they never see anybody in this God-forsaken hole. I expect you will want to get back to Pontywen now.'

'Do you mind if we come in for a few minutes?' my wife asked. 'It's ages since we have seen you.'

I had never seen anyone so reluctant to say Yes. After a pause, Mrs Wentworth-Baxter, flushed with embarrass-ment, said, 'Well, only for a few minutes. I've got to get the children to bed and then tidy up all the mess they made everywhere.'

'Mess' was an understatement. The house was indeed a pigsty, as Charles had told me. As soon as we entered the hall, our nostrils were assaulted by a combination of smells, all of them unpleasant. Bronwen, still holding the baby, was about to take us into the sitting room when Eleanor said, 'Perhaps we had better get back. It is getting late. I'll give you a ring tomorrow morning and we'll fix a date for lunch at the Tudor Arms. Charles will mind the children, won't you?' She smiled sweetly at him.

'Of course,' he mumbled.

'I'll come and pick you up sometime next week,' added Eleanor.

'If that's all right with you, Charles,' said Bronwen.

'I've said it's all right, haven't I,' he snarled.

As we drove back to Pontywen my wife was fuming with anger about what she had seen and heard in Penglais Vicarage. 'That man is not only a disaster in a parish. He is an even bigger one in his home. If something is not done soon, the wreckage will be beyond repair.'

'So then, doctor,' I asked, 'what course of treatment do you prescribe?'

'I'll tell you after I have examined the patient next week,' she replied.

## 5

'I wish we did not have to go?' sighed Eleanor, as she fastened her nylons to her suspender belt. 'I suppose there is no escape since they are both my patients and your parishioners. C'*est la vie*.'

It was the Saturday after our visit to the Wentworth-Baxter Vicarage. Apart from the occasional late wedding, Saturday afternoon and evening provided an opportunity for us to enjoy each other's company without let or hindrance. The majority of weddings were scheduled for the morning or early afternoon and my wife's duties were over by midday. Sometimes she took the children for a drive in the countryside, and once or twice a month Marlene looked after the children to allow the two of us to enjoy a visit to Cardiff or Newport.

Today was different. It was the golden wedding of Mr and Mrs Arthur Davies of Inkerman Street. Edwina Davies was a large talkative lady who was a regular attendant at St Padarn's Church. Her hair was dyed an unnatural black. Thickly applied eyebrow pencil gave her the appearance of a female George Robey. She was liberal in her application of face powder and equally so in her use of rouge. Her thin lips were neatly painted with red lipstick emphasising her rat trap of a mouth, underneath which was a formidable lantern jaw. Long earrings drooped incongruously from her large ears. For a seventy-year-old lady she presented a picture of someone trying to catch up with her youth fifty years late.

Active in the Mothers' Union, the Townswomen's Guild, and the local Labour Party, she was well known in Pontywen as someone to be avoided in the street if discerned on the horizon. Once trapped, there was no escape. 'How are you, Mrs Davies?' would be the signal for her to unfold her medical history, with appropriate quotations from doctors and consultants, going back into the distant past and ending with the very latest diagnosis. In church life, she was the equivalent of Bertie Owen, a Vicar's nightmare, an agitator at meetings and occasionally prone to create a disruption in church. For example, we held our patronal festival earlier that year when the Very Reverend James Williams-Ellis was the preacher. He had been in the pulpit for some twenty minutes, giving a history of the Celtic Church and the place of St Padarn's in its hierarchy. To relieve the boredom Mrs Davies decided to delve into her purse to find a three-penny bit to put on the collection plate. She was not a generous woman. So when she dropped the coin on the floor she began to search for that which she had lost, like the woman in the parable, except that, unlike Edwina, she had mislaid a gold coin. As she bent down to discover the whereabouts of her offering to the Lord, she toppled against the chair of the worshipper in front of her. That lady was jerked forward, so that her head collided with the back of the church warden. This chain reaction halted the preacher as he was about to connect St Padarn with St David.

Despite 'tut-tuts' and 'shushes' from the congregation, she persisted in her attempt to find the coin, her large posterior dislodging her chair, which was pressing into

the knees of Mrs Hughes, the organist's wife, behind her.

'My dear sister,' said the Dean, through gritted teeth, 'would you kindly leave your search for whatever it is you have lost until I have finished my sermon.' By now she was on the floor sweeping it with her hands to try to discover the lost treasure. The remonstrance from the dignitary brought an instant response. Puffing and blowing she struggled to get back into her chair, only to tilt it backwards, landing with her chair in the lap of Mrs Hughes and her legs up in the air. The Dean was still silent, unamused by the circus act of which he had a bird's eye view. In the meanwhile the congregation were beginning to enjoy the diversion, realising that Edwina

Davies was providing more entertainment than St Padarn and St David. All heads were turned towards her and none towards the pulpit. It was with a sense of anticlimax that they resumed their attention to the preacher once order had been restored.

A year previously, the old lady had broken her hip after falling in the street in an attempt to run after the bus which was about to leave the square in Pontywen. This entailed a stay for some months in the local hospital. After causing chaos in the ward, the doctor and the sister were only too pleased to allow her out to attend her granddaughter's wedding in the parish church. Unfortunately the ambulance was late arriving, and everybody, including the bride, was present except Granny Davies. After waiting ten minutes in the porch, I suggested to the bride that it would be advisable to proceed with the service since I had another wedding booked for three quarters of an hour later. 'I wouldn't dare, Vicar,' said the bride. 'You know what my gran is like.' At that moment, the ambulance drew up outside the church gates and soon the old lady was being trundled in her wheelchair up the path.

The customary signal to the organist to begin the Wedding March was the opening of the door at the west end of the church. I had forgotten to warn him about the arrival of Mrs Davies. The door was opened noisily to admit her. 'Here comes the bride,' thundered the organ. The congregation stood and turned to greet her. Instead of a vision in bridal array they saw a flustered old lady in a wheelchair clutching her handbag coming down the aisle and loudly instructing an even more flustered ambulance man to get her down to the front on the bride-side. 'I thought it was supposed to be my day,' said the bride.

These were but two instances of Edwina's ability to draw attention to herself either by accident or design. On the other hand her husband was content to stay out of the limelight, ensconced in his wooden armchair at the fireside and filling the living room with obnoxious fumes from his beloved pipe and its contents of 'Digger's Shag'. He was a little man with a walrus moustache, somewhat discoloured by his tobacco habits. The only time he enjoyed any kudos was in his early married days when he played at outside half for the Pontywen first fifteen. He was good enough to attract the attention of the Cardiff Club. Sadly, Arthur's rugby career came to an abrupt end when his wife paid her first visit to see him play. He was handled with unnecessary vigour by an opposing wing forward and was laid out for a few seconds. On his return home, Edwina threw his boots on the fire and issued an edict that he must never set foot on that field again. He was more afraid of her than any wing forward and a potential international was sacrificed on the altar of matrimonial obedience. As Full Back Jones the grave digger told me, 'If ever there was a martyr, Arthur Davies was one at that time.' Then he added, 'Mind you, he still is.'

The venue for the golden wedding celebration party was the Labour Club, known locally as the 'Glue Pot', from the reluctance of the members to leave there, even after closing time. It was a corrugated-iron structure, which had received its first coat of paint only recently, since its erection in 1933. The Committee had decided on old gold as a suitable shade with scarlet doors and window frames to complete the Labour Party colours. As the Chairman said at the function to mark the occasion,

'We can be proud of our identification with the battle colours of our cause and of the way in which we are brightening up the Valley.' Other inhabitants of Pontywen were not so lyrical about the new look. The Chairman of the British Legion Club described it as 'a bloody red and yellow monstrosity'; Idris the Milk said that it should be known as the 'mustard pot', since so many members got plastered there.

By the time we arrived at the club, there was enough noise coming through the opened windows to be heard in the next valley. Mr and Mrs Davies had four sons, and the three daughters who had begotten twenty-one children, one grandson and two granddaughters had added to the tally by supplying five great-grandchildren. It was obvious that all were present, not to mention well wishers, including the Mayor whose car adorned the car park. As we made our way to the entrance we were almost bowled over by two young boys who were chasing each other and loudly exchanging insults as they ran. It was then that we decided that, as soon as the telegram from the Queen had been read out and the cake had been cut, we would make our excuses and leave the scene as quickly as possible.

Once inside the metal construction, it was difficult to assess which was more unbearable, the temperature or the decibels. To add to the discomfort was the amount of human flesh crammed into such a limited space, which made the Black Hole of Calcutta seem like Wembley Stadium. As we elbowed our way through the throng to discover the whereabouts of the happy couple responsible for the occasion, we were confronted by Bertie Owen who was grinning like a Cheshire Cat. 'She's been waiting for you to come,' he said. 'It will make her evening. By the way, I'm the compère for tonight. Follow me.'

As we followed him, Eleanor murmured, 'That's going to make our evening. Featuring the two biggest bores in Pontywen – Edwina and Bertie.'

'Not only that,' I replied, 'but he makes it sound as if she is a widow. I assume that Arthur must be here, if only in a supporting role.'

After some strenuous physical effort more appropriate to a rugby scrum than the prelude to a meeting with the two people in whose honour the festivities had been arranged, we arrived at a table set out at the foot of the stage. There, in all her glory in a black evening gown of some silky material, with her George Robey facial make up and her fingers decorated with several rings plus purple varnished nails, was Edwina Davies. At her side was an uncomfortable Arthur suffocating in a stiff collar and black bow. On either side of the couple were the Mayor and Mayoress, wearing their chains of office, both sweating profusely and looking as if they were eager to get to their next official engagement.

'The Vicar and Dr Secombe,' announced Bertie.

'I can see that,' said Edwina sharply. 'This is our Vicar and his wife,' she explained to the Mayor and Mayoress.

'We have met before several times when the Vicar was Mayor's Chaplain some years ago,' replied the Mayor.

'I began to think you weren't coming,' she went on. 'We've been holding up proceedings until you were here. There's a nice little do arranged. I think you'll enjoy yourselves. Bertie, bring 'em to order.'

Bertie produced a whistle from his pocket and blew a loud blast. To no avail. The noise continued unabated. It took three more blasts before there was any semblance of order. 'Now then, take your seats, please,' shouted the compère, red in the face after his vigorous blowing. This produced a scramble for the chairs which were lined against the walls. Since the number of persons present was at least three times that of available seats an impromptu game of 'musical chairs' ensued, with the children running around like headless chickens and the adults trying to find their respective family groups, some carrying chairs at the same time. Eventually the chaos subsided. The children sat on the floor and the men either stood behind their seated spouses or joined the large contingent of standing spectators at the back of the hall.

'Now you all know why we are gathered together here today,' began Bertie. 'This is an important occasion. You can tell that by the fact that we have got our chief citizen and his lady wife in our midst. Let's put our hands together and give them a big welcome.' Not enough hands came together to produce a big welcome. It was more in the nature of a polite gesture of goodwill. 'Now then, not only have we got our Mayor and Mayoress here but on this table is a message from our young Queen. I know she hasn't got her crown yet but she is still our sovereign as she is now, whether she is sitting on the throne or not. In a moment or two I will read it out to you. So then, what is all this fuss about? It's because we are honouring two people who have been together for fifty years.' At this point he broke into song: 'And it don't seem a day too much'. After a cough he carried on. 'Mr and Mrs Davies have lived all their lives in Pontywen. Mr Arthur Davies spent all his working life at the Colliery and was in charge of the pit ponies at one time. Mrs

Edwina Davies. Now there's a lady for you. Everybody in Pontywen knows Edwina. The Labour Party, the Mothers' Union, the Townswomen's Guild, St Padarn's Parochial Church Council. You name it, she's in it and at her age too.' Edwina frowned. 'I'm hoping she'll do her party piece for us later on to show how young in heart she is.' Edwina smiled a thin-lipped smile.

'Heaven preserve us,' whispered my wife.

'I could go on for the rest of the evening telling of all the things she has done for the people of Pontywen but we have a long programme arranged to celebrate this golden wedding.'

By now his audience was getting restive. 'Well, get on with it, Bertie,' shouted someone at the back of the hall.

'So then, without any more ado, I will read out the message from Her Majesty the Queen.' Bertie took the large envelope from the table and extracted the telegram. He made a great show of taking his spectacles from his pocket and placing them on his red nose. He cleared his throat and took a deep breath. "Heartiest congratulations on your golden wedding. Elizabeth R".'

'Is that it?' said Idris the Milk, who was standing near by.

'I now call on his Worship the Mayor to say a few words before he leaves for another engagement further down the valley.'

Alderman William Evans rose to his feet with alacrity, ready to make a quick getaway. 'Mr and Mrs Davies, you have reached a great millstone – er – milestone in your lives. Not many marriages go on as long as yours has done. Yet here you are surrounded by your family and your friends having survived fifty years of being together in the – er – estate of matrimony. I hope you have a happy evening and that you will have many more years of – er – being together. Good night to you all.'

He turned to the Mayoress, who was bestowing a kiss on Edwina's countenance. 'Come on, Annie,' he said to her, 'we're late already. We don't want to keep them waiting at the Chamber of Trade dinner, like we did last week at the Co-op dinner dance.'

'Give them one more clap,' requested Bertie. That is precisely what they had, contributed by me as a solo effort.

Once they had left, the noise reached deafening proportions again, prompting the use of the compère's whistle. When the pandemonium had been reduced to a tolerable level of murmured conversation, Bertie was on his feet. 'Next,' he shouted, 'I will ask the Vicar to say a few words.'

'Another of your occupational hazards,' said Eleanor out of the side of her mouth.

'Mr and Mrs Davies, relatives and friends. I am not going to keep you long,' I began.

'Hear! Hear!' came from several quarters.

'You were married not long after the turn of this century. During that time the world has become a different place. It has shrunk into a globe which aeroplanes can encircle in a matter of days and the wireless in a couple of seconds. For you your world has been one tiny dot on that little globe. Pontywen is that dot but it has been big enough to provide you with a large family and all the love that comes with it. Congratulations to you both and may that love continue to be with you until the end of your days, whatever changes that time will bring. God bless you and keep you.'

No sooner had I finished my 'few words' than there was a concerted dash towards the bar at the side of the hall. Bertie indicated to Eleanor and myself that we should occupy the seats vacated by the Mayor and Mayoress. We looked at each other and acknowledged that we were trapped. We would be unable to emulate the chief citizen and his wife and escape whatever else the evening had to unfold. 'Thank you, Vicar,' said Edwina as I sat beside her. 'That was very nice. Now they will bring the refreshments out on to the tables. We didn't have them brought out before, otherwise the kids would have been eating everything in sight before you could look round. You know what they're like. We'll have the cake cut later on. Perhaps you'll say grace when everything is ready.' Two long tables were set out on either side of the hall, covered with a mixture of lace and plain tablecloths brought from the various homes of the Davies progeny. Soon the daughters and daughters-in-law emerged from the kitchen carrying trays loaded with sandwiches, cakes and trifles.

Whilst I sat and listened to Mrs Davies's non-stop monologue Eleanor was making a vain attempt to engage Arthur in conversation. His contribution to the *tête-à-tête* consisted of monosyllables delivered from a face more appropriate to a funeral than a golden wedding celebration. It was obvious that Edwina had forbidden him to bring his beloved foul-smelling pipe. Add to that deprivation the discomfort of the stiff collar and it was small wonder that he was longing for the return to his armchair. His countenance grew longer by the minute. The din

caused by the shouting and the antics of the excited
children, plus the loud laughter and badinage coming
from the alcoholic contingent around the bar, was reaching an unbearable level. It was a great relief when Alice
the eldest daughter came up to us and announced that the
food was ready.

'Quiet!' bellowed her mother. She had a strong contralto voice which rivalled that of Dame Clara Butt. It
caused more of a hush than the compère's whistle. 'Come
and get your plates filled.' A stampede ensued, led by the
hungry children. Our table was already laden with the
festive fare.

'Help yourselves,' commanded Edwina. 'When you've
done that I'll ask Bertie to get you to say grace, Vicar.'

'I don't think you'll need him, Mrs Davies,' I replied.
'You are much more in charge than he is.'

'You've got to have a compère at the club,' she said.
'He offered his services and I didn't want to offend him.'
I was about to add that Bertie always offered his services
because no one else would ever recommend him but
thought better of it when my wife gave me one of her
reproving looks.

It must have taken at least a quarter of an hour before
Mrs Davies decided to call upon the services of the
compère.

'Now I will call upon the Vicar to say grace. Will you
all stand, please,' he announced in lay-reader tones. Since
most people were standing already and those who were
sitting were trying to balance plates on their laps and
hold a drink at the same time, it caused some confusion
and a few upturned plates of sandwiches.

I attempted to say an impromptu prayer suitable for

the occasion. 'For these thy gifts of food, O Lord, and for all the blessings of this life, especially for those which thou hast bestowed upon these two persons, gathered together here.' I stopped and coughed as I realised that it was impossible for two persons to gather together. '. . . present here, in the midst of their loved ones.' I decided to call it a day. 'Amen,' I said and sat down. I could see that my wife was struggling to stifle an outburst of laughter.

'Thank you, Vicar,' said Edwina. 'That was lovely, wasn't it, Arthur?' He nodded and ate a sandwich. I suppose that as long as he filled his mouth with food, he thought there would be no need for him to speak.

The next item in what Bertie called 'a long programme' was the cutting of the cake. Alice brought to the top table a large iced cake with fifty candles on it. 'She made that herself,' said Edwina, 'and our Liz did the icing. Our Mary bought the candles. They're good girls, aren't they?'

'I must say, they have made a great job of it,' Eleanor replied.

'Liz was up all last night, doing the icing with all those fiddly bits, wasn't she, Alice?'

'Not as long as I was making the cake,' she said petulantly to her mother.

'There you are all three of you getting together to make a wonderful tribute to your mother and father,' I commented, in an effort to keep the peace.

'Let's hope it tastes as good as it looks.' The matriarch's remark evoked a scowl from her eldest.

'Suck it and see,' was her response as she walked away.

'We are now going to light the cake,' Bertie told his

audience. 'We' were Liz and Mary, who advanced upon the work of art with a box of matches each.

'You take that side, Mary,' ordered Liz. After contending with a number of stubborn wicks, eventually all the candles were lit by the sisters, who stood admiring their handiwork.

'Mr and Mrs Davies will now blow out the fifty candles,' shouted Bertie. Edwina's quota was soon extinguished.

'Shall I help,' said Eleanor to Arthur. He nodded with his mouth still half full. She completed his task with myself grateful for deliverance from whatever might be blown in my direction. Everybody clapped and cheered.

'Come on, Mam and Dad, cut the cake, then,' said Liz. 'You've got the knife by there.'

'All right, calm down,' replied her mother. 'I can see where the knife is. Stand up, Arthur, you've got to help me.' Her husband rose reluctantly. 'Put your hand over mine and I'll do the rest.' She pressed the knife firmly into the cake. Once again there were cheers and claps.

'It's a pity the photographer from the *Gazette* isn't here,' Eleanor said.

'He came to the house this morning to take a picture of us with the telegram from the Queen,' Edwina replied. 'I suppose he couldn't come twice. In any case, I expect he's down at that hotel with the Mayor and Mayoress. The Chamber of Trade is more important than a couple of pensioners having a "do" in the Labour Club. The nobs always come first.'

'Raise your glasses and drink to Edwina and Arthur,' said Bertie. Eleanor and I looked at each other as we drank a modicum of sweet British sherry from the thimble glasses provided, grateful that it was confined to a modicum.

When we sat down Edwina said to me, 'Thank you for the grace and your little speech.' She sipped at her sherry. 'It's very nice, isn't it?'

I felt ashamed at the smug way I had looked at my wife, scorning the drink which celebrated the occasion. I remembered my parents, my aunts and my uncles when I was a boy, to whom a Christmas cheap sherry was one of the highlights of the festive season. 'Very nice indeed,' I replied.

'Drink that, Arthur,' said one of his former workmates as he put a pint of beer in front of him. 'You deserve that after fifty years of penal servitude. Sorry, Edwina, only joking.' He departed rapidly, leaving Arthur with a foaming tankard in front of him and a glowering wife beside him. Such was her husband's desperation that he chose to seize the receptacle and empty its contents with barely a pause in the process. For a little man with a restrictive collar it was a most impressive performance.

His wife looked at him as if she were seeing a different person from the one with whom she had shared fifty years of married life. 'You'll be up all night after that, Arthur Davies,' she warned him.

'Do you know what, Edwina?' he replied. 'I think I'll have another one. I enjoyed that.'

'Would you let me buy you another one?' asked Eleanor.

'Thank you, doctor,' he said quickly before his spouse could intervene.

As my wife went to the bar, Edwina said to me, 'Well, Vicar, I hope my husband realises what he is doing. He only rarely drinks except at Christmas and then only a drop of sherry like just now. Perhaps the doctor thinks he is used to drinking.'

'I don't think one more pint will do him any harm, will it, Mr Davies?' I replied.

'I used to drink a lot more than that when I played rugby.' It was the first full sentence Arthur had spoken that evening.

'And a lot of good that did you,' snapped his wife. 'You leave it at one more, "boyo".'

My wife returned with a tray full of drinks. A pint for 'boyo', a sherry for Edwina, and two whiskies for ourselves. 'I hope a sherry is what you want, Mrs Davies,' she said.

'Lovely,' was the reply. 'Thank you, doctor. It's very kind of you. I've been telling Arthur that he mustn't have any more after this. It will go to his head otherwise. You see, he doesn't drink normally.'

'I could see that,' said my wife. 'Still, one more pint won't hurt him.'

At this point in the conversation, Bertie arrived to tell us that he was about to introduce the entertainment. 'Do you want to do your party piece first or later in the programme,' he asked Edwina. 'The pianist has got the music for you.'

'I think I had better do it now before I get too tired,' she said, and made her way from the table to the side of the little stage.

Eleanor came and sat by me. 'What is the betting it is a Clara Butt rendering of "Home Sweet Home"?' she whispered.

In the meanwhile Arthur had swallowed his second

pint. 'We had better move our chairs, Mr Davies, to have a better view,' I suggested.

'You can,' he replied, 'but I see it every Christmas.'

'It doesn't sound like "Home Sweet Home" to me,' I said to my wife.

A few minutes later the compère appeared in front of the curtains. 'Put your hands together and give a big welcome to the Belle of the Ball for this evening, Edwina Davies!' The curtains opened to reveal the lady standing centre stage and acknowledging the applause with a bow.

'Ready!' shouted the pianist.

'Off you go,' she shouted back. He launched into a version of the sailors' hornpipe. Soon the performer was in full swing from climbing the ropes to pulling them but, when she decided to fold her arms and dance with her legs outstretched, with her bottom almost at floor level, Eleanor expressed some alarm.

'Her hip,' she murmured. The alarm was justified. Suddenly Edwina was stretched out on the floor, in agony. The curtain came across and my wife was up on the stage seconds later. There was an apprehensive silence.

'It's her own fault,' said Arthur about his partner of fifty years. 'She's too headstrong, that's her trouble. I told her not to do it but she wouldn't listen.'

When I arrived on the scene, all the Davies family were there, surrounding their mother. 'She has dislocated her hip once again,' said my wife to me. Then she addressed the throng. 'I think it's best that you all go back to your places in the hall. The steward has rung for the ambulance and it should be here before long.'

'Where's Arthur?' demanded the patient. Liz pushed her way through the curtains.

'Dad,' she shouted to her father who was finishing his third pint, with his collar undone and his bow tie dangling down his shirt front, 'Mam wants to see you.'

'I'm coming,' he replied and made his way slowly up the steps to the stage.

'What do you look like, Arthur Davies?' said his wife, her face contorted with pain but with her tongue still razor sharp. 'Liz, do his collar up and put his tie right. I told you not to drink any more. You'd better come with me to the hospital. Then you won't be able to wet your whistle. When you've seen to his collar, Liz, tell Bertie Owen to carry on with the programme once the ambulance has taken me.'

It was not long before the ambulance arrived. They took her out through the side entrance to avoid parading her through the hall. As some Valley news reporter remarked of a funeral, 'The death had cast a gloom over the proceedings.' Despite the best efforts of Bertie to carry on with the programme it was like a performance of *Hamlet* without the Prince.

Eleanor and I made our apologies to the family and left early. As we drove home, I said to her, 'What a dotty thing to do with her hip in that condition!'

'You should have expected that after what you said in your "few words",' she replied.

'What do you mean?' I asked.

'Well, you said that Pontywen was a dot on the globe. In which case everybody who lives in it must be dotty.'

'Very funny, Eleanor.'

'You don't sound amused, Frederick. Never mind, love, at least we have avoided Bertie telling us to put our hands together several more times during the rest of the evening. I am sure he thought he was back in charge of St Padarn's Sunday School.'

'And he made as much of a mess of that as he did of the celebrations tonight.'

'Vicar, you are in a mood. You had better get rid of that by tomorrow. Otherwise your congregation will not know what has hit them.'

'Only playing,' I said.

'You weren't, you know,' she replied, 'but I love you just the same.'

## 6

'It's not going to be a nice morning. I've given you fair warning,' announced Jack the Fish as he arrived on our doorstep. Jack Williams, travelling fishmonger, came once a week to the Vicarage in his ancient van, bringing fresh fish collected early that morning from the trawlers' catches at Swansea Docks. It was always a nostalgic occasion for me. I had spent my boyhood amongst the trawler men and the dockers when we lived in our council house overlooking Swansea Bay. Unfortunately the nostalgia was tempered by the inane rhyming inflicted on his customers by the little man, adorned in his striped apron and sporting his battered straw boater.

'Now what shall it be today? I can offer you some cod or some ray or perhaps a steak of hake.' His beady little eyes looked past me as Eleanor came behind me. 'Ah. The lady of the house, come to assist her reverend spouse.'

'Now then, Jack,' said my wife, 'if you keep on like this you can take your fresh fish back.'

'Very good, Dr Secombe.' His expression made it plain that he thought Eleanor was not in the same league of poets as himself.

'Since my husband will be dining alone for lunch, I should think a small steak of hake will not my pocket break.' This second attempt at verse had a much more appreciative acceptance. 'By the way,' she added, 'I hope your weather forecast is incorrect. I have to drive into the countryside to pick up someone who needs sunshine, not rain.' As she paid him for the fish, he ended the transaction with a typical flourish.

'I know my forecast of coming rain has caused you mental pain. I can only hope my wireless set from which my weather news I get is wrong about the rain, as it is again and again.'

As he drove off up the drive, I said to Eleanor, 'I think he should have his meter examined.'

'I would have said it is his head, Fred.' She burst into laughter. 'See how contagious his rhyming is, if you'll pardon my effort.'

'I'm afraid that is unpardonable by any priest, including your husband,' I replied.

Half an hour later, she was on her way to pick up Bronwen Wentworth-Baxter for their lunch date, leaving me with the task of coping with our two children since it was Marlene's day off. Mrs Watkins was preparing my 'steak of hake' and its garnishments. Elspeth, our baby daughter, had been fed and watered by her mother and was soundly asleep in her cot. David, our three-year-old son, had come with me to the front door to wave goodbye to his mother. He was a sturdy child who had grown out of his habit of trying to eat lumps of coal and of using his head as a hammer against the wall of his bedroom. Eleanor explained that the latter was due to the protracted labour which brought him into the world, caused by the largeness of his head, inherited from his father. I had strict instructions to put him to bed at three o'clock, despite any protestations he might make. I was looking forward to the next few hours in his company. He had ceased to be a baby and had become a little boy who could carry on a conversation.

'What about a game of football, David?' I suggested.

'Yes, please,' he said enthusiastically. 'Can I be the goalie, Dad? I like being the goalie. Don't kick the ball too hard, though.'

'I promise I won't,' I replied. He ran back into the house to get the ball from the play room upstairs. As he did so, the telephone rang. 'Pontywen 342,' I said. I suppose I should have said 'Vicar of Pontywen speaking' or 'Pontywen Vicarage'. For some psychological reason, I preferred to remain anonymous, unlike the porter at St Woolos Hospital in Newport who always picked up the phone and announced that he was 'St Woolos'.

'Is that by chance the Vicar of Pontywen?' inquired a lady whose accent was distinctly transatlantic. The shock of encountering a voice from the New World stunned me into a momentary silence. 'Hello! Are you there?' she continued.

'Yes, indeed. This is the Vicar of Pontywen,' I replied in the best ecclesiastical manner I could manage.

'Vicar, I am Mrs Susannah Price from Austin, Texas and I am over here for a few months taking in Europe and coming back for your wonderful coronation on 2 June.' Before I could explain that it was not mine she launched into a long account of her reason for contacting the Vicar of Pontywen. Apparently her great-grandfather had been a miner at Pontywen Colliery and his son had emigrated to the United States in 1882 to find work in the coal mines of Pennsylvania. She was married to a lawyer who was also of Welsh extraction and they were both 'enjoying a pilgrimage back to their roots,' as she put it.

At this juncture in the conversation, David came into earshot shouting, 'Dad! Come on! I've got the ball.'

I put my hand over the receiver. 'You go out on the lawn and I'll be with you in two ticks,' I told him. 'Excuse me,' I said to her, 'that was my young son wanting me to play football with him.'

'How cute,' she gushed.

'Well, Mrs Price, what can I do for you?' I asked.

'My husband and I are coming to Cardiff next week. He is going to the Rhondda to try to trace his roots and I am coming to Pontywen to trace mine.' It sounded more like a botanical expedition than a pilgrimage. 'I don't want to hold up your little boy's game. Shall I just say that I shall be in Pontywen next Monday and I should like to have a look at your church registers and the tombstones in your church cemetery some time in the afternoon, if it is convenient.'

'By all means,' I replied. 'Shall we say three thirty?'

'OK by me,' she said, 'and thank you for all your help. See you Monday, Vicar.'

I put the phone down and turned to face David who was looking at me with his large white football clasped against his stomach. 'Come on then, Dad,' he demanded. 'Mrs Watkins says we mustn't be too long because dinner will be ready soon.'

'In that case,' I said, 'we had better get cracking, otherwise she'll be giving us a row and we don't want that, do we?' He shook his head.

We moved out on the balcony with David hugging the football to his chest. 'Come on then,' I shouted, 'throw me the ball.'

'I'm not ready yet,' said my son. 'I've got to go and get my gloves.'

On the few occasions I had taken him to see Pontywen United play in the local league, Dai Phillips, the goal-keeper, the younger son of Phillips the Grocer, always wore gloves and made a great show of adjusting them every five minutes or so. While I waited for him to come back with his gloves, there was a click as the Vicarage gates were opened and Emlyn Howells, my curate, came down the drive. His normal high colour had intensified into a deep puce.

As he walked across the lawn to me, I could see that his breathing was causing him distress. 'Vicar,' he gasped. 'Sorry to trouble you, but I have just been in the vestry to write in the details for tomorrow's wedding and the safe has gone. What's more, the carpet down the aisle has disappeared with it.'

There had been only one 'break in' since I came to the parish eight years ago and that was at the tin church of St Padarn's, perpetrated by two young boys from the local council estate – a piece of juvenile bravado. Evidently this was much more sinister and much more brazen. The church adjoined the Vicarage and I had been in the church for morning service at eight o'clock, accompanied by my curate. Four hours later, despite my living next door to the church, thieves had managed to carry away a very heavy safe and a long length of carpet in full daylight without anyone being aware of what had happened. By now David had appeared, wearing his winter gloves, and still carrying his beloved football. 'Ready, Dad?' he asked.

Emlyn and I rushed into the Vicarage, leaving my son bewildered on the lawn. I dialled '999' and waited impatiently for the answer. 'Your local constable will be there shortly. The CID will be along later on.'

'Would you mind playing football with David while I go and see for myself what has happened?' I asked the curate. 'By the way, you have to dribble with the ball and then shoot, gently, of course, at the goalkeeper.'

'He won't have any trouble saving the ball. I'm the world's worst footballer,' he replied. 'Not only that, I'm out of breath.'

When I entered the church it was quite a shock to see the bare stone floor of the aisle. The expensive red carpet had been a gift to celebrate the centenary of the church. Inside the safe were the solid silver chalice, paten and flagon presented to the church at its opening one hundred and four years ago. So, too, were the church registers covering that period. Since I always kept the church open for private prayer during the daylight hours, and the vestry door had no lock, it would be a simple exercise to remove the safe. The patch of wall against which it had reposed displayed a lack of paint and a plethora of ancient webs long vacated by the spiders.

As I waited for Will Book and Pencil, PC William Davies, the local constable, I remembered the phone call of earlier that morning and the lady from Austin, Texas, who was due to inspect the registers on Monday afternoon. My musings were interrupted by heavy footsteps down the stone floor accompanied by much puffing and blowing, heralding the arrival of the strong arm of law. Six foot tall and solidly built, he was a formidable figure but whose physical stature was not commensurate with his mental capacity.

'You haven't touched anything, have you, Vicar?' he said, as he came through the door of the vestry.

'There is nothing for me to touch,' I replied. 'The

vestry door was open and so was the door at the west end. What amazes me is how they were able to carry that very heavy safe out of the church.'

He pondered that problem for a while. 'Perhaps the safe wasn't all that heavy and if you had two strong men they would be able to carry it. Mind, they wouldn't be able to carry it down the street without being detected. So they must have had some kind of van to take it away.' He produced his famous note book from his pocket and then his pencil from inside his jacket. 'Do you mind if I sit down, Vicar?' he inquired and then moved a chair beside the desk.

'Excuse me saying this, PC Davies,' I said to him, 'but shouldn't you have avoided touching that chair in case there were fingerprints on it?'

'Oh, I doubt if they would touch the chair; they wouldn't need to do that. I'm more concerned about fingerprints on the door handles. Now then, do you keep the church locked?'

'No, Constable. I have always believed that the church should be open to anyone who wishes to come in and say their private prayers. A number of people have told me how grateful they were to come into the quiet and sanctity in times of personal distress. Others just want to sit down and get away from it all, without saying any prayer. My predecessors kept the church open for that purpose and I intend to follow their example.'

He pursed his lips and then looked me in the eye. 'In that case, Vicar, you can't say anything if the place gets burgled. It's an invitation to any crook who happens to be around. Well, I tell you what, if you are going to leave the church open, the least you can do is to see that the vestry is locked up. I know it is like locking the stable door after the horse has bolted, but there you are. Now then, Vicar, what were the contents of the safe.' Laboriously he took down all the details about the safe and the carpet. Then he said, 'The boys from the CID will be here before long. In the meantime, I'll go and make inquiries around the houses in Church Street to see if they noticed anything suspicious. I shouldn't be surprised if somebody or other has seen something.'

I sat down in my seat in the chancel and stared at the table on the wall opposite. 'To the glory of God and in memory of Joseph Lloyd Morgan, Vicar of Pontywen 1871 to 1898. A faithful pastor and a friend of the fatherless and widows.' How many fatherless and widows were the price paid to King Coal, I wondered. What is more, how would Joseph Lloyd Morgan react if he were in my shoes? Would he consider that the loss of a safe and a carpet were a price worth paying to provide a place of prayer for those who needed it? I could almost hear him saying, 'Don't let a couple of thieves shut down your church, my boy. The Holy Communion does not depend upon the quality of silver. It is simply the giving of consecrated bread and wine, just as valid if it comes from an ordinary plate and a cup as it would be from the most valuable of antique silver.'

Before I could congratulate myself further on my policy of an open church, the two plain clothes men of the CID entered the church. I came out of my stall and went to meet them as they came down the aisle, instantly recognisable by their height and their feet. They were younger than 'Will Book and Pencil' and seemed to be more intelligent.

'I am Detective Sergeant Wilcox,' said the red-faced corpulent one of the duo, 'and this is my colleague, Detective Constable Pugh.' The junior member of the partnership was taller but considerably thinner. As a choreographer at a weekend drama school I attended in the Valley once informed us, people can be divided into balls and pins. Sergeant Wilcox was decidedly a large ball while Detective Pugh would have made an excellent Cleopatra's Needle.

'So, you've had a little bit of trouble, Vicar.' The detective sergeant made it sound as if someone had walked off with a hymn book.

'More than a little bit, I would say,' I replied. 'That safe contained valuable silver Communion vessels and all the registers dating back more than a hundred years. The carpet can be replaced but not the contents of the safe.'

'Obviously a professional job. We'll get our fingerprint man out here but I should think they would have used gloves in any case. It was the silver they were after and just took your nice carpet as a bonus. I take it that you leave the church open.'

'Yes, I feel it should always be there as a place of comfort for anybody who needs it.'

'And a place of profit for any thief,' said Detective Pugh.

His colleague ignored that remark and proceeded with his interrogation. 'When were you last in the church?'

'My curate and I were here at eight o'clock this morning for our daily service.'

'When was the theft discovered?'

'The curate went to the church about twelve o'clock to fill in details for a wedding tomorrow. He came to tell me and I dialled 999 immediately. What amazes me,' I said, 'was how they could remove such a heavy safe.'

'Easy,' he replied. 'They probably used a trolley. With a van outside and a ramp to wheel the trolley, the whole operation would be over in a matter of minutes. Now then, has there been any publicity at all about your valuable church silver?'

'Not that I know of, Sergeant. I think there was a mention of it when we celebrated our centenary four years ago but nothing since then. I do mention it in the little guide I have written for visitors to the church, not that we have many in Pontywen.'

'May I see it, Vicar?' he asked.

I took him down to the shelves at the back of the church where we kept copies of the parish magazine on the ledge over the rows of hymn books and prayer books. He thumbed through the few pages of the guide. In it I had written, 'The only treasures in this parish church are the elaborate chalice paten and flagon in sterling silver presented by Sir David Jones-Williams, in 1849.'

'Well, Vicar,' said the detective, 'unless they are securely protected, it is an open invitation to any thief to take them. In the years to come, if churches are going to look after their treasures they will have to take adequate safeguards to protect them. In other words, if you don't mind me saying so, you are asking for trouble. There's a big wide world outside and the people in it are not like those inside a church. As you can see from what has happened here.'

As we spoke, Will Book and Pencil made a noisy entrance, looking very pleased with himself and producing his beloved note book from his pocket excitedly in his

progress down the aisle. 'I've just come from number 4, Church Street, where somebody witnessed the robbery, without realising that it was one,' he announced when he came up to us. 'Mrs Myfanwy Hopkins said that when she was making the bed in the front room, she happened to look out of the window. She saw two men in white coats pulling a trolley down the church path, with a large object on it, covered by what looked like some kind of carpet. They opened the back of a white van which was outside. One of them bent into it and pulled out some kind of metal support. They then pushed the trolley up it, closed the door and went off. I asked her what they looked like. She said that one was about thirty, short and fair haired and the other was older, about forty, with a dark moustache and dark hair. He was bigger than the other one. She thought it was somebody doing repair work in the church. I asked her what time it was when she saw them. She said she thought it must have been about ten thirty since that was the time she always made the beds. Nobody else in the street had noticed anything.' He put his notebook in his pocket with an air of achievement.

'Thank you, Will. That confirms what I thought had happened,' said the senior detective. 'I am afraid, Vicar, that you will not see your valuable silver again. By tomorrow, it will probably have been melted down somewhere. On the other hand, I shouldn't be surprised if your registers turn up somewhere in the vicinity of Pontywen in the next day or so. Let's hope they will not be exposed to the elements for too long. I am afraid there is not much more we can do at the moment. We shall let you know immediately if we find anything.' He shook hands with me and went off briskly accompanied by his lanky colleague who managed to catch him up by the church door.

'I'd better be getting off, too,' said Will Book and Pencil. 'Sorry about this, Vicar, but that's how it goes. I'll have a look round down the dell later on. It's surprising what you can find down there sometimes.' The 'dell' was a little wooded ravine on the outskirts of the town, frequented by courting couples and those who wished to dispose of unwanted items of household equipment.

When I left the church, I did something I had never done before. I locked it. The thought of the house of God being open to desecration suddenly made me feel guilty of dereliction. 'What I shall do,' I said to myself, 'is to put up a notice outside the church informing anyone who wishes to use the building for private prayer or meditation they could obtain the key from the Vicarage.' If I was not at home, there was always Eleanor or Mrs Watkins available.

To my surprise, I found Emlyn Howells and David still engaged in a game of football on the lawn. 'This is a long game,' I said.

'To be honest,' replied the curate, 'we have only just restarted after half time when Mrs Watkins brought us some pop and a biscuit.'

'I've saved all the goals, Dad,' said my son proudly.

'They need him in the Welsh team against England next week,' gasped Emlyn, as he ran to secure the ball David had thrown into the rose bushes.

'Dinner's ready,' shouted Mrs Watkins, as she saw us on the lawn.

'I don't want any, Dad,' said David.

'I should think not, too,' chided our domestic help. 'You've already had your pop and biscuits. This is for your father.'

'What do the police say,' asked Emlyn, clutching the football.

'Apparently the theft is the work of professionals and it is extremely doubtful if we shall recover the Communion set. However, the detectives said that it is most likely that we shall be able to get the registers back, discarded somewhere after the safe had been broken open. Will Book and Pencil is going to search the dell to see what he can find.'

'Let's hope he can do that by tomorrow. How on earth

can the marriage take place tomorrow if there is no marriage register?' the curate enquired. 'There has to be some kind of official form to be signed.'

'I think the first thing I have to do is to phone David Fitzgerald to get his advice. There must be some kind of procedure in a case like this. When I have done that I had better have my dinner before Mrs Watkins gets at me.' The diocesan register was very helpful. He told me to use the return forms which came every quarter from the local register office. Then, if the registers were recovered, the bride and groom and the two witnesses would have to come back and sign them. Otherwise, the signatures would have to be made in the new registers.

Our domestic help was looking disgruntled when I went into the kitchen for my meal. 'Your dinner's not very warm. I would have put it in the oven if I had known you was going to go on that old phone again.' No sooner had I tasted my first mouthful of hake than there was a ring on the doorbell. Mrs Watkins exploded, 'You carry on, Vicar. I'll go to the door. I'll tell them you are having your dinner.' She stamped out of the room with David at her heels. She was back in an instant. 'It's Will Book and Pencil with those books that have been stolen. I'd better put your dinner in the oven.'

'You had, indeed,' I shouted joyfully as I jumped to my feet. 'Come on in PC, Davies. What an angel of mercy you are!' I effused. The constables's cup of self-satisfaction was overflowing at his second triumph of detection that morning. He put down the registers on my desk.

'There you are, Vicar, intact as far as I can see. It's a good job it's dry today. They were out in the open, alongside your safe down in the dell. They had bashed in the back of the safe and the Communion cup and plate and flagon have gone of course. Anyway you've got your registers back. Well, if you don't mind I'll be on my way. If you don't mind me saying so once again, you'll have to start locking the church up if you want to look after the contents. Next time it could be the candlesticks and the cross.' He strode up the drive with the jauntiness of a man of achievement, a Sherlock Holmes with yet another case solved.

When Eleanor returned from her lunch with Bronwen a few hours later, she was looking unusually serious.

'You have missed all the excitement, love,' I said as she came through the door.

'I could do with some exciting news after all the tale of woe I have been hearing. Tell me your story and then I'll tell you mine,' she replied and then listened to my account of the brazen theft and of Will Book and Pencil's starring role in the thriller. 'So the church is minus its valuable silver and its expensive carpet but our local constable has retrieved the left-overs,' she commented.

'Oh! be fair,' I replied. 'They are not just left-overs. All the history of Pontywen church is contained in these registers – all the baptisms, the marriages and the details of every service that has taken place within its hallowed walls.'

'My! we are waxing poetic, aren't we? Well, I wish that I could be as poetic about all the stories I have heard about your erstwhile colleague,' she said in acid tones. It was not like Eleanor to be so bitter.

'I think you had better tell me what you have heard from Bronwen. Evidently it is not exactly the happiest of sagas.' We were sitting together on the settee in the lounge. I put my hand on top of hers and clutched it tightly. For a while she said nothing and then, after a deep breath, she began.

'Charles Wentworth-Baxter is a lazy, self-indulgent brute and I mean brute, Fred, a brute. That poor girl has had to put up with verbal and occasionally physical abuse. Apparently he has forced his attentions upon her as soon as he could after each child has been born. He has not hit her but he has gripped her by the arms in some of his rages. The bruises are still evident. He has forbidden her to get in touch with her mother because he says that she will only cause trouble since she is a strict Baptist and did not want her to marry him in the first place. He has hit little Llewellyn across the face, leaving marks there for hours afterwards. He is very rarely in the house and when he does come home he expects a meal to be ready for him instantly. That girl is going through hell, Fred.'

She began to cry. I put my arms around her and cuddled her. 'As a doctor,' she said, 'I should be able to look at their domestic scene dispassionately but I can't. We know them too intimately. What can we do, Fred? If something is not done soon, she will either put a carving knife into him or, if she is wise, she will take the children with her and take refuge with her mother. Either way it is the end of their marriage.'

We sat in silence for a while. 'There are two alternatives,' I replied. 'The first is that I confront the lion in his den. I have done that already – not in his den, admittedly. I am sure that will be counter-productive. The other is that I should get in touch with the Bishop and let him know what is happening in Penglais Vicarage. I think that is the only way to approach this. The Bishop knows Charles and all his deficiencies. I hope that he will deliver him an ultimatum. If Charles does not comply then he will have to leave Penglais and his family. I am sure her mother will take her back but with an attitude of 'I told you so'. At least she will have some comfort from her father who loves her and has the distinct advantage of being a sensible person and a non-strict Baptist.'

We decided that this was the best course to follow and that I should ring the Bishop the next morning. When I went to church for service the following day I was able to assure Emlyn Howells that he could proceed with the wedding that afternoon without any difficulty. 'I must say,' he told me, 'I take my hat off to Will Book and Pencil for that piece of detection. It is not often he gets an accolade for anything.'

'Oh, he is quite proud of it,' I replied. 'He left the Vicarage yesterday afternoon with all the aplomb of a Sexton Blake or Sherlock Holmes. By the way, I think it wiser to keep the church locked as from now on. I shall get you a key made. Now we have to buy a new safe, a new Communion set and a new carpet for the aisle. I wonder if our transatlantic visitor will be able to help in this direction.'

'Who is that?' he enquired. When I told him, he said, 'If this is any encouragement, Vicar, a lady from Chicago whose ancestors were buried in the churchyard of my last parish paid for the renovation of the organ and the rebuilding of the churchyard wall.'

'Emlyn, you are a tower of strength to your Vicar,' I replied. 'I only wish you could have come as a curate before Charles Wentworth-Baxter was foisted upon the parish. It would have saved me, the parish and his wife and children a great deal of aggravation.

When I went back to the Vicarage, Eleanor was on the phone, looking very agitated. 'I'll be with you in half an hour,' she said, and rang off. 'That was Bronwen. There was quite a scene after I dropped her off at the Vicarage. Charles accused her of letting us try to run her life. Then this morning things erupted once again. Only this time he turned violent and gave her a black eye. He stormed out, got into the car and drove off. She is getting the children ready to take them to her mother. Since she hasn't any transport, she has asked me to pick them up. What a mess! Her mother hasn't a phone so she has rung her aunt who lives a few doors away. Mrs Williams is going to have quite a shock because Bronwen has told her nothing of what has been happening.'

A few minutes later, she was in her car. She wound down the window. 'Sorry to leave you with the children once again. Marlene should be along soon anyway. Keep your fingers crossed that our friend Charles has not returned by the time I get there.' Then she was up the drive, ploughing up the gravel as she shot off from the starting mark, leaving my call to the Bishop in abeyance. As Will Book and Pencil had said about the need for ensuring that the theft in the church would not be repeated, it would be like locking up the stable door after the horse had bolted.

## 7

She was a short, corpulent, ageing, peroxide blond with an expensive coiffure, and even more expensive outfit which was fighting a losing battle with her figure. The taxi driver who had driven her from Cardiff General station asked me if I could recommend a good café for 'something to eat' while he waited to transport his fare back to the capital city. His face gave the happy expression of a man who had struck oil, as he left his cab to walk to Cascarini's in Pontywen Square.

Mrs Susannah Price of Austin, Texas arrived at the Vicarage punctually at the appointed time of 3.30 p.m. As the taxi driver walked up the drive she stood on the doorstep, admiring the lawn and the rose bushes, which had come into flower only recently. 'You certainly live in a green and pleasant land, as your poet says,' she commented.

Eleanor said afterwards, 'Perhaps she thinks that Wales is just a province of England, in which case we could claim Blake as one of our bards.'

'Where is your little boy?' asked our visitor when she came into the lounge. 'He sounded so cute asking you to play football when you were on the phone.'

'He's in bed,' replied my wife. 'David is only three and needs his afternoon sleep.'

'Have you any other children?'

'One daughter, Elspeth. She is only six months old and

is also aloft. This is what we call our breathing space, an hour or so's peace before it is disrupted once again. Still, they are both good children, if you count a six-month-old as a child.'

'My three children are well past that stage in their lives. In fact one of them has a baby daughter of her own. She certainly should know how to look after her. Isabel is a doctor in Houston. What's more, her husband is a paediatrician in the biggest hospital in Texas. So between them they should be able to give Sarah Louise the best possible start in life, I guess.' Mrs Price preened herself in such an ostentatious fashion that I could see Eleanor's face showing signs of instant irritation. My hope of overseas aid for the replacement of the safe and the carpet began to fade.

'Well, Mrs Price,' replied my wife, 'I am afraid my husband is no top paediatrician but I am a doctor like your daughter. Since my husband is a Vicar, between us we should be able to give our children the best possible start in life, the one to care for their souls and the other to care for their bodies. Would you like a cup of tea before you do your research into your ancestry?' To my great relief, the irony of my wife's reply passed unnoticed.

'I sure would like some of your excellent English tea but with no milk, please. I am allergic to milk.'

'Are you allergic to sugar?' inquired Eleanor.

'Only as far as my weight is concerned, Mrs Secombe. In other words, one teaspoonful of sugar would be just fine.'

When my wife went out to make the tea, I came into the conversation for the first time. 'How quaint, Vicar, that you are married to a doctor. Does she still practise her medicine? My daughter has given that up for the next four or five years at least, according to her schedule. They are planning another child in two years' time.'

'Eleanor has cut down on her commitments at the surgery and is a part-time practitioner at the moment. She is fortunate to have an excellent colleague whose work rate is phenomenal. However, she is hoping to be more active in the practice in a year or so's time. We have a very reliable nursemaid.'

'Do you have any other help in your Vicarage? It must be a great strain on your lovely wife to run a home and be involved in your parochial duties, if you'll pardon me saying so. I am an Episcopalian and I know how much our rector's wife has to do back home, being part of the prayer groups, the social committee and all that jazz.'

By now Mrs Susannah Price's inquisitional attitude was beginning to penetrate what Eleanor called my 'shell of clerical politeness'. I wondered how long it would be before I joined Eleanor in an aversion to our visitor.

'We have a treasure in Mrs Watkins, our part-time housekeeper, who is only too pleased to assist her part-time employee in running a well-organised household. Neither the parish nor its parish priest are the worse for the presence of a doctor in the Vicarage. I am sure the congregationers in Pontywen would testify to that.'

At this stage in the conversation my wife came into the room with a tea tray laden with our best china and a plate of biscuits. 'Your husband has just been telling me how well you have been able to schedule all your duties in what must be a very busy life. You are sure lucky to have such useful people at your elbow.'

As she put down the tray on the table, Eleanor replied,

'Without seeming to be big headed, that was not luck but was due to our unerring selective judgement. Would you like your tea weak, medium or strong?'

'Weak, please,' she replied. 'Anything more would upset my stomach. My daughter says I must keep a strict watch on my digestion. The slightest miscalculation could cause a reaction. I have a very delicate constitution.' My wife looked at me and I found it difficult to control an overwhelming desire to burst into mirth.

'It is a good thing you have come today and not a few days earlier, Mrs Price,' I said. 'Otherwise there would have been no registers for you to look at. We have had a daylight robbery at the church in the course of which the safe in the vestry and the carpet down the aisle were stolen.'

Her eyes and her mouth opened wide. 'You don't say! I would never have believed it in a place like this. We are used to hearing about robberies in the big cities in the USA though there are not many thefts in Austin. It is the capital city of Texas and very law abiding. So how come your registers are here for me to inspect?'

'Our local constable, commonly known as Will Book and Pencil, found the safe broken open and minus our valuable church silver but with the registers intact strewn alongside it. Fortunately the weather had been kind and no rain had fallen to damage the records. They are in my study, immaculate and ready for your perusal. You did not give me any details of your great-grandfather, otherwise I could have done some research before you arrived. In any case, it will not take long to trace your ancestry.'

'My!' she said. 'To think I could have come all this way to find out about my family roots and then to hear that everything had been destroyed. I sure am grateful to your Will Book and Pencil, as you call him, for his help. Do you think I could give him something to show my gratitude?'

'I am afraid,' I replied, 'that you would not be allowed to do that. As it would be said officially, it was all in the course of his duty. The great thing is that the church is once again in possession of its historic records, even if it is missing a safe at the moment. What is distressing is the loss of its priceless silver chalice, paten and flagon given to St Mary's by the forebears of Sir David Jones-Williams who were responsible for the building of this church. The carpet is easily replaced but not the silver.'

By the time I had finished my shameless, indirect appeal to the Texan pocket I received one of Eleanor's disapproving glances. However, the effect it had on Mrs Price was most encouraging. 'I hope you don't mind, Reverend Secombe,' she said, 'but I should sure like to help towards buying some of the best silver you can get for your new Communion set. Perhaps we could talk about it when we have had a look at your registers. I just can't wait to see them.'

After the tea and biscuits, I ushered our visitor into my study for the search into her Pontywen 'roots'.

'What a fine lot of books you have here,' she remarked. 'When do you get time to read in a busy life like yours?'

'I have not read them all by any means,' I replied. 'Most of them are here for reference rather than reading for pleasure. Now then, let's begin at the beginning, which is the best way to start, I suppose.' My attempt at humour passed unnoticed.

'I guess so,' she said. 'So where are the wonderful registers I have come to see. To think that I might be seeing the handwriting of my ancestors, perhaps.'

'Only if it is in a marriage register, of course, not if it is a baptism or a funeral.' Once again my schoolboy witticism failed to find the target. It was met with a dead-pan face.

'I guess not,' she replied.

'What was your maiden name, Mrs Price?' I enquired.

'My what?' she exclaimed.

'What was your name before you were married?'

'It is a strange name – Cadwallader.'

'That is not strange in Wales. It is another form of Caractacus, the famous King of the Celtic people in Mid Wales, a man who fought the Romans, a great hero of the Welsh.'

She looked at me in wide-eyed astonishment. 'You mean, I am descended from a famous King?'

'Well, it may be so. There must be thousands of Cadwalladers in Wales. The sexton at our sister church, St Illtyd's, is a Cadwallader. Perhaps you are related to him.'

'What do you mean by "sexton", Vicar?'

'He is the grave-digger.'

Her face fell. To be related to the equivalent of Hamlet was something wonderful, to be related to his grave-digger was not in the same category. It was evident that she had no intention of tracing any kinship with Tom but at least she could go back to Texas and trumpet the claim that buried in the distant past there was a royal ancestor.

'Well, what do you know?' she murmured. 'Wait till I get back home and tell the folks that I have royal blood in my veins.' When we found the first Cadwallader in the marriage registers it was in the year 1851. David William Cadwallader, collier, married Emily Elizabeth Davies, domestic servant. He was twenty-two years of age and she was seventeen. They had nine children recorded in the baptismal register and three recorded in the burial register in infancy. The fourth son, Albert Edward, baptised 20 May 1857, was the great-grandfather Susannah had come to trace. She clapped her hands as soon as she saw his name. David William died at the age of thirty-seven. Albert Edward, collier, married Agnes May Thomas, laundress, on 30 June 1880 and two years later set sail for Pennsylvania. Mrs Price recorded each entry meticulously in a notebook she had brought with her. By the time she had finished, her cup of happiness was running over. To discover her roots was one thing. To find they went back to Roman times and to a king was something else. I could imagine the éclat in Texas which would greet the revelation of her ancestry.

I took her for a tour of St Mary's, Pontywen, with its tasteless Victorian glass in the east window donated by the Jones-Williams family and with little else to offer. The bare stone floor of the aisle added to the uninspiring aspect of the church. However, Mrs Price seemed to find it attractive. 'I love these old churches,' she said. Back at the Vicarage, she drew a cheque book out of her handbag. 'This is in dollars,' she said, 'but I am sure your bank can translate it into your money. It is just a big thank you for all your kindness and help.' She proceeded to write out a cheque for a thousand dollars. 'Now, I think I had better go. I am due to meet my husband in Cardiff at six o'clock. I bet he hasn't had the luck I've had in finding my roots.'

As she waved goodbye, going down the drive in her taxi, Eleanor said, 'There goes your fairy godmother. Heaven knows, you worked hard enough to make her one. It reminded me of a story I once read about an American benefactor who had been responsible for the renovation of an ancient parish church. He came back for the re-dedication service and when the Vicar gave thanks during the service for "this unexpected succour", the bene-factor got up and walked out of the church in high indignation. I hope you will rephrase your thanksgiving if you are thinking of inviting her back for something similar.'

'I noticed you looking at me when I was letting her know how impoverished we were in Pontywen,' I replied.

'What is more I must admit to a feeling of guilt about my unwarranted imposition on her generosity.'

'Unwarranted imposition, my foot. I thought you exploited her kindness to the 'nth degree, Secombe. She may have been gullible but she was a good Christian lady who would help anyone in need. I happen to think you exaggerated the extent of St Mary's need far beyond what was required.'

'Before you say any more, my sweet,' I said, 'who sprayed her with sarcastic remarks? I know they went over her head, fortunately, but none the less they are hardly in accord with your description of her as a good Christian lady!'

'Touché,' admitted my wife. 'I suppose I should have made allowances for the Texan tendency to have the biggest and the best of everything and to show an inordinate amount of interest in other people's affairs. She is still a good Christian lady for all that.'

When I handed the cheque to David Vaughan-Jenkins, bank manager-cum-churchwarden, he whistled his astonishment at the amount. 'What with the money from the insurance plus this donation, St Mary's will be much better off than before the theft,' he remarked.

'That's exactly what my wife said,' I replied. 'She felt I had taken Mrs Susannah Price for a ride.'

'Knowing you, Vicar, I am sure you did no such thing, but whatever you did, I can tell you that the congregation will appreciate this boost to their finances. By the way, you will be pleased to know that we have purchased a twenty-four-inch television set, large enough to provide a view of the coronation for about a dozen members of the congregation in our lounge. I suppose that before long we had better begin to make out a list of viewers for the great day. What a headache that is going to be!'

This became apparent at the meeting of the coronation committee later that evening. After reports from those responsible for the various activities being organised as part of the celebrations, Idris the Milk raised the matter of the television audience. 'As you know, Vicar,' he said, 'we have nearly two hundred in the electoral roll of the parish and an average congregation per Sunday in the two churches of about a hundred and twenty. How on earth are we going to decide on who are going to watch the coronation in the respective houses which have got sets? I know we can all listen to the service on the wireless, but that's not the same as seeing it, is it?'

I sent up an urgent prayer for guidance and then launched into the deep. 'First of all, we must be very grateful to Mr and Mrs Vaughan-Jenkins and to Mr and Mrs Nicholls for their kindness in inviting members of the congregation to join them in viewing the great events of next 2 June. If the Vicarage was big enough I would gladly invite all our church people to come to see the coronation. As things are, that is impossible; I am sure that nobody thinks that they have a right to watch it on television. Many families will want to be together and listen to it on their wireless sets. Not all that long ago, they would not have been able to do that, so let's get matters in perspective.

'I think the emphasis must be on the family. Talking of rights, the children have as much right to be in on the occasion as the grown ups. It is *their* future which will be bound up with what is going to happen on Coronation Day. As far as I can make out, there will be provision for about fifty people at most to view the proceedings, so let me put it this way, how many of the congregation would be willing to leave their families to come and watch it without their children?'

There was what might be termed a pregnant pause as the committee considered my emphasis on the family. Inevitably it was Idris who was the first to speak. 'Thank you, Vicar, for bringing us back to earth. Isn't it strange how selfish we can become. Never mind the kids, let's get in on the act ourselves.'

Then David Vaughan-Jenkins was on his feet. 'As one who is to be host to twelve viewers, I echo the Vicar's sentiment in wishing that I could give hospitality to ten times that number. As that is impossible, might I suggest that we put up a list in both of the churches, limiting the number of – er – applicants, as it were, to two from each family. Further, might I suggest that the Vicar writes an article in next month's magazine based on what he has said here tonight.' This was greeted with a number of grunted 'Hear! Hear!s' and silence from the rest of the congregation. It was obvious that the advent of television in Pontywen was going to sow the seeds of discontent in our two churches.

'Thank you for those suggestions, Mr Vaughan-Jenkins,' I said. 'I shall be writing about the televising of the coronation in any case. As for the placing of a list on the noticeboard of each church, I think that is an excellent idea. However, I think it would be wise to delay that until I have written my article in the magazine and addressed both congregations on the matter. In the meanwhile let us get on with our preparations for the celebrations after the coronation is over. There is more than enough to keep us occupied, what with organising the tea in the church hall, the purchase of mugs for the children, the Punch and Judy show, the concert, the dance and so on. So let's get our priorities right.'

When I went back to the Vicarage and told Eleanor of what had happened, she said. 'What a devious man you are! Earlier today you extracted a thousand dollars from the Texan lady and now you have used the children as pawns in your attempt to avoid blood letting over the television problem – but I must say, Frederick, I take my hat off to you. I don't think any of the clergy in this neck of the wood would have been able to rise to the occasion like you.' She kissed me lightly on the cheek. 'Now then, my dear, you have another problem to solve. While you were engaged in your tactical manoeuvres in the church hall, I had a telephone call from our mutual friend and pain in the neck, Charles Wentworth-Baxter. He is begging you to go to Bronwen and plead on his behalf for her return to the matrimonial home. I told him in no uncertain terms what I thought of him and that he had a nerve to ask you to intervene in what is essentially their own private affair. According to him he has turned over a new leaf. I told him he had turned over so many new leaves that he has gone through the whole book already. He is terrified that the Bishop will get to hear of what has happened and that he will be suspended from the living. I said I would tell you about his call when you came in.'

'Oh, no!' I exclaimed.

'Oh, yes!' she replied.

'I can't possibly talk to him tonight; my head is in a whirl. How can I go to that poor girl and ask her to return to a husband who has physically abused her and even ill treated one of his children. I'll sleep on it and give him a ring in the morning.' I put my arms around her and hugged her.

'I think you are being very wise, my love,' she said. 'Let him stew in his own juice until the morning. I hope he doesn't have a single minute's sleep. He doesn't deserve a second, let alone a minute.'

No sooner had she said that than the telephone rang. 'Sorry, Fred,' murmured my wife, 'but it's that man again.'

I picked up the receiver. 'Hello!' I snapped.

'Fred, thank God it's you. Has Eleanor told you I phoned?' He sounded like a man at the end of his tether. His voice was shrill and unnatural.

'She has indeed, Charles. I have only just come in from a committee meeting.'

Before I could say anything more he broke down and began wailing. 'I'm sorry, Fred. I've been a fool, a big fool. I don't deserve her, she's far too good for me. If she doesn't come back I'll do away with myself. I will, I tell you that. It's only now I realise how much I love her and how much I have hurt her.'

'Hurt her,' I shouted. 'You have hurt her body as well as her soul. Now you want me to ask her back to be hurt all over again. Look, Charles. How much is this repentance due to your fear that the Bishop will have it in for you if he finds out what you have done to her. How much is due to genuine regret that you could have been such a callous brute.'

The wailing continued, 'I know I have been beastly to her but I miss her so much as well as the children.'

'They have only been away for a day or so, Charles.

You haven't had time to miss her much and if you think I am going to her mother's place to ask her to come back to you, you are very much mistaken. You go and do it for yourself. I have done enough hauling you out of trouble in the past. It's time that you stood on your own two feet. Goodnight.' I slammed the phone down.

'Good for you,' said Eleanor. 'Let's get to bed.'

We went to bed but I could not sleep; my mind was in a turmoil. I kept thinking of my former curate's threats to do away with himself. If he did that, would I be partly to blame because I refused to help him, I asked myself. When I did sleep, I was plagued with dreams, culminating with me finding Charles with his head in a gas oven. I awoke in a cold sweat and sat up suddenly, waking Eleanor in the process.

'What's the matter, love?' she asked drowsily.

'I've just had a horrible dream. I found Charles with his head in a gas oven.'

'No such luck,' she replied and turned over on her side.

The dream was so vivid that I could not get back to sleep. I was glad when the day dawned and Eleanor got up to feed the baby. As she sat beside me in bed cradling Elspeth in her arms, she said, 'You've had a disturbed night.'

'I can't get Charles out of my mind after that awful dream,' I replied.

'What dream?' she asked.

'I told you that I had found him with his head in a gas oven and you said "No such luck" and went back to sleep.'

'I don't remember that, love. Anyway they are still my sentiments. Bronwen and the kids would be far better off

540

without him. That man is a menace. He is one leopard who will never change his spots. If you are worried about the gas oven dream, don't forget they haven't any gas in Penglais. Secondly, if they did Charles would bungle his suicide attempt. Thirdly, he would never have the nerve to do anything of that nature anyway. He likes his own life too much to do that. You have wasted some precious sleep, Frederick. What about a nice cup of tea, then? I don't see why the baby should be the only one to get some light refreshment.'

When I went across to the church to open up for morning service I was surprised to see Miss Harding, the headmistress of the Infant School in Pontywen. A large lady, in height and weight, with a booming voice, she was a member of the congregation at St Padarn's. As she was not a regular worshipper there her presence at daily Matins in the church which normally consisted of a dialogue between Vicar and Curate was unexpected, to say the least. She was in earnest conversation with Emlyn Howells who looked relieved to see me coming up the path. Her powerful contralto tones drowned the clergy's contribution to the general confession and the Lord's Prayer. When we came to the psalms appointed for the morning, her recital of the alternate verses proceeded at a gallop, leaving Emlyn a poor second both in pace and in volume. After the service she was waiting outside as Emlyn and I came from the vestry door. 'Are you coming my way, Mr Howells?' she inquired in an affectedly coy fashion.

'I am afraid Mr Howells has to come to the Vicarage for our daily parish strategy meeting, Miss Harding,' I said.

'See you Sunday, Mr Howells,' she cooed loudly and made her ungainly way towards the lych gate.

'Daily parish strategy meeting,' said my curate. 'That's a new one, but thank you all the same for the deliverance. Miss Virginia Harding is becoming a big nuisance, I can assure you.'

'I could see that,' I replied. 'Well, do you want to come in for a cup of coffee and a dose of strategy or would you rather get straight back home?'

'I think a cup of coffee would be very welcome, Vicar, and perhaps a chat about the big nuisance would be in order. I have been meaning to talk to you about her for some time. Your advice on the subject will be as welcome as the coffee, believe me.'

As we sat drinking coffee, I said to Emlyn, 'I thought it strange to see Miss Harding there this morning. It's not as if she were a regular worshipper at St Padarn's.'

'Oh, but she is now,' he replied. 'She is there at every service I take and always hangs around to speak to me afterwards. She has insisted on lending me books I don't want and on bringing them round to my house. If I ask for volunteers for any function at St Padarn's she is always first in the queue. The trouble is that the congregation have noticed this and are beginning to assume that there is some relationship between us. God forbid! The last thing I want is any kind of relationship with that lady. She terrifies me, as I believe she does her pupils.'

'Well, Emlyn,' I said, 'sooner or later you will have to be very frank with her and make it plain that you have no interest in her whatsoever. You are such a tolerant person that you will find it difficult to be rude – but rude you will have to be, otherwise she will make your life a misery. She is such an overpowering person. No wonder she has "Jumbo" as her nickname.'

He began to laugh. 'That's very unkind but very appropriate, I'm afraid. I have never known such a clumsy person. She has knocked over my standard lamp and broken two wine glasses on the few occasions she has been at my place.'

'All the more fool you for inviting her in,' I told him. 'From now on, if she comes with a book, keep her standing on the doorstep. If she hangs around after service find a way of going out by the vestry door. She will soon get the message. The sooner the better, Emlyn. Miss Harding is a formidable lady, so don't delay.'

Eleanor was highly amused when I told her about the Harding obsession with the curate. 'She is at least twenty years older than Emlyn,' she said. 'Perhaps you could help by paying a visit to the Infant School and inventing a fiancée for the poor man to get him out of her clutches. Tell her that his young lady is very attractive and has not been able to visit Pontywen yet because she lives in the Shetland Isles.'

'You accused me yesterday of being devious in my dealings with Mrs Susannah Price,' I replied. 'At least I did not tell lies. Now you are inciting me to tell whoppers of which Baron Munchausen would be proud. I take it that you are not being serious. In any case, if he takes my advice, I don't think he will be troubled any further.'

'We'll see,' she said and proceeded to change the baby's napkin. 'At least if they did get married, she would not have to be lumbered with this routine.'

Before she could say anything further on the unlikely possibility of Miss Harding becoming Mrs Howells, the telephone rang. It was the lady in question. 'Vicar!' her voice had the resonance of a town crier.

'Ah, Miss Harding,' I said.

'How did you recognise my voice so instantly? I am most impressed,' she boomed.

'You have one of those voices which are unmistakable. Good to see you at Matins this morning. What can I do for you?'

'Well, Vicar, I have been thinking of ways in which those children in my school who have no connection with organised Christianity could at least be in touch with the clergy in this town. The most obvious way is to get the clergy into the school. So I have been wondering if you would allow the Reverend Emlyn Howells to come in occasionally and speak to the children. He has a rare gift for speaking to the age groups we have here. I am sure that my pupils would benefit enormously and, who knows, the church as well.'

I sent up an arrow prayer for the second time in less than twenty-four hours. 'If you don't mind me saying so, Miss Harding, I think it would be better if the Vicar came rather than the curate. He is the persona of the parish. Curates come and go but the incumbent is more or less a permanent fixture. I, too, like talking to children. All the more so since I have a young son myself. So, if you can put up with me, I shall be pleased to come whenever you invite me.'

There was a long silence at the other end of the phone. When she spoke, the boom gave way to a more moderate but acid tone. 'As you please, Vicar. I just thought it would be a useful experience for Mr Howells. I shall be in touch with you.'

After the abrupt ending to the conversation, Eleanor came into the study. 'Miss Harding?' she inquired.

I told her of the way in which I had rescued poor Emlyn Howells from her clutches once again. 'She said that it would have been a useful experience for the curate,' I added.

'Useful for her, she meant,' my wife replied.

# 8

A red-headed leprechaun with vivid blue eyes and a strong Belfast accent stood on my doorstep later that morning. 'My apologies, Vicar, for coming uninvited,' he said, 'but as I was in the neighbourhood I thought I would take the opportunity to call on you with a proposition. Joe McNally, Catholic priest at Abergelly. How do you do?' He put out his hand and held mine firmly, looking me in the eye whilst doing so.

'Come on in, Father. I am very pleased to meet you.' I led him into my study. He looked around at my books and expressed his approval.

'Quite a good library you have here. More than enough to keep you occupied. I am afraid mine is very limited in comparison, but there you are, perhaps I spend too much time outside and not enough indoors.'

'The same goes for me,' I said. 'Don't be misled by the quantity of books. I just use them to make an impression on my Bishop. Now would you like a cup of coffee? I am afraid it is too early in the day to offer you whisky.'

'My dear Vicar, it is never too early in the day to offer me a whisky – that is, if you have any available.'

As we sat drinking the aqua vitae he broached the subject of his proposition. 'There are quite a few Catholics in Pontywen – not enough to warrant the building of a church, you know. Still, there are sufficient to have their own opportunity to worship. Abergelly is a fair distance away and on a Sunday morning the bus service is non existent, so it is. I was wondering whether you would be prepared to allow us the use of your altar at St Padarn's after your Mass is finished. We would give you a reasonable amount of money for that, of course. I know it sounds like a piece of impertinence on our part but I can tell you that your co-operation would be appreciated, so it would be.'

'Well, Father McNally, I must confess that this is an unusual request. As far as I am concerned I shall be only too pleased to allow you to worship in St Padarn's. However, I shall have to ask the Bishop's permission and I will have to get the consent of the Parochial Church Council. Once this is done, there is no reason why you should not have your Mass at St Padarn's.'

A broad smile spread over the face of Father Joe McNally. 'Now that's what I call a really Christian attitude. I am afraid we give the impression that we are the only authorised children of God. I don't know whether you have heard the story of someone who was taken up to heaven to do a kind of Cook's tour. He was met by an angel guide who led him first of all to a crowd of people who were singing Sankey and Moody hymns lustily. "They are the Pentecostals," he said. Then he led him to a small group who were sitting in silence and contemplating their navels. "That's the Quakers," he explained. After that they moved on to another group of boys and men who were singing the psalms so beautifully that the visitor to heaven was moved to tears. "That's the Church of England," the angel said. Then he was taken to another part of heaven which was surrounded by a big wall. "Where are we now?" he asked his guide. The angel said to him, "Keep your voice down. These are the Roman Catholics. They think they are the only people up here." I can tell you, Vicar, that there are some of us who are only too willing to acknowledge the presence of other workers in the Lord's vineyard and that we have not the monopoly of the faith.'

'How big a congregation would you expect at the altar?' I asked.

He looked at the ceiling and made a mental calculation. 'About forty or fifty, I should say, with the Italian element predominating. You know, I sometimes think that there are more Italians in the valleys than there are in Rome. Then there are a few Murphys and Ryans who have found their way to Pontywen. A few of my colleagues have started to learn Welsh. I have told them that they are wasting their sweetness on the desert air. The natives of the valleys know as much about their mother tongue as they would about Swahili, excepting their National Anthem, of course. They've got to know about that to sing their team to victory at Cardiff Arms Park, so they have.'

'By the way,' I said, 'do you know Father Eamon McCarthy who was a curate at St Bernadette's in Swansea in the early nineteen forties? I expect he has left there by now but I was very friendly with him. We both used to run soccer teams in the youth league and his church was just down the road from mine. On many occasions, we used to have chats about ecumenical relations. He was prepared to accept the Anglicans but drew the line at any other denomination.'

'Would you believe it? I know him quite well. He has left Swansea and he has gone to his own church in

Cardiff – Our Lady of the Sea. You must pay him a visit one day. Eamon comes from my part of Belfast and I remember him as just a wee lad who served at the altar in my home church. Father Francis, the parish priest, thought the world of him. It is a small world, that it is.' Our conversation continued for another half hour or so by the end of which we had arrived at Christian name terms and I had promised to let him know in a week's time whether his flock could worship in St Padarn's. 'You must come down and have a meal at my place. My housekeeper is a very good cook and I keep an excellent cellar.'

I debated with myself whether I should write to the Bishop or telephone him. In view of the fact that I had promised to let Joe know within a week about the Bishop and the Parochial Church Council's response I decided to ring his lordship immediately. His secretary answered.

'Would you mind delaying your call for another quarter of an hour, shall we say? The Bishop has someone with him at the moment. I shall tell him you have phoned.'

I spent the next quarter of an hour ruminating about possible opponents to the proposition in the Parochial Church Council. Ezekiel Evans, the lay reader, was a certainty. Bertie Owen was another. On the other hand such an alliance would be sufficient to persuade the rest of the Council to vote in favour, just to spite them. My speculation was ended abruptly by the telephone bell. It was the Bishop inquiring about the purpose of my call.

'Can you make it short, Vicar? I have to go out very soon.'

'It is a somewhat unusual request, my lord.'

'Nothing to do with Charles Wentworth-Baxter, I trust.'

'Not at all, the Roman Catholic priest at Abergelly has asked me whether I would be prepared to let him have the use of the altar at St Padarn's once a Sunday after the morning service was over. Apparently he has between forty and fifty worshippers in Pontywen who are more or less cut off because of the poor bus service on Sundays. He is prepared to make a regular payment to be agreed if permission is granted. I told him I would have to consult you first and also the Parochial Church Council.'

'I see,' said his lordship. I waited quite a while before he spoke again.

'As you say, it is an unusual request. I have heard of it done in a few English dioceses but this is the first occasion I have been asked to give permission for such an arrangement in this diocese. Well, if the Parochial Church Council are agreeable, I would be willing to allow it for an experimental period of twelve months. Should everything be congenial after such a trial, then I would probably be prepared to let the agreement go on indefinitely.'

'Thank you very much, my lord,' I replied.

'Oh, by the way, what has happened about Wentworth-Baxter's request to serve as an extra unpaid curate?' he inquired. Obviously he had heard nothing of Charles's matrimonial troubles about which I thought it wise to be silent.

'When I gave him a list of what I would require him to do if he came to Pontywen, he decided he would rather stay in his own parish. I had no need to consult the Parochial Church Council. All he wanted was an excuse to escape from Penglais.'

'Typical of that young man,' said the Bishop. 'Sometimes I wonder what will become of him. I am afraid he has no sense of vocation. I think he must have been railroaded into the ministry by his father who insisted that his one and only son should follow in his footsteps. There have been many such cases. Inevitably they result in unfortunate clerical misfits. Well, I must go now, Vicar. I hope the experimental cooperation with the Roman Catholic Church proves more fruitful than the Wentworth-Baxter proposition.'

When Eleanor came in after one of her occasional morning surgeries, I told her of my visit by Father Joe McNally and then of my conversation with the Bishop. 'Well, Frederick,' she said, 'I am afraid the Wentworth-Baxter saga continues to unfold. Earlier this morning I had a phone call from Bronwen. She had rung the Vicarage but could not get a reply.'

'That must have been when I went to get my newspaper,' I replied. 'Marlene had taken the children out and evidently Mrs Watkins either did not hear the phone or, more likely, chose to ignore it and get on with her work.'

'Whatever the reason, that time there was no reply, and she rang the surgery. It seems that Charles appeared at her parent's house, banging on the door and demanding to see his wife and children. Fortunately Bronwen's father was working afternoons and was at home. Apparently he took Charles apart and told him that he was lucky not to be in a police court that morning. He warned him that if ever he assaulted his daughter again, he would beat the daylights out of him. Now the silly girl has decided to go back for a trial period. She has told him that if there is any more violence she will leave him for good. I think she is on a hiding to nothing, if you will excuse the dreadful pun. Anyway, I have told her that I will keep a close eye on her and that she must ring me immediately if she gets any more trouble from her stupid spouse.'

That afternoon I had been invited to speak at the weekly old-age pensioners' meeting which was held at the Miners' Welfare Hall. The Pontywen building was modest, compared with the grandiose complex at Abergelly, with its pillared frontage, large theatre, and several reception facilities. Its main feature was an excellent library, little used nowadays, according to Idris the Milk.

'Most of the miners go to the clubs or to Abergelly,' he told me. 'It's only the old-age pensioners that keep it going. A sign of the times, that's what it is. Once upon a time they used to have debates there and have really good speakers. Now it's the clubs that get the numbers with the booze and the so-called entertainment. There's so much money about that the wives want to be in on the act. You can't blame them, I suppose. What's good for the goose is good for the gander.'

I was due to be there at three o'clock. I arrived at five minutes to three, to find the committee room which was used as their meeting place full of noisy chattering elderly people, all seated on uncomfortable tubular chairs. There was an ancient wooden table in front of the gathering, out of place with the rest of the furniture. Behind it were three chairs of the tubular variety, two occupied and the other waiting to seat me. The Chairman, Dan Evans, stood up to shake my hand and to welcome me.

'Well, Vicar, it's a pleasure to see you. We are looking forward to your address. If you don't mind, we have some business to attend to before you begin to speak. Take a seat and make yourself comfortable.'

I would defy anyone to make himself comfortable on a piece of plastic held together by aluminium supports. I did my best.

On the other side of Dan, was the secretary, Miss Mabel Jones, retired schoolteacher and an active citizen of Pontywen, prominent in the Townswomen's Guild and local Labour Party. She raised her head from a perusal of the opened minute book and murmured a greeting, after which she turned over the page to read the other side. There was a tumbler of water in front of me, beside a lectern. Evidently they expected a lengthy address.

'Now then,' said the Chairman. 'First of all, let's welcome our speaker, no stranger to you all by any means. He has been in Pontywen for about eight years now. I think I am right.' He turned to me and I nodded. 'There you are, eight years. He must like us a lot to be here for such a length of time. Anyway, during that time he has done much. None of us will forget how he has stood up for the miners and what's more what his wife did for them in that terrible accident which took so many lives.' There was spontaneous applause at this point. 'Anyway let's get down to business. Shall we have the minutes of the last meeting, Miss Jones.' She adjusted her spectacles, cleared her throat and declared rather than read the minutes. It was an impressive performance worthy of a better text than a minute book.

'Matters arising?' asked the Chairman. There were several matters arising and it was half past three before I was called upon to address the meeting. 'Mr Chairman,' I began, 'thank you for your kind words earlier on. Yes, I have always had a great admiration for the miners. Any man who earns his living by crawling about in the bowels of the earth inhaling coal dust and risking life and limb is worthy of admiration. The history of coal mining in this country is littered with examples of shameless exploitation not only of men but women and children who rarely saw daylight and were paid a pittance. When I took my history degree I chose as my special subject Anthony Ashley Cooper, the seventh Earl of Shaftesbury, who devoted his political life to releasing women and children from their slavery in the mines, fighting the vested interests of the coal magnates.' As I proceeded to describe in detail the life of the noble lord from his early years to his death as an old man, I could see many pairs of eyes glazed over and I could hear many sighs from around the room. It was when the coughing began that I decided that enough was enough and I brought my lecture to an abrupt end. There was half-hearted applause. Then the Chairman rose to speak.

'Thank you for your talk about Lord Shaftesbury, Vicar. By a strange coincidence we had another talk about him a fortnight ago from Professor Tudor Matthews. So it's like what you say when you read the banns, it's for the second time of asking. You weren't to know that, were you? That's life, I suppose. Are there any questions for our speaker?' It seemed that no one wanted to ask a question. Evidently they had used up their quota of questions on Lord Shaftesbury a fortnight ago. Then suddenly an old man with a scarf tucked into his jacket spoke from his seat at the back of the room.

'Mr Chairman,' he breathed in bronchitic fashion, 'would the speaker like to tell us why he is on the side of the miners when he has never seen the inside of a coal mine and his bishops at the time of Lord Shaftesbury were supporting the coal owners in the House of Lords while the Earl as a Christian was trying to rescue the poor women and children from a life of slavery. Either he is a hypocrite or he is in the wrong job. I don't seem to hear of the bishops today defending the miners.'

I was so confused by the question that I did not know where to begin the answer, back in the nineteenth century or in the nineteen fifties. I decided to plump for the present day.

'You ask why I am on the side of the miners. Well, first of all, I am of working-class origins. I was brought up on a council estate in the docks district of Swansea. The people where I lived were steelworkers, dockers and trawler men. The steelworkers and the trawler men had to face risks in their employment. I may not have been inside the heat and dust of a steelworks or on a trawler facing the hazards of the Bristol Channel or the Irish Sea, but I could imagine what they had to face. Once I went out into Swansea Bay with a docker who lived a few doors away from us. I think I was about twelve at the time. I was thrilled to be going out in a rowing boat with him. After half an hour when we were away from the shelter of the harbour I was violently sick. I had to watch him eat the sandwiches my mother had prepared for me. It was like Chinese torture. I did not stop being sick until we reached dry land. Another day I went to the steelworks and felt suffocated in the heat and the dust. I don't have to go down the mines to realise what the miners have to endure. I heard enough from my wife when she came back from that terrible disaster to know the conditions under which they have to work. As for the bishops in the time of Lord Shaftesbury, they were the creatures of their own environment, their episcopal palaces and their pleasant pastures. They were blind to the realities of coal mining. I am not and I am no hypocrite, I can assure you.'

I spoke with such vehemence that my listeners were moved to give me a hand clap, which was deafening in comparison with my earlier reception. The man with the scarf sat unmoved. 'After that', said the Chairman, 'I think we had better have our tea and biscuits.'

As we sat drinking our tea Dan Evans commented, 'I tell you what, your answer to Llew Jones was better than Professor Matthews's and your lecture rolled into one. You spoke with such conviction that you made us feel you were one of us and not one of them. What more can you ask of a Vicar than that? As for Llew, unless you had spent years in a pit, he would never accept you as one of us.'

The following Monday evening I had to preside at the hastily convened Parochial Church Council meeting to discuss the possible use of St Padarn's altar by Father Joe McNally. I had mentioned the purpose of the special session to Idris the Milk and Charlie Hughes, the two churchwardens, after the service on Sunday. 'That's a turn up for the book,' said Idris, 'to have the Roman Catholics wanting to worship in our church. I think it's marvellous.' It took Charlie, who was now deafer than ever, at least a couple of minutes adjusting his hearing aid to understand the reason for the meeting.

'What about the Roman Catholics, Vicar? They want to buy our church. Never.'

'No, Charlie, they would like to rent our church to have their own service after we have had ours.'

'Oh, that's different. You mean that they are going to pay us something each Sunday. We could do with the money, that's certain. Mind, you'll have to watch them to see they pay every Sunday.' Charlie was in charge of counting the collection.

Before the meeting began, I could see Ezekiel Evans and Bertie Owen working in tandem to persuade members of the Council to reject the proposition, as I had foreseen. The more they proceeded to browbeat their visitors the more convinced I became that this unholy alliance would ensure that the motion to accept the proposition would be passed with only two voting against. When the minutes of the last meeting had been read and confirmed I recounted the details of my meeting with Father McNally. 'I can only say,' I went on, 'that I was most impressed by his breadth of vision. He is a Catholic in the true sense of the word, broadminded and tolerant. I am positive that if we allow them to share the use of the altar in St Padarn's it will be a significant advance in ecumenical relations in this valley. The Bishop is quite prepared to give his blessing to the enterprise for an experimental period of twelve months and then to extend it indefinitely if it proves successful.'

Immediately Ezekiel Evans was on his feet, his face flushed with righteous indignation. 'H'is this the thin h'edge h'of the wedge? Can't you see that 'e is 'oping to h'attract members of our congregation who might stay on to see 'ow 'e conducts 'is service? 'E's only pretending to be broadminded. They h'intend to take over h'our church one of these days, believe me. H'as far h'as they are concerned, we are the h'infidels in 'is eyes. H'I can't h'understand why our Bishop 'as been bamboozled, let alone you, Vicar.'

Next Bertie Owen jumped up. 'I would like to support what Mr Evans has said. For years, in fact, all my life, the Roman Catholics have despised us. They don't even recognise weddings that take place in our churches. Now, suddenly, they want to take over one of our buildings for their own purpose. Why haven't they asked you, Vicar, if they could have the parish church instead of St Padarn's? How would you like to have the stink of incense there instead of us suffering it in our little church? I tell you what, if the Council vote for this to go ahead, they'll need to have their heads read.'

It was the turn of Idris the Milk to say his piece. 'Well, Vicar, if you listen to what Ezekiel and Bertie have been saying, it seems that the end of the world has come because we are doing our fellow Christians an act of kindness. There are Roman Catholics in Pontywen who can't get down to Abergelly for Mass, because the bus service on Sundays is hopeless. Are we going to deny them the right to have Communion because we are small-minded? If you are worried about the stink of incense, Bertie, as you put it, you needn't be because, by the time Sunday comes around once again, the church will have been cleaned and aired. What's more, if I may say so, you have been very insulting to the rest of us in the Council by saying that we need to have our heads read if we don't agree with you. The boot is on the other foot.'

'And if the cap fits, wear it,' murmured David Vaughan-Jenkins, who was at my side. Charlie Hughes was having trouble with his hearing aid, which had been whistling ever since the meeting began. Now he stood up to make his contribution.

'I didn't hear much of what has been said, my battery has been going, but I would like to say this. I'm all for the Roman Catholics being able to rent our church. The collections have not been all that great these past few months and every little bit helps, as you know. The sooner they start the better, as far as I am concerned.' He sat down and switched off his hearing aid to save his battery.

Ten minutes later the Council had made their decision, to accept the proposition, with only two votes against. When the meeting was over, Emlyn Howells asked if he could have a word with me after Matins next morning. 'Why not come back to the Vicarage now for a cup of coffee?' I suggested. He accepted the invitation gladly. He had been looking glum throughout the proceedings. Normally he would have been enjoying the spectacle of Ezekiel and Bertie making fools of themselves.

When we sat down to drink the coffee in my study, he explained his desire to 'have a word'. 'It's that woman, Harding,' he said, with more than a hint of desperation in his voice. 'I think I am a tolerant bloke, but my limit of tolerance has reached breaking point. I am sorry I ever suggested that the PCC might agree to me having a phone. Ever since it was installed a month ago and the number was printed in the church magazine, she has been driving me crazy with her incessant ringing. Whenever I answer, she has the most implausible excuse for the call. During this last week or two she has developed another technique. The phone rings. I pick it up and say my number, then the dialler puts down the phone. It is getting to the stage where it is playing on my mind. I have even had one of those calls at two o'clock in the morning. I have no proof that it is she but I am positive that it is. I don't know whether you can do anything to help, Vicar. You have helped quite a lot already with keeping her away from me. This is a different problem altogether. I have been very curt to her when she calls. It seems to have no effect. Next day she is back on the phone. I suppose sooner or later I shall have to cut her off as soon as she speaks, rude as it may be. Even that will not end these anonymous calls.'

'Let's go in the lounge and talk to Eleanor to see if she has any suggestions to make. You can have a whisky as well to soothe your shattered nerves. Tell Eleanor about your phone calls while I go to the kitchen for some aqua vitae,' I said.

'Not from the tap, I hope, dear,' she called as I went down the passage. By the time I returned with a bottle and a jug of water, Emlyn was coming to the end of his tale of woe.

'That two o'clock ring was the last straw.'

'I can see that,' my wife replied. 'You could go ex-directory, of course, but that would be the last straw in another sense, since you have had the phone put in for your parish work. I suppose you could use that device as a temporary measure. Better still would be a direct con-frontation with the old battleaxe in the course of which you could warn her not to pester you any more, otherwise you will have to take some kind of legal action. I should think that would frighten her off. If it doesn't, then you can go to a solicitor and get an injunction. I am sorry, Emlyn, but unless you do something drastic she will not let go! She is at the time of life when women are subject to obsessional fantasies as well as hot flushes. As a stranded spinster left behind by the tides of the passing years, she sees you as her last chance of happiness.'

The prospect of a face-to-face encounter with the formidable Virginia Harding did nothing to lift the gloom which had enveloped my curate. By the time he left the Vicarage he looked even more miserable than when he came in. When I returned to the lounge, Eleanor said, 'It is a pity that he is such a nice man. I suppose it is one of the tragedies of life that people like Emlyn seem to attract such man-eating types as "Jumbo" Harding. Well, either he braces himself for the fray or he has a nervous breakdown.'

'I haven't told you about my talk to the old-age pensioners, have I?' I asked.

'No, you haven't. If you will arrange to do these things while I am out on my rounds, that's your fault, Frederick. Why, did anything interesting happen? One more nightcap before I listen to your account.' She poured us both a generous refill.

'Well, I decided to give them my talk on Lord Shaftesbury, which has gone down well, as you know, on several occasions. I couldn't understand why my riveting *tour de force* was leaving them stone cold. As a matter of fact, there was a fair amount of coughing and half-closed eyes. So I finished as quickly as I could. When Dan Evans got up to speak, the reason became obvious. A fortnight ago Professor Tudor Matthews from Cardiff University had also given a talk on Anthony Ashley Cooper. Then an old man with a scarf round his neck accused me of being a hypocrite to be on the side of the miners when all the bishops at the time of Shaftesbury were supporters of the coal owners and that I myself had never been down a coal mine. Apparently his name was Llew Jones. I must say he sounded full of dust. His voice and his breathing showed he must have spent his life underground.'

She began to laugh uproariously. 'Llew Jones is a patient of mine. Otherwise known as Llew the Scarf. He is a pain in the neck. That cough and his breathing are the product of heavy smoking. He never worked underground. He was employed as winder at the pit head.'

## 9

Next morning I rang Father McNally to inform him that the Bishop and the Parochial Church Council had agreed to an experimental period of one year's use of the altar at St Padarn's for his Sunday Mass in Pontywen.

His response was one of profuse gratitude. 'How wonderful! My dear Fred, you're a miracle worker, that's what you are. Between me and that old gate post they talk about, I thought that your bishop would have put his episcopal foot down, that I did. Now then, would you like to come over to the presbytery and work out the details over a nice little meal and some lubricant for the throat?' We agreed that we would meet in a week's time. Before he rang off, he said, 'Oh, by the way, would you like to bring a music copy of *Hymns Ancient and Modern* with you? I think your hymns are much better than ours, and I have quite a reasonable piano here. We can have a *cymanfa ganu* of our own.' Considering that he had said in our first conversation that he saw no point in his colleagues learning Welsh, at least he knew the Welsh for a singing get-together.

'I shall look forward to that,' I said. 'I hope your housekeeper can sing soprano. Then we can sing parts.'

'She's tone deaf,' he replied, 'but I tell you this, she can certainly cook and that's what matters in a housekeeper.'

That afternoon, it was my turn to do the hospital visiting. How times had changed since I first came to

Pontywen as a curate. Then I was terrified of the sisters and even more of entering the women's wards. Now, with a wife who was a doctor, I was treated with the utmost respect both by patients and staff. My first visit was to old Mr Tapscott who had been taken into hospital, suffering from incessant hiccups. When I went into the ward, he was sitting up in bed, looking a picture of health reading the *Daily Herald*. He was in his seventies and married to a wife some thirty years younger. They had a fourteen-year-old daughter who had been confirmed recently.

'How are you feeling, Mr Tapscott?' I asked.

The response was a hiccup. 'Apart from these b-blasted things I am fine.' There followed another 'blasted thing'. He looked around the ward furtively and then turned to me, lowering his voice. 'They say they don't know what's causing it (hiccup). I think it's what they're doing (hiccup) to the water. You know, every Tuesday (hiccup) they put that distemper in our taps. Before long there'll be lots of people in bed like (hiccup) me. I don't know whether Doctor (hiccup) Secombe can do anything to stop it before it's (hiccup) too late.'

'I'll have a word with her when I get home,' I replied, 'but I shouldn't think it's the water, it's more likely to be you and your digestive system.'

Our conversation continued for a few more minutes about the chlorination of the water supply, which he still insisted was responsible for his hiccups. I had gone to see old man Tapscott as a soft option before being confronted with the formidable Edwina Davies in the Princess Royal ward. After listening to an endless series of hiccups, I

began to wonder if any other hospital visit could be more insufferable. I should have known better.

As soon as I entered the ward, I met Sister Mary Rogers who was striding towards the door in high dudgeon. 'Well, Vicar,' she said, speaking through the corner of her mouth, 'she's all yours and may the best man win because I can't.'

There was no missing Edwina. She was in the bottom bed on the left. She was waving and shouting 'Vicar!' at the same time. 'Where have you been?' she demanded when I reached her. 'I thought you had left the parish.'

'Now, come on, Mrs Davies,' I replied. 'I was here a fortnight ago and Mr Howells was here last week.'

'All I can say', she replied, 'is that it seems donkey's

years since you were here last. You don't know what it's like to be stuck here in this place – nobody to talk to. All these old girls around here have got their heads stuck under the bedclothes, except when they're having their meals. I can't read because I need new glasses. My eyesight's getting worse. I think it's got a lot worse since I've been in here. The light is terrible. I tell you what, I'll be glad to get out of here. They say it will be another three weeks at least before they will let me get up. The last time I was in I was out of bed much earlier. It's this new specialist. He's a real dictator! "I know what's best for you, Miss Davies," he said. "So you obey my instructions and what's more you obey them when you go home. Otherwise you'll be a cripple for the rest of your life. If you had been a wise woman, you would not have been in here in the first place. Doing the sailor's hornpipe with a hip like yours. You should have known better." How was I to know I was going to dislocate my hip? I've been doing the hornpipe ever since I was a kid. Who does he think he is, the young whipper snapper? He is not long out of his nappies. You'd think he'd have more respect for his elders. I began to wish that she had caught distemper from the water like Mr Tapscott. At least it would have staunched the torrent of words. As she paused for breath, I ventured a remark. 'I'm sure that he must have respect for you, Mrs Davies. I am told that Mr Michael is one of the finest hip specialists in South Wales. So it would be just as well to listen to what he says.'

Almost before I could finish my last sentence, she continued her monologue, as if she had not heard a single word I had said. 'I told Sister Rogers that young men like that should not treat their elders as if they were little children. They will be old themselves one day. Then they will know what it is like to be scolded as if you were in infant school. All I hope is that I will be out of here in time for the coronation. Somebody was telling me the other day that you will be having some of the congregation to see it on the television you are going to have. I'll look forward to that. I remember the coronation of King Edward the Seventh. Mind, they didn't make the fuss of it that they are doing for this one. I expect it's because she is so young, poor soul. Have you seen that big crown she's going to have on her head. It's a wonder it won't break her neck. I don't know how she's going to wear that for such a long time. Let's hope the Archbishop of Canterbury gets a move on, not like that Pentecostal who took a service in the ward last Sunday. I thought he was never going to finish. Half the old girls were snoring long before he came to an end. That's the only good thing I could say about the Reverend Wentworth-Baxter – the service was over before you could say Jack Robinson. How is he doing out in the country, Vicar? I expect he misses Pontywen.'

'He certainly does, Mrs Davies,' I replied. 'Still, he has a lot to keep him occupied with his large family.'

'I should say so,' she said. 'They've got four, haven't they? It's about time they put a stop to things now, I should say. I don't know how that poor little woman can cope with everything, stuck away in the back of beyond like that.'

'I think I had better go, Mrs Davies,' I whispered. 'It looks as if your specialist is coming to see you.'

'You don't have to leave. You can wait outside until he has finished,' she ordered.

'I am afraid not. I have some more people to see.' It was a white lie. I did have other people to see but they were not in the hospital.

As I passed the time of the day with Mr Michael I could see his furrowed brow as he contemplated another encounter with Edwina. 'Nice afternoon,' I said. My greeting received a grunt as a reply.

I strode down the hill from the hospital, which was perched on the hillside outside the town, its red brick standing out against the sparse grass which had survived the fumes of the Valley industry. The sun was shining and I had been rescued from at least another half hour's thraldom with Edwina. My euphoria evaporated as the Rural Dean's bullnosed Morris drew up beside me, on its way downhill from the hospital car park.

'Ah! Vicar!' he bellowed through the open window of his ancient vehicle. 'The very man I want to see!' My heart sank. 'Can you come in beside me for a few moments?' I went in beside him, expecting the worst. Every time I had been in contact with the Reverend Daniel Thomas it meant trouble ahead. 'Well, how are you and how is Dr Sembone?' He was incapable of pronouncing my surname correctly.

'We are both quite well, thank you,' I replied, 'and what can I do for you?' I am afraid I have always led with my chin exposed. My mother used to tell me that my grandfather made the same mistake, which was why he ended up as a docker, and not a headmaster, as he was intended to be, when a promising school teacher.

'Well, Vicar, it's like this,' he intoned through his nose.

'As you know, you are easily the youngest incumbent in our deanery and you have plenty of new ideas and so on. Last Monday the Bishop called a meeting of rural deans and he wants us to move with the times, as he put it. One of the things he wants us to do is to get all our people together for a talk, illustrated with slides which the diocese will provide, and it is about – er – our bodies and how – er –' he paused for a moment, 'babies are – er – conceived, and so on. Now, as far as I can see, you are the only one who can do it, or perhaps Doctor Seaforth wouldn't mind coming along. After all, that's her job, isn't it, and she is a Christian. So if I leave it with you, whether you would mind taking this on or whether you would prefer to ask your good lady, the doctor, to do it, would that be all right?'

The sun was shining through the windscreen. He had wound up his window before I had entered the car. As a result the stale smell of humanity was overpowering, especially when heightened by a strong aroma of moth-balls. I felt an urgent desire to escape. It had been a claustrophobic afternoon. 'By all means, Mr Rural Dean,' I said. 'I shall have a word with my wife this evening and let you know later which of us will do the talk.'

'Splendid,' he replied. 'I would think it would be a good idea if we all came down to your church hall for it. After all, it is bigger than anything else we have in the deanery. Give my kind regards to Dr Seebolm.'

When I told Eleanor of the projected talk, illustrated with slides, she was highly amused. 'A talk about bodies,' she said. 'I would have thought it better to get Matthews the undertaker to do it, with interludes from Full Back Jones on "bodies and how I have buried them". Can you imagine the audience we shall have – an average age of sixty? If they do not know by now about their bodies and what to do with them, nothing I can tell them will be of any use.'

'Don't elaborate any further, my sweet,' I replied.

'Thank you very much. I was not exactly thrilled at the idea.'

I went on to tell her how Edwina had invited herself to our coronation extravaganza at the Vicarage. 'Let's hope that she will still be in hospital then.'

'Don't you believe it,' said Eleanor. 'Should she be in hospital she will have her bed transported here on the back of a lorry if needs be. Once she is determined to do something, nothing will prevent it, come hell or high water. You had better resign yourself to the pleasure of her company on Coronation Day, even if the Queen does not get a word in edgeways. I promise you, Frederick, that she will be in the front row of the audience, giving a running commentary.'

'I think I had better phone the Rural Dean and let him know that you will be giving the birds and the bees lesson,' I said.

'Don't give him the impression that I am eager to oblige,' replied my wife, 'otherwise he will be telling his cronies in the deanery that I am available for Mothers' Union talks on woman's problems at the drop of a hat. Make it appear that I am doing this as a great favour in the middle of an extremely busy schedule. It's a one-off effort, tell him.'

It took some time before he answered the phone. 'Have you been ringing long?' he said. 'We were listening to a programme on the wireless about Westminster Abbey – very interesting.'

'Don't you let me keep you, Mr Rural Dean. I am just letting you know that my wife is willing to give the talk about our bodies. She is a very busy lady but she will try to fit it in to her schedule of work. Perhaps you will let me know a date as soon as possible. In the meanwhile, I think I had better let you get back to your programme.'

'Oh, thank you very much, Vicar. Tell Dr Seymour that we are delighted she can do it. Talking about Westminster Abbey . . .' my heart sank for the second time that day, 'I was at the bank with Mr Vaughan-Jenkins after I left you. He tells me that you are going to have a television set from your brother so that you can watch the coronation. Isn't that kind of him? I am afraid that we are not going to be so lucky. I wonder if you wouldn't mind Mrs Thomas and myself joining some of your congregation at the Vicarage to see the service. We haven't anybody in the parish who has a television set. You know what these old farmers are like. They won't part with their pennies, will they?'

I took a deep breath. 'Come along by all means, Mr Rural Dean. I am afraid you will have to put up with some very cramped seating arrangements because so many people want to come. Let me know the suggested date for the talk as soon as possible, would you please?'

'Well, thank you very much for inviting us to see the coronation at your Vicarage. That is very kind of you, indeed. Mrs Thomas will be delighted. Thank you very much indeed.' With that he put the phone down.

I came into the sitting room where Eleanor was listening to Beethoven's Seventh Symphony on the Third Programme. 'You should have been listening to a talk on Westminster Abbey on the other wavelength,' I said. 'It has so intrigued the Rural Dean that he has invited himself and his wife to view the coronation in this Vicarage, together with half of the population of Pontywen.'

'Do you know what?' said my wife. 'I think our viewers will provide much more amusement than any coronation service. What a wonderful mixture, the Rural Dean, Edwina Davies, Charlie Hughes manipulating his hearing aid, our son and daughter who must be there to witness the historic occasion, not to mention Bertie Owen who is bound to gatecrash the party. I can't wait for 2 June. Incidentally did he give any indication of when he wants this "moving with the times" educational project?'

'My dear love,' I replied, 'once he knew that he had a reserved seat for the great day, he had forgotten about the Bishop's pioneering adventure into the sociological and biological realms. All that mattered was that he and his good lady would be in Pontywen Vicarage on 2 June. I hope we don't get any more self-invited people for the occasion.'

'I can only think of one other invasion,' said Eleanor.

'And who is that?' I asked.

'Charles and Bronwen plus their four, just to make up the number.'

'Don't tempt fate, there's a dear,' I said.

'Stranger things than that have happened,' she replied.

Next morning the curate appeared at Matins with a smile on his face. 'You are looking happy, Emlyn. I take it that you have slain the dragon.'

He answered my comment with a chuckle. 'Something like that. I'll tell you all after the service.' Considering that it was the last day before Holy Week, there was a noticeable lack of solemnity in our devotions. He looked as if a load had been lifted from his shoulders and I was glad for his sake. He was too good natured to be persecuted by a frustrated fifty-year-old headmistress. Emlyn stayed on his knees for quite a while after Matins was over, evidently giving thanks for his deliverance.

'Coming in for coffee?' I asked when he joined me eventually.

'Yes, please, Vicar, and you can have a blow by blow account of the *coup de grâce* which laid low the dragon, as you put it, yesterday evening, thanks to Dr Secombe's advice.'

We were joined in the sitting room by Eleanor, who was anxious to here what had transpired. 'Well, Dr Secombe . . .' he began.

'I think it's about time you started calling me Eleanor,' she said, 'but carry on, do.'

'Well, Eleanor, you advised me that a face-to-face confrontation with Miss Harding was the only way I could end this constant chasing after me, so I invited her to come to my place last night. I must admit that I filled myself with Dutch courage before she arrived. It was the only way I was going to say my piece. When I opened the door to her knock, there she was in her best clothes, a special hair do and enough perfume to drown the whisky on my breath and that was a lot, believe me. Evidently she thought her big moment had come. "Sit down, Miss Harding," I said in my best scout-master voice once we were in the front room. "Virginia, please." She tried to sound like a sex kitten. It was grotesque – so grotesque I felt sorry for her. "Now then, Miss Harding," I went on, "I think the time has come to put all the cards on the

573

table. You have been ringing me up incessantly, even at two o'clock in the morning. I have had enough. I want nothing to do with you, Miss Harding. I have my own life to live and I am asking you to keep out of it. You have your own life to live and I would have thought that your career would have a lot of satisfaction in it. That's all I want to say, Miss Harding. I am sorry to have to be so blunt but you give me no choice." I had learnt that speech by heart. I rehearsed it over and over again until I could say it in my sleep. You can have no idea of how she looked when I had finished. I had a dog once. I spoilt it but one day it made a mess all over the place. I belted it right, left and centre. It looked at me just as she did. She got up and went out of the house. She didn't say a single word and that was it. I hated doing it but it was the only way, wasn't it?' He looked for reassurance from us both.

'My dear Emlyn,' said my wife, 'there was no alternative. You had to be cruel to be kind. She will get over it in the fullness of time. Everything heals after the surgeon's knife has been applied.'

That afternoon we had a family outing into the surrounding countryside to pick bunches of pussy willow for the Palm Sunday service the following morning. It was the custom for the children to bring 'English palm', the old name for the willow buds, in procession to the altar while the hymn 'All glory, laud and honour' was sung. I had never forgotten how when I first came to Pontywen the children from the council estate who were unable to escape by car into the countryside had to beg a few scrawny twiglets from the privileged few whose parents had cars. I remember particularly one incident when a spoiled child arrived outside the church with his arms full of pussy willow. I asked him to share some of his abundance with two little boys alongside him. He searched amongst the profusion until he found two little pieces with a few buds on them. He presented one each to his classmates with an air of generosity which was more appropriate to a golden handshake than the mean spirited response to my request. After that I organised a search for bundles of 'English palm' every Saturday before Palm Sunday and each child had an ample supply to hold in procession. This year David was going to join the parade for the first time and he was more excited about that than he was at the thought of the Easter egg a week later. Baby Elspeth would have to be content with receiving a palm cross when her mother brought her to the altar rails. Unlike David when he was an infant in arms, she had been a model of good behaviour at morning service, receiving the equivalent of four gold stars from the elderly ladies in the congregation for her behaviour.

The weather was warm and sunny. We decided to drive to Abergavenny to collect our Palm Sunday bunches on the way and then to spend on hour or so in the pleasant little market town to do a little shopping and to have tea in one of its cafés. We stopped at a river bank on the way and Eleanor joined me in a very productive haul of willow buds, while David watched from inside the car, alongside his sleeping sister. We loaded the greenery into the boot, after presenting my son with a twig or two to keep him quiet.

'Are these mine for tomorrow?' he asked.

'If you are a good boy you can have a lot more tomorrow,' I said.

'Can't Elspeth have some, Dad?'

'She's too small to be in the procession. She can't walk yet, can she?'

'Can't mummy carry her?'

'No, David, the procession is only for children who can walk. Mummy will bring her up to the altar to have a palm cross.'

'Can I have a palm cross as well?'

'Of course you can. Don't you remember coming up for one last year? The one you've got pinned on the wall above your bed? Elspeth wasn't born then. So she can have one on the wall over her cot this year.'

When we pulled into the car park in Abergavenny Eleanor said, 'Don't look now, keep your head down, there's a dear.'

'Don't look at what?' I asked.

'It's a family group just disappearing in the distance. Bronwen carrying one on her arm and the other hand holding another as the child tried to walk. Charles inevitably walking ahead with the two eldest on either hand, like a Middle Eastern husband accustomed to having his wife bringing up the rear. So let's stay here for a few minutes and let them get away. I'm afraid, if we meet them I shall have to explode and spoil a lovely afternoon.'

'After what you said last night about Charles and Bronwen joining our coronation audience I think we should abandon our shopping expedition in Abergavenny and have it in Pontywen instead.'

'Having come all this way, Frederick, I don't feel inclined to turn back simply because we have seen Mr and Mrs Wentworth-Baxter and family. Why should they spoil our afternoon out? Another couple of minutes and they will have gone out of sight. All we have to do is to avoid the market. Charles is sure to be in there after a bargain. They won't be in a café. He won't want to fork out for a meal there. So avoid the market and avoid the main street but, first of all, let's find a café and have something to eat. I'm starving.'

'Righto. Upon your head be it. There's a café down that street by the market.'

We waited another five minutes to be sure that we were in the clear and then made our way out of the car park. Eleanor was pushing Elspeth in the pushchair and I had a firm hold on David's hand, which was tugging me like an unruly colt resenting its constraint. When we reached the café we found it full. If we wished to wait for a table, we could do so, we were told. We had no wish to wait for a table and came out to look for somewhere else to eat. The streets were full of half the farming population around Abergavenny, not to mention the day trippers who had come up from the valleys.

'For heaven's sake,' exclaimed Eleanor, 'let's put our hands in our pockets and go to the hotel across the road. Whatever we have to pay, it will be worth it, just to avoid all this shoving and pushing. I know one thing. We shan't find Charles and his family there; that's for certain.'

We crossed the street and passed through the portals of the three-star hotel. Once inside we found a haven of peace. It was a Georgian building where time had stood still. There was a young lady whose white blouse and black tie surmounted the reception desk.

'Can I help you?' she inquired in an accent she had

evidently acquired only recently since her rural origins were barely concealed.

'Do you serve afternoon teas?' said Eleanor.

'Not until four o'clock, madam. You can wait in the lounge until then, if you like.' It was half past three. We decided to wait. Elspeth was fast asleep in the push chair and David's eyelids were beginning to droop. There was no one in the lounge. Copies of the *Daily Telegraph* and *The Times* were on the highly polished table in the centre of the room. Soon David was asleep beside us on the big settee by the window. I was attempting to solve *The Times* crossword without using a pencil and my wife was reading the Saturday features page in the *Telegraph*. Suddenly the peace of our oasis was shattered by an all too familiar voice telling Simon to be quiet. We both dropped our newspapers and looked at each other in dismay. The very person we had planned to avoid was about to descend on us. Four-year-old Simon led the invasion, followed by his father shouting at him to stop running. Charles Wentworth-Baxter caught sight of us on the settee and stood transfixed. His dismay seemed to be much greater than ours. To use one of Idris the Milk's favourite expressions, he was trapped 'like a fly in a jam jar'.

Charles was rescued from his predicament by Bronwen's appearance from behind him. She was coping with three children but found enough breath to exclaim, 'Look, Charles! Fred and Eleanor.' He was still speechless. However, Eleanor was not.

'How nice to see you, Bronwen.' She stood up and moved towards her, ignoring her husband. 'Let me take the baby from you for a moment,' she added. 'It looks as if you could do with some assistance.'

By now Charles had ceased to be a statue and had grabbed Simon by his coat collar. 'Now, behave yourself,' he warned him, 'or I'll have to smack you.'

'Hello, Simon,' I said. 'You are going to be a good boy, aren't you?' He nodded his head. 'When are you going to start school?'

'In September, tell the Vicar,' said Bronwen. 'Fancy meeting you here. We are celebrating Charles's birthday. So we thought we would come somewhere decent for our tea.'

She was a changed person since my last encounter with her. Her self-confidence had returned and she looked well groomed, unlike the slattern of not so long ago. I managed to squeeze out a half-hearted 'Happy birthday, Charles.' My wife stayed silent.

Ten minutes later when we went into the restaurant for tea, Eleanor and Bronwen were in animated conversation and I was left with a sullen ex-curate whose birthday was apparently far from happy. Our two families occupied adjoining tables. David was now wide awake and was very interested in Simon who was not very interested in David. Every overture from my son to the eldest Wentworth-Baxter child was rejected out of hand, despite the encouragement from Bronwen to get her offspring to talk to David. He was as reticent as his father, who spoke no more than a few sentences all through tea. It was a most uncomfortable experience. I was very glad when the time came to settle the bills.

'See you soon,' said Eleanor to Bronwen when we went our different ways. Charles glared at her. The glare was returned. As we sauntered up the main street, with my wife manoeuvring the push chair past a multitude of legs, I said to her. 'What a pain in the neck that was!'

'For you, maybe,' she replied, 'but I was delighted to see the transformation in Bronwen. Her father must have frightened the life out of Charles. From what she said to me in the "Ladies", he now helps out in the house, even if it is a grudging assistance. He knows that if he falls out of line again that will mean curtains for him.'

'Falls out of line!' I exclaimed. 'From my past experience with Charles, I would say that is inevitable.'

'Well,' said Eleanor, 'that will be his funeral, not hers. Her parents are more than willing to look after her, should it come to the worst. In the meanwhile we must give her all the support we can. That's why I have invited her over to join our throng of coronation viewers, together with the children. If he wants to come, I suppose he can. I told you I had a hunch about it. Anyway, I said she could include him in the invite. What else was I to do?'

I was about to suggest an alternative and then decided against it, in case I was accused of a lack of Christian charity. 'As you please,' I replied, 'but it sounds like a manufactured hunch to me.'

The next morning, a sunny beginning to Palm Sunday, the children from the two Sunday Schools were forming a noisy scrum outside the parish church. Some had come with their own bunches of 'pussy willow'. Included amongst them was my young son, standing on the fringe, hopping excitedly from foot to foot. The others were waiting impatiently to be supplied with their share of the barrow load being wheeled up the path by Bertie Owen in his capacity as Superintendent of St Padarn's Sunday School. 'Bertie!' shouted Idris the Milk, who had been trying to keep order unsuccessfully. 'You are dropping more branches than you've got on the barrow.' Whereupon there was a rush from several of the branchless to retrieve pieces for themselves.

'Quiet!' I bellowed. 'Now get into line.'

Emlyn Howells and I had just followed the choir on their way from the vestry door to the front of the church, ready to lead the procession of palm bearers. When all the children had been provided with bunches I moved into the church to announce the hymn 'All glory, laud and honour'. As the organ blasted the opening notes, with all the stops pulled out by Mr Greenfield, the cross bearer came to the fore, prepared for action. Harry Llewellyn, a tall, pimply youth, lowered the processional cross to get it through the door as if it were a lance. He struck Bertie Owen between the shoulder blades as he was about to make his way down the aisle to collect the 'pussy willow' in the sanctuary. The Sunday School superintendent was propelled into a collision with a pile of hymn books and ended up lying spreadeagled at my feet, face down and covered with *Hymns Ancient and Modern*. In the meanwhile the congregation had launched into a lusty rendering of the first verse. I bent down to help Bertie to his feet but he was back to a standing position before I could render assistance. He had been an athlete in his time and was a very fit man. If his mental ability had matched his physical attributes, he would have been a force to be reckoned with. As it was, all his strength was in his body. To quote Idris, he had 'a vacuum upstairs'.

'You be careful with that thing, Harry,' he said. 'Next time it could be an old lady and a hospital job.'

It took another verse before the procession could get

moving. During the hold up, some of the children had begun to have 'pussy willow' contests to while away the time. As my curate said afterwards, it was not a procession but a shambling amble when it reached the altar rails – young David arrived at the end of the line and refused to surrender his 'English palm' to Bertie. Instead he invaded the sanctuary to present it to me, much to the delight of the old ladies in the congregation who told me after the service that they thought it was 'lovely'. Having made his presentation, he proceeded to dash down the chancel and then fall flat on his face. Like Bertie, he was up on his feet quickly and proudly joined his mother and his sister in the front pew.

I began my pulpit address by questioning the children about the events of Palm Sunday. 'How did Jesus come into Jerusalem on Palm Sunday?' I asked. A host of hands went up. I picked on Shirley Evans, the nine-year-old daughter of one of the sidesmen.

'He was riding on a donkey.'

'Why do you think he did that?' There was a pause before Selwyn Owen raised his hand. He was a twelve-year-old who fancied himself as a wag in my confirmation class.

'Because he couldn't find a horse.' There was an outburst of laughter from the children and a few from the adults. It was confrontation time.

'Selwyn,' I said, 'do you realise that we are entering the most sacred week of the year and all you can do is try to be funny about someone who gave his life for you on Good Friday? He chose to ride on a donkey because in the Old Testament the prophet Zechariah told the Jews that when the Messiah came to Jerusalem he would be riding on a donkey. In those days, the donkey was regarded as a noble animal. Nowadays a donkey is a term applied to someone foolish and empty headed. I need say no more.'

The silence that followed my remark was sufficient to ensure that the rest of my address made its full impact. The distribution of palm crosses at the conclusion of the service was followed sometimes by sword fights with them in the pews. Today there were none. Selwyn Owen had been the catalyst for a most effective Palm Sunday service.

As I was shaking hands with the congregation as they left, Idris the Milk come up behind me and whispered in my ear that he would like to speak to me later. When the last worshipper had left me, he joined me. 'I don't know whether you have heard, Vicar, but it seems that the Council are arranging a big fireworks display at the Welfare Ground on the night of the coronation. It won't be anything like that fiasco after VS day, when Bertie Owen set off all the fireworks at once in the square and we all had to dive for cover when that rocket went through Protheroe's plate-glass window. This is going to be well run with show pieces and all that jazz. What about our big concert that night? Everybody will want to go to the Welfare Ground.'

'No, I hadn't heard about that, Idris,' I replied.

'We had better call an emergency meeting of the Committee as soon as possible.'

'Can you let everybody know by Wednesday?'

'Easily, Vicar. Perhaps we can have an eve of the coronation "do", but let's see what the others have got to say.'

By the time we met on the Wednesday evening, full details of the Council's programme of celebrations had been published in the local newspaper. All the schools would be giving coronation mugs. The Pontywen Silver Band was booked to play on the Welfare Ground in the afternoon. The Mayor would be visiting all the street parties and attending the fireworks spectacular later in the evening. A grand dance was to take place at Abergelly Miners' Welfare Hall, admission free.

'Well, Mr Chairman,' said David Vaughan-Jenkins, 'I think our programme compares with that. We have a slap-up tea arranged for our children and, by the way, I think the Mayor should visit that. We have pony rides and boxes of coronation chocolates for the children. We have a dance, too, to finish up the evening, admission free, and in Pontywen, not Abergelly. Our big headache is what to do about our splendid concert. Everybody will want to go to the fireworks, that's positive. If we hold it later in the week that will be an anticlimax. All the excitement will have gone by then, I am afraid.'

'If I may make a suggestion, Mr Chairman, why not have our big concert on the eve of the coronation,' Idris suggested. 'As you know, I had a word with you about this after church on Sunday. Since then I have been in touch with Aneurin Williams who is going to be responsible for putting it on and he says that he is quite prepared to have the show the night before. It will be one up for us as a church to be the first to get the festivities going in Pontywen.'

This suggestion brought Mrs Agnes Collier to her feet. She had been made responsible for the catering. 'Now hold on,' she warned. 'What is going to happen to all the arrangements we have made to get the hall ready for the tea the night before? If you are going to have this big concert, there will be all the chairs and tables to get ready. You can't expect the women to be working late into the night. We'll all be wanting to listen to the service or watch it, if we are one of the lucky ones, the next morning. So I don't see how you are going to be able to have your concert. It's one thing to say that Aneurin Williams is prepared to do it. He doesn't have to clear away and get everything ready.'

There was a lull in the proceedings as the Committee members sought to find ideas which would overcome the obstacle raised by the catering supremo.

'What about a working party, ready to begin the clearing away, etc. as soon as the concert was over! There are plenty of men who would be willing to lend a hand.' This contribution came from Harold Jones, builder and Vicar's warden. 'Perhaps we could start the concert earlier so that there would be that much more time to get on with things.'

'I don't know about starting the concert earlier,' said Idris. 'Some of the men won't finish work until five o'clock at the earliest and then they've got to have their meal and clean up before they leave the house.'

'Come off it,' retorted Harold. 'Most of the men are on shift work. That means that those working six till two will be OK. Anybody doing the two till ten would not be able to take part anyway, except by taking French leave. You are just talking about the white-collar workers and there aren't many of them. I still think that starting the concert at half past six could solve the problem. What do you think, Agnes?'

'I suppose that would be all right, as long as there's this working party of men to get cracking straight away after the concert,' she said somewhat reluctantly. 'Mind, the women will still have to get the cloths on the table and see to the crockery and so on. It's going to be a late night for everybody, I can see, but let me tell you now if there's no working party when we want them, don't ever ask the women to do anything like this again.' I put Harold Jones's proposition to the meeting, and they voted unanimously in favour.

'Now, then, Vicar,' Agnes was on her feet once again, 'what about these lists you are going to put up in the porch for people to sign if they want to come and watch the television? I think you said, only two from one family can come. It's fine for me because I am a widow, as you know, but it's a bit hard on some of the families.'

'Look, Mrs Collier,' I said heatedly, 'I have said it before and must say it again: nobody has a right to enter someone else's house to watch the ceremony. It's only through the kindness of television set owners that they are invited. I can tell you now that already we have a number of people coming to the Vicarage to see the programme and I know that Mr Vaughan-Jenkins and Mr Nicholls are similarly placed. I shall put up a list in St Mary's and St Padarn's on Easter Day. There is no guarantee that there will be room for them. The only thing that will be fair is to put all the names into a hat and call out the lucky numbers. If I had a set the size of a cinema screen and put it in the hall it still would not be enough to cope with all those who would want to come. To be quite frank, I am beginning to wish I had not been given a set, if it is going to cause any animosity. I would have been quite content to listen to the service on the wireless as I did in 1937 at the last coronation.' Very rarely did I lose my temper at meetings of any kind but the self-invitations of the Rural Dean and Edwina Davies plus Eleanor's open-house invite to Bronwen, Charles and family had exacerbated the soreness of a raw nerve. To have Agnes Collier adding to the discomfort was too much to bear.

The sight of the Vicar losing his temper was sufficient to end any further discussion of the television issue. It was decided to hold the next meeting in a fortnight's time.

'I can appreciate how you feel,' said David Vaughan-Jenkins as we left the church hall. 'It is amazing how friendly people become when they know you will be watching the big day on your own set. I expect by the time the next coronation comes, everybody will have their own.'

'I wish that time had arrived in 1952,' I replied. 'It would have saved me a lot of worry. How on earth are we going to cope with the Rural Dean and his wife, Edwina Davies, the Wentworth-Baxters and a crowd from the congregation, I do not know.'

'I'll tell you one thing, Vicar, between you and me and the gatepost, your wife will be much more of a help that day than mine.' With that remark from the churchwarden we went our different ways, leaving me to regret my fit of sulks at Eleanor's invitation to Bronwen.

The following day was the date for my visit to Father Joe McNally's residence to finalise details of the renting of St Padarn's for a late-morning Sunday morning Mass. He rang me during the morning to remind me to bring a music copy of *Hymns Ancient and Modern* with me. 'What with your tenor and my bass we should be able to do it justice, that we should.'

Before I left, Eleanor warned me to be careful about the quantity of alcohol I might be tempted to drink. 'Remember Bill Jackson,' she said. He was Vicar of a neighbouring parish who had been arrested for being drunk in charge of his Austin Seven. His parishioners said that he always drove as if he was drunk in charge, not knowing his right hand from his left hand and since he drove so slowly his miniature car would be in greater danger of damage than any pedestrian with whom it might collide. 'Remember you have a bigger car and drive much faster than that unfortunate gentleman,' she added. With these words ringing in my ears I proceeded up the drive circumspectly to impress my spouse. Once outside the gates I reverted to my normal speed, as undoubtedly she guessed I would.

'St Francis of Assisi' was a small red brick church on the outskirts of Abergelly and alongside it was the presbytery, which was almost as big as the place of worship. The drive gates were open, ready to accommodate my car. As soon as I pulled up, Father Joe came from the house.

'Irish territory in splendid isolation,' he said as he put his arm around my shoulders and escorted me into the lounge. There by the window, was an upright piano, bearing the name 'Challen', its polished exterior paying tribute to the handiwork of his housekeeper.

'I see you have brought your means of singing for your supper,' he said, opening the lid of the piano and taking the hymn book from me. He placed it on the music stand

and drew the music stool to the piano. Then he paused. 'But before we raise the roof we must anoint our throats with some Irish embrocation,' he ordered. He went to a side table on which was a full bottle of whiskey. 'Now, by the time you leave tonight, that bottle has to be emptied,' he ordered. He poured out half a tumblerful each for us. 'Here's to a long and enjoyable friendship.' We touched glasses and he sat down at the piano. 'What shall we have as our introit?' he asked.

'To get us off to a rousing start,' I suggested, 'I would say Hymn Number 196. People have told me that they can hear this being sung at Cardiff Arms Park half a mile away, known to every rugby supporter as 'Guidemeo'.

'Good old Cwm Rhondda,' he replied. 'Do you know the story of the millionaire who used to sing in the second verse "land my safe on Jordan's side", instead of "land me safe on Jordan's side"? Somebody should have told him that he couldn't take it with him.' He turned the pages till he found 196 and then played through the tune with the touch of a skilled pianist. 'Are you ready, Freddy?' he asked.

For the next half hour or so, we sang all the old favourites. He had a deep rich voice and sang almost as well as he played. Then there was a knock on the door after we had finished 'The day thou gavest, Lord, has ended'.

'Dinner's ready, Father,' announced a female Irish voice.

'It certainly has not ended,' he said. 'We must carry on with our hymns of praise once our stomachs are full, after a decent rest, of course.'

We went into the dining room. My heart sank when I

saw two bottles of wine on the table, one white, one red. 'Joe!' I gasped, 'how do you expect me to drive back to Pontywen after imbibing all that lot? My wife has already warned me not to drink to excess.'

'Now then, Fred, don't panic, there's a good lad. We are going to fill our stomachs with three courses of excellent food. That will absorb a lot of alcohol. If you can't finish the whiskey afterwards, I'll do it for you. I shall see that you are in a fit state to drive back, even if it means making you walk a straight line down the path before you get into your car.'

If he was not right about the absorption of alcohol he was certainly right about the excellent food. We began with a creamed vegetable soup, followed by a delicious steak and kidney pie and attendant vegetables and crowned by a sherry trifle with apricots and almonds and a liberal application from the bottle of sherry. This was rounded off with Stilton cheese and biscuits, accompanied by a glass of port. It was one of the best meals I had ever eaten and the cook was a little old Irish lady with a thick accent which seemed to indicate that she had spent most of her life in some remote village in south-west Ireland. When she came to collect our plates, prior to our moving back into the lounge, I said to her, 'I must thank you for a wonderful meal. I can recommend your cooking to anybody who wants to know what good food tastes like.' She blushed, murmured her appreciation and made a bee-line for the door.

Back in the lounge, I said to Joe, 'Where did she learn to cook like that? You have a treasure in that housekeeper of yours.'

'You needn't tell me that,' he replied. 'As it happens,

she is an aunt of mine, several times removed. She came to London many years ago to find work, like so many others. Eventually she became cook housekeeper to a moneyed family in Kensington. She stayed with them until the husband left his wife, just before the war. After that she kept house for a priest in Chelsea. He died suddenly five years ago. I was moving into this, my first parish, and I needed a housekeeper and that's it.'

'You're a lucky man, Joe,' I said.

'Now, come off it, Fred,' he replied, 'the boot is on the other foot. You have a charming and very capable wife and you have two children. Would you care to swap with me?'

'Touché,' I murmured. Then I went on, 'May I ask you a question? There must be times when you feel very lonely. When you came to welcome me, you mentioned the words "splendid isolation". You are obviously a man who enjoys life, very much an extrovert, if I may say so. With a personality like yours, surely you must miss the companionship of a woman and the love of a family. You would be an excellent family man. If the time ever came when the Pope decreed that married clergy would be allowed within the priesthood, would you settle down with a wife?'

'That,' he said with a certain amount of vehemence, 'is a question I will not answer. Shall we get down to working out the details of our lease-lend agreement, to use a wartime phrase?' I could see that I had done an 'Agnes Collier' and touched a raw nerve. I determined that I would never again question the celibacy of the priesthood in our conversations.

We agreed that he should have the use of the altar

from 11.30 a.m. until 12.30 p.m., every Sunday for the next three months for a rental of ten pounds a Sunday. Since the rental provided an income almost equal to our normal Sunday collection at St Padarn's, it was a lucrative transaction. After we had shaken hands on the deal we sang some more hymns 'Ancient and Modern' concluded with 'Now thank we all our God'. There was still a half bottle of whiskey.

'If you don't mind,' I said, 'in the interests of road safety and the condition of my liver, may I suggest that you have a very large nightcap while I remove my vehicle from your drive and go back to Pontywen while I still know the way.'

'It is a wise man who knows his own limits,' he replied. He came to see me off the premises, ignoring the heavy rain which was falling. When I had reversed on to the road, he said, 'If you drive forwards as well as you drive backwards, you'll have no trouble in getting home at all. May God and St Christopher go with you; see you at St Padarn's one of these days.' With that, he patted the bonnet of the car and waved me away.

I drove off in a euphoric haze. 'Brimful of the friendliness that in an RC presbytery I have found,' I said to myself, quoting a revised line from one of Keats's sonnets. Fortified by Joe's prayer that God and St Christopher should protect me, I was relishing the prospect of an open road with not a car in sight. Suddenly it happened. A rabbit darted out from a hedge and froze into immobility in the glare of my headlights. On my one and only excursion into the realm of field sports, I had maimed a rabbit with my one and only attempt at marksmanship. I had the repugnant obligation to club it to death with the

x

593

shotgun. After that, I vowed I would never kill another rabbit.

I slammed my foot on the brake and swerved at the same time to avoid the creature. The car skidded on the wet road. It ended up on its roof with the wheels spinning and with my head in a similar condition. In a daze I reached out for the ignition key and turned off the engine. My right shoulder and my ribs felt as if they had been hit by a two-ton truck. I lay on my back, still for a minute or so. Then I decided to clamber out. Since the driving seat was only inches away from the hedge there was no alternative but to make my escape through the other door. As I strove to move towards it, lifting my leg over the gear lever, my whole body was racked with pain. 'I am here for the night,' I thought.

It was then that in the distance the headlights of a car appeared. I prayed that God and St Christopher had sent them. Sure enough, as the vehicle approached, it slowed down and stopped. Four men got out. In no time at all, they turned the car over on to its four wheels. Next, one of them squeezed himself between the hedge and the door of the driving seat. He opened it and inquired, 'Are you hurt, Reverend?'

'I don't think so,' I replied hesitantly.

'Can you manage to get out this side?' he asked. I raised myself from the seat painfully and took his hand. Between us I managed to edge myself out on the grass verge.

'My shoulder and my ribs are aching but, apart from that, I feel all right,' I said.

'Sure now?' he inquired again.

'Yes, sure,' I replied.

The other three came to join him. 'I tell you what,

Reverend,' one of them said, his speech slurred by alcohol, 'we thought you'd 'ad it when we saw the car first, didn't we, Mal?'

Mal was evidently the driver since his friends seemed incapable. 'All right, boys, you get back in,' he ordered. After they had seated themselves he said, 'Let's watch you go on your way first, Reverend. Just to see that you're all right.' Then lowering his voice, he added, 'It's been my turn to drive tonight. We go out once a week for a booze up but one of us is always the unlucky one to be on orange juice. Still, you can't risk life and limb when you're driving, can you?'

When I arrived at the Vicarage, Eleanor was still up. 'Good heavens!' she exclaimed, 'What has happened to you, love? You look as pale as a ghost.'

I recounted the story of my misadventure.

'Come on, take your shirt off. Let's examine you,' she ordered. After a brief examination, she pronounced the verdict. 'No bones broken, but you'll have some lovely bruises in the morning.'

'It's a good thing that God and St Christopher were protecting me,' I said.

She replied, 'Since you smell like a brewery, you can thank them that you did not end up in a police station. Let that be a lesson to you, my lad.' I was never allowed to forget that lesson thereafter.

## 11

'All I can say about these slides and the accompanying notes is that they would be far more suitable for infant schools.' Eleanor's comment came after a brief perusal of the so-called 'information pack' to be used in the moral welfare project for sex education in the rural deanery. I had ignored her suggestion that the Rural Dean should 'keep his slides', as she put it.

Now they had arrived at the Vicarage on the Tuesday morning, ready for showing to our rural deanery in Pontywen church hall on the following Friday evening. 'To expect me, as a doctor, to lecture adults, most of whom are long past their teens, in the meaning of sex in such terms is an insult to my vocation and training. As for those who are to be lectured, it treats them as if they still believed that babies were delivered by storks and found behind gooseberry bushes. I shall borrow some illustrated material from the sister tutor at the hospital and give the lecture in my own way. If some of them find it shocking, so be it. Most of the teenage pregnancies nowadays stem from the lack of guidance from parents, who either think it is not quite nice to talk about sexual relations or who pretend that "the kids will find out for themselves soon enough, the same as we did". It is not good enough, Fred. It really isn't.' Her face was flushed with anger.

'I shall look forward to next Friday evening,' I replied.

'I shall spend most of my time looking at the old ladies' faces and a fair amount watching the Rural Dean's reaction. It will have the same effect as if they had been taken to see an X film in Cardiff, with disbelief and horror at what is being unfolded before their very eyes.'

'Not so much before their eyes, dope,' she said, 'as what is assaulting their ears. Almost all of my lecture will be with no illustrations. What a pity Charles is no longer in the deanery. He would have learned a lot about the right way to treat a woman.'

Any further discussion was prevented by a ring on the door bell. It was Heather Andrews with Christine, her baby daughter. 'I've taken advantage of this lovely sunny morning to walk down from Ashburnham Close to get some exercise. If I am to be running alongside my pony, giving children rides in a few week' time, I shall have to be fit, believe me,' she said.

'Coming down was easy,' replied my wife. 'You wait until you push that big pram back up the hill. Now that really will be exercise. So I suggest a cup of coffee and some biscuits to build you up for the return journey.'

'If you don't mind,' I said, 'I shall leave you two ladies alone for your *tête-à-tête* while I get on with some sick visiting.'

'Before you go, Fred, I suppose that everything has been cleared for me to give the rides for the afternoon of D-Day.' Heather sounded concerned. 'I understand that they are planning a big firework display on the Welfare Ground in the evening, which means that there will be plenty of activity going on while I am doing my thing with the children.'

'As far as I know, Idris the Milk, who is the secretary

of our organising committee, has checked with the council that everything is OK. He is very reliable. Anyway I'll pop into his house on my way back from visiting just to make sure.' So saying, I left them in the lounge and went into the study to collect my robes and sick Communion set for my monthly celebrations of Holy Communion in the homes of house-bound parishioners. No sooner had I gone into the study than there was a telephone call.

'Good morning, Vicar.' It was my Bishop.

'Good morning, my lord,' I replied.

'I expect you have heard that Canon Joseph Morris is retiring at Abergelly. As you know, he has been there for nearly forty years and his health is beginning to deteriorate. The parish needs an infusion of young blood in the Vicarage. The living is in my gift and I wondered if you might be interested. As you know, it is a much larger parish than Pontywen and dominates the valley industrially, but not, I am afraid, ecclesiastically. You have now been in Pontywen for eight years and I wondered whether you would like a change. I would suggest that you go to see the parish and its church and to have a word with Canon Morris. If you do not leave Pontywen, after you have been to see Abergelly, I shall understand fully how you feel. However, please pay it a visit and then let me know in your own good time your decision.' The unexpected offer of a new living rendered me speechless for a few moments. Then I recovered my senses.

'Thank you for considering me for this important parish,' I breathed. 'I shall certainly pay it a visit, as you suggest, and then talk things over with my wife who has her practice in Pontywen. It will have to be a joint decision, as you will appreciate, my lord.'

'Of course,' he replied. 'There is no hurry. The Canon is not due to retire until the end of May, in any case.'

I put the phone down and went back to the lounge, where Eleanor and Heather were engaged in a conversation about breast feeding, as far as I could gather.'

'I thought you were on your way out,' said my wife.

'I'm afraid I was delayed by his lordship,' I replied. 'I'll tell you about it when I get back. It involves you as well as me.'

'Tell me now,' she demanded.

'When I come back,' I reiterated.

'You rotten thing,' she shouted as I went out to the car. On my way to Mrs Turvey in Balaclava Street, my mind was in a turmoil. I had assumed that I would be in Pontywen for many years to come as part of a 'working partnership' – myself: the local parson; my wife: the local doctor. This offer had come like a bolt from the blue and threatened our domestic bliss. I began to wish the Bishop had never phoned.

When I arrived at the Turvey residence, the district nurse answered the door. Beryl Evans had been one of the bridesmaids at the Wentworth-Baxter wedding. A contemporary of Bronwen's at Pontywen Hospital, she had been appointed only recently to work in the town. A tall, talkative young lady, she made an ideal visitor for the bed-ridden, ready for a chat at any time and strong enough to lift any invalid who needed a bed change or a bed bath.

'She's ready for you, Vicar,' she announced. 'Is there anything you want for the service? I've put a nice clean cloth on the table by her bed and a little jug of water.'

'That's fine,' I said.

'How is Bronwen these days?' she asked. 'I hear she has four children already. I never thought Charles could be such a fast worker.'

'Oh, she's OK,' I replied. 'Her hands are tied with such a large family, not to mention the fast worker. You must call on her one day. I am sure she will be glad to see you. She needs to see fresh faces, stuck out in the country, as she is.'

'I must do that,' she answered. 'When I get a break from this busy routine.' Then she lowered her voice. 'By the way, Mrs Turvey is going downhill, I'm afraid. The doctor doesn't give her long to live, a few months at the most, but she is very cheerful, all the same.' She led me into the front room, where the old lady was sitting up, propped up by two big pillows. She was a tiny lady whose body was bent in half by rheumatoid arthritis, her hands were clenched permanently by the cruel disease and her legs were locked in an equally permanent bent position. Her white hair had been brushed and combed. Despite the incessant pain and discomfort, her face was always beaming whenever I came to visit her.

'Good morning, Vicar. Isn't it a lovely day.' She made a valiant effort to lift her head to look at me, her little face alight with a smile of greeting.

'It certainly is, Mrs Turvey,' I said, 'and all the better for seeing you.'

'I expect you say that to all the girls,' she replied. She had never lost her sense of humour despite the suffering which afflicted her. Her daughter said it was her secret weapon and that without it she would have been dead years ago.

'Our Ethel is working this morning but Nurse Evans has been very good and has put everything ready.'

As I prepared the Communion vessels and robed for the service, she engaged in a monologue. 'I hear they're going to have fireworks on the Welfare Ground for the coronation. I hope they make a better show of that than they did for VE day in the square. That was the last time I was out of the house. Our Ethel took me there in a wheelchair. I said to her, I don't know why Bertie Owen wasted all these rockets in one go. I could have done with one of them behind my wheelchair. It would have saved you pushing and what's more I would have been home on time. I can remember King George the Fifth's coronation quite well. It was the same year that I got married. Eighteen I was and Stan my husband was twenty-nine. He took me down to Porthcawl the day after our wedding to celebrate. Do you know what? That was my first time at the sea side. Oh, you're ready now, are you? I do keep on, don't I? I suppose it's because I'm on my own so much that when anyone comes, I can't stop talking. Sorry, Vicar.'

'Please, don't be sorry, Mrs Turvey,' I replied. 'It's always a pleasure to listen to you, but now it's down to business. Let us pray.' She knew the service by heart, which was just as well, because she could not hold a prayer book. I had to communicate her by dipping the wafer into the wine and placing it in her mouth. When I finished she remained silent with her eyes closed for quite a while, as I cleansed the vessels and removed my surplice and stole. Then she looked at me, painfully raising her head a little.

'Thank you, Vicar. That was lovely. I do look forward

to my Communion but I'm afraid I won't be here to have it much more. I know it looks as if I have plenty of breath to talk to you but, when you have gone, there won't be much left. I save it up for when anybody calls. Anyway, I'm more than ready to meet my maker. I've had a good life and now I feel very tired. I'm sure the Lord will soon be saying that my time is up, and I'll be very grateful, believe me.'

The other three parishioners were not as talkative and long before lunchtime I was back at the Vicarage where Eleanor was waiting impatiently to hear about the Bishop's telephone call. Heather Andrews had gone and she was on the doorstep before I could get out of the car.

'Come on, spoilsport,' she said. 'Let's have an account of what his lordship has told you.'

'Hold on, woman,' I replied. 'Keep control of yourself, please.'

'Really, Secombe, you can be most exasperating at times. I'll have to have words with your mother about you.' There was an edge to her voice which indicated that any further delay in imparting the information would be most unwise. With my one arm holding my surplice, and the other arm round her waist, I led her into the house.

'In a nutshell, my love,' I said, 'his lordship has offered me a living.' She stopped suddenly as we were about to enter my study.

'Say that again,' she demanded.

'He has offered me the parish of Abergelly and wants us to see the Vicarage and the church before giving him a reply. I have told him it will have to be a joint decision, because you have your practice here in Pontywen.'

'You can say that again,' she commented forcefully. 'I thought he said to you when he offered you this parish that he wanted someone who would stay here for a long time.'

'I know that, love, but evidently he feels that I am the man who can revive church life in a large parish which has become run down after the present incumbent has been there for nearly forty years. It needs a young man with plenty of energy, and new ideas.'

She cut me short. 'Stop bragging, Secombe. I could say that I have revived a practice after the previous practitioner had been there for nearly forty years. It would hardly be fair to expect me to walk out on it just as I have managed with the help of David Andrews to put it on its feet.'

'Calm down, Eleanor. His lordship said that if I did not wish to leave Pontywen he would understand fully. He just wants us both to have a look at Abergelly and then let him know "in our own good time", to quote him, our decision. So I suppose the least we can do is to drive down to the place, have a word with Canon Morris, look at everything and then report back to him if it is yea or nay.'

She looked at me with narrowed eyelids, a look I had learned to treat with caution. 'I tell you now, it will be nay. By all means let's go down to Abergelly, if that is what he wants. How can you expect me to give up everything I have been trained to do, apart from the financial side of things, to become just a vicar's wife. I am a doctor, Fred, just as you are a vicar. In Pontywen we can be both and live in perfect harmony.' She caught hold of me and held me tight. I raised her head and kissed her.

'My dear love,' I said, 'whatever we do, it will be a mutual decision, you should know that by now. I love Pontywen and its people and so do you. Abergelly will have to be something tremendous to make us change horses.'

'World shattering, I would say,' she replied and returned my kiss.

'I think we should get it over and done with. What about a phone call to Canon Morris and a trip to Abergelly tomorrow morning?' I suggested.

'Agreed,' she said. 'The sooner we get this out of our system the better.'

Once I had taken off my cassock and had been fortified by an aperitif before our lunch of sausage and mash, I rang the Vicar of Abergelly. It was some time before there was an answer.

'Abergelly Vicarage,' said a deep voice at the other end.

'This is Fred Secombe, Vicar of Pontywen,' I replied. 'The Bishop has asked me if I would come down to your parish and have a look around with a view to becoming the next Vicar. Would it be convenient if my wife and I came to Abergelly tomorrow morning? I know it is short notice but we shall not be able to visit the parish until next week, otherwise.'

A silence ensued. 'I should think that will be all right. We are a bit upside down in the Vicarage, getting ready to go in a few weeks' time, but I suppose it is better for you to come now rather than later on when everything will be topsy-turvy. I have heard you have been doing great things at Pontywen. It would be good for Abergelly to have some young blood in the parish. One day, Vicar, you will be old and unable to do what you always found straightforward and easy to do. I have gone long past that stage and if we had been financially situated to have somewhere to live, my wife and I would have gone some time ago. Now we have bought a cottage in Breconshire and we are eager to go, I can tell you.'

The next morning we made our way to Abergelly, a town with a population of ten thousand and the administrative centre for the valley. On the fringes were a large aluminium works, a colliery, and a tinplate works. Amongst its many shops, it boasted a Woolworths store, a Burton's tailoring establishment and a branch of Boots the chemist. It was a thriving place where unemployment belonged to its past and had no part in its present and future. Moreover, its rugby team included Newport and Cardiff in its fixture list. In other words, Abergelly had an importance that Pontywen would never equal.

As I drove through its streets to the Vicarage, I began to feel an urge to become the Vicar of such a hive of activity and to wish that my wife was not a doctor tied to a practice in a less desirable parish. I glanced quickly at Eleanor to see what effect the town was having on her. She had been quiet ever since we entered its environs and now was looking out through the window at the cavalcade of shoppers on the pavements.

'Very busy here,' I ventured to remark. 'It's like Piccadilly Circus compared to Pontywen.'

'Now then, Frederick,' she replied, 'don't start getting big ideas. Pontywen suits me.' A few minutes later, we entered the Vicarage drive through the opened rusty gates which could not have received a coat of paint since Hitler invaded Poland, as I said to Eleanor.

'More like the Kaiser's invasion of Belgium,' she replied.

Abergelly Vicarage was a Victorian building, constructed with stones hewn out of the local quarry, which had also supplied the material for the parish church adjoining it. Both were grey-brown monuments to the lack of taste which afflicted the church architects of the time. They provided an antidote to the ambition which the streets of Abergelly had kindled in my breast. 'This is the reality!' I said to myself. 'This is where I would live and work. This is where my children would be brought up.' The Vicarage at Pontywen was decorated by the elegant lawns which bordered the long drive leading to the front of the house. Here the drive was no more than a few yards long and not a blade of grass was to be seen.

'What a dump!' exclaimed my wife as she got out of the car. 'Living on the main road and listening to the constant noise of the traffic day and night. No, thank you.'

Before I could get to the porch to announce our arrival, Canon Joseph Morris appeared on the doorstep. He was a tall, thin, sallow-faced man with a prominent nose and with a twinkle in his eyes. 'Welcome to Abergelly, Vicar,' he proclaimed in a fruity bass voice which I would have recruited for my Gilbert and Sullivan productions, despite his age. He advanced on Eleanor and shook her hand warmly. 'And a hearty welcome to you, my dear. I understand that you are the local doctor in Pontywen. If you come here I am sure that you will find plenty of work in Abergelly. We are not exactly well blessed with medical care in this town, I'm afraid.'

He led us into the lounge, a large, airy room which

looked out on the hills beyond the town. There were two tea chests in a corner but, apart from that, there was little sign that a removal was imminent. An expensive three-piece suite bordered the big bow windows, flanked by two standard lamps. The centre of the room was occupied by a Persian rug and along the inside wall was a mahogany cabinet surmounted by silverware and an eight-day clock. On either side of the cabinet were two easy chairs with chintz covers. The opulence of the lounge was totally at variance with the impression given by the entrance to the drive. 'Please, sit down and make yourselves comfortable,' he said. 'I'll go and get my wife. She has just come in after her morning's shopping. Would you care for some tea or coffee? It's a little early to offer you anything stronger.'

'Coffee for me,' I replied.

'Ditto!' added Eleanor.

'Strong, weak or indifferent?' asked the Canon.

'We are neither weak nor indifferent,' I said. 'I'm sure my wife will bear me out on that score.'

'You must excuse my husband's bombast, Vicar.' She narrowed her eyes as she looked at me. It was the second time in two days. At that moment Mrs Morris entered the room.

'Edna,' he exclaimed. 'I was just coming to get you from the kitchen. Here are Mr and Mrs Secombe, or should I say Mr and Dr Secombe.'

She was as tall as her husband, a well-preserved lady whose hair still showed signs of the auburn which had given place to grey. Many years younger than the Vicar, she had a ready smile. Dressed in tweeds and wearing a necklace over her brown jumper, she looked more the kind of lady to be seen on the pages of the *Tatler* than those of the *South Wales Echo*.

'How nice to meet you!' she said. Her accent matched her tweeds. It reminded me of Eleanor's mother with her public school background far removed from the ambivalence of the valleys. I wondered how it had managed to survive such a long exposure to her stay in Abergelly.

'They have just expressed a preference for a strong cup of coffee,' said Canon Morris.

'I vote for that,' replied his wife, 'and I expect you do, as well, dear.' She disappeared into the kitchen while her husband proceeded to give us a brief outline of the church history of Abergelly and its contemporary situation. Apparently there was a need for a new church to be built on a post-war council estate. The roof of the parish church was badly in need of repair and the church organ was in a similar state. Attendance at services had been declining and there was an urgent need of a break from the dated pattern of worship which had continued unchanged since the church was built more than a hundred years ago. 'I warn you,' he said, 'if you take this parish on, it will require a lot of guts for you to interfere with the laws of the Medes and Persians and give the services a completely new look. I can tell you this, too, unless you do that the church in Abergelly will end up as an irrelevance in a community which is expanding as each year goes by. Believe me, Vicar, it will be quite a challenge and only a young man like yourself with energy and vision will be able to face up to it.' Mrs Morris appeared with a tray laden with coffee and biscuits as he finished his job description facing the next Vicar of Abergelly.

'I hope you don't find it too daunting, young man, but it is just as well to be honest when describing what is involved. I shall just say one thing more. If you are prepared to accept the challenge, there are quite a number of parishioners who will support you. There are also quite a number of stick-in-the-muds who will say, "As it was in the beginning, is now and ever shall be". However, I am sure that, once the congregation see what you have in mind, you will have more support than opposition. Of that, I am certain.'

'Milk and sugar?' inquired the Vicar's wife. 'That's enough shop for the moment,' she added.

After the light refreshments, we visited the church. Unlike St Mary's Pontywen, St Peter's boasted a tower and a peal of eight bells. It was a large building with a nave which could seat six hundred people and a spacious chancel where an elaborate east window, depicting scenes involving its patron saint, looked down on a sanctuary twice the size of that in my own church. It was most impressive. 'I think a visit to the Waunfelin estate is the next step,' said the Vicar. 'It will give you an idea of the challenge facing you if you come here.' Half an hour later, we were on top of a hill looking down on the town, standing on a derelict patch of land surrounded by numerous rows of newly built terraced barracks, meriting the description of a concrete jungle. There was not a shop to be seen. 'This is to be the site of the new church and a parsonage adjoining it,' announced Canon Morris.

'At the moment, it looks as if any priest coming to live here would be a clerical Robinson Crusoe, stranded in an area of mindless development,' I replied. 'I should imagine that all the inhabitants of these so-called houses must feel that they have been banished into exile. There is no sense of community here whatsoever. It's just a barren wilderness.'

'Now you can see why I called it a challenge,' remarked the old priest quietly. 'Some vicar will have to face it. These people have no facilities of any kind. As you say, there are no shops, no pubs, no meeting place of any kind. There is no doctor's surgery, the nearest is down in the town. That's what I meant, Dr Secombe, when I said that there would be plenty of work for you if you decided to come to Abergelly. You can see, that is no exaggeration.'

As we drove home, we were both silent. I could see that the abandonment of the population of the Waunfelin housing estate presented as much of a challenge to her as it did to me. My wife's sense of vocation was very strong. It was not until we were seated in the lounge of the Vicarage drinking the coffee Mrs Watkins had prepared for us that I broached the subject. 'Well?' I asked. 'Do I phone the Bishop this afternoon and tell him that I am not interested or do we wait a few days to weigh up the pros and cons?'

'Let's put it another way,' she said. 'Are we prepared to become missionaries or are we not? That estate comes into the category of a mission field. I have a well established medical practice here and you have a comfortable living with few problems. We have a nice house and a large garden where our children can run wild as they grow older. At Abergelly Vicarage there is nowhere for them to play.'

'Those are the cons,' I replied. 'Now let's have the pros, if any. As far as I am concerned I would relish the challenge of a large parish. I much prefer the parish church there to ours here. As far as shopping facilities are concerned, there is no comparison with Pontywen. It is a thriving town. If I stay here, I could develop into a turnip.'

'Very funny,' she said. 'To become a turnip is not in your nature any more than it is in mine. Yes, I must admit that I felt a strong urge to get up off my backside and do some pioneering work on that estate.'

'In that case,' I suggested, 'let's think about it for a few days before I let his lordship know about my decision.'

'Done,' she replied.

Two days later Pontywen church hall was full for the rural deanery's venture into sex education. The Mothers' Union groups figured prominently in the audience. There was a sprinkling of men, mainly from our own Saints' Club. Young people were conspicuous by their absence, that is apart from two young curates who had been dragooned into coming by their incumbents. The average age of the clergy present was nearer seventy than sixty. Eleanor had borrowed the blackboard from St Padarn's Sunday School to complement that belonging to the St Mary's Sunday School. Each was decorated by a large anatomical representation of the human body, male and female, supplied by Pontywen Hospital. A sense of excitement mingled with foreboding was in the air when the Rural Dean rose from behind the table at the front of the hall to begin the proceedings. My wife was seated beside him, surveying the elderly assembly in front of her who had come to be instructed in the basics of sexual relations.

'Now then,' began the Rural Dean, 'I am sure we are

all grateful to Dr Secombe for giving of her time to give us this lecture about the – er – way in which God has arranged for our – er – human race to be carried down through the ages. There is nobody better than a doctor to – er – talk about such things but, before she starts, will you all stand for a prayer?' A noisy scraping of chairs on the block floor ensued, drowning the opening words of his address to the Almighty. Even when there was silence for the rest of his prayer, he had rattled through it at such a speed that Eleanor waited until the last chair had come to rest and then stood to address her listeners.

'Mr Rural Dean, fellow Christians,' she began, 'at the beginning of creation, according to the first chapters of the book of Genesis, God created male and female and told them to be fruitful and multiply. This they have done, as the Rural Dean has said, "down through the ages". Tonight we are going to look at the way in which God arranged for this to happen. Here on my left is the anatomy of the female and on my right that of the male. Let us consider first of all the female body.' She then went on to describe in detail the female genitals and the way in which they were connected to the ovary. By now the Rural Dean was showing distinct signs of embarrassment. When she turned to the male body, describing the function of the penis, he became acutely uneasy, looking anywhere but at the figure on the blackboard. This disquiet was shared by the Mothers' Union contingent and was further compounded when my wife proceeded to emphasise that the sexual act was not invented by God simply to reproduce the human species but also to give pleasure to those engaged in it. By the time she had elaborated on the way in which this pleasure could be obtained there was an outbreak of coughing and shuffling of chairs. 'Finally,' she said, 'I think it is time that this essential part of human relationships should be brought out into the open. I wonder how many of you who are parents have given any guidance to your children in these matters. So many teenage pregnancies are the result of woeful ignorance on the part of youngsters who know nothing about their bodies. If you want to ask questions on what I have been speaking about, I shall be only too pleased to answer them.'

The Rural Dean was on his feet immediately. 'I am afraid there is no time for questions. If you will all stand, we shall finish with a prayer.' This was said at such a rate that even the Almighty would find it difficult to decipher it. Evidently the dignitary was anxious to escape as quickly as possible, as were the Mothers' Union members. The only listeners were the two curates, who could scarce contain their glee at the discomfort felt by their elders. They thanked Eleanor as they left, the only two to do so.

On the contrary, as the Rural Dean left, he said, 'It is a pity you did not use those lantern slides, Dr Secombe. They were much more suitable for a mixed audience. By the way, my wife and I have been invited to see the coronation at the Mansion with Sir Edward and Lady Davies. So I am afraid we shall not be with you for it!'

When we returned to the Vicarage, Eleanor said to me, 'I have made my mind up. As far as I am concerned I am quite prepared to go to Abergelly. It will be a different rural deanery and not the back woods of the diocese, as this one appears to be. It's now up to you.'

'I am more than ready to move,' I replied, 'but let's sleep on it before I contact the Bishop.'

Next morning, as we enjoyed our morning cup of tea in bed, I asked her if she was still of the same mind. 'I meant what I said last night, Fred. You can phone the Bishop this morning if you want to. I think the Lord has decided it is time for us to go.'

Promptly at nine o'clock I rang his worship to tell him I would accept the living of Abergelly.

'Splendid,' he said, 'both for you and Abergelly.'

## 12

'Vicar,' said Idris the Milk, 'you can't do this to us! You and Dr Secombe are part of Pontywen. We all thought that you would be here for thirty years or longer, like Canon Llewellyn.'

The news of my appointment to the living of Abergelly had caused consternation in the parish – and not only in the parish but in the surgery. David Andrews told Eleanor that he was 'shell-shocked' for only the second time in his life. The first occasion was during the closing stages of the war. 'That,' he said, 'I was prepared for, but not this. Our partnership is beginning to flourish. We have the monopoly of medical practice in Pontywen.' Had we not been so determined to move, the reaction to the announcement had been so strong that I might have been tempted to withdraw my acceptance of the living.

So we began to make plans for our departure. Eleanor was engaged in negotiating with David over the sale of the practice and also with Abergelly Town Council about the building of a surgery on the Waunfelin housing estate. I had to cope with the disappointment of Emlyn Howells, my curate, the first assistant priest with whom I had any rapport. 'I'm sorry, Emlyn,' I told him, 'that I have to leave so soon after you have come here. Still, you have settled in very quickly and your help will be invaluable to my successor. Who knows, after a couple of years you could come and join me as priest in charge of the Waunfelin estate. You would be the ideal man for that position. In the interregnum you will have plenty of experience of looking after a parish until the new man comes. I hate to think of what would happen to it if Charles Wentworth-Baxter were here.'

It was fortunate that the coronation was imminent and that a frenzy of anticipation had gripped the country. Pontywen was no exception. By now all the arrangements for the parish's celebrations were completed. The eve of the service in Westminster Abbey would be marked by a concert in the church hall featuring the Gilbert and Sullivan Society at the unusually early time of six thirty. Immediately the concert was over, the hall would undergo a quick transformation from a theatre into a dining place for the children of the parish the next day. They were to be regaled with cakes and sandwiches and an endless supply of Emmanuel Thomas's fizzy pop. Then they would parade down to the Welfare Ground where they would be treated to pony rides by Heather Andrews and would take part in races, in which the grown-ups would also participate. That had been the easiest part of the programme to arrange. What had been the most difficult activity to organise was the allocation of television viewers to the only possessors of sets in the parish. As Eleanor said. It was the biggest cross I had been given to bear since I came to the parish, apart from Charles. As far as I was concerned, John Logie Baird had done mankind a great disservice by discovering that it was possible to convey images through the air and into a receptacle in every living room. I could see that once a family could afford to rent a set or pay for one, that box, be it plastic or wooden, would take precedence over any other household appliance, come what may. All I knew was that it was the source of the bitterest animosity I had ever experienced in Pontywen. To that extent it made our departure more desirable.

The morning before the coronation, I went down to the church hall to watch the preparations for the evening's concert. Inevitably it was Bertie Owen who had appointed himself as foreman. When I arrived he was allotting various tasks to the volunteers who had turned up to help. 'Dai and Harry, can you manage to get the piano up on the stage? If you need any extra help, Llew is cleaning the toilets at the moment but I'm sure he'll lend a hand.'

'Hold on, Bertie,' I shouted from the back of the hall, 'that piano stays down on the floor. Didn't you hear Aneurin say that it would take up too much room when everybody is on stage for the choruses? In any case, since when where you given the authority to be ordering people about? I thought Idris had been given that job.'

'Well, as you can see, Vicar,' he retorted, 'he hasn't shown up yet and the sooner things get done the better.'

'It's more than likely that he has been held up on his milk round, as you well know, Bertie. In which case he will be here as soon as possible and I don't think he will take kindly to your butting in.'

At that moment Idris appeared behind me in the doorway. 'Right, Bertie,' he instructed, 'get that coat off and your sleeves rolled up and prepare to sweat a bit for a change. How about starting to unstack the chairs in the cloakroom?' Dai Williams and Harry Evans indulged in a snigger as the would-be foreman took off his coat angrily and glared at Idris, whose five feet five inches had dared to command his six feet one inch. It was a long-running contest which Bertie lost every time.

'Do you want me to render assistance, Idris?' I asked.

'Certainly not, Vicar,' he replied. 'You save all your energy for rendering those duets with your good lady this evening. Since it is the last time we'll have the pleasure of listening to them, you had better make sure they're of top quality. I wouldn't be surprised, by the way, if the Abergelly Operatic put in a bid for your services.'

After watching the hive of activity for half an hour I returned to the Vicarage where I found Jones the Wireless on top of the roof fixing the television aerial to the chimney. We had received the set from my brother a week ago but it was only now that the one and only expert in Pontywen had time to put it in working order, probably because we had not bought the set from him. When I went into the kitchen, I found Eleanor in a state of high indignation. 'Look at this,' she said and thrust a letter into my hand. 'Read it and tell me what you think.' It was on Mothers' Union notepaper and bore the address of the Diocesan President, the Hon. Octavia Jones-Anderson of Hengam Castle.

Dear Dr Secombe,

I have received a number of complaints from members of the Mothers' Union in your deanery. They have asked me to express their concern about your talk on sex education held under the auspices of the Moral Welfare Council of the diocese. Apparently you ignored the approved lantern slides issued by the Council and proceeded to give an exceedingly explicit talk on sexual relations which those present found most offensive. I must remind you that there is a vast difference between an audience of medical students and the Christian lay persons of a typical deanery. I trust that if ever you are invited to address a similar assembly in the future you will temper your remarks accordingly.

Yours truly, Octavia Jones-Anderson, JP.

When I had finished my perusal of the missive I was silent for a moment. 'Well, come on, Secombe,' demanded my wife, 'pronounce judgement.'

'First of all,' I replied, 'I can only say that she had a cheek to write this letter since she was not present to hear you and form her own opinion. Secondly, I am proud to be the husband of someone who has the courage of her own convictions. If you keep on doing that as long as you are my wife, I shall always take my hat off to you.' I caught hold of her and kissed her.

'Hang on, my love,' she replied, 'and what do you mean "as long as I am your wife?" Are you contemplating a change of partner?'

I gave her a hard smack on her bottom. 'You deserve that for such an outrageous suggestion.'

'Only checking,' she said. She decided that she would wait a few days before replying, if only to couch the letter in terms appropriate to the JP's social position.

Early that afternoon, Aneurin Williams, musical director of the Pontywen Gilbert and Sullivan Society, came in to give us a rehearsal of the duets we had to perform that evening. Before he sat down to play he said, 'I feel I have to warn you that you are going to leave chaos behind you in this Society. Not only do we have to find a tenor and soprano lead but we also have to appoint a producer and a chairman of the casting committee. It is going to be mayhem. Either the Bishop will have to appoint an incumbent who has a wife who can sing and who is capable of being a benevolent dictator as you have been or there will be complete disintegration.'

'Come off it,' replied Eleanor, 'who is better to assume the role of the benevolent dictator than yourself? You have all the musical expertise, not to mention the stature of a pillar of the community. You have been musical master at Pontywen Grammar School for the past twenty years or so and, not only that, you have the respect of every member of the Society.'

'There are two things I haven't got,' he said. 'The first is my complete lack of any histrionic ability. The second is my lack of a clerical collar to give me any authority. For those two reasons I predict that there will be squabbles over casting and over the direction by whoever is unfortunate to have to correct the gestures or the interpretations of the principals in the next production. My apologies for beginning our final music rehearsal in such a negative way. Now then, let's get down to work.'

Before we could 'get down to work' there was a ring on the front door. 'Blast!' exclaimed my wife. 'Pardon my language. That must be Ernie Jones, coming to connect the television to the aerial. He said he would be here in the late afternoon. I can't ask him to come back, otherwise we may all be looking at a blank screen tomorrow. He has to bore a hole through the window sill to make the connection. Let me check first.' She made a quick exit to the front door. Back she came accompanied by Ernie.

'Sorry to interrupt your music practice, Vicar, but unless

I do the work now I don't know when I can finish it. I'm up to my eyes in it.'

'I suggest we go down to the church hall,' said Aneurin. Ten minutes later Eleanor and I were launched into the lovely duet from *The Pirates of Penzance*, 'Stay, Frederick, stay'. As we finished it, Aneurin said, 'What could be more appropriate to express the sentiments of your audience tonight?' The second duet we had chosen to sing was the kissing duet between Nanki-Poo and Yum-Yum from *The Mikado*, 'Were you not Ko-ko plighted?'

'If you don't mind my saying so,' said our pianist, 'you couldn't have chosen two more sloppy duets than these.'

'With a wife like mine,' I replied, 'what else would you expect me to choose.'

'Flattery,' said Eleanor, 'can get you anywhere, even as far as Abergelly, and that applies to you, Aneurin. As far as your remark about our first effort is concerned, it's Abergelly here we come, no mistake.'

When we went back to the Vicarage we found Jones the Wireless still in attendance, with his van proclaiming, 'Jones, Wireless and Television suppliers. Beat us if you can.' Since there was no one else in Pontywen to beat him it was a pointless boast. As we entered the sitting room we were confronted with a blur of images which Ernie was trying to focus into something recognisable. 'I may have to adjust the aerial,' he said. 'You are down in a dip here and it makes the reception difficult. It's much better in Ashburnham Close, I can tell you.'

'Well, since we don't live in Ashburnham Close,' my wife replied acidly, 'it is your job to see that we can have a reasonable picture on our set. If you have to twiddle the aerial for the next few hours, you are not going from here until we can at least have some idea of what is supposed to be shown on that screen.'

Jones the Wireless winced at the onslaught. 'Right, Dr Secombe,' he murmured, avoiding her gaze. 'I'll see if I can get it more in line with the transmitter in Cardiff. It's the hills, you see.'

'I don't care if it is Mount Everest,' she exploded, 'at least I am sure that you can do better than that Picasso picture you've got at the moment.'

In the kitchen Mrs Watkins and our nursemaid Marlene were in earnest conversation when we entered. 'I've just been saying to Marlene,' said our daily, 'I expect the children will miss being in this nice big Vicarage and all that lovely garden. Marlene was saying that one in Abergelly is stuck right in the middle of the town with all that traffic and that.' Marlene blushed at being caught talking behind her employer's back. Mrs Watkins had no such inhibitions. As Arthur, our part-time gardener used to say, 'She's like a gramophone record, playing the same old tune but a little bit cracked.'

'Well,' said Eleanor, 'the house in Abergelly is just as big as this one. In fact the downstairs rooms are even a little bigger than in this one. What's more, across the road is a lovely park with a splendid playground for the children – I am more concerned that the children will miss you, Marlene, much more than they will miss the house. The Vicar and I have been talking this over. How would you like to come with us?'

Marlene blushed more than she did at being overheard. 'I'd love to,' she stammered, 'that is if my mother will let me. I'd miss the children so much if I couldn't look after them anymore. In any case, there's nothing to keep me in

Pontywen. There's a lot more going on in Abergelly, like the cinema and the dances in the Welfare.'

'Since we are on this subject,' I added, 'how do you feel, Mrs Watkins, about coming as well? There are six bedrooms in the Vicarage. You would be able to have a sitting room which you could share with Marlene.' The prospect of sharing a sitting room with Marlene did not appeal to her, it was evident.

'Well, thank you, Vicar, but I don't think I can leave Pontywen. I've been here all my life and I'm too old to make a move now. I'm sure there will be plenty of women down there who will be only too glad of a job helping in the Vicarage. It's been lovely being here with you but I think the time has come for me to live on my pension and that. By the way, Dr Secombe, I've just put the sausage rolls in the oven for the television party tomorrow. I thought I would leave the Welsh cakes until first thing in the morning. They are always better when they are made fresh, like.'

'I know that,' I said. 'I used to take them hot from the baking stone when my mother was cooking them.'

'It's no wonder you suffer from indigestion,' remarked my wife. 'Don't you let him do that tomorrow, Mrs Watkins, otherwise he will be disrupting the audience by dashing into the kitchen for some bicarbonate of soda midway through the crowning ceremony.'

At six o'clock we made our way down to the church hall, leaving Marlene in charge of the children. 'Thank God we shall be taking her with us to Abergelly,' Eleanor said. 'The children would be heartbroken if she stayed in Pontywen. Let's hope that her mother will raise no objection. They are a very close family, as you know.'

'I'm sure her mother would rather that she was with us than in a factory,' I replied. The audience was already queueing outside the doors when we reached the hall.

'Hardly surprising,' said my wife, 'when you think it is a free show by the only musical society in the town, and not only that, but one of top quality.'

'Self-praise is no recommendation,' I retorted.

Inside the hall there was the usual chaos as the bow-tied and the pseudo dinner-suited male members of the chorus mingled on the stage with the young ladies, who were clad in a variety of attire which encompassed the tasteful and the positively garish. All were excited as if they were on some kind of outing. As Idris the Milk remarked about the last-night performance of *The Pirates of Penzance*, 'the adrenalin was overflowing'. The Secombe era had reached its grand finale. In view of the coronation, it could be described as its crowning glory. I mentioned this to my wife as I watched the antics on the stage. 'Big head,' she said.

In front of a full house with latecomers standing at the back of the hall I stood in front of the curtains to introduce the concert. 'I am proud to present the finest operatic society in the Valley' (cheers) 'who are to entertain you this evening. They will present excerpts from their great successes over the past five years from *The Pirates of Penzance* to *The Mikado*, and here to conduct the chorus and principals is the musical director and their inspiration, Mr Aneurin Williams!' Aneurin came forward and took his bow amidst great applause. He beckoned to his talented student at the piano, David Protheroe, graduate with distinction RAM, and the roof was raised with a spirited rendering of 'Dance a Chachucha' from *The*

*Gondoliers*. Then came Iorwerth Ellis, my tenor under-study since the inception of the society, desperate to prove his worthiness as my successor. He sang 'Is life a boon?' from *The Yeoman of the Guard*. He had a fine tenor voice but no histrionic ability. It would have been better if he had confined himself to his singing but he attempted some inappropriate gestures which seemed to indicate that he was a puppet whose manipulator had not read the script. However, his singing won the day and he received a warm round of applause. Next came Idris the Milk accompanied by the chorus, who sang the famous song from *The Pirates of Penzance*, where the sergeant of police complains about his unfortunate vocation, 'A policeman's lot is not a happy one'. To this he added a third verse: 'When our Vicar's got a living in the offing and decides his days in Pontywen are done. When his missis tires with coping with the endless coughing which plagues her waiting room from ten to one, she thinks the time has come to be a mother. By looking after both her daughter and her son. Ah, take one consideration with another, a warden's lot is not a happy one.' This piece of doggerel was the hit of the evening and had a reception which was even more rousing than that for our duets.

It was a happy evening which ended all too soon and was followed by a frantic transformation of the hall into a suitable venue for the beanfeast to come next afternoon. Tables were laid and were decorated with the coronation mugs that the organising committee had bought for the children. Agnes Collier was on her best behaviour in charge of the kitchen and twice managed to control her temper when Bertie Owen tried to invade her realm. As

Idris said, 'It is a landmark in their relationship.' Then he added, 'Mind, I hope he keeps out of her way tomorrow.'

When we came back to the Vicarage, we found Marlene watching the television in the sitting room. Ernie had succeeded in producing a 'reasonable' picture as requested by Eleanor. The definition was not of the best but since the landscape of Pontywen was not very cooperative that was not his fault. Our babysitter thought the picture was 'wonderful' and could not wait for tomorrow to come. After going to bed, we talked long into the night, so much had happened in the course of just a few days that our heads were in a whirl. It would not be long before we would be leaving Pontywen for ever. I began to wonder what the churchwardens would be like and whether they would be cooperative. The present Vicar seemed to indicate that there were a fair number of backwoodsmen in the parish who would not take kindly to changes of any kind. What was more disturbing was the disinclination of the Town Council to be helpful to Eleanor in her negotiations for the building of a surgery on the Waunfelin estate. We talked ourselves to sleep.

We awoke to the sound of Elspeth crying in the next room. Eleanor jumped out of bed and pulled back the curtains to reveal a sunny June day. She went off to the nursery singing, 'Oh, what a beautiful morning'. I arose, put on my dressing gown and was about to go downstairs to make the tea when my wife returned, cradling the baby who was still crying loudly.

'I take back what I was singing. I am afraid, my love, that she has all the symptoms of parotitis.'

'What on earth is that?' I asked. 'Is it dangerous?'

'Not particularly,' she said. 'In other words, your daughter has mumps. Her glands are swollen and obviously painful and she has a high temperature.'

'I remember having that when I was about seven or eight and it certainly was painful. I looked like Fatty Arbuckle. When my mother brought me a mirror to look at myself, I started to laugh and cause myself even more pain.'

'It's just as well that you had it then because if you contracted it at your age it could affect your virility. It is quite contagious. Fortunately, like you, I had it in my early childhood. I hope Marlene is the same, otherwise she will have to stay away until they are getting over it. You hold the patient, while I go to see whether David is in the same boat.'

Nothing I could do would pacify Elspeth. If anything she was exercising her lungs more fully than ever. Eleanor came back with the news that our son was affected by the same bug. 'Do you think that we should cancel the television jamboree?' I asked.

'As long as the children are quarantined upstairs I should think it would be all right. The only question mark is Bronwen and her brood. If they haven't had mumps, there might be an element of risk. I'll phone her and ask her if she is prepared to take a chance. You know how devoted she is to her family.'

After we had drunk our quota of morning tea, she telephoned the Wentworth-Baxter household – I was getting ready to take Matins, putting on my cassock and standing alongside her as she rang – she pulled a face when the call was answered by her *bête noire*. 'Could I speak to Bronwen, please?' she inquired. She put her hand over the phone as she waited to speak to Mrs W-B.

'He's hardly full of the joys of spring,' she commented. When his wife came on at the other end a long conversation ensued which was still continuing as I left the Vicarage. There was a handful of parishioners stand outside the porch when I made my way up the church path.

'Mr Howells has gone round to the vestry, Vicar,' said Agnes Collier, whose name had been at the top of the list of potential viewers at our house. The next minute the door was opened and the small congregation trooped into the chancel for the service.

'Have you had mumps?' I asked Emlyn in the vestry. He looked at me quizzically.

'That is a strange question this time of the morning, Vicar,' he replied. 'As a matter of fact I have. I had it when I was five and it came upon me on my birthday and spoilt it. Why do you ask?'

'In that case you will have a permit to view the coronation without any threat to your manhood.'

'You say the strangest things, Vicar. Would you mind explaining yourself?'

'David and Elspeth have chosen to mark the coronation by going down with mumps. According to my wife, if you had not suffered from it, you would have been in danger of impaired virility by being in contact with a stricken household. So, my dear Emlyn, I look forward to your company this morning if only to offset the effect of being in the presence of Bertie Owen and his wife, Agnes Collier, the formidable Mrs Davies in her wheelchair and possibly your predecessor the Reverend Charles Wentworth-Baxter.'

'I think I would rather have the mumps,' he said.

When I arrived at the Vicarage after the service, Marlene opened the door to me before I could put my key in it. 'I saw you coming, Vicar,' she said, 'so I thought I would beat you to it.'

'This means you have had the mumps, I take it, and what is more that your mother has said that you can come with us to Abergelly.'

'That's right and I'm so excited. Mind, I'm sorry about Elspeth and David but I'll look after them, I really will.'

'I'm sure you will, Marlene. Now then, where is my wife?'

'She's in the kitchen with Mrs Watkins and they're making sandwiches for the people coming to see the coronation.'

'A word with you in the study,' Eleanor said as I came through the door. 'I'm afraid I have had bad news from your ex-curate,' she informed me when we were on our own.

'You surprise me,' I replied.

'Bronwen decided that she would rather miss the coronation on television and listen to it on the wireless to avoid any risk of her children getting mumps. Dear Charles was most upset, like the spoilt child that he is. He has not had parotitis. However, he's coming solo, despite the possibility of contracting it. I would suggest that some time during the viewing we bring Elspeth down and place her in his lap. If it means that he could become sterile, we should be doing Bronwen the greatest of favours, don't you agree?'

'I agree on that,' I replied, 'but I don't see why we should inconvenience our daughter to that extent. Let's hope a stray germ invades the room and nobbles him.'

By the time all our guests were crammed into our

sitting room, where the seating capacity had been augmented by chairs borrowed from the church hall, there was an audience of twenty to watch the birth of the new Elizabethan age. Fitting Mrs Davies's wheelchair into a convenient position had been the bone of contention. She

had insisted on having her chair centrally placed at the front, which meant that half a dozen viewers behind her had either to develop swan-like necks or see nothing. Eleanor solved this problem by importing the lectern platform from the church to the back of the room, setting up Edwina on high, a position greatly to her liking. Bertie Owen had been comparatively silent from the moment he had entered the Vicarage. This phenomenon was due to the fact that he was accompanied by his wife, a little women of forbidding appearance, with penetrating blue eyes. She had but to say 'Herbert' to bring him to heel at once. Idris the Milk said it was a pity she wasn't a churchgoer. 'Can't you get her confirmed, Vicar?' he said, after one bad burst of 'Bertieitis'. 'The congregation would double your Easter offering if you managed that.'

Charles was seated next to Emlyn Howells. 'It's a cross you have to bear just for a few hours,' I told my curate. 'I had to carry it for nearly four years.' There was an air of great excitement as the television cameras showed the crowds along the route to Westminster Abbey and then the honoured guests assembled in the great church.

'I remember King Edward the Seventh's coronation,' announced Edwina.

'Are you sure it wasn't Queen Victoria's?' inquired Agnes Collier, who voted Conservative and had no time at all for a woman who was a prominent member of the local Labour Party. 'Anyway,' she went on, 'I don't know why you're here. I remember you in the thirties when you said you'd like to see the Red Flag flying over Buckingham Palace.'

'Look here, Aggie,' shouted Edwina, 'if it wasn't for being stuck in this wheelchair, I'd give you more than a piece of my mind. Everybody's entitled to change their view.'

By now there were loud protests from some of the viewers that they couldn't hear what Richard Dimbleby was saying because of the noise from the back. 'Ladies!' I said. 'That's enough of that. I suggest we watch in silence from now on and enjoy the spectacle on the screen.'

At this stage of the proceedings, Eleanor and Mrs Watkins came into the room with the light refreshments to be enjoyed before the service began. Sandwiches and Welsh cakes were passed around, together with cups of coffee and tea. Inevitably it was Charles who found he could not balance his plate of sandwiches on his lap without dropping it on the floor. In stooping down to retrieve it and its contents he jerked Emlyn's elbow as he was about to drink his cup of coffee. The curate's best suit was drenched with the hot liquid. 'Charles!' exclaimed my wife. 'For heaven's sake watch what you're doing. Trust you to do something like this.'

'I am not staying here to be insulted,' he said. The two clergymen rose simultaneously, the one to go to the kitchen for running repairs and the other to go out through the door in high dudgeon and speed off up the drive with a roar of the engine which drowned the commentary on the television set.

Bertie Owen spoke for the one and only time during the morning. 'Thank God for that,' he said. After receiving one of his wife's special looks he turned his attention to his cucumber sandwich.

A little later Emlyn left the Vicarage to go back to his house and change his suit. He was back in time to see the beginning of the service. As I opened the door to him I whispered, 'I told you Charles was a cross you had to bear for a few hours; you were lucky. It was less than an hour.'

'You have my sympathy, Vicar. Job pales into insignificance compared with you.'

From then on there was a reverent silence as the coronation service unfolded the secrets of its ancient ritual before the gaze of millions of Her Majesty's subjects who were privileged to watch what had been the prerogative of the few hitherto. When the young woman's head was crowned by the Archbishop of Canterbury both Edwina and Aggie were at one in their appreciation of the solemnity of the occasion. There were further refreshments as the Abbey bells rang out and the impressive cavalcade of regal pomp made its way back to Buckingham Palace. When the programme came to an end, Agnes Collier was first out of the room to dash down to the church hall to supervise the children's tea. As we surveyed the chaos left after the last viewer had gone, Eleanor said, 'What a relief that we don't have to take David and Elspeth to the jamboree this afternoon. At least we shall be able to clear up at our leisure, the three of us females, that is. You can go down to the hall and do your Father Christmas act by all means. My only regret is that David will not be able to have a ride on Heather's pony. He was so looking forward to it.'

'In a week or so's time, my love, I'm sure that Heather will give him a ride on her pony and, what's more, he won't have to queue for it,' I replied.

After I had presided at the children's tea, I went down to the Welfare Ground where Heather Andrews was about to cope with a long queue of children eager for a ride on Daisy, her pony. 'Where's David?' she asked.

'In bed with mumps,' I said, 'so please can you give him a ride on Daisy when he's up and about once again.'

'My dear Fred, he can have as many rides as he likes, you know that. By the way, we enjoyed our viewing of the coronation with the Nicholls. They did us proud. How did your lot like it?'

'Apart from Charles, who left in a huff, they loved it,' I replied.

'What was that all about?' she inquired.

'Over nothing, really,' I said. 'Just another Wentworth-Baxter episode.'

Later that evening Eleanor and I looked out of David's bedroom window to see if there was any sign of the fireworks display on the Welfare Ground. Our son was awake and had been crying with the pain of his ailment. Suddenly a fusillade of rockets shot up into the dying sunlight of 2 June. 'Come on, David,' said my wife, 'and watch the fireworks, or, to use your father's expression, "the crowning glory", ending the Secombe era and beginning the Elizabethan era.'